IN SEARCH OF REALITY

IN SEARCH OF REALITY

A Layman's Journey Through Indian Philosophy

O.N. KRISHNAN

MOTILAL BANARSIDASS PUBLISHERS
PRIVATE LIMITED • DELHI

First Edition: Delhi, 2004

ISBN: 81-208-2012-6 (Cloth)
ISBN: 81-208-2021-5 (Paper)

Also available at:

MOTILAL BANARSIDASS

41 U.A. Bungalow Road, Jawahar Nagar, Delhi 110 007
8 Mahalaxmi Chamber, 22 Bhulabhai Desai Road, Mumbai 400 026
120 Royapettah High Road, Mylapore, Chennai 600 004
236, 9th Main III Block, Jayanagar, Bangalore 560 011
Sanas Plaza, 1302 Baji Rao Road, Pune 411 002
8 Camac Street, Kolkata 700 017
Ashok Rajpath, Patna 800 004
Chowk, Varanasi 221 001

Printed in India

BY JAINENDRA PRAKASH JAIN AT SHRI JAINENDRA PRESS,
A-45 NARAINA, PHASE-I, NEW DELHI 110 028
AND PUBLISHED BY NARENDRA PRAKASH JAIN FOR
MOTILAL BANARSIDASS PUBLISHERS PRIVATE LIMITED,
BUNGALOW ROAD, DELHI -110 007

To

VENGU

boyhood mentor, and
daughters & sons
with the fond hope
they will read this.

Contents

PART III
BUDDHISM

Part V
ADVAITA OF ŚAṄKARA

Part VI
ULTIMATE TRUTH

List of Figures

FIGURES

Foreword

The present work "A Layman's Journey Through Indian Philosophy" by O.N. Krishnan is a philosophical treatise in itself. Although the title claims that it is a 'layman's journey', this is indeed an erudite attempt and a sincere search to know the ultimate truth of existence and to grasp the essentials of the Indian philosophical teachings over the ages on the sources of pains and miseries of beings and the means of attaining liberation from these pains and miseries. It is an attempt with an objective to gain an insight into the ultimate reality and a realisation of the *summum bonum* of life.

One, who is seriously interested to know the teachings of Indian philosophical works throughout the ages, is easily bewildered by the innate complexities and enormous contradictions coupled with the lofty linguistic difficulties he comes across in these works. The author has spared no pains to present, in a swift, smooth and exegetic way, what all he has learned from the wealthy treasures of Indian philosophical works, so as to fill the brains of readers only with a clear and comprehensive analysis of the essential elements of these teachings. Hair splitting, dogmatic and enigmatic presentations in abstruse style usual for philosophical works are studiously avoided in this work. In his search for profound philosophical truths, the author has unveiled many a hidden golden discs.

This Indian philosophical journey starts at a natural spot, the beginning portions of *Vedas*. Polytheism of the *Vedas* is analysed and presented objectively. How polytheism of Vedic period has evolved into monotheism is lucidly depicted by the author. The anachronistic fundamentals of *varṇa* theory are boldly brought out in this study. Vedic study is followed by a comprehensive study of the *Upaniṣads* in a very systematic and analytical manner bringing out all the essences of their teachings. In his study the author has covered many minor *Upaniṣads* as well, such as *Maitrī Upaniṣad.* This is a different approach, but all the more welcome.

The significance of *Sāṁkhya,* as the earliest theory of evolution far ahead of Darwinism, is wisely imparted in this work. After journeying through the timeless *darśanas* of Indian philosophy, the author enters the golden vistas of Buddhism. All different schools of Buddhism are closely analysed.

Gauḍapādīya-kārikā is the original fore-runner of *Śaṅkara's Vedānta* and, in its turn, *Gauḍapādīya-kārikā* has inherited a lion's share of its teachings from Buddhism. This little-exposed truth and the indebtedness of *Vedānta* to Buddhism are brought into daylight by this present work very authentically with a brilliant comparison. The last chapter gives a concise overview of the various philosophies and ends with a clear exposition of what ultimate truth is. Attaining Buddha consciousness is the ultimate end; this is the consciousness, that is an incarnation of selflessness itself, suffused with love and compassion. This can be realised by one in oneself.

This work is an unbiased and undaunting study of Indian philosophy which is unusual in the tradition where faith is more praised than reason. The author has travelled throughout the breath-taking marvellous hills and vales of Indian philosophy and has brought to us many a treasure of lofty logical conclusions as gifts. Any student of philosophy as well as any common man can gain much from this work- not only as a food for thought but also as a memento for motivation and a searchlight for finding the path to realise the ultimate reality.

I personally consider this work as a very significant contribution that no seeker after Truth can afford to miss.

Those with eyes cannot miss to see.
Those with ears should not miss to hear.
This is a book to be perused ever and ever.

DR. V. SIDDARTHA PERIYARDHASAN
Professor, Dept. of Philosophy,
Pachaiyappa's College, Chennai - 600030

HON. DIRECTOR,
DR. AMBEDKAR INSTITUTE OF BUDDHIST RESEARCH
21, I-Phase, ICL Hometown
Noombal, Thiruverkadu, Chennai - 600077

Preface

Having come under the spell of Spinoza's Ethics in the formative years of life, I hold strongly to the rationalist view that life should be guided by reason and intellect and not by blind belief or faith. No doubt faith has a unique place and plays a very important role in the religious life of individuals; but this faith also should be based on reason and logic and not rest solely on imaginary constructions of the mind. With the mind having been conditioned by Spinoza's mathematical method of philosophizing with axioms and proofs, when I first started reading Indian philosophical and religious works like Upaniṣads, Bhagavad Gītā and Advaita Vedānta, I was at a loss to understand and grasp them. But my accidental foray into the Buddhist philosophy dramatically altered the position I found myself in with respect to the Indian philosophy. I then came to discern a rational foundation for the faiths because Buddhist teachings happen to be more a rational philosophy than a religion.

Like any ordinary Hindu brought up in the religious, cultural and social milieu dominated by Brahmanical world-view and traditional belief systems, I had earlier—I should not say an antipathy-but an ambivalent attitude to Buddhism. Accidentally I drifted into Buddhist works in the course of my search when I could not understand the philosophical works of Hinduism. Only after I started reading Buddhist philosophical literatures, could I actually comprehend the Vedantic views and what they mean and place them in the proper perspective. From then onwards, my interest has been in the comparative study of the philosophical ideas of the two traditions.

Even though Gautama, the Buddha, is considered an avatar of Supreme God Viṣṇu in Hinduism, the study of his religious teachings and philosophical ideas is neglected in India and in fact, not encouraged, The Hindus normally take it for granted that the best of the Buddha's teachings have been absorbed in their religion and that there is no need for them to undertake a separate study of the teachings and philosophies of Buddhism. They do not realize how far away they are from the truth and what they miss. Even scholars like Dr. Radhakrishnan had not been fair to Buddhism when they tried to establish that it is but only an off-shoot of the Upanisadic thoughts. The radical philosophical differences in the two religious traditions have been overlooked or brushed aside by them. They also tend to interpret wrongly the passages in the Buddhist literatures like Udāna and read an affirmation of the Upaniṣadic view of Self or Brahman in the Buddha's concept of Nirvāṇa. The import of the concepts of śūnya and selflessness in Buddhism has been missed by them. It is also not generally recognized and appreciated how the middle and later Upaniṣads and the philosophy of the Advaita Vedānta have been influenced by the Buddhist thoughts.

Hinduism and Buddhism are undoubtedly the two most outstanding philosophical and religious traditions of India. They are vibrant living religious traditions which have played and continue to play most significant roles in the lives not only of countless individuals but also of a great many communities. They are the objects of study not only for the respective religious communities and professionals and researchers but also for any seeker of Truth. These traditions have not grown in a cultural vacuum and in separate independent water-tight compartments. They have interacted with and impinged on each other, in the process each affecting the other and itself getting affected. Hinduism was enriched by its interaction with Buddhism and transformed itself from a crass materialistic religion to one of high ethical ideals. Buddhism evolved into Mahāyāna Buddhism with the devotional (bhakti) element drawn from Hinduism and the Bhagavad Gītā. The decline of Buddhism in India and the circumstances leading to its extinction in the land of its birth are subject matters for separate study by scholars and researchers. But what is of interest and relevance to any seeker of Truth is the study of their teachings and what they offer as philosophical solutions for application to our problems in modern times.

This work is an attempt to undertake an analytical study of the teachings of Vedānta and the various Buddhist schools in a comprehensive manner and present a comparative assessment of the philosophical ideas of the two traditions. In spite of its coming from a layman and any limitations or shortcomings that may be perceived in this work, its purpose will be deemed to have been served if it evokes interest in such a comparative study and succeeds in generating a flow of further works from more able and learned hands in the scholastic community as a counter to this one or as providing more insight and knowledge into the philosophical questions discussed and compared here.

O.N. Krishnan

March 10, 2003
Bellary

Acknowledgments

This work is an attempt to understand the ultimate truth and establish logical rational basis for the practices to realize the same through a comparative study of the philosophical teachings in Hindu and Buddhist traditions.

It will be appreciated that a work of this nature depends on many sources for its development. Among those authors, to whose works I am deeply indebted, special mention should be made of Dr. S. Radhakrishnan, Swami Gambhirananda and Professors G.M. Nagao, Paul Williams and Richard King. I have attempted to climb on their shoulders and gain a wider vision in the search for reality. I am grateful for the insights provided by them.

I should thank my colleagues Ms.Parimala, Venkata Swamy, Krishna Mohan and Kiran Kumar for their immense help in giving a shape to this work and making it presentable.

I must also thank the publishers, Motilal Banarsidass, for coming forward to publish this work.

Last though, but not the least, I should thank Dr. V. Siddartha Periyardhasan, Professor, Department of Philosophy, Pachaiyappa's College, Chennai, for finding time in spite of his numerous preoccupations to go through this work and for readily contributing a Foreword to the book. I am grateful to him for his kind gesture and encouragement.

Abbreviations

A.U.	Aitareya Upaniṣad
B.G.	Bhagavad-gītā
B.U.	Bṛhad-āraṇyaka Upaniṣad
B.S.	Brahma Sūtra
C.U.	Chāndogya Upaniṣad
G.K.	Gauḍapādīya Kārikā
Īśa.	Īśa Upaniṣad
Kena	Kena Upaniṣad
Kaṭha	Kaṭha Upaniṣad
K.U.	Kauṣītakī Upaniṣad
M.B.	Mahābhārata
Maitrī	Maitrī Upaniṣad
Mā.U.	Māṇḍūkya Upaniṣad
M.U.	Muṇḍaka Upaniṣad
Paiṅgala	Paiṅgala Upaniṣad
Praśna	Praśna Upaniṣad
R.V.	Ṛg Veda
S.U.	Śvetāśvatara Upaniṣad
Subāla	Subāla Upaniṣad
T.U.	Taittirīya Upaniṣad
Upad.	Upadeśasāhasrī

BUDDHIST TEXTS

A.	Aṅguttara Nikāya
Dh.	Dhammapada
Dh A.	Dhammapada Aṭṭhakathā
D.	Dīgha Nikāya
K.	Khuddaka Nikāya
MV.	Madhyāntavibhāga
MSA	Mahāyānasūtrālaṃkāra

M.	Majjhima Nikāya
MMK.	Mūla-Madhyamaka-Kārikā
RGV.	Ratnagotravibhāga
S.	Saṃyutta Nikāya
Śrīmālā	Śrīmālādevīsiṃhanāda Sūtra
Sn.	Sutta-nipāta

Introduction

Fundamental Philosophical Questions

The mysteries of the universe and the existential questions have exercised the minds of the Indian sages from time immemorial. How has the universe originated? What is sustaining it and "the stellar dance of teeming suns and planets that are whirling through the vast etherial space?" How has life emerged? What is the fundamental principle underlying existence? Is there any first cause of existence? Is there any supra-cosmic Reality, a transcendent God or Creator? Is there any soul? What happens to the individual after his death? Is there any life after death? Is there any purpose or meaning in life? What is the ultimate goal of human existence?

In the *Upaniṣads* dating back some 2200 to 2600 years in time, we find such philosophical and existential questions being asked by devout disciples desirous of gaining the saving knowledge.

".............. What is the cause? Is it Brahman? Whence are we born? By what do we live? And on what are we established? O Ye who know Brahman, tell us, presided over by whom do we live in our different conditions of pleasures and pains, happiness and miseries?" (*S.U.* I.1)

"By whom willed and directed does the mind light on its objects? By whom commanded does life, the first, move? At whose will have the people gained the power of speech? And what God is it that energies the eye and the ear?" (*Kena* I.1)

"........ O Venerable Sir, from where is this *prāṇa* (life-force) born? How does he come into this body? How again does he distribute himself in the body and carry out the different functions? How does he depart?........" (*Praśna* III. 1)

"...... This body is like a cart without intelligence. To what superior being belongs such power by which such a sort of body has been made intelligent? In other words, who is its mover? ...." (*Maitrī* II.3)

Who is the mover and energizer of this body which is only just like a cart without intelligence? How have the eyes and ears gained their respective powers of seeing and powers of hearing? How is the mind cognizing the objects and how has it gained the power of thought, intellect and discrimination? How has the tongue gained the power of speech? How has the power of speech emanated?

The world is surfeit with pain and misery. What is the source of these pains and miseries? Are there any means of liberation from these pains and miseries, sufferings and sorrows? What is the ultimate goal? What is the ultimate reality behind the ever-changing flux of things experienced in this world?

These are the profound philosophical questions to which the Indian seers have attempted to find satisfactory answers since the dawn of Indian civilisation. Their search has been for the ultimate truth, ultimate reality behind the impermanent scheme of things in this phenomenal world. Their soul-stirring cries and prayers have been:

"From the unreal lead me to the real, from darkness lead me to light, from death lead me to immortality (life-eternal, *amaratvam*)" (*B.U.* I.3.28).

"The face of truth is covered with a golden disc. Unveil it, O *Pūṣan*, so that I who love the truth may see it" (*Īśa.* 15)

Early man in his primitive past when faced with the inimical forces of nature was struck with awe and fear. His instinctual fears were the ones which first gave rise to the ideas of supernatural powers and gods controlling these forces of nature. As he evolved, his intellectual powers and analytical reasoning developed and his ideas became more and more refined and new thoughts and discoveries added to the collective wisdom of men.

In the fertile cultural ground and climate of India grew many different systems of philosophical thoughts and spiritual insights answering to the different human needs and meeting the different levels of understanding and spiritual consciousness of men. A vast corpus of philosophical and spiritual wisdom has been developed and bequeathed from ancient times as precious legacies for the posterity. But bewildering complexities and contradictions characterize these Indian philosophical systems. The present attempt is a search through the maze of these teachings from a layman's point of view to find out the core meanings of the answers given by some important philosophical systems to the above profound existential questions.

The basic objective, as in any such enquiry, is to gain an insight into the ultimate reality or ultimate truth of existence and an understanding of ultimate goal in life, the *summum bonum* of life. For, unlike western philosophy, Indian philosophy is closely linked to the way of life. The enquiry into the truth or reality here is not for the sake of knowledge or love of wisdom alone, but also for the sake of defining the ultimate goal in life. Here the knowledge of ultimate reality determines and fixes the ultimate goal in life and also dictates the path to be traversed in life to achieve this ultimate goal and realize the ultimate reality.

At the outset, it would be appropriate to define clearly what we understand by the term ultimate reality. What is it that qualifies to be designated as the ultimate reality? Reality, as generally understood, is the one that must always be. It is the one that is ever present in all the states of existence conceivable and without which no state of existence can be conceived. The test of reality is existence for all times. It remains unchanged through all the changes of existence. It is eternal and immutable. It is birthless, deathless, it is unborn, uncreated, uncaused. It was, it has always been, it is and it always will be. Further, as the *Chāndogya Upaniṣad* describes, it is the one "that is free from evil, free from old age, free from death, free from grief, free from hunger and thirst" (*C.U.* VIII 7.1). Having defined thus, is there any thing we find in existence that answers these criteria? Is it God, *Īśvara* or Brahman as variously described?

First let us study the concepts of many gods in the *Vedas*.

Part I

VEDIC IDEAS

CHAPTER 1

Vedic Ideas

1. Polytheism in the Vedas

Fear of the destructive forces of nature, fear of death and feelings of gratitude and adoration over the benefits bestowed to mankind by nature were the principal factors that gave rise to the ideas of gods in the initial stages of development of human thought.

There exist innumerable inexplicable mysteries of the universe and whenever man failed to reason out and comprehend their cause, they attributed them to be the work of an unknown power which was conveniently called God. Observing the various phenomena of nature, man attributed divine powers to different aspects of nature and deified them. Thus came about the concepts of many gods and goddesses. *Indra, Agni, Varuṇa* and *Mitra* are the gods personifying such forces of nature as thunder, fire, the sky and the sun respectively. In *Ṛg Veda,* we find hymns in praise of these gods and also deities such as *Sūrya* (sun), *Sōma* (moon), *Pṛthvī*(earth), *Maruts* (storm winds), *Vāyu* (wind), *Ap* (water) and *Uṣas* (dawn).

Thus many gods and goddesses were imagined, identified with the forces of nature, invoked and worshipped with prayers and offerings. They were imagined to be in the likeness of human beings, and human qualities of love, hatred, passion and mercy came to be attributed to them. Sacrifices were made to please them and seek their blessings for secular welfare, wealth and progeny. *Agni,* the god of fire, occupied a special position in the pantheon of gods because it was vital for providing heat and food and also because it has the capacity to defy gravity and raise up. *Agni* alone was believed to have the capacity to consume the sacrificial offerings, thereby transforming them from their gross state and deliver them to the gods in the acceptable form of smoke. *Agni* was the deliverer of the sacrificial offerings to the gods.

Gradually there emerged a trend in the *Vedas* to question the multiplicity of gods and move towards monotheism unifying all the gods into one. This unifying trend came about with the realisation of the close connection and inter-relationship among the various powers and forces of nature which the multiplicity of gods represented. The *Ṛta* or order in the functioning of the elements of nature was recognised and this had contributed greatly to this unification drive. Does not the Sun god raise water from the oceans as the rain-bearing clouds and does not the *Varuṇa* God drive these clouds over the fields? Do not lightning and thunder accompany the rains? Is not food produced from rain? From rain is produced food. From food come forth the beings. All the natural phenomena are linked and inter-related to each other.

Thus the vast multiplicity of gods which earlier epitomized the Vedic thought came to be recognised as subject to *Ṛta*, the regulating force, supposed to be at the heart of the cosmos. *Ṛta* was the regulating pulse which governed manifest existence, both at the microcosmic and the macrocosmic levels. *Ṛta* it was which gave the planets their orbits, caused the sun to rise and set, the seasons to come and go and the nature to flourish. *Ṛta* was also supposed to set the norms for social and moral behaviour. Those who did not conform to these norms were answerable to *Varuṇa*, the custodian of *Ṛta*. This concept of *Ṛta* seems to have given rise later in Hinduism to the concept of '*dharma*' ('What is right').

With the gradual progression and evolution of thought, the concepts of many gods in the *Vedas* gave way to the concept of one God. All gods were then seen to be manifestations of one God or deriving their power from one God. This one God was also supposed to uphold *Ṛta*, the universal law.

2. Vedic Scriptures

The *Vedas* which constitute the core canonical scriptures of Hinduism are four in number: the *Ṛg*, the *Yajur*, the *Sāma* and the *Atharva*, each traditionally divided into four segments: *Saṃhitā*, *Brāhmaṇa*, *Āraṇyaka* and *Upaniṣads*. The earliest is the *Ṛg Saṃhitā* which was a compilation of sacred hymns and prayers addressed to the various deities, and the chief purpose of these hymns was to use in the sacrificial rituals. The way these hymns were used in the sacrificial rituals gave rise to two further *Saṃhitās* or collections: the *Sāma* and the *Yajur*. The *Sāma Saṃhitā* (sometimes simply called the *Sāma Veda*) consists of hymns mostly taken from the *Ṛg Veda* and arranged according to their respective timings of recitation in the sacrificial rites. This also has a second section consisting of notated chants (*sāmans*) to which the hymns were set. They were meant to be sung in the sacrifices with the specified chants and melodies. The *Yajur Saṃhitā* or *Veda* contains hymns found in the *Ṛg*, as also prose and verse formulas (*Yajurs*) which were muttered (as opposed to chanted) by the priests during the performances of the rituals.

The fourth *Saṃhitā* called *Atharva* seems to have come from a different stream of thought and absorbed later into the Vedic family. Though it contains hymns of prayer to gods and makes ample references to the devas and devis of the *Ṛg*, it is largely composed of earthly verse-spells for protection against life's problems (fevers and sicknesses, enemies, snake-bites, bad dreams and so on) and charms and sorcery for bringing about some desired results (eg. the goodwill of others, victory in battle, success in love, healthy cattle, good crops and rain, virility, power in society and so on).

Thus, the four *Saṃhitās* (collections)– the *Ṛg*, the *Yajur*, the *Sama* and the *Atharva*–first came to be established as a canonical block. Then followed the other three stages of development of the Vedic scriptures: the *Brāhmaṇas*, the *Āraṇyakas* and the *Upaniṣads*. The *Brāhmaṇas* contain the descriptions and explanations of the various sacrificial rites. Here the Vedic hymns and prayers have been analyzed and detailed instructions given on what hymns to be applied to which sacrifices, what hymns to be sung at which time and when a particular oblation to be offered to a god in a sacrificial fire. The values and significance of the various ceremonial rites have also been described in the *Brāhmaṇas*. These *Brāhmaṇas* are in prose form whereas the *Saṃhitās* are poetical. There are *Brāhmaṇas* attached to each *Veda*.

The third section of each *Veda*, called *Āraṇyaka*, is mainly in prose and contains deeper reflections of the pious men who had retired to forest life after fulfilling their house-hold duties. They no longer performed sacrificial rites. The central goal of the *Saṃhitās* and *Brāhmaṇas* was the efficacious performance of the sacrificial rituals. This gradually transformed into more symbolic reflections in the *Āraṇyakas* into the meaning and purpose (*artha*) behind the rituals. The main theme of the *Āraṇyakas* is philosophical contemplation of the supreme power or reality. Some explanations of the hymns of the *Ṛg veda* are also found in the *Āraṇyakas.*

The fourth and last section of each *Veda* is called the *Upaniṣad.* The *Upaniṣads* are known as *Vedānta* (the end of the *Veda*) by virtue of the fact that they are the concluding portions of the *Vedas* and also since these represent the chief aim and goal of the *Vedas*. They aim at *Brahma-jñāna* or the knowledge of Brahman, the ultimate reality. Thus , they represent the *Jñāna-kāṇḍa* or the knowledge portion of the *Vedas* whereas the *Saṃhitās* and the *Brāhmaṇas* represent the *Karma-kāṇḍa* or ritual portion. The *Upaniṣadic* teachings have been composed in prose as well as verse forms. We shall consider these teachings in the next section.

The present-day scholarship is of the view that the actual literary development and composition of the *Vedas*-from the beginning of compilation of the *Saṃhitās* to the composition of the *Upaniṣads*–may have been over a period of a millennium and half from C.1200 BCE to C.500 CE.

The *Vedas* are venerated as of divine origination, as the "voices heard"(*śrutis*) by the seers in their direct intuitive perception. They are said to contain infallible truths directly revealed or breathed out to the seers by Brahman, the ultimate God, himself. As such, they are considered to be most sacred. *Vāc,* word, wisdom, breathed out by Brahman, came to be called the first created thing, *Brahmā* and also *prathamajam* (first born).

3. Sacrificial Rituals

The Vedic religion was dominated by the practices of sacrificial ritual performances (*yajña*) with the objective of bending the cosmic powers represented by the various gods to serve the earthly needs of the individual or the individuals. The individuals go in for the rituals and sponsor them desiring progeny, cattle, wealth, health, power, victory in battle, success in the various mundane endeavours or reward of immortal life in heaven. Sacrifices were conducted for rains to ward off drought, cosmic stability and social well-being as well. The rituals involved setting up of three fires: the *gārhapatya* (household fire), the *āhavanīya* (fire-of-the-offering) and the *dakṣiṇāgni* (southern fire), for pouring the sacrificial offerings so that these offerings are carried and transmitted to the gods by the *Agni deva* (fire god). The rituals involved animal sacrifices also in addition to other sacrificial offerings. *Aśvamedha yajña* (horse sacrifice) is the famous sacrifice prescribed for the kings desirous of extending their domains. The practice of offering *soma* juice to the deities and imbibing this intoxicating drink during the rituals ostensibly for the purpose of enhancing the mystic vision were also common.

The belief underlying the performances of these sacrificial rituals was that the hymns, prayers and mantras invoked and recited in these sacrifices had the magical power and potency to influence the cosmic powers and bring about the desired results. The Vedic utterances in these sacrifices with their intonation and vibrational patterns and prosody (i.e. the patterns of sounds and rhythms) were believed to be the key to the success of the rituals. This sacrificial culture and tradition gave prominence and importance to the priestly class (brahmins) who were the professionals well-versed in the Vedic teachings and who had the requisite specialized knowledge and skill to carry out these sacrificial rituals for the benefit of the individuals. This priestly class acted as intermediaries between the individual humans and the divine powers and in their role as such intermediaries, they exercised considerable influence over the lives of their fellow beings working on the psychological fears and anxieties of the latter. With such gain of power over others, they elevated themselves to a higher pedestal of superior class. They were called *deva-puruṣas* (godmen), and the concept of purity came to be attached to them. Because of their purity, they were considered most suited to perform the sacrificial rituals on behalf of the sacrificers and ensure granting of their wishes by gods. To maintain ritual purity, they had to be a separate class of special birth.

4. Varṇa Theory

The *Vedas*, 'the voices heard' (*śrutis*), issued forth from the mouth of Brahman and likewise, the class of brahmins, destined to become proficient in the *Vedas* and eligible to perform sacrificial rituals enjoined in the *Vedas*, also came forth from the mouth of Brahman, the ultimate reality. What makes a *Brahmin* is such special birth that ensures his knowledge of the *Vedas* and the ritual purity required by the *Vedas*. This class distinction had the divine sanction giving a sacrosanct status to it, for, in a late hymn of the *Ṛg veda* (10.90, the hymn of the generative sacrifice of the cosmic person), it has been described how different human beings emerged out of the cosmic person. "His mouth became the *Brahmin,* his arms became those who protect and rule (*rājanya*), his thighs became those who trade (*vaiśya*), from his feet those who serve (*śūdra*) were born." Thus a distinctive class hierarchy has been ordained in the *Veda* and this may be interpreted as a division of labour in the society, but it is also a division assigning relative purity to the different levels of human beings. The class of brahmins has been blessed with the highest purity and the highest social status. Each succeeding class is less and less pure with corresponding inferior social status. The last one was so impure that it became a group of outcastes.

How this class division or *varṇa* (colour or race?) division degenerated into the odious caste distinctions is a very complex issue and a matter of considerable debate. This calls for a separate detailed study. It may only be stated here that this distinction is hardly justifiable, however much the conservative revivalists and fundamentalists may tend to argue that this hierarchy is somehow organic and natural. It is not only anachronistic, but also militates against the fundamental universal principles of equality and justice.

5. Vedic Philosophy

For our present purpose, what concerns us here is what the Vedas teach on the reality or the truth in the existences. We gather from the *Saṃhitās* and the *Brāhmaṇas* that what they consider reality are the various gods. These gods in point of fact are only the personifications of the various cosmic powers or forces of nature. What concern them are these cosmic powers and the means to win the favours of these powers. The path they prescribe is the path of sacrificial rites to please these cosmic powers and achieve the desired ends. All goal here in this religion is earthly, mundane and materialistic. Sometimes immortal life in heaven is talked about as the goal. The inner workings or dynamics of the universe are conceived as influenced by the sacrificial rituals with their offerings and recitations of mantras, hymns and prayers which are believed to possess magical power and potency of their own to bring about the desired results. According to this religion, the sacrifices uphold and sustain the cosmic stability and natural order, *Ṛta.*

A trend towards monotheism is discerned in the later portions of the *Vedas*. The one God, the supreme, is variously called as *'Puruṣa'*, *'Viśvakarman'*, *'Hiraṇyagarbha'* and *'Prajāpati'*. The underlying philosophy in this religion is that the cosmic powers support and sustain the universe and its beings, and sacrificial offerings have to be made to satisfy these cosmic powers and keep them in their course or *Ṛta*.

Even though we do not come across profound philosophical insights in the *Vedas*, poetical and soul-stirring prayers and descriptions of nature abound in them. An evocative description of creation is given in the Hymn of Creation (X.129, *Nāsadīya*) in the *Ṛg Veda*.

> There was neither non-existence nor existence then;
> there was neither the realm of space
> nor the sky which is beyond.
> What stirrred? Where? In whose protection?
> Was there water there, bottomlessly deep?
> There was neither death nor immortality then.
> There was no distinguishing sign of night nor of day.
> The one breathed, windless, by its own impulse.
> Other than that there was nothing beyond.
> Darkness was hidden by darkness in the beginning;
> with no distinguishing sign, all this was water,
> The life-force that was covered with emptiness,
> that one arose through the power of heat.

What was the principle behind the creation of the world? The above *Ṛg Vedic* hymn postulates life-force as this principle. That was covered with emptiness. There was neither existence nor non-existence then. All this was water. That one was breathing without breath. This creation hymn seems to be a metaphorical description extending the analogy of the microcosmic sperm cell floating in the waters in the mother's womb to the cosmic level. The life-force is identified as *Hiraṇyagarbha* at the macrocosmic level. *Hiraṇyagarbha* is the golden germ from which the world grows. How did the life-force or *Hiraṇyagarbha* arise? The suggestion here seems to be that in creation water came first and all this was water before consciousness(life-principle) evolved from it through the power of heat. This power of heat may be interpreted either as desire

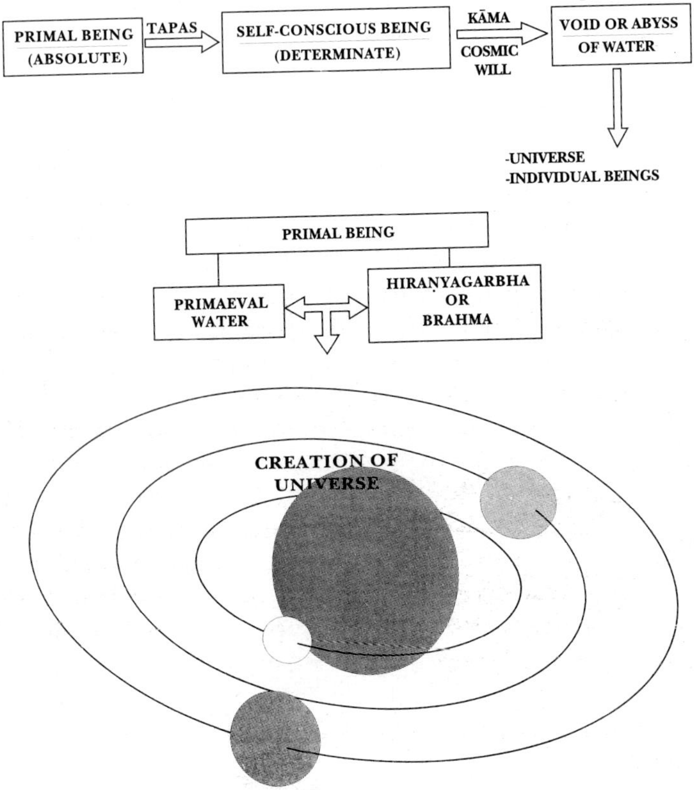

Fig. 1 Vedic Ideas on Creation

(*kāma*) or as *tapas* (the contemplative power). The desire propelling the life-force in the human embryo is transmuted to the contemplative power, *tapas*, in the conception of creation at the macrocosmic level (Figure 1).

There are a number of instances in the *Saṃhitās*, however, where desire (*kāma*) is specifically associated with the creation of the universe (RV X.190). The *Ṛg Vedic* hymn I.10-72 describes not-being (*asat*) as lying "with outstretched feet" like a woman in the throes of child-birth. As the first product of the divine mind, the mind's first fruit, came forth *kāma*, desire. This is seen as the cosmic will, the primal source of all existence. In this *kāma*, "the wise, searching in their hearts, have by contemplation discovered the connection between the existent and the non-existent".

In the above hymns of creation quoted, there is no mention of a god like *Indra* or *Varuṇa, Prajāpati* or *Viśvakarman.* All these gods seem to be of late or of secondary origin. They are ignorant of their origin and what was in the beginning.

In some hymns in the *Ṛg Veda* (X.82, IV.58.5, I.10.121), *Prajāpati* (the lord of creatures) is praised as the creator and preserver of the world and as the one God. In hymn I.10.121, *Prajāpati* is described as the first existent being facing the chaos of waters. He impregnates the waters and becomes manifest in them in the form of a golden egg or germ from which the whole universe develops. He is called the one life or soul of the gods (*devānām asuḥ*). The chaos of water here may be the precursor to the later *Sāṃkhyan* principle of *prakṛti.*

In some accounts, a primal being has been recognized and he is said to produce spontaneously the primeval water; "from this comes the primordial God as the first born of the divine order, the golden germ of the world, who was the first seed resting on the navel of the unborn. *Hiraṇyagarbha* who is the world-soul expresses his spirit through the environment. He manifests the forms contained within himself. The world is fixed in him as are the spokes in the hub of a wheel. He is the thread, *sūtrātman,* on which all beings and all worlds are strung like the beads of necklace. He is the first-born, *prathamaja*". (Dr. S. Radhakrishnan, Basic Writings, p.122). He is also known mythologically as *Brahmā,* the four-headed creator God. He is the golden germ containing within himself all the forms and the entire universe. He is said to enter into creation and manifest all these forms and the universe.

In these accounts of creation, we find a tension between non-existence and existence, non-being and being, and duality and non-douality. There is wonder and surmise, questioning and doubt in these theories. It is asked whether existence came from non-existence and whether being was produced from non-being. Also there is a question whether there was only one primal being from the beginning or there was a duality of primal waters (*prakṛti*) and primal being (*Puruṣa)*. With characteristic humility, doubts on the various theories of creation are expressed in the following hymn in the *Ṛg Veda* :

> "He, the first origin of this creation, whether he formed
> it all or did not form it,
> Whose eye controls this world in highest heaven,
> He, verily, knows it or perhaps he knows not."
> (RV X 129.7)

When we come to the *Brāhmaṇas,* we find that they consider *Brahmā* or Brahman as the central principle of the universe. Brahman denoted the ritual as well as the *mantra* (prayer). Gradually it acquired the meaning of mysterious power to turn on the universe. Thus, in the *Brāhmaṇa*s, the objective working of the universe came to be regarded as based on the performance of sacrificial rituals and the potency of the mantras chanted or uttered in the rituals. The hymns of the *Saṃhitās* are the mantras that came from Brahman. Brahman is also ritual. By knowing Brahman, by performing sacrifices and by reciting his *mantras,* one controls the universe. He who knows Brahman knows and controls the universe. This is the central teaching of the *Brāhmaṇas.*

6. Ultimate Goal

The ultimate goal in the Vedic religion is longevity (living for a hundred autumns) or immortality in a heavenly realm after death. The concept of immortality as the final goal of human existence has undergone change, in the *Vedas* themselves and in their subsequent interpretations. The concept in the *Saṃhitās* is circumscribed by a narrow vision and focus on heavenly enjoyments with attendant sensual pleasures of all kinds. As Julius Lipner points out:

"......... immortality as understood in the *Upaniṣads* (and by their interpreters, the *Vedāntins*) differ from the immortality intimated by the *Saṃhitās*. This may also be said about the (means for) attainment of immortality. In the religion of the *Saṃhitās*, immortality is attained by ritual performances and in that of the *Upaniṣads* by the contemplative and recitative interiorization of the ritual. But it is immortality according to either understanding, and the way to attain it, that is the central concern of the Vedic corpus" (Hindus, Julius Lipner. p.41).

The validity and the truth of these teachings rest solely on the scriptural authority of the *Vedas*. The *Vedas* are considered infallible because of their divine origination. It is stressed that human intellect and reasoning powers cannot comprehend and uncover these truths. These are made the articles of faith.

Even in this modern age of scientific temper and rational spirit, the fundamentalists tend to project the *varṇa* theory, the social order based on *varṇa* and caste distinctions and the world-view based on the sacrificial rituals as infallible truths and as divinely ordained. If the belief in the efficacy of the ritualistic sacrifices and prayers prescribed in the *Vedas* still holds sway in the minds of the masses, it is simply because they appeal to their imaginations and work on their psychological fears, hopes and desires. Impelled by desires and hopes, the people ignorant of the true nature of things tend to grasp whatever means and devices offered to them which hold the promise of bringing material gains. Rational thinking and enquiry yield place to blind faiths and superstitious beliefs. Instinctual fears, desires and hopes are the grounds breeding the blind faiths and beliefs.

The *Upaniṣads (Vedānta)* and the *Bhagavad Gītā* tend to turn away from the traditional ritualistic sacrifices and *yajñas* enjoined in the Vedic teachings and practices and direct the efforts to new spiritual levels weaning the mind away from mundane goals. They emphasize and assign importance to wisdom as against the ritualistic actions prescribed in the earlier *Vedas* and add new meanings and dimensions to the concept of immortality.

With this brief on the Vedic ideas, we now turn over to the study of the *Upaniṣads*.

Part II

UPANIṢADS

CHAPTER 2

Basic Ideas

As we have already seen, the *Upaniṣads* are the concluding portions of the *Vedas* and represent the *Jñāna-kāṇḍa* or the knowledge portion of the *Vedas*.

The scholars interpret the word '*Upaniṣad*' as derived from *upa* (near), *ni* (down) and *sad* (to sit), i.e. sitting down near. Thus, the term '*Upaniṣad* ' is interpreted to signify the secret doctrine learnt sitting down at the feet of the teacher and hearing from him. In the quietude of the forest hermitages, the sages of the *Upaniṣads* pondered on the deep philosophical questions and communicated their knowledge to the deserving disciples gathered around them.

Śaṅkara, in his introduction to the *Kaṭha Upaniṣad*, interprets the word '*Upaniṣad*' as derived by adding *upa* (near) and *ni* (with certainty) as prefixes and *kvip* as a suffix to the root *sad*, meaning 'to split up', 'to loosen' or 'to destroy'. According to this interpretation, *Upaniṣad* is the knowledge that splits up, injures or destroys the seeds of worldly existence such as ignorance etc. It is the *Brahma-jñāna* i.e., the knowledge of Brahman gained by those seekers of emancipation who, after discarding desires, approach a teacher and receive through his instruction the knowledge (*upa sad*) and who then contemplate or deliberate on it with steadiness and certainty (*ni*). It is the knowledge, "knowing that, one becomes freed from the jaws of death" (*Kaṭha* I.3.15) (*Eight Upaniṣads* with the commentary of Śaṅkarācārya, Trans. By Swāmī Gambhīrānanda, Vol.I, P.99/100).

In *Muktika Upaniṣad* (I.30-39), it is said that salvation may be attained by a study of the hundred and eight *Upaniṣads*. From this, it may be seen that Indian tradition has generally recognized and acknowledged one hundred and eight *Upaniṣads* even though in actual number they may be more than two hundred.

The principal *Upaniṣads* are said to be ten. Śaṅkara has commented on eleven: *Bṛhad-āraṇyaka, Chāndogya, Īśa, Kena, Kaṭha, Taittirīya, Aitareya, Muṇḍaka, Māṇḍūkya, Praśna* and

Śvetāśvatara. He also refers to the *Kauṣītakī, Jābāla, Mahānārāyaṇa* and *Paiṅgala Upaniṣads* in his commentary on the *Brahma Sūtra.* These together with the *Maitrī Upaniṣad* constitute the principal *Upaniṣads.*

Rāmānuja has used all these *Upaniṣads* as also the *Subāla* and the *Cūlikā.* He mentions also the Garbha, the *Jābāla* and the *Mahā Upaniṣads.*

The other *Upaniṣads* which have come down are more religious than philosophical. They belong more to the Purāṇa and the Tantra than to the *Veda.*

As Richard King has summarized in his book "Early *Advaita Vedānta and Buddhism*"(p.52), there are roughly four historical layers to the development of the main *Upaniṣadic* texts i.e. early, middle, late and new *Upaniṣads.*

"It is generally accepted that the earliest stratum contains the *Bṛhad-āraṇyaka* and *Chāndogya Upaniṣads.* These are said to contain material that is pre-Buddhist, placing them at some time before the fifth century (before the common era) BCE.

"The middle period covers such *Upaniṣads* as the *Aitareya,* the *Kauṣītakī,* the *Taittirīya,* the *Kāṭhaka,* the *Muṇḍaka,* the *Praśna* and the *Śvetāśvatara Upaniṣads,* which show evidence of Buddhist influences and must therefore have been compiled after the fifth century BCE.

"The late *Upaniṣads* dating from the first two centuries of the common era are the *Kena,* the *Īśa,* the *Māṇḍūkya* and lastly the *Maitrayāṇīya* (or *Maitrī*) *Upaniṣad.*

"Of the new *Upaniṣads* (which are not usually accepted as valid by the *Advaita Vedānta* school) nine are pure *Vedānta* texts, eleven are yoga *Upaniṣads,* seven are *saṃnyāsa Upaniṣads* and twelve are sectarian (five *Śaiva* and seven *Vaiṣṇava*)."

The names of the authors of the *Upaniṣads* are not known. Since these have been composed by many different authors, they do not present a coherent unified religious or philosophical system. Several philosophical ideas have been suggested in the *Upaniṣads,* some of which are even mutually conflicting. What is attempted here is an overview of the main trends of the philosophical thoughts pervading the *Upaniṣadic* literature.

The unification drive discerned in the later portions of the *Saṃhitās* and *Brāhmaṇas* to identify the different deities as one God finds its culmination in the *Upaniṣads.* All gods are now seen as manifestations of one supreme God, Brahman. Brahman is now recognized as the ultimate supreme reality and the one God, underlying all the powers in the universe and uniting all of them.

1. *Ṛta* at the Command of the Imperishable

"From fear of Him does the wind blow; from fear of Him does the sun rise; from fear of Him do *Agni* and *Indra* act and death, the fifth, doth run." (T.U.II.8.1) (*Kaṭha* II. 3.3).

These *Upaniṣadic* sages see the proof of Brahman in the laws of the universe and in the order, rhythm and arrangement in the scheme of nature.

"Verily, at the command of that Imperishable, O *Gārgī*, the sun and the moon stand in their respective positions. At the command of that Imperishable, O *Gārgī*, heaven and earth stand in their respective positions. At the command of that Imperishable, O *Gārgī*, what are called moments, hours, days and nights, half-months, months, seasons, years, flow by. At the command of that Imperishable, O *Gārgī*, some rivers flow to the east from the white snowy mountains, others to the west, in whatever direction each flows ...." (B.U.III 8.9).

The orderly movements of the sun and the moon and the various planets and the heaven and the earth are suggested here as operating at the command of that Imperishable Brahman. From the relative movement of sun and earth arises the concept of time-days, half-months, months and years. This also is at His command. The maintenance of the rhythm, order and the invariable laws of nature is not considered possible without the guidance and control of a superconscious intelligent principle. From within, He is operating as the prime-mover and controller.

2. Supremacy of Brahman Parable in the *Kena Upaniṣad*

The *Upaniṣads* take the view that all the Vedic gods derive their respective powers from Brahman who is the ultimate God and supreme one.

The story of the Vedic gods in *Kena Upaniṣad* (III. 1 to 12 and IV. 1 to 3) vividly illustrates how these gods are devoid of their power without the supreme Brahman.

Brahman asks: "What power is there in thee?". *Agni* conceitedly replies, "I can burn everything whatever is there on earth".

Brahman places a blade of grass before him saying, 'Burn this'. *Agni* goes towards it with all speed, but could not burn it.

Likewise, *Vāyu* (who boasts that he can blow off everything whatever there is on earth) could not blow the blade of grass placed by Brahman.

Then, *Agni, Vāyu* and *Indra* learn from *Umā* (the daughter of Himavat) that it is from Brahman that they derive their power and that it is through his grace alone the gods enjoy their greatness. This story affirms the supremacy and the ultimate power of Brahman most graphically.

3. Divine Powers in the Universe and Individual Self

Whereas the Vedic seers were struck or overwhelmed by the wonderous mystery of the external cosmic universe and identified the powers and divinity behind the different natural phenomena as various gods and goddesses, the sages of the *Upaniṣads* extended their search and enquiry inwardly as well as outwardly-inwardly to what is within them or within the individual self and outwardly exploring the cosmic manifestations. They saw the divinities ruling within the individual self and also recognised a correspondence or identity between the macrocosm of nature and microcosm of man.

In the *Bṛhad-āraṇyaka Upaniṣad* (III. 9.1), *Vidagdha Śakalya* asks *Yājñavalkya:* "How many gods are there, *Yājñavalkya*?"

Yājñavalkya first quotes the *nivid* i.e. the group of verses that enumerates the number of gods invoked in the hymns of praise to the *Viśve-devas* and replies that there are as many as three-thousand and three gods. On repeated questioning, he progressively reduces the number of gods to three-hundred and three, thirty-three, six, three, two, one and a half and ultimately to one.

The enquiry proceeds inwardly as well as outwardly.

First analysing the external universe, the sage *Yājñavalkya* identifies the following eight divine powers as constituting the essence and existence of the universe: the fire, the earth, the air, the sky, the sun, the heaven, the moon and the stars. These are called the eight Vasus because they constitute the universe and also provide support and sustenance for life on the earth.

Next, analysing the individual self, the sage finds the following powers constituting the essence and existence of the self: the powers of the five sensory organs (seeing, hearing, smelling, tasting and touching), the powers of the five motor organs (hands, feet, speech-tongue, genitals and excretionary organs), and the mind. These are the eleven Rudras that make up the individual.

The eight *Vasus*, the eleven *Rudras*, the twelve *Ādityas* (i.e. the twelve months of the year), *Indra* (the thunder) and *Prajāpati* (the sacrifice) are considered the thirty-three gods ruling over the universe and the individual self. Progressively, the sage reduces the number of gods to six, three, two, one and a half and ultimately to one.

"............... Which are the two gods?" "Food (*anna*) and breath (*prāṇa*)".

"Which is the one and a half?" "This one here who blows the air". "How is he one and a half?" Because, combining with food, he becomes one and a half and, when he blows, all this grow up".

"Which is the one God?" "The breath. He is Brahman. They call him *tyat* (that)"(B.U. III. 9.8 & 9).

In the above analysis, progressively, the entire universe (macrocosm) and the individual (microcosm) are reduced to two fundamental principles:food (*anna*) and breath (*prāṇa*). Food (*anna*) represents matter which becomes food for the life-forms and their senses and which constitutes their bodies. Breath (*prāṇa*) is the life-force. Out of the union of these two develop all the rest. Because of its importance and vital function, *prāṇa* is accorded a certain primacy out of the two and is identified with the one God, the ultimate Brahman, considering the fact that without the breath all the bodily functions of the individual self cease.

4. Supremacy of *Prāṇa* and *Prāṇa* as *Prajñātmā*

In an allegorical story in the *Bṛhad-āraṇyaka Upaniṣad*, the divinities controlling the six bodily functions – life-breath, speech, eye, ear, mind and semen (procreation) – dispute among themselves as to who is superior and the most excellent. They go to *Brahmā* and put their question. Brahma answers that he is the most excellent whose departure makes the body the worst. (*B.U.* VI. 1.7)

"(The organ of) speech departed and having remained absent for a year came back and asked: "How have you been able to live without me?" They said: "As the dumb, not speaking with speech but breathing with the breath, seeing with the eye, hearing with the ear, thinking with the mind, procreating with semen. Thus have we lived". Then speech entered in" (*B.U.* VI. 1.8).

When the eye departed for a year, the others lived as the blind. With the ear departed, the others lived as the deaf. With the mind departed, the rest lived as the stupid. With the semen (the organ of procreation) departed, the rest lived as the impotent (*B.U.* VI. 1.9 to 12).

"Then as the life-breath tended to depart, even as a large fine horse of the Sindhu land might pull up the pegs to which his feet are tied, even so did it pull up those vital breaths (i.e. the divinities controlling the other sense organs) together. They cried out: "Venerable Sir, do not go out; verily, we shall not be able to live without you." "If I am such, make me an offering", said the life-breath. "So be it", answered the others." (*B.U.* VI 1.13)

In the microcosm of man, *prāṇa* (life-breath) has thus been identified as the central principle, core reality. The *Upaniṣad* concludes that the divine power bestowing the power of seeing, the one bestowing the power of hearing, the one bestowing the power of thinking, the one bestowing the power of speech, the one bestowing the power of procreation–all spring from the same source and all have the same fountain-head. This fountain-head is the *prāṇa*, Progressively, as the enquiry deepens further, an inner immortal person is recognized as the higher divinity within, behind *prāṇa*, and this is the one who breaths and sustains the life. This one who breaths is now called in the *Kauṣītakī Upaniṣad* as *prajñātmā*. "What is the breathing spirit is the intelligence self (*prajñātmā*). What is the intelligence self, that is the breathing spirit".

It is the *prajñātmā* that animates all the sense-organs, co-ordinates and integrates all the sense perceptions and makes them intelligible. Without this *prajñātmā*, the sense perceptions will remain scattered and fragmentary and no knowledge will be possible. The *prāṇa* now becomes identified with *prajñātmā*.

Kauṣītakī Upaniṣad proclaims that it is the true understanding of this truth and meditation on this truth that leads one to immortality. Indra conceived as the supreme being in *K.U.* III.2 says:

"I am the breathing spirit, meditate on me as the intelligence self (*prajñāmā*), as life, as immortality. Life is breath and breath is life. For, as long as breath remains in the body, so long is there life. For indeed with the breathing spirit one obtains immortality in this world, by intelligence true conception. So he who meditates on me as life, as immortality reaches his full (term of) life in this world and obtains immortality and indestructibility in the heavenly world....... (*K.U.*III.2)

The sacrificial rites prescribed in the early Vedic religion as the means for attaining longevity in this world and immortality in heaven are replaced here by meditation on the interior intelligence self (*prajñātmā*) and we see a shift towards interiorisation, deeper probing and search for the inner self. This *Upaniṣad* teaches us to look within for the inner self behind all the external manifestations. Speech is not what one should desire to understand, but one should know the speaker. Likewise,

One should desire to understand

Not odour	- but the inner self who smells the odour.
Not form	- but him who sees the form (the seer)
Not sound	- but the hearer
Not taste	- but the discerner of the taste of food
Not the deed	- but the doer
Not the pleasure and pain	- but the enjoyer
Not bliss, delight and procreation	- but the discerner of bliss, delight and procreation.
Not the movement	- but the mover
Not the thought	- but the thinker

".... These ten existential elements are with reference to intelligence. The ten intelligence elements are with reference to existence. For, truly, if there were no elements of existence, there would be no elements of intelligence. Verily, if there were no elements of intelligence, there would be no elements of existence. For, from either alone, no form whatsoever would be possible. And this self (the self of intelligence) is not many. For, as in a chariot the felly is fixed on the spokes and the spokes are fixed on the hub, even so these elements of existence are fixed on the elements of intelligence and the elements of intelligence are fixed in the breathing spirit. This same breathing spirit is truly the intelligence self, bliss, ageless, immortal............" (K.U. III.8)

The inter-relatedness and inter-dependence of the sense-objects, senses and the sense–consciousnesses and their anchoring (rootedness) in the breathing spirit (*prajñātmā*) are clearly brought out in these *Upaniṣadic* passages. This breathing spirit is considered the ultimate reality in the person because it is the one which is present in all the three states of waking, dreaming and deep sleep. When a person falls into dreamless deep sleep, all the five senses and the mind lose their identity and merge in the breathing spirit which alone remains ever shining. (*K.U.* III.3)

5. The Five Vital Breaths

The breathing spirit is the most fundamental element, fundamental reality in the make-up of the person because, as we have already noted, it is the mover or activator of the unintelligent mass (i.e. the body) that animates it and makes it conscious and intelligent. It gives to the five senses and the mind their sensing and mental powers respectively and integrates and co-ordinates their functionings. It controls not only all the conscious faculties of the mind but also all the sub-conscious drives and impulses coursing through the body beneath the surface of the mind. It controls all the vital functions of the body like breathing, circulation of blood through the body, digestion of food and assimilation of energy, excretions from the body, production of semen etc. The *Praśna Upaniṣad* describes how the breathing spirit assigns these functions to the vital breaths: *prāṇa, apāna, samāna, vyāna* and *udāna* just as a sovereign assigns areas and functions to his officers (*Praśna* III.4).

Prāṇa

Prāṇa acts as the sovereign and allots the other vital breaths their respective places and functions. *Prāṇa* is the link between the individual being and the external cosmos. The breath is the thread through which *prāṇa* travels from the cosmos to the individual and from the individual to the cosmos and which weaves the individual being with the cosmos to form an integral unity.

In the sub-division of *prāṇa* into the five vital breaths, the first mentioned *prāṇa* is the vital force of inspiration. In this context, the word *prāṇa* means 'that which draws in or takes in' (*pra+ana*). The vital force, which issues through the mouth and nostrils, acts on the eyes and ears, and controls their functions. The revelation of objects like colour, sound, etc., that constitutes what is known as seeing, hearing etc is caused and controlled by *prāṇa*.

Apāna

Apāna is a division of *prāṇa* and *prāṇa* ordains it to control the excretory organs. Expulsive movements occurring in the bowels, bladder, uterus, seminal vessels and pores during defecation, urination, menstruation, procreation, perspiration and all other kinds of excretions are due to the function of *apāna.*

Samāna

In between the places of *prāṇa* and *apāna* is *samāna* which controls the digestive and assimilating force so as to make all that is eaten or drunk suitable for absorption, and then assimilates the same. It is called *samāna* because it distributes equally, to all parts of the body all that is eaten or drunk, the food that is poured as a libation in the digestive fire in the stomach. (*Praśna* III.5)

Vyāna

Vyāna is the contractile vital force. *Vyāna* exists pervading the body wholly through the nerves, which, like rays from the sun, issue in all directions from the heart, and controls all rhythmic or non-rhythmic contractions in the body. It governs the process of relaxing and contracting the voluntary and involuntary muscles. This force also governs the movements of the ligaments and sends sensory and motor impulses through the nervous tissues. It is the performer of deeds.

Udāna

Udāna means 'energy that uplifts'. It is the force that causes contraction in the thoraic muscles, thereby pushing air out through the vocal chords. It is, therefore, the main cause of the production of sound.

Udāna moves everywhere from the soles of the feet to the head. Among the one hundred and seven nerves said to issue in all directions from the heart, like rays from the sun, is one vital nerve known as *Suṣumnā* which proceeds upwards to the crown of the head. At the time of the death of the person, the vital breath *udāna* departs through this nerve *Suṣumnā* and the crown of the head upwards carrying with it the impressions of mind and intellect. It leads to a virtuous world (such as the world of gods) as a result of deeds that are virtuous, or it leads to a sinful world, to hell or to birth among beasts, if the deeds of the person are sinful, or to the human world if the deeds are virtuous and vicious mixed. (*Praśna* III. 6 & 7).

Next, *Praśna Upaniṣad* talks about the correlation and interdependency of the elements of the macrocosm and microcosm. (*Praśna* III.8)

The sun, indeed, is the external *prāṇa* in the cosmic context. It rises up favouring *prāṇa* (the vital breath) that exists in the eye in the individual body and helps its vital functions. That is, the sun facilitates the perception of form by the vital force *prāṇa* in the eye by providing light for the eye.

That deity which is in the earth, by its power of attracting or pulling, keeps the body rooted in earth and also facilitates the functions of the vital breath *apāna*.

The same air, which is in the middle in the space between heaven and earth, is in *samāna* also, the space within the body.

The air in general that exists externally is *vyāna* because of the similarity of pervasivness. Air pervades the world and *vyāna* pervades the body.

Luminosity is common for the sun (special manifestation in the external universe) and *udāna* in the body. *Udāna* that causes one's leaving the body is of the nature of luminosity just like the sun and while functioning in the body it is favoured by the external light of sun. When the individual dies, this luminosity leaves as *udāna* and rises above with the subtle body and the impressions of the past deeds to attain another body (rebirth).

6. The Dual Principles and the One Brahman

As seen above, in the progressive development of *Upaniṣadic* thought, there comes a stage where multiplicity of divine powers or gods is rejected and duality of *anna* (matter) and *prāṇa* (life-principle) proposed. But, the seers of the *Upaniṣads* are not satisfied with this concept of dual principles as they probe further the facts of life. They deduce an underlying unity behind these principles by a logical analysis of the inter-relationships and interdependency between them.

" 'Brahman is food', say some. This is not so, for, verily food becomes putrid without life. 'Life is Brahman', say some. This is not so, for life dries up without food. But these two deities when they become united attain their highest state......... ." (*B.U.* V.13.1)

The individual cannot survive without air, water, food and light which come from the external universe. He is inextricably woven into the fabric of the universe with these basic elements of nature. He and the external universe are interrelated and interdependent.

His body depends upon food and hence upon the earth that produces food. He toils upon the earth and produces food.

The seed depends on water to sprout and grow into a plant or tree. Speech depends on the fire (heat) in the body. There is no breath without air. Eye depends on the light of sun for its functioning and the ear on sound through the space. Like these, instances can be multiplied. Nothing in this world is independent or self-contained.

All things evolve and develop out of the union of these two fundamental principles – *anna* (matter) and *prāṇa* (life-principle). This unifying principle is Brahman. He is the supreme one guiding and governing the union of these two. He is the ultimate divine power and there is none above Him.

7. Interdependency of Cosmic Universe and Individual Self

Honey Doctrine (*Madhu Vidyā*) B.U.

The honey-doctrine (*Madhu-Vidyā*) enunciated in the fifth *Brāhmaṇa* of the *Bṛhad-āraṇyaka Upaniṣad* brings out beautifully the inter-relatedness and inter-dependency of the elements of nature in the external universe and the elements of the individual being, and the unity underlying them(Figure 2).

The interdependency is likened to that existing between the bees and the honey. The honey supports the bees and the bees produce honey from the juices in the flowers.

"This earth is (like) honey for all creatures and all creatures are (like) honey for this earth. This shining, immortal person who is in this earth, and with reference to one self, this shining, immortal person who is in the body, he indeed is just this self. This is immortal, this is Brahman, this is all"(*B.U.* II.5.1).

The earth and all living beings are mutually dependent even as the honey and bees are. The earth produces food but it also depends upon the man and the creatures in the production of food. Man tills the earth and enriches it to produce food for him. From food man grows and multiplies his race. Since the earth and the living creatures are thus mutually dependent and interwoven in the fabric of the universe, it is but logical that their causes should also be interlinked. As such, it follows that the ultimate cause of the earth and the living creatures and the fountain-head from which all these spring should be the same one. This leads to the realisation of the truth that the immortal person who causes the earth and who is in the earth supporting it and the one who causes all beings and who is in all the beings

BṚHAD-ĀRAṆYAKA UPANIṢAD
II.5.1 TO 14 and III.9.1 to 9

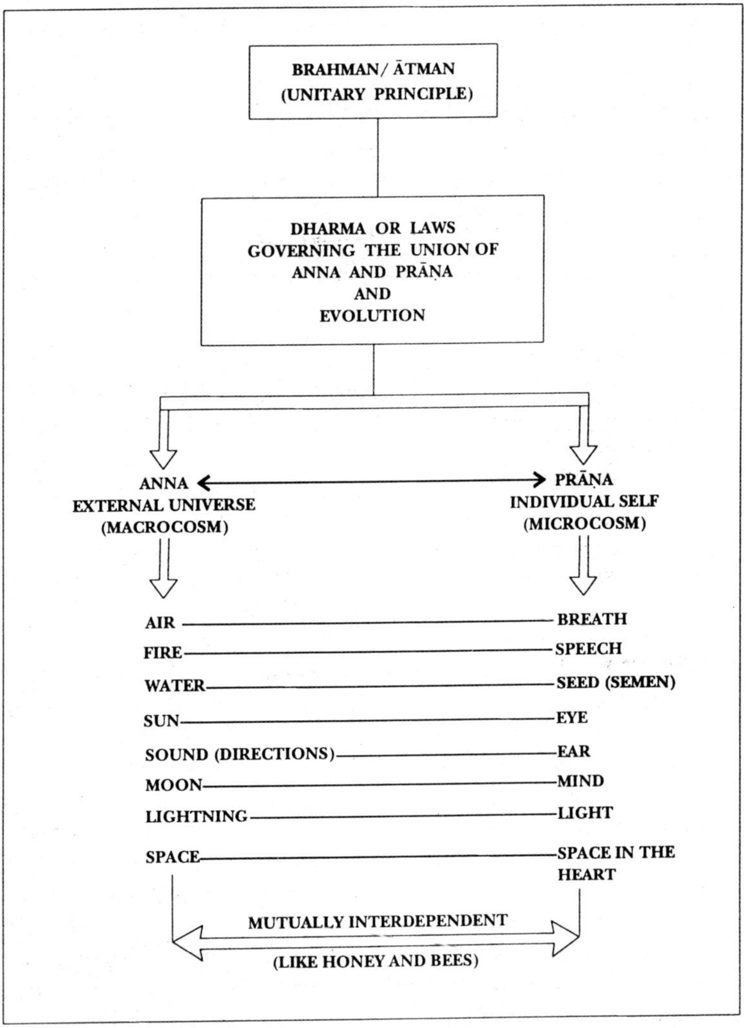

Fig. 2 Interdependency of Universe and Self

supporting and sustaining them are not two different deities but one and the same deity. Brahman is this supporting deity in each – in the earth and also in each individual being. He is the ruling Self in everything.

Like earth, every other principal element or principle in nature in the external universe is analysed and compared with the corresponding element constituting the individual self, and their interdependency highlighted in the subsequent verses II. 5.2 to 14 in the *Bṛhad-āraṇyaka Upaniṣad.* The correspondence and interrelationship between the macrocosm (the external universe) and the microcosm (the individual self) can be seen from the following comparison:

In the external (Macrocosm)	**In the Individual Self Universe (Microcosm)**
Water	Seed (Semen)
Fire	Speech
Air	Breath
Sun	Eye
Sound	Ear
Moon	Mind
Lightning	Light
Space	Space in the heart

From this close relationship and interdependency between the elements of macrocosm and the elements of microcosm, B.U. concludes that the two shining immortal deities – the one underlying the external universe (macrocosm) and the one underlying the individual being (microcosm) – are one and the same. They are nothing but Brahman who is the governing deity, the supreme.

It is very interesting and instructive to note that this honey-doctrine equates or identifies Brahman with the law (*Dharma*)– the universal laws governing the essence and existence of *anna* (matter) i.e. the external universe and *prāṇa* (life-principle) i.e. the individual self, their interactions and their union and the evolutions therefrom.

"This law (*Dharma*) is like honey for all beings and all beings are like honey for this law. This shining immortal person who is in this law with respect to the universe and this shining immortal person who exists in the law-abidingness (righteousness) with respect to the individual–both are just this Self, this is immortal, this is Brahman, this is all"(*B.U.* II.5.11).

The concept of *Dharma* as law-abidingness and righteousness is also suggested here.

"This self (cosmic self) is like honey for all beings and all beings are like honey for this (cosmic) self. This shining immortal person who is in this (cosmic) Self and the shining immortal person who is in this (individual) self of beings – both are just this Self, this is immortal, this is Brahman, this is all" (*B.U.* II.5.14).

"This Self, verily, is the lord of all beings, the king of all beings. As all the spokes are held together in the hub and felly of a wheel, just so, in this Self, all beings, all gods, all worlds, all living creatures, all these selves are held together" (*B.U.* II.5.15).

Traditionally the ultimate power in the external cosmic universe (macrocosm) i.e. shining immortal person in the cosmic universe is called Brahman and the innermost being, the shining immortal person supporting and sustaining the individual being, is called *Ātman.* Even though, as we shall see later, there are some differences in the teachings of the various *Upaniṣad* sages and conflicting viewpoints, yet all the *Upaniṣads* are unanimous in confirming the identity of Brahman and *Ātman.* Brahman in the cosmic universe is the same as the *Ātman* in the individual self. This follows from an analysis of the facts of experience and the doctrine of interdependency and interrelatedness observed in the two systems – macrocosm and microcosm. This interdependency proves that the two ruling principles – Brahman and *Ātman* – cannot be different.

To summarize, the above mantras in the fifth *Brāhmaṇa* of *Bṛhad-āraṇyaka Upaniṣad* establish the following truths:

(1) The correspondence and interrelationships between the elements of the external world and the individual beings are analogous to those existing between the honey and the bees.

(2) There is only one supreme God and that is Brahman. All the divine powers witnessed in the macrocosm (i.e. the external world) and microcosm (i.e. the individual being) are but his manifestations. Brahman behind the cosmic universe is the same as the *Ātman* underlying the individual self.

(3) Brahman exists within each and every element of the external universe and also within the individual beings as their essence (*Dharma* or law). He is immanent through and through. The idea of a transcendent God

separate from the external universe and the inidividual beings has been rejected.

(4) The eternal laws governing the union of the two fundamental principles – *anna* (matter) and the *prāṇa* (the life-breath) – and the interactions between the elements of the macrocosm and microcosm and the evolutions from these interactions and union are also Brahman.

(5) Brahman is an integral whole and unity like a wheel. Just as in a wheel all the spokes are held together in its hub and felly, in Brahman are held together all the elements of the external universe, all worlds, all divinities and all breathing creatures.

This is the *Madhu-Vidyā*, the Honey Doctrine, preached by *Dadhyaṅ* to the two *Aśvins.* The story goes that Indra was afraid of the spread of this sacred doctrine because it was bound to undermine his authority and supremacy. Therefore, he had threatened *Dadhyaṅ* that he would cut off his head if he taught this Honey-Doctrine to anyone else.

At the insistence of the two *Aśvins, Dadhyaṅ* had to take recourse to wearing a horse's head given by them in place of his own, before venturing to teach this doctrine to them. Since he disseminated this doctrine, Indra became angry and carried out his threat. But, the *Aśvins* restored to *Dadhyaṅ* his own head. This is considered such a sacred and secret doctrine.

Chāndogya Upaniṣad

The same truth is proclaimed by *Chāndogya Upaniṣad* also in many of its verses. The idea of the individual self and the external world interwoven together as an integrated whole or unity is stressed in verses *C.U.* III.18. 1 to 6.

8. Progressive Definition of Brahman

A *Kṣatriya's* Teaching on Brahman (B.U. Chapter II, First *Brāhmaṇa*)

In this section of *Bṛhad-āraṇyaka Upaniṣad* occurs the famous dialogue between *Dṛpta-Bālāki* of the *Gārgya* clan (a *Brāhmaṇa* by birth) and *Ajātaśatru* of *Kāsī* (a *kṣatriya* by birth) regarding the definition of Brahman and how he is known.

Gārgya says: "The person who is yonder in the sun, on him, indeed, do I meditate as Brahman" (*B.U.* II 1.2).

He further states:
"The person –
- who is yonder in the moon
- who is yonder in the lightning
- who is yonder in the ether
- who is here in air
- who is here in fire
- who is here in water
- who is here in a mirror
- who is in the quarters (of heaven)

On him, indeed, do I meditate as Brahman"

(*B.U.* II 1.3 to 13)

Ajātaśatru asks: "Is that all?" "That is all", says *Gārgya*.

Ajātaśatru refutes and says:; "With that much only, it is not known" (B.U. II 1.14)

Gārgya identifies Brahman with the divinities he comprehends in the external universe – the sun, the moon, the lightning, the air, etc. *Ajātaśatru* is not satisfied and tells that this is not all and that, with this much only, Brahman is not known. Thereupon, *Gārgya*, the *Brāhmaṇa*, asks the *kṣatriya* king to impart him the knowledge of Brahman. It is contrary to the usual practice that a *Brāhmaṇa* should come as a pupil to a *kṣatriya* for a teaching on Brahman. *Ajātaśatru* takes *Gārgya* to a person who is asleep. The sleeping person does not get up even when addressed and called. *Ajātaśatru* wakes up the person by rubbing him with his hand.

Ajātaśatru questions *Gārgya*: "When this person, who consists of intelligence, fell asleep thus, where was his intelligence and whence did it come back?"(*B.U.* II. 1.16).

Gārgya is clueless. *Ajātaśatru* teaches him that Brahman is not only the cosmic elements meditated upon by him but also that Self (*Ātman*) within the person who is only known or surmised when analysing the sleeping state. He is also that Self who by his intelligence or power takes into himself and absorbs the intelligence or power he gave to the senses of the person to be active in the waking state and restrains them in the sleeping state. He is the one who has struck down the senses dormant and who is himself active in the sleeping state supporting the life's vital unconscious activities in the person. He is the Self (*Ātman*) who projects the senses and the intelligence in the waking state of the person and restrains them in the sleeping state. He is also the one who is ever present in all the states of existence of the person – the embryonic state, the waking state, the dreaming state and the sound sleep state. He resides within the space of the heart. He remains rooted in the summit of bliss, in the pinnacle of peace, in all these states, just as he experiences the perfect bliss in the sound-sleep state.

In the deep sleep state when the breath is restrained, the speech is restrained, the eye is restrained, the ear is restrained, the mind is restrained, (when one falls sound asleep, when he knows nothing), the self (*Ātman*) alone remains active and rests in the summit of bliss, in its own self within the space of the heart. (*B.U.* II. 1.17)

It is from this Self (*Ātman*) or Brahman that all the breaths, all the worlds (including the worlds in the waking state, the worlds in the dream state and the worlds in the deep sleep state), all the divinities, all the beings come forth, issue forth, just as the fine thread comes forth from the spider and the sparks issue forth from the fire (*B.U.* II 1.20).

The teaching here is that by exploring the external universe, we come across conflicting and contradictory natures and attributes of Brahman. The true nature of Brahman is not known, not realized in this process. By delving deep within the individual self only, the true nature of Brahman can be known because Brahman is not different from the Self (*Ātman*). The Self in the deep sleep state points to the true nature of Brahman. His nature is nothing but bliss (*ānanda*).

Universal Self – *Chāndogya Upaniṣad*

A discussion on Brahman similar to the one described above takes place in *Chāndogya Upaniṣad* also (*C.U.* Chapter V, Sections 11 to 18).

The conceptions of sky, sun, air, space, water and earth as Self are here accepted by the king *Aśvapati* as only partially true. He says: "Sky is only the head of the Self; the sun is only the eye of the Self; the air is only the breath of the Self; the space is only the body of the Self; the water is only the bladder of the Self and the earth is only the feet of the Universal Self (Brahman)". He corrects the wrong notions of the pupils who mistake the parts for the whole (i.e. Self) even as blind men mistake parts of the elephant for the elephant.

Aśvapati describes universal Self (Brahman) as of the measure of the span (*prādeśa-mātra*), that is, Brahman is of the measure spanning from the heaven to earth. The idea conveyed here is that the universal Self has the entire universe as his body and, residing in space, he has assumed the shape of the whole universe. He is non-different from the universe. It is also taught here in this mantra that the Universal Self who resides in space is identical with the *Ātman* or Self in man who resides in the secret place of the heart.

He Who is Yonder in the Sun and He Who is Here in the Heart, They are One—*Maitrī Upaniṣad*

Maitrī Upaniṣad also proclaims the fundamental truth of the identity of Brahman and *Ātman* most eloquently in the following passages.

"He (the Self) manifests himself in two ways, as he who is breath and he who is the sun. ________ Yonder sun, verily, is the outer self; the inner self is breath. _____ Now that golden person who is within the sun, who looks on this earth from his golden place, is even he who has entered into the lotus of the heart and eats food" (*Maitrī* VI.1).

"Now, he who has entered the lotus of the heart and eats food is the same as that fire of the sun which enters the sky, called Time the invisible, who eats all beings as his food.........." (*Maitrī* VI.2).

The secret and mysterious power that lies within the heart continuously pumping the same and whose fire digests the food consumed is the same as the fire in the sun. The digestive fire in the stomach of the individual (*vaiśvānara* fire) is equated here with the fire in the sun.

The sun-rise in the east and the sun-set in the west lead to the concept of time and give rise to the ideas of creation and dissolution with the passage of time. Thus time becomes the eater of all beings. Time is conceived as eating all beings as his food. The divine cosmic power that is behind the sun, behind the evolution and dissolution of the universe and all its beings and behind time eating all these beings as his food, is the same as the power within the individual self and within the heart of man that eats food, grows the individual and finally dissolves the individual.

"............. He is that luminous form which gives heat in the yonder sun, the wonderful light on the smokless fire, as also the fire in the stomach that cooks (digests) food. For thus has it been said, He who is in the fire, and he who is here in the heart and he who is yonder in the sun-he is one. He who knows this goes to the oneness of the One"(*Maitrī* VI. 17).

Thus, the *Upaniṣads* proclaim the ideal oneness of the breath within the man, the fire within the man i.e. the Self of the individual with the cosmic power sustaining and supporting the universe i.e. Brahman.

"God's dwelling place", says Dr. Radhakrishnan in his exposition of the philosophy of the *Upaniṣads*, "is the heart of man. The inner immortal Self and the great cosmic power are one and the same. Brahman is *Ātman* and *Ātman* is Brahman. The one supreme power through which all things have been brought into being is one with the inmost Self in each man's heart."

9. Theories on Self (*Ātman*)

We see a progressive evolution of thoughts in the *Upaniṣads*. In the initial stages of enquiry, two fundamental principles–*anna* (food or material principle) and *prāṇa* (life-breath)–were identified as accounting for the evolution of the universe. Recognizing the importance and the vital nature of *prāṇa*, a certain supremacy was accorded to the same among the divine powers within the individual being and it was even equated with the supreme power Brahman at some stages. At some point in the early *Upaniṣadic* period, the theories of Law of Karma and transmigration of the soul or the life-spirit, that were the products of the alien *śramaṇic* culture outside the main stream Vedic religion, came to be absorbed in the *Upaniṣadic* philosophy. These involved the notion of a permanent inner self in each individual being and continuity of the same birth after birth. *Prāṇa*, breath, is absent in the course of life in the mother's womb as the embryo and also in the post-mortem journey. The search for the reality or the underlying principle (self) in each living being culminated in the recognition of an inner immortal person behind the *prāṇa* (breath). He is the one who breaths and who is ever present in all the states of existence. Thus, with the progressive development of thoughts, the focus shifted from *prāṇa* (life-breath) to the person behind the same who breaths, and the *prāṇa* came to be called as *Jīvātma*, *Prajñātma*, inner immortal person or *Ātman*.

The word '*Ātman*' is understood to be derived from '*an*' ('breathe'), and gradually its meaning was extended to include the life-spirit *Jīvātma*, intelligence self (*Prajñātma*), soul, the inner immortal person and the transmigrating self continuing birth after birth. *Ātman* or Self is the new metaphysical term used in the *Upaniṣads* to denote that true essence in each individual living being or that principle of reality animating life, senses, mind and intellect. We shall now study some important theories of the *Upaniṣads* on the Self (*Ātman*).

Self is Birthless and Deathless – Wisdom Declared by Death *(Yama) (Kaṭha Upaniṣad)*

A very important core teaching of the *Upaniṣads* is that the Self of the person is birthless and deathless. It is immortal. It is only the body that dies and not the Self. Even if the body is slain, the Self survives.

This is the supreme wisdom revealed and taught by Death (Yama, the god of Death) himself to the young boy Naciketā in the famous dialogue in the *Kaṭha Upaniṣad.*

Young boy Naciketā's father, a poor and pious *brahmin,* performs a sacrifice desirous of rewards and presents a few old and feeble cows (which are all that he possessed on earth) as sacrificial offerings to the priests. Seeing that the cows presented are too old to drink water or eat grass and too feeble to give milk or bear calves, the son realizes the utter worthlessness of such sacrificial offerings made by his father and feels worried that "Joyless, verily, are those worlds to which he, who presents such worthless gifts, goes." He wants his father's sacrifice to be more worth-while and more meaningful, not only in name and form. He wants to avert the evil result that would befall his father as a consequence of the imperfect sacrifice. He offers himself to perfect the sacrifice and make it more significant and worthwhile and asks his father: "To whom will thou give me, Sir?" Even though initially ignored by his father, he goes on repeating the question.

Getting angered that a mere boy should be so impertinent as to interfere in his sacrificial acts, the father replies: "Unto Death (Yama) shall I give thee". Naciketā takes his father's words literally and feels that it is his duty to keep his father's words. He is not afraid of death. He has the maturity to understand that life is only transitory and that he will not be the first mortal to die nor will he be the last. Birth and death are the laws of nature. "A mortal ripens like corn, and like corn, is born again."

Thinking thus he offfers himself to Death (Yama) and goes to the abode of Yama. There he waits for three nights because Yama has gone out and is not there. When the latter returns, he feels remorse that a venerable guest has to remain in his house unattended and without food for three nights. Therefore, he wants to make amends and asks the boy to choose three boons.

As a first boon, the boy asks Yama to release him from the words of his father and set him free to return to his father. This granted, the boy asks Yama, as a second boon, to describe to him the fire sacrifice that will lead him to heaven. Yama describes to the boy how that fire sacrifice should be conducted, what kind of bricks are to be used in building the sacrificial altar, how many and in what manner.

As Dr. Radhakrishnan points out, this passage in the *Kaṭha Upaniṣad* advocating sacrifices and rituals as means to attaining to heaven shows the loyalty of the *Upaniṣads* to the tradition of Vedic religion which runs concurrently with the spirit of reform against the soulless rituals and sacrifices. Both the strands of thoughts and teachings are found in the *Upaniṣads.*

Pleased with the boy Naciketā, Yama further tells him that, henceforth, that fire sacrifice will be known by his name as 'Naciketā fire' and that "one who lights the Naciketā fire thrice daily or who makes obeisance to and worships the three (mother, father and guru) and who performs the three acts (of sacrifice, study of scriptures and almsgiving) will cross over birth and death and obtain everlasting peace"(*Kaṭha* I. 1.17).

In addition to the ritualistic sacrifice, meditation on the Naciketa fire as the beginning of the world and as Brahman is also prescribed by Yama in the next verse (*Kaṭha* I. 1.18).

Thereafter, Yama asks Naciketā to choose his third boon. As the third boon, the boy wants to be enlightened as to what happens to a man after his death.

"(Yama said): Even the gods of old had doubt on this point. It is not easy to understand ; (so) subtle is this truth. Choose another boon, O Naciketā. Do not press me. Release me from this"(*Kaṭha* I. 1.21).

Yama offers the boy valuable worldly possessions, wealth, worldly pleasures and long life. But, the boy is not tempted and rejects them as they are transient and wear out the vigour of all the senses of men. Of what avail are these in the face of disease, old age, decay and death? "Can we enjoy wealth when we have seen death?" These are not the fit things to enjoy.

Undeflected, the boy insists on knowing the truth and the specific answer to the question on the mystery of death. "What is there in the great passing on?". "What is there after death?" (*Kaṭha* I. 1.29).

Naciketā asks to know if there is life after death. The answer to this question is given by Yama in the next section in the following verses:

"The intelligent Self is never born; nor does he die at any time. He did not originate from anything, nor did anything originate from him. He is unborn, eternal, abiding and primeval (*purāṇaḥ* new even in old times). He is not slain when the body is slain (*Kaṭha* I. 2.18).

"If the slayer thinks that he slays or if the slain think that he is slain, both of them do not understand. He neither slays nor is he slain" (*Kaṭha* I. 2.19).

Lord *Kṛṣṇa* begins his teachings in the *Gītā* with the very same famous words. Here Death (i.e. Yama) teaches the very same truth. Death takes only the body and not the soul or the self in man. The self in man is unborn, eternal. This is the answer to the question of Naciketā.

"The person of the size of a thumb, the inner Self *(Puruṣa)*, abides always in the hearts of men. Him one should draw out unerringly from the body, as (one may do) stalk from the *muñja* grass. Him one should know as the pure, the immortal, yea, Him one should know as the pure, the immortal" (*Kaṭha* II. 3.17).

"Knowing the separate nature of the senses which spring separately (from the various subtle elements) and (knowing also) that their rising and setting (are separate and do not belong to the self), the wise man does not grieve" (*Kaṭha* II. 3.6).

The discrimination of the self from the sense organisms and the body is taught here by Yama. What rises and falls, what is born and what decays and dies according to the laws of nature is only the body and the sense organisms. The self is different from the senses. When it leaves the body on decay and death of the body, the wise man does not grieve because he knows that our bodies are only vehicles or chariots ruled by the inner immortal Self within (*Kaṭha* I. 3.3). He is the lord of the chariot and it is only because of ignorance we wrongly identify this true Self (*Ātman*) with the ephemeral embodied self. This Self has experienced a myriad of different existences in different bodies and in different circumstances. This is the transmigrating Self which constitutes the permanent essence, the intrinsic nature of each living being.

"Look (here). I shall explain to you the mystery of Brahman, the eternal, and also how the soul fares after death, O Gautama" (*Kaṭha* II. 2.6).

"Some souls enter into a womb for embodiment; others enter stationary objects (like trees) according to their deeds and according to their thoughts"(*Kaṭha* II. 2.7).

Yama teaches here the law of karma as the divine mystery, the mystery of Brahman. This law determines the association of the soul with the body. In this passage and other verses, the *Kaṭha Upaniṣad* seems to affirm the reality of the individual souls as well as the reality of the supreme Self (Brahman).

The Theory of Two Selves

We have so far been considering the Self (Soul) as the inner divinity or ruler of each living being, as the true essence and reality of each being. But this inner controller causes evil things to be done and suffers the consequences of these actions. It is not the arbiter of its own destiny. It is unhappy and it is whirled through the endless cycles of birth, death, rebirth and redeath. Can this be considered the true reality which is free from sin, free from old age, free from death and grief, free from hunger and thirst? Here comes in the theory of the two selves—the *jīvātman* and *Paramātman*.

Two selves have been postulated and described in the *Muṇḍaka* and the *Śvetāśvatara Upaniṣads* in identical languages.

"Two birds, companions (who are) always united, cling to the self-same tree. Of these two, the one eats the fruits of different tastes and the other looks on without eating" (*M.U.* III.1.1 and *S.U.* IV.6)

"On the self-same tree, one *puruṣa* person immersed (in the sorrows of the world) is deluded and grieves on account of his helplessness. When he sees the other, the lord who is worshipped, and His greatness, he becomes freed from sorrow"(*M.U.* III.1.2 & *S.U.* IV.7).

The two selves in the body are compared to two birds perched on the same tree. The *jīvātman* is released from its sorrows and miseries when it realizes the other self, the supreme Self (*Paramātman*) and gets merged in it annihilating itself.

The supreme Self is not subject to the pains and pleasures of experience and is said to be witness to the activities of the other self. *Maitrī Upaniṣad* calls theses two selves as witnessing Self and the experiencing Self respectively.

"....... The two selves are the witnessing self and the experiencing self. The former is tranquil and the latter is full of activity." (*Maitrī* VI.36)

Kaṭha Upaniṣad describes the experiencing self as the shade of the supreme Self (*Paramātman*).

"There are two selves that experience the inevitable results of *karma*. Both are lodged in the secret place (of the heart), the chief seat of the Supreme. The knowers of Brahman speak of them as shade and light ...." (*Kaṭha* I. 3.1)

Here the supreme Self is likened to light and the other self *jīvātman* is spoken of as its shade. Unlike the other *Upaniṣads*, *Kaṭha* talks of both the selves as eating the sweet and bitter fruits of the deeds. How can the supreme Self, which is represented as looking on without eating the fruits of actions in the other *Upaniṣads*, be treated as experiencing the rewards?

Madhava interprets and justifies the above as follows: "The Lord Hari dwells in the hearts of beings and accepts the pure pleasure arising from their good works".

Śaṅkara interprets that the supreme Self is also called an enjoyer here because of association with the experiencing self.

What constitutes the supreme Self (*Paramātman*) and what its precise nature is, have not been clearly brought out in the above passages. Just as Brahman is the cause, ground and support of the macrocosm of the universe, the supreme Self (*Paramātman*) is taken as the foundational reality of the microcosm of man. *Paramātman* is said to be the conscious support of experience and the immanent inner-controller (*antaryāmin*) of the living beings (*B.U.* III. 7.1). "It is the light of man" (*B.U.* IV. 3.6). It is *Sat* (Truth), *Cit* (Consciousness) and *Ānandam* (bliss) as we shall see in subsequent *Upaniṣadic* passages. It is self-illuminating (*svaprakāśa*) and its essence is bliss.

But the precise relationship between the *Ātman*/Brahman and the individual *Jīvātman* is far from clear. This question of relationship has led to different interpretations of the *Upaniṣadic* teachings in later ages, and different schools of philosophy–*Dvaita, Advaita* and *Viśiṣṭādvaita*–have arisen all quoting Vedic and *Upaniṣadic* passages in support of their respective theories. Basically the Vedic religion and *Upaniṣadic* philosophy rest on the fundamental concept of Brahman as the root, origin and source of the universe and all its beings. If Brahman (*Paramātman*) is considered as the ultimate reality and cause of everything, then the question arises as to how to reconcile the evils in the world without violating the integrity and purity of Brahman. *Karmic* intentions with their unwholesome aspects of evil nature and defilements are alien to the concept of ultimate pure Being and cannot be associated with it. The theories on *karma* absorbed by the *Upaniṣads* from the *śramaṇic* tradition do not seem to merge seamlessly in their system without philosophical inconsistencies. If Brahman or *Ātman* is considered as the ordainer and operator of the divine law of karma and also at the same time the inner controller of the other lower self, then He will simultaneously be the cause of evil actions and also the dispenser of justice against the very same evil actions that flow from His own cause and controls. This seems to be incongruous. Some explanations offered are reviewed below but these will appeal only to religious faith and not to logical analysis and reasoning.

Supreme Self is Not Tainted by the Sorrows and Imperfections of the World *(Kaṭha Upaniṣad)*

Do the joys and sorrows of the individual selves and the miseries and imperfections of the world not touch the Supreme Self (*Paramātman*)? Is He not responsible for them and is He not tainted by them? These are the same questions we considered above relating to the purity of the Supreme Self.

Kaṭha Upaniṣad gives answers to these questions in the following passages:

"Just as the sun, which is the eye of the whole world, is not defiled by (or tainted by) the external faults seen by the (human) eye, similarly the Self, that is but one in all beings, is not tainted by the sorrows of the world, It being transcendental"(*Kaṭha* II.2.11).

"The one, controller of all, the inner Self of all, who makes His one form manifold – to the wise who perceive Him as abiding in the soul, to them is eternal bliss, to no others"(*Kaṭha* II.2.12).

The first passage seems to suggest that just as the sun is not defiled by the defects in the eye, the Self is not affected by the sorrows of the world. But, is the world or the lower Self different from the supreme Self as the eye is different from the sun? Is not the supreme Self inner controller and cause of the world as affirmed in the next passage? The world is what it is because of the supreme Self. Is not it? There seems to be an inner contradiction and tension here which is irreconcilable. Attempt is made in some systems to reject these contradictions on the ground that the imperfections of the eye are superimposed on the sun and these are only appearances and not real. Such theories are advanced as religious truths and appeal to faith only. These do not stand to logical enquiry. This will be further discussed later.

Supreme Self is Doer in Seeming Only *(Maitrī Upaniṣad)*

The question of how to reconcile the imperfections, iniquities and evils experienced in this world with the supreme Self who "is pure, clean, void, tranquil, breathless, mindless, endless, undecaying, steadfast, eternal, unborn and independent" (*Maitrī* II.4) is taken up and considered in *Maitrī Upaniṣad* also.

Here, *Vālikhilyas* repeatedly question *Kratu Prajāpati* how such a great Self and such a desireless being can be the mover of the body and become the individual afflicted with desires and passions and how such a desireless being can become the cause of the desiring self. *Kratu Prajāpati* answers that the supreme Self (which is full of pure consciousness and intelligence) dwells in the body with a part of Himself. That part of Him which is intelligent and which sets up the body as possessing intelligence is called *Prajāpati* or *Viśva* at the macrocosmic level and the elemental self (*bhūtātma*) at the microcosmic level associated with an individual body. The individual self in this view is a part (*aṃśa*) of the supreme Self. This self derives his intelligence or consciousness from the supreme Self and he is the knower of the body and the mover of the body.

Because of his association with the body, he develops the characteristics of sensation, perception, conception, determination or volition and self-love. The universal fire within him (*Vaiśvānara* fire) cooks (digests) the food eaten by him and releases energy to act and enjoy. Everything external to him becomes food for his senses, and, with his intelligence, he discriminates what is useful to him, what satisfies his hungers and desires, what is conducive to his pleasures and what is not. He develops likes and dislikes, attachment and hatred. He is consumed of self-love and *ahaṃkāra*, sense of 'I' and 'mine', that separates him from all others.

This elemental self, verily is affected by the *guṇas* (forces in nature: *rajas, tamas* and *sattva*). Being affected by these *guṇas*, he gets confused and bewildered. Because of confusion and bewilderment, he sees not the blessed Lord (the Supreme Self) who dwells in himself and who is the inner controller. Borne along and defiled by the stream of *guṇas*, unstable, wavering, bewildered, full of desire, he gets to the state of self-love and selfish actions. Thinking only of himself with the notions of 'I' and 'mine', he binds himself with his selfishness and selfish actions, like a bird in a snare. He has to reap the sweet and bitter fruits of his actions. He enters a good or an evil womb so that his course is downward or upward according to his actions and he wanders about in the cycle of birth and death, affected by the pairs of opposites (i.e. pleasures and pains, joys and sorrows, happiness and miseries, etc.) (*Maitrī* II.6, III.1 to 5).

Thus, the *Upaniṣad* affirms that the doer and sufferer is this elemental self only and not the Supreme Self who is within as the inner controller.

"Verily, this (inner) self, the seers declare, wanders here on earth in every body (from body to body) unaffected, as it seems, by the sweet or bitter fruits of action. On account of this unmanifestness, subtlity, imperceptibility, ungraspability, freedom from self-sense, (the self) is unabiding and a doer only in seeming, truly is not a doer,- - - - . Verily, he is pure, stead-fast, unswerving, stainless, unagitated, free from desire, remains fixed like a spectator and abiding in his own self. As an enjoyer of righteous work, He covers himself with a veil made of qualities, but He remains fixed, yea, He remains fixed" (*Maitrī* II.7).

The points stressed in this verse are:

- The inner immortal Self is devoid of self-sense and desire; is stainless, pure.
- He is a doer in seeming only and not truly
- He remains fixed like a spectator or witness to the actions of the elemental self
- This pure inner self has cast over itself a veil made of the three fundamental forces (*guṇas*) in nature– *tamas, rajas* and *sattva.* These forces or *guṇas* only cause the elemental self to act. The various desires impelling the latter to act are manifestations of these three *guṇas.*

To drive home the point of non-doer; *Maitrī Upaniṣad* III.3 uses the follwing analogy:

"....... Now even as a ball of iron, overcome by fire and beaten by workmen takes many forms, the elemental self overcome by the inner person and beaten by the qualities takes many forms. The mode of that form has four fold covering, is fourteen-fold, is transformed in eighty-four different ways, is a host of beings, is verily manifold. All these varieties, verily, are impelled by the person even as the wheel by the potter. Now, as when a ball of iron is being beaten, the fire is not overcome, even so the person is not overcome. The elemental self is overcome because of its attachment (to qualities)" (*Maitrī* III.3).

Here the elemental self is compared with ball of iron, the supreme Self with fire heating it and the *guṇas* (i.e. the forces of nature – *sattva, rajas* and *tamas*) with the blacksmiths beating and working on the ball of iron.

Prajāpati at the macrocosmic level and the elemental self at the microcosmic level take many forms and undergo changes and sufferings because of the forces or *guṇas* in nature. The inner laws of the supreme Self may be said to govern these modifications as the fire facilitates the modifications on the ball of iron. Due to these two sets of causes – the *guṇas* and the inner laws-, the *Prajāpati* and the individual elemental self take on the foul-fold sheath (matter, *prāṇa*, mental consciousness and intelligence) and become manifold developing the organs of perception and organs of action. Thus, the evolution of the universe and the individual beings is traced to the modifications wrought by the *guṇas* and the inner laws of cause and effect.

Of the two causes for the ball of iron suffering changes – the inner fire and the external blows of the blacksmiths-the first is qualitatively of different nature and is a passive facilitating one and not a direct and active cause as the blows. In the same manner, the two causes for the sufferings of the individual elemental self – the inner laws and the forces or *guṇas* in nature – differ qualitatively. The active cause is the *guṇas* and not the inner laws governing the modifications and sufferings. It follows from this that the supreme Self is not the direct and active cause of the actions and sufferings of the elemental self. He is the doer only in seeming, not truly, as *Maitrī Upaniṣad* teaches in the above passage.

From this, can we deduce that the supreme Self is equated here with the eternal and immutable laws as later day Spinoza has defined God? It seems a reasonable interpretation that according to this *Upaniṣad*, these laws are decreed by God and the universe and the individual selves evolve according to these laws. The suggestion here also seems to be that the supreme Self is not an absolutely free agent in the world creation because he is dependent on other factors like the *guṇas*. Are the *guṇas* independent of Him? Are they different from Him? This goes against the basic unitary concept generally held in the *Upaniṣads* that reality is one. Conflicting interpretations and theories have arisen. The *Upaniṣads* being the works of different authors have not presented a unified definitive view on the subject of relationship between the supreme Self, the individual *jīva* or elemental self and the *guṇas*.

On the understanding of the universe as evolving according to the laws decreed by God, Stephen Hawking has the following pertinent philosophical question:

".............. With the success of scientific theories in describing events, most people have come to believe that God allows the universe to evolve according to a set of laws and does not intervene in the universe to break these laws. However, the laws do not tell us what the universe should have looked like when it started, it would still be up to God to wind up the clockwork and choose how to start it off. So long as the universe had a beginning we would suppose it had a creator. But if the universe is really completely self-contained, having no boundary or edge, it would have neither beginning nor end: it would simply be. What place, then, for a creator?" (A Brief History of Time, p.149)

If God is conceived as kicking off and starting the world process then he cannot escape the criticism of unequal and unjust creation. If the universe is understood as evolving according to a set of laws established on the basis of scientific enquiries and experiments and if it is beginningless and endless, then there is no place for a creator God. As we shall see later, this is the position taken by Buddhism contrary to the teachings in the *Upaniṣads.*

No Multiplicity of Selves

Different interpretations are given to the *Upaniṣadic* teachings on the identity or difference between these two selves – *Jīvātman* and *Paramātman,* or elemental self and supreme Self. As regards *Jīvātman,* a multiplicity is apparently seen in different individual beings, in different bodies. Is this multiplicity true? The *Upaniṣads* are of the view that this multiplicity is not true. The self appears different only because of its association with different bodies. The bodies only vary and not the self. We cannot distinguish any variety in the self just as we cannot see any distinction of variety in *prāṇa,* breath or air. *Prāṇa* which is the precursor to the concept of soul is one, and as such, the soul also has to be one only.

Kaṭha Upaniṣad gives two analogies to illustrate the truth.

"As fire, which is one, entering this world, becomes varied in shape according to the object it burns, so also the one self within all beings becomes varied according to whatever it enters and also exists outside them all" (*Kaṭha* II.2.9).

"As air, which is one, entering this world, becomes varied in shape according to the object it enters, so also the one self within all beings becomes varied according to whatever it enters and also exists outside them all"(*Kaṭha* II 2.10).

Prāṇa (life-force) or the self is one only just as the space or air is one only. The self within individual beings is like the space circumscribed by the pots. The variation is only because of the limiting adjuncts of the pots. The space takes the shape of the pot limiting it and in the same manner, the self becomes varied according to the bodies it enters into. Then what about the bodies? How do they arise? Have they any independent existence? We cannot get a correct idea of the relationship between the self and the bodies from this analogy.

CHAPTER 3

Theories on Origination of the Universe

Based on the analysis of the facts of life and their intuitive perceptions, the *Upaniṣadic* sages identified two fundamental constituent principles of the existences in the universe – *anna* (matter) and *prāṇa* (breath) or self or *puruṣa* (who breaths) – together with a higher underlying and unifying principle Brahman (*Ātman*), which form the subject matters of the core teachings of the *Upaniṣads*. Unlike in *Sāṃkhya* philosophy, these two fundamental principles – *anna* (matter) and *puruṣa* (self) – are not recognized as two separate, independent and ultimate principles in the *Upaniṣads*. A superordinate overarching principle of *Ātman* (Brahman) has been postulated as a unifier of the two or a unity from which these two fundamental principles emerge. Whereas *Sāṃkhya* philosophy is dualistic in concept acknowledging two independent principles – *prakṛti* and *puruṣa* – as the ultimate aspects of reality, *Upaniṣadic* teachings are monistic in content accepting no duality.

While there is a broad agreement in the *Upaniṣads* on the fundamental principles, the view-points on how *anna* and *prāṇa* have originated and what their relationship is with the highest Self (*Ātman*/Brahman) differ in detail. The *Upaniṣads* are unique in the sense that they do not all work out a single system of thought or dwell on a single theory; but contain a wealth of ideas, suggestions and theories of different sages on the mysteries of the universe based on their experiences and direct intuitive perceptions. There has been a progressive development of different shades of thoughts and postulations on the origination of the universe. It is very difficult to summarize the immense variety of views and theories propounded in the various *Upaniṣads*.

The different theories may however be classified as under :-

(1) Creation from non-being (*asat*).
(2) Creation by a personal creator God–*Prajāpati* or *Brahmā* creating the universe (This theory is basically an extension of the Vedic ideas).
(3) Emanation from or transformation of Brahman–Brahman as an organic unity from which the universe and life-forms evolve and develop (*pariṇāmavāda*).
(4) From *guṇas* arise the universe.
(5) The universe with all its beings is an appearance only superimposed on Brahman and not real (Brahman-*Vivarta vāda, Māyāvāda*).

The last mentioned theory of *māyā* or illusion will be treated separately in a later section. The other theories as propounded in the *Upaniṣads* are discussed here.

1. Creation from non-being *(Asat)*

In the Hymn of Creation (X.129) in *Ṛg Veda*, we have seen how the Vedic seer has described that, before creation, all this was darkness shrouded in darkness, an impenetrable void or abyss of waters on which the Primal Being superimposed His will (*tapas* or *kāma*) and created the world.

Similar accounts of creation and of existence arising out of non-existence are found in the *Upaniṣads* also.

Bṛhad-āraṇyaka Upaniṣad

"There was nothing whatsoever here in the beginning. By death indeed was this covered or by hunger, for hunger is death. He created the mind, thinking 'let me have a self (mind)'. Then he moved about worshipping. From him, thus worshipping water was produced.————" (*B.U.* I. 2.1).

"———— That which was the froth of the water became solidified that became the earth. On it, he rested. From him, thus rested and heated (from the practice of *tapas*), his essence of brightness came forth (as) fire" (*B.U.* I.2.2).

A philosophical model based on these concepts is schematically shown in Figure 3.

In this account, *Bṛhad-āraṇyaka Upaniṣad* considers death or hunger (craving) as the ruling principle and as the source of creation of everything. There was nothing whatsoever in

BṚHAD-ĀRAṆYAKA UPANIṢAD I.2.1 & 2.2

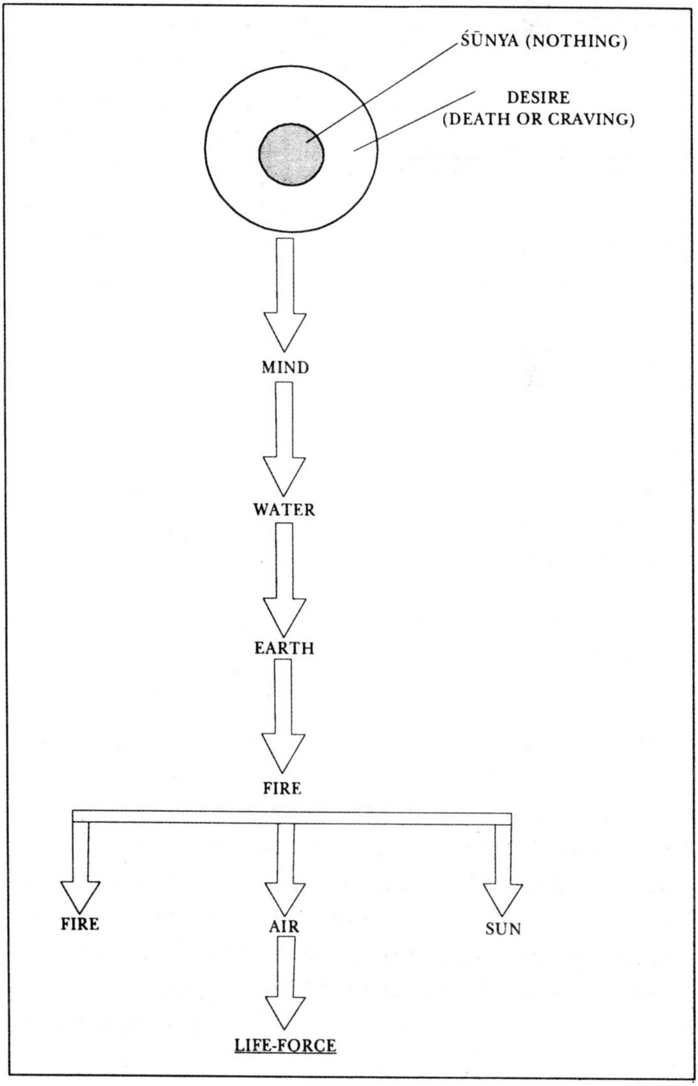

Fig. 3 From Death (Craving) Creation

the beginning. Only death was there. Death here is hunger, craving or desire. Through his creative power of *tapas,* death (desire) created the mind and then progressively water, earth and fire as the constituents of the body. With the body, he brought about the union of speech and mind ; that is, he evolved speech out of the union of body and mind. The whole world has thus arisen from the death or craving (desire).

The similarity of the concept in this account with Buddhist philosophy can be easily discerned. Desire is considered the sole source of creation of both mind and matter (body). There is nothing else apart from desire.

Taittirīya Upaniṣad

In T.U. II.6.1, it has been suggested that Brahman is non-being (*asat*). Brahman that is existing here and that is the cause of this world is the embodied soul of Brahman who is non-being (*asat*). Similar idea of *sat* arising from *asat* is again borne out in the following mantra also:

"Non-existent, verily, was this (world) in the beginning. Therefrom, verily, was existence produced. The Brahman created Itself by Itself. Therefore, it is called the well-made i.e. self-created (*T.U.* II.7.1).

Brahman who accounts for the universe is described here as the self-created spirit or soul arising out of *śūnya* or nothingnes.

Subāla Upaniṣad

In *Subāla Upaniṣad,* which is in the form of a dialogue between the sage *Subāla* and *Brahmā,* the former asks *Brahmā:* "What was there then (i.e in the beginning)"? To him, *Brahmā* replies:

" ———— It was not existent, not non-existent, neither existent, nor non-existent. From that emerged darkness, from darkness the subtle element ether, from ether air, from air fire, from fire water, from water earth ; then there came into being the egg. That egg after incubation for a year split into two : the lower one being the earth and the upper one being the sky. In the middle (between the two parts) there came into being the divine person with a thousand heads, a thousand eyes, a thousand feet and a thousand arms. This (person) created death the foremost of all beings ——" (*Subāla* I .1).

This *Upaniṣad* says that in the beginning there was neither existence nor non-existence. Unlike B.U.I.2.1 & 2.2, this *Upaniṣad* seems to suggest that consciousness in the form of desire arose through a natural process of evolution from the subtle elements. The darkness here had the potential to give rise to the non-mental and mental worlds progressively.

2. Creation by God

Bṛhad-āraṇyaka Upaniṣad

From the primaeval waters emerged Brahman the real, who is the only truth. Brahman produced *Prajāpati* who in turn created all this world, all the gods and all the creatures. They are ephemeral, transient and ever-changing and, as such, are unreal (untruth). They are produced from Brahman and dissolved in Brahman. As such, all this creation (which is untruth) is enclosed on both sides by the Truth that is Brahman. The eternal truth contains within itself the ephemeral, evanescent untruth (*B.U.* V.5.1).

Aitareya Upaniṣad

Aitareya Upaniṣad (Part I, chapters 1 to 3) gives a graphic account of creation by the transcendental Being which it calls *Ātman.*

In the beginning, *Ātman* (the Absolute Self) was one only with all the universe unmanifest within it. There was nothing else whatsoever that winked. It thought, "Let me create the worlds."

That Self created these worlds just as an architect builds a palace according to a well laid-out plan. A schematic presentation of this account of creation is given in Figure 4.

Having created the worlds, the food and the *Virāṭ* Self and from *Virāṭ* Self (cosmic Self) the man, the God split open the crown of his head and entered the body as an individual soul that animates and rules over his body and organs. He thus entered the body for sake of realizing His own Self. And having entered there, He realized directly His own Self in its reality. He is the only one Self in all the bodies and there is none besides.

The correspondence and the interdependence of man and the external world as envisioned in the creative scheme of the divine are also shown in Figure 4.

This scheme of creation is characterized by the following five distinctive features:

(1) The idea of creation by a transcendental Being or God.

AITAREYA UPANIṢAD (PART I, CHAPTERS 1 to 3)

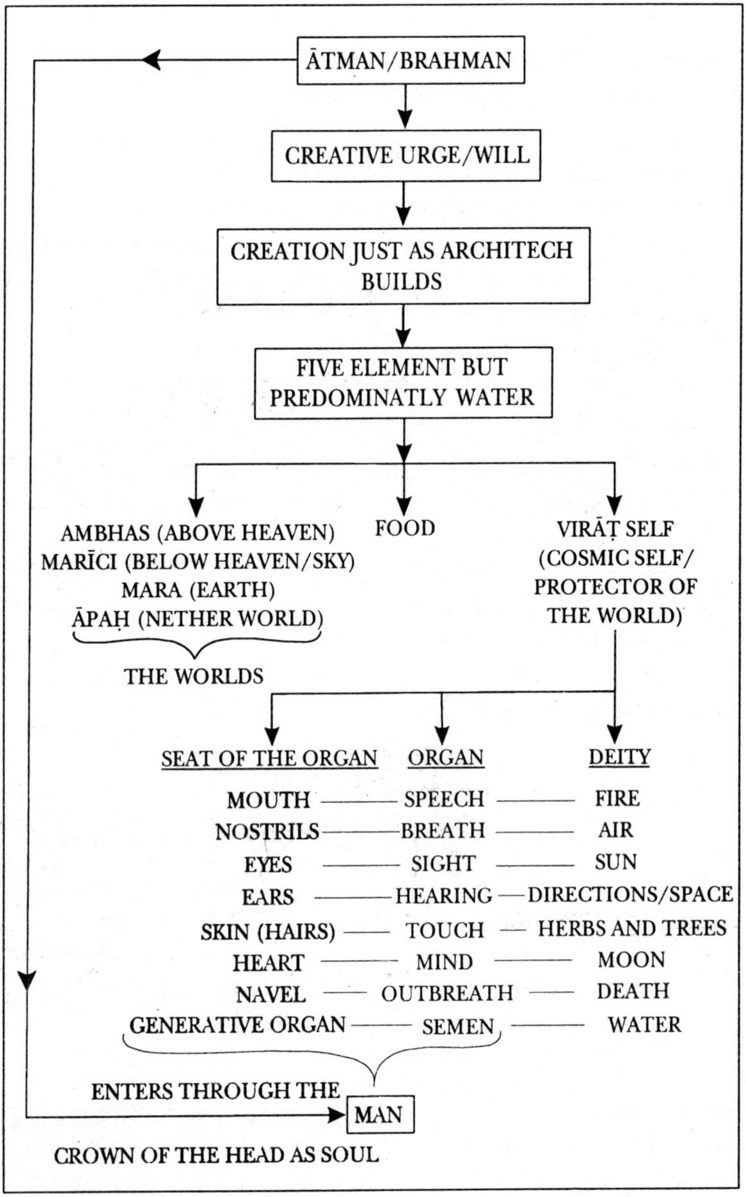

Fig. 4 Creation

(2) The idea of creation according to a well-laid out design after thoughtful deliberation and contemplation.
(3) The idea of creation just like a potter creates a pot using external substance, but with the difference that the substance also has been created by God from Himself
(4) He creates the aggregate of body and organs and Himself enters it as an individual living soul. Thus, He is the one Self in all the bodies.
(5) He enters the body for the sake of realizing His own Self.

Praśna Upaniṣad

In this *Upaniṣad,* we find four successive evolutions of thought.

In the first proposition, it is held that *Prajāpati* (the Lord of creatures, also called *Hiraṇyagarbha*), through his intense *tapas* creates the dual principles (couple)–*anna* (food) and *prāṇa* (breath)–which in turn produce creatures multifariously for him (*Praśna* I.4) (Figure 5). Next, *prāṇa* itself is identified with *Prajāpati* because of its pre-eminence and greatness and because mind, speech, intellect and all Vedic knowledge evolve from *prāṇa.* (*Praśna* II.5).

This is further clarified by the venerable *Pippalāda* (who is answering the questions of his disciples) in the next section. While answering the third question put to him, *Pippalāda* says that this *prāṇa* identified with *Prajāpati* (*Hiraṇyagarbha*) is born from the *Ātman* (the Self or the Supreme *Puruṣa*). This birth or relation between the *prāṇa*/ *Prajāpati* and the *Ātman* is further amplified. Just as there is shadow when a man is there, in the same manner this *prāṇa* is fixed on the *Ātman* or the Self. That is, this *prāṇa* is thus affirmed as the shadow of the *Ātman.* Śaṅkara interprets this to mean that the principle of *prāṇa* or *Prajāpati* is false by nature as this is analogous to a shadow. As such, according to him, *prāṇa* or *Prajāpati* is unreal.

For *Praśna Upaniṣad, prāṇa* or *Prajāpati* is the shadow of the *Ātman* (Brahman) whereas, for *Śaṅkara,* it is *māyā* of Brahman. One is a shadow cast by the *Ātman* or Brahman in His own likeness and the other view is that it is a *māyā,* veil, magic cast by the Brahman. These are different interpretations of the teaching in *Praśna Upaniṣad.*

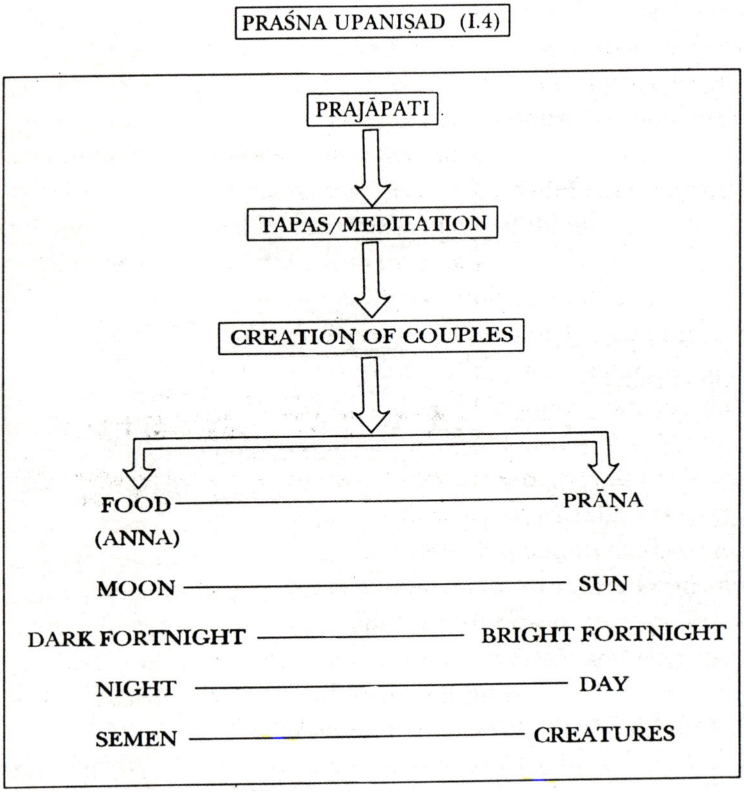

Fig. 5 Couples Instrumental to Creation

PRAŚNA UPANIṢAD (VI. 2 to 4)

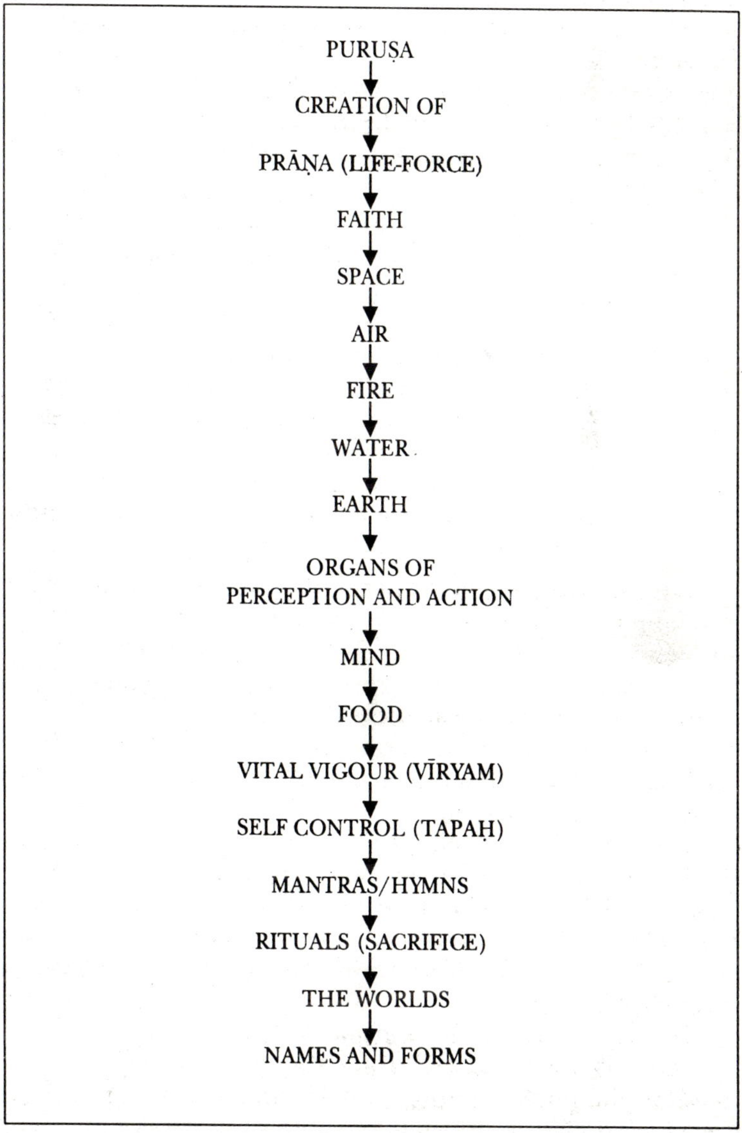

Fig. 6 Puruṣa with Sixteen Parts

Next *Ātman* is described as the *Puruṣa* with sixteen parts or limbs (*Praśna* VI. 2 & 3) (Figure 6).

The first product of his creation is *prāṇa*. From *prāṇa*, He created faith that is the source of stimulus for all beings to do good works. From that, He created the great elements that support life by becoming the material constituents of the physical body and also providing sustenance to the body. These are:

- Space, possessed of the quality of sound.
- Air, possessed of two attributes, its own attribute of touch and the attribute sound of its source (space).
- Fire, possessed of three attributes or qualities, its own quality of colour and the qualities of sound and touch belonging to the earlier two.
- Water, possessed of four attributes – its own individual quality of taste and the infusion of the three earlier qualities (sound, touch and colour).
- Earth, endowed with five qualities by virtue of its possession of smell and the permeation of the four earlier qualities (sound, touch, colour and taste).

So also, He created indriyam, the organs – the organs of perception and the organs of action, total ten in number – constituted from the above elements. Then, He created the mind to control these organs. Having thus created the body and organs of the creatures, He created for their sustenance food constituted of paddy, barley etc. From that food, when eaten, arises *vīryam* (ability, vigour) which is the root of engaging in all kinds of works and procreation.

After that, He created *tapaḥ* (self-control) characterized by intellect from which arise the mantras comprising the *Ṛg*, *Yajur*, *Sāma* and *Atharva* texts and the various means of religious activities. Then follow the *karmas* (the rites) and the worlds as the result of the rites. In these worlds, He created the names, the individual beings.

In all these, He enters as *prāṇa*, the inner soul.

Multiplicity or duality of independent principles (as in *Sāṃkhya* philosophy – *puruṣas* and *prakṛti*) is not accepted by the *Upaniṣad*. Reality or the ultimate cause is One from which arise all the principles, elements and constituents of the body and organs, from *prāṇa* down to the individual names and forms. The conclusion of this *Upaniṣad* is that *puruṣa* or *Ātman* creates all these and enters all of them as the inner soul, the *prāṇa*.

3. Brahman-*Pariṇāmavāda*

The concept of Brahman as an organic unity from which the entire universe with all its beings evolves finds beautiful expression in many *Upaniṣadic* passages.

The word 'Brahman' is derived from the root, '*Bṛh*', which means 'that grows', 'that expands' or 'that develops'. Brahman grows or develops into all these things.

Chāndogya Upaniṣad defines Brahman as *tajjalān*, as that (*tat*), which gives rise to (*ja*), absorbs (*la*) and sustains (*an*) this whole world (*C.U.* III.14.1). All this arise from Brahman.

Taittirīya Upaniṣad teaches : "That, verily, from which these beings are born, that by which, when born, they live, that into which, when departing, they enter – that seek to know. That is Brahman" (*T.U.* III.1.1).

The theory of *pariṇāmavāda* – evolution or development of the universe from Brahman – as propounded by *Rāmānuja* and others can be traced to the following passages in the *Upaniṣads*. The *Upaniṣads* are replete with teachings lending support to this view.

Bṛhad-āraṇyaka Upaniṣad

"As a spider moves along the thread(or spins its thread), as small sparks issue forth from the fire, even so from this Self (*Ātman*) come forth all breaths, all worlds, all divinities, all beings. Its secret meaning is the truth of the truth. Vital breaths are the truth and their truth is this Self" (*B.U.* II. 1.20).

All the vital breaths (*prāṇa*, vital energy), all the matter, all the divinities governing the interaction of the life-breaths and the matter, and the functions of the various sense organs, and all beings emanate from the *Ātman* (Self). How do they emanate? The analogies given are : Just as the spider weaves its thread using no other material but its own self, just as blazing fire gives forth sparks of its own nature, in a similar way the *Ātman* gives rise to all breaths, all worlds and all beings. The underlying truth or the fundamental reality behind all these emanations is the *Ātman*. This is the ultimate truth or the truth of the truth (*Satyasya satyam*).

There is no suggestion here to support the view of the later day Advaitins that the world is unreal. All the worlds and all the beings should be real because, as this *Upaniṣad* asserts, all these are born of the *Ātman*, *Ātman* being the material cause as well as efficient cause of all of them. They are from *Ātman* just as spider's thread is from spider and sparks of fire are from fire.

Just as the trees and plants are sprouting and growing from the earth and are ultimately dissolved into the earth as matter, the individual beings are born from Brahman and dissolved into Brahman. Just as the growth and decay are for the plants and trees only and not for the vast earth, in the same manner, the births and the deaths are for the individual creatures only and not for Brahman. What we call these births, deaths and changes, these are taking place in Him and not of Him. These things will not affect the Infinite Being that is Brahman.

"That is full, this is full. From fullness, fulness proceeds. If we take away the fullness from fullness, even then remains fullness ——————" (*B.U.* V. 2.1).

It is the fundamental axiomatic truth that even if we take away infinity from infinity, infinity still remains. Conditioned by the finite modes, if we talk of changes affecting the fullness or integrity of Brahman that is meaningless and has no validity for Brahman.

Chāndogya Upaniṣad

The three elements and the living self that evolve from *Sat:*

"In the beginning, my dear, this was Being (*Sat*) alone, one only without a second. Some people say, in the beginning, this was non-being (*asat*) alone, one only without a second. From that non-being, being was produced" (*C.U.* VI.2.1).

"But how, indeed, my dear, could it be thus? said he. How could being be produced from non-being? On the contrary, my dear, in the beginning, this was being alone, one only, without a second" (*C.U.* VI 2.2).

"It thought, May I be many, may I grow forth. It sent forth fire. That fire thought, May I be many, may I grow forth. It sent forth water ——————" (*C.U.* VI.2.4).

"That water thought, May I be many , may I grow froth. It sent forth food——————" (*C.U.* VI.2.4).

After an initial uncertainty and doubt over the question whether Being (Existence or *Sat*) was produced from non-being (non-existence or *asat*), *C.U.* here asserts that non-existence cannot convert itself into existence and that in the beginning *Sat* existed. This was Being (ultimate reality), one only without a second. It grew and issued forth into the three elements – fire, water and food (*anna*). In relation to the three-elements which are called the three divinities or the *devatās,* Sat is called the *para-devatā* (the highest *devatā*).

Sat further developed into the living-self (life-spirit or *jīva*) and caused the union of the same with the three divinities earlier developed i.e. the three elements. That is, *Sat* evolves into the two fundamental principles – matter (the elements) and life-force – and remains as the higher unifying principle. By this union, names and forms are developed and all the varied manifestations of the world arise (*C.U.* VI.3.2).

All the variations in the manifestations and the multiplicity seen in the world arise through a process of splitting up of each of the basic elements and mixing up of these parts in varying proportions. These elements are the fundamental constituents of all the varied things in the universe. All are only combinations of these elements and their modifications as brought out by the Primal Being (*Sat*) through the living-self.

"Whatever red form the sun has, it is the form of *tejas* (fire); whatever is white, it is the form of water. Whatever is dark, it is the form of earth. Thus vanishes the quality of the sun from the sun, the modification being only a name arising from speech while the truth is that it is only the three forms" (*C.U.* VI.4.2).

The *Upaniṣad* affirms that the same is the case with moon, lightning and everything else because everything is constituted of these three basic elements and from these three everything is known. It may be noted that the qualities of red, white and black talked here are the precursors to the theory of the three *guṇas* developed later in the *Sāṃkhya* philosophy.

The later *Upaniṣads* identify the basic elements as five including space (ether) and air in addition to the three mentioned above. Manifestation takes place according to a systematic process of splitting up of elements and recombination in innumerable ways.

"That art thou, *Śvetaketu*"

Śvetaketu in a philosophical dialogue with his father *Uddālaka Āruṇi* raises a doubt as to how this vast universe with its multitudinous variety can be produced from non-being.

> "Fetch a fruit of that nyagrodha tree", asked the father.
> "Here is one, Sir,"said *Śvetaketu.*
> "Break it and tell me what you see therein", asked the father.
> "I see some tiny seeds," said *Śvetaketu.*
> "Crush one of the tiny seeds", said the father.
> "Yes, I have done it, Sir".

"What do you see therein?".
"Nothing at all, Venerable Sir".

Then, the father said to the son:

"My dear, that subtle essence which you do not perceive, verily my dear, from that very essence, this great nyagrodha tree arises. Believe me, my dear" (*C.U.* VI. 12. 1 & 2).

"That which is the subtle essence, this whole world has for its self. That is the truth. That is the Self. That art thou, *Śvetaketu*" (*C.U.* VI. 12 .3).

The seeds of different trees or plants have different potentialities. But behind the different potentialities, the *Upaniṣad* identifies a subtle essence.

That subtle essence which is in the seed but not perceivable gives rise to the huge nyagrodha tree. That is the soul (or self) of the huge tree. The very same subtle essence in that seed exists as the soul of the universe as well as the soul of the individual being. From that evolves the entire universe and all the individual beings just as the huge tree grows from the seed. That principle of subtle essence which is in the seed is common to the seed of the universe and also to the seeds of the individual beings. **"That art thou, *Śvetaketu*".** That principle of subtle essence which is in the seed is the same as the one within you (thou).

This is the acme, the highest point of *Upaniṣadic* teachings, and the most sacred mantra.

Taittirīya Upaniṣad

Brahman, the real, who resides in the secret place of the heart of individual being and also in the highest heaven is the source of all.

"____________From this Self (Brahman), verily ether arose; from ether air; from air fire; from fire water; from water the earth ; from the earth herbs ; from herbs food ; from food the person *(Puruṣa)*.______" (*T.U.* II.1.1).

Chāndogya Upaniṣad talked of the three elements and the living-self as emerging from the *Sat.* Here T.U. teaches that the five elements and the *puruṣa* (i.e. the living-self) arose from Brahman, the highest reality.

Muṇḍaka Upaniṣad

A number of mantras can be quoted from *Muṇḍaka Upaniṣad* in support of the theory of evolution or *pariṇāmavāda.*

M.U. also gives the same analogies of spider-its thread and fire – its sparks found in *B.U.* II.1.20 to illustrate the relation between the Brahman (*Ātman*) and the universe. *M.U.* quotes further analogies as well to reinforce the concept of Brahman as an organic unity giving rise to the universe with its multitudinous varieties.

"As a spider sends forth and draws in its thread, as herbs grow on the earth, as the hair grows on the head and body of a living person, so from the Imperishable arises here the universe" (*M.U.* I.1. 7).

Just as the spider, by itself and from within itself independent of any other auxiliary spreads out the threads that are indeed non-different from its own body and again withdraws those very threads making them one with its self, just as herbs and trees grow from the bowels of the earth firmly rooted in it and just as from a living person grow hairs on head and other parts of the body, in similar manner from the Imperishable Brahman issues forth this entire universe with all its beings. No other auxiliary is involved in this growth but for the Brahman himself. He is the source, sustenance and cause of all the evolution and growth.

"By contemplative power (*tapas*), Brahman expands like a seed sending out its sprout. From that grows food. From food, life (*prāṇa*), thence mind, thence the rituals (*karmas*) and in the rituals immortality" (*M.U.*I. 1.8).

"This is the truth. As from a blazing fire, sparks of like nature issue forth by the thousands, even so, O beloved, many kinds of beings issue forth from the Imperishable (*Akṣara*) and into it again they merge" (*M.U.*II.1.1).

"From Him are born *prāṇa* (vital force, life), mind, all the senses, space, air, fire, water and earth that supports everything". (*M.U.* II.1.3).

"From Him emerges the heaven (the fire) with fuel as the sun. From the moon (that evolves out of heaven) emerges cloud, and from cloud, the rains, the herbs and corns on the earth. From food originates semen. Thus from the Supreme *Puruṣa* have originated many creatures" (*M.U.* II.1.5).

It is not creation but emanation or growth that is suggested in these passages. All are in Him and are manifested in succession as causes and effects according to His divine laws or will. *Sāṃkhya* theory treats the manifested *prakṛti* (primordial nature) as an independent principle *(tattva)* separate from *Puruṣa*. The *Upaniṣad* here holds the contrary view that all nature, universe and the individual living selves, all are in Him and from Him only they emerge. Uncompromising monism is taught here.

The sun, moon, all quarters of space, all knowledge and the souls of all existing beings are parts and manifestations of that single all–immanent Being. All life and all qualities, functions and activities, are evolutions of that single Energy. He is the fire that makes the very sun burn obediently like a faggot in the fire. The rain does not rain, but it is He that rains through and by means of the clouds. Living beings do not multiply, but indeed it is He that multiplies through them. The mountains and the seas, the rivers, the trees and shrubs and their essences – all issue forth from that Supreme Self (Brahman) who is immanent in everything and who also dwells in the secret place of the heart of the individual self.

Realize this, O dear boy, and cut asunder the knots of ignorance that bind (*M.U.* II.1.9 & 10).

Maitrī Upaniṣad

The above truths taught in *Muṇḍaka Upaniṣad* are echoed in *Maitrī Upaniṣad* also (*Maitrī* VI. 31).

Just as the sprouts issue forth from the seed, and smoke, light and sparks from fire, even so the breath (*prāṇa*), hearing, sight, mind, speech, understanding, steadfastness, memory and wisdom – all these arise from Him who is the Self. From the sprout, we infer the invisible seed. From the smoke, we infer the fire. Even so from the breath, the speech, the hearing, the sight, the mind etc we infer the underlying causative principle, the Self. The whole universe with all its creatures springs from Him just as the sprouts from the seed, the sparks from fire and the rays from the sun. The relationship between Him and the universe is akin to the one between the sprouts and the seed, between the sparks and the fire or between the sun-rays and the sun. He is not only the root cause of all but also the essence of all. He becomes all. An organic and integral unity of the whole universe and all the creatures in it with Brahman is affirmed here.

"From him, indeed, who is in the self come forth all living creatures, all worlds, all *Vedas,* all the gods and all the beings. Its mystic meaning is that it is the truth of the truth (*Satyasya satyam*)" (*Maitrī* VI. 32).

Just as, when a fire laid with damp wood is kindled, clouds of smoke issue forth, likewise, verily from this great being come forth all worlds, all beings all the *Vedas,* all the legends, all the doctrines.

Ancient Fig Tree With Roots in Heaven

Kaṭha Upaniṣad, *Śvetāśvatara Upaniṣad* and *Maitrī Upaniṣad* describe this world as the "ancient fig tree with its roots established in heaven and branches below". The tree of life with all its branches (creatures), leaves (their good and bad deeds) and fruits (the sweet and bitter fruits of their actions) grows from the Imperishable Brahman and rests on Him (*Kaṭha* II. 3.1, *S.U.* III. 9 and *Maitrī* VI.4).

He is the butter in the milk, the oil in sesamum seeds, water in the river beds and the fire in the fire sticks (*S.U.* I 16).

He is the essence of all and He is in all. This is the highest mystic doctrine.

4. From Guṇas Arise the Universe

In the *Upaniṣadic* concepts we have seen so far, the fundamental constituents of the universe are the five basic elements (or matter) and the living self (*prāṇa* or life-force), either created by or evolving from the Primal Being or Brahman.

But in the parallel philosophical tradition of *Sāṃkhya* which is considered to be oldest of all Indian philosophical systems, the basic elements are replaced by the three *guṇas* or forces in nature–*sattva, rajas* and *tamas* – which are said to be the fundamental constituents of the universe. *Sāṃkhya* is a dualistic philosophy which believes in two separate coexistent realities: the conscious *puruṣa* and the unconscious *prakṛti* and a multiplicity of *puruṣas*. *Prakṛti* is said to be the material cause of the universe and is composed of the three *guṇas*. Under the influence of the proximate conscious principle *puruṣa, prakṛti* is said to spin into evolution and cause the universe with its twenty-three evolutes (Figure 7).

Sāṃkhya Theory

According to *Sāṃkhya, guṇa* is not quality or attribute, but it is force or energy with specific characteristics. The *guṇas* literally mean threads or strands which make up the rope of *prakṛti* and which bind the *puruṣa* with it. The three *guṇas* – *sattva, rajas* and *tamas* – represent the three modes in which we find the energies: intelligence, passion and inertia respectively. The characteristics of *sattva* are weightlessness, light and knowledge, and of *rajas* motion, activity and passion. And *tamas* is heaviness, darkness and ignorance.

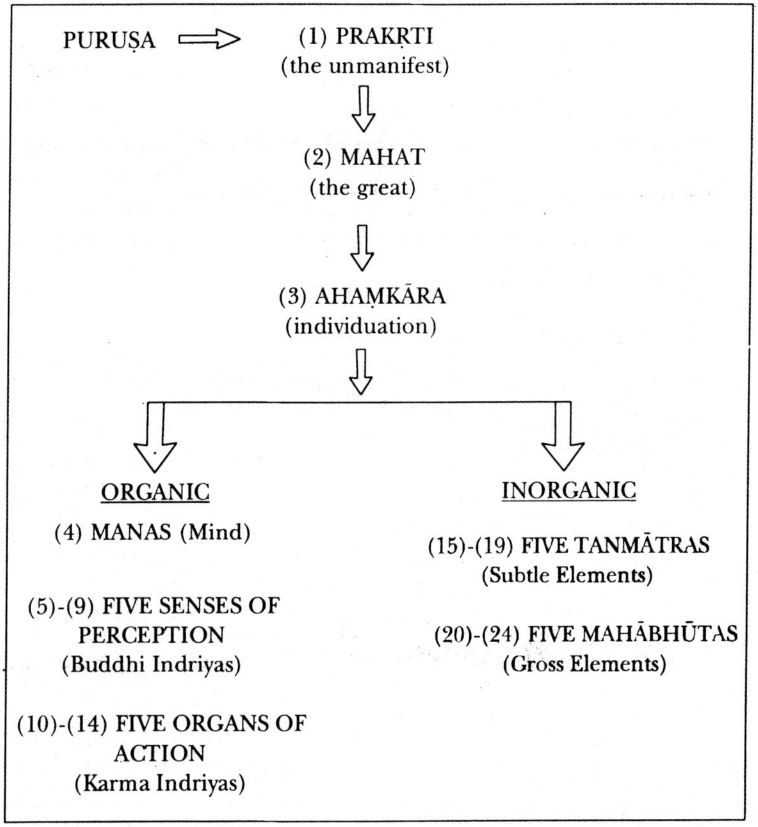

Fig. 7 Evolution in Sāṃkhya

These three *guṇas* exist only in combination; none can exist separately. *Prakṛti* is the unmanifested state in which the three *guṇas* balance out and remain in perfect equilibrium. The *guṇas* are formless and omnipresent in this state of equilibrium having completely given up their specific characteristics and submerged in each other. But when *prakṛti* is influenced by *puruṣa,* the equilibrium of the three *guṇas* in the *prakṛti* gets disturbed and *prakṛti* begins to evolve into differentiated material universe.

On the physical side, *sattva* gives rise to brightness, lightness and related material properties and is associated with the colour white. *Rajas* is responsible for mobility of various kinds and is associated with the colour red, while tamas associated with the colour black produces darkness, inertia, decay and related phenomena. With different degrees of combination of these *guṇas,* the physical universe gets manifested progressively in stages. According to *Sāṃkhya,* the process of manifestation originates from the unmanifested unity of *prakṛti* and completes its cycle with the manifestation of twenty-three evolutes (Figure 7).

Our moral and mental make-ups are also derived from the *guṇas.* Not only does sattva give rise to certain physical phenomenon, but at the level of the individual it undergoes modifications so as to produce characteristics such as serenity, peace, love, compassion, forbearance, intelligence, clarity of mind, purity etc. Likewise, *rajas* produces passionate mental and moral activities like wrath, lust, passion, mercurial temperament etc, while the modifications of *tamas* give rise to such things as sloth, torpor, stupidity, mental confusion, cowardice and so on.

We can see the influence of *Sāṃkhya* in the teachings of the later *Upaniṣads* which have adopted the theory of the three *guṇas.* The three forms – red, white and dark – earlier mentioned in the passages on three-fold development in *Chāndogya Upaniṣad* (C.U. VI. 4.1 to 4.7) may be considered as the precursors of the three *guṇas* developed in *Sāṃkhya* philosophy.

Śvetāśvatara Upaniṣad

"Time, inherent nature, necessity, chance, the elements, the womb or the person *(Puruṣa)* – should they be considered as the cause? It cannot be a combination of these because of the existence of the soul. Even the soul is powerless in respect of the cause of pleasure and pain" (*S.U.* I.2).

"Those who were adepts in meditation and contemplation saw the self-power of the Divine (*Devātma-śakti*) hidden in its own qualities. He is the one who rules over all these causes from time to the soul" (*S.U.* I.3).

The universe with all its beings is not self-caused. The *Upaniṣad* here talks about the different theories prevalent at various points of time on the cause of the universe. Is the cause time, inherent nature, necessity, chance, the elements or the womb (*Yoniḥ* or *prakṛti*)? The *Upaniṣad* considers these theories and rejects them on the ground that conscious soul is seen to exist and such conscious being with mind, intellect and ego cannot arise from a non-conscious thing or from a combination non-conscious things. Even the *puruṣa* or soul is not the ultimate cause because it cannot determine its own destiny. It is also a powerless being subject to the laws of cause and effect and goes through the cycles of birth and death, pleasures and pains. It is not the arbiter of its own destiny.

The truth directly perceived by the sages through their meditative and contemplative powers is that the ultimate cause of the universe with all its beings is the self-power of the divine (*Devātma-śakti*) hidden in the three forces or *guṇas* of nature.

The three *guṇas* – *sattva, rajas* and *tamas* – are the three kinds of forces or energies experienced in nature. As is now well-known, according to modern scientific theories, matter can be divided into the basic elements (ether, air, fire, water and earth), the basic elements into molecules, molecules into atoms and atoms into protons and electrons or into waves of energies. Energies are the most basic and fundamental components of nature. Here the suggestion is that nature or *prakṛti* is composed of the three *guṇas* and the divine power of Brahman hidden in these *guṇas* becomes the cause of creation, maintenance and dissolution of the universe. The *guṇas* are the material cause and He is the efficient cause. He exists hidden behind the three *guṇas*.

Maitrī Upaniṣad

The suggestion contained in mantra S.U.I.3 in *Śvetāśvatara Upaniṣad* finds expression in a slightly more developed form in *Maitrī Upaniṣad* in the following passage:

"Verily, in the beginning, this (world) was darkness (*tamas*) alone. That was in the Highest. When impelled by the Highest it moves on to differentiation. That form verily is passion (*rajas*). That passion, when impelled, moves on to differentiation. That, verily, is the form of goodness (*sattva*). That goodness, when impelled, the essence flowed forth. That part is what the intelligence principle in every person is, the knower of the body, which has the marks of conception, determination and self-love, *Prajāpati* (the lord of creation) called *Viśva.*

"Now then, indeed, the part of him which is characterized by darkness (*tamas*), that, O students of sacred knowledge, is this Rudra. Now then, indeed, that part of him which is characterized by passion (*rajas*), that, O students of sacred knowledge, is this *Brahmā.* Now then, indeed, that part of him which is characterized by goodness (*sattva*), that, O students of sacred knowledge, is this *Viṣṇu.*

"Verily, that One becomes threefold. He developed forth eightfold, elevenfold, twelvefold, in unlimited parts. Because he thus developed, he is a being, he moves about, having entered all beings. He became the lord of beings. That is the self within and without, yea, within and without" (*Maitrī* V.2.).

Rudra (representing *tamas,* darkness,) *Brahmā* (representing *rajas,* passion) and *Viṣṇu* (representing *sattva,* goodness) are the three-fold manifestations of the Highest i.e. the Supreme Brahman. From the essence of *sattva* arises the intelligent principle –*Prajāpati* in the cosmic context and *Viśva* as the individual.

The eightfold development of *Prajāpati* covers the five vital airs, the sun, moon and stars or the five elements, the sun, moon and stars. The eleven developments are the ten organs of cognition and action plus the mind. With intellect, it becomes twelvefold development.

CHAPTER 4

Karma and Rebirth

1. Evolution of the Ideas in the Upaniṣads

The Vedic religion dominated by the *Brāhmaṇas* centred around the performance of rituals and sacrifices which are believed to have the magical power and potency to bestow safety, longevity, progeny, wealth, fame and celestial happiness in the heavens to those who sponsor these sacrifices and pay for them. As we have already seen, the highest goal of the humans according to these Brahmanical codes is the attainment of heaven in a 'glorified' body and blissful life therein for ever or as long as possible in the company of gods and beautiful maidens. The thrust and aim of the teachings in the *Brāhmaṇa* portions of the *Vedas* is the proper performance of the prescribed sacrifices and rituals for the attainment of such mundane goals.

The theory of Karma which affirms that the future of man is determined by his own acts – virtuous and vicious – and not by external rituals or sacrifices runs counter to the concepts and injunctions in the *Brāhmaṇas.* If man himself can shape the future course of his life through his acts, then all rituals, sacrifices, priests and gods cease to be indispensable. Thus, this theory of Karma is alien to the concepts in the *Brāhmaṇas.* This is not found in the *Vedas* and *Brāhmaṇas* and appears for the first time in *Bṛhad-āraṇyaka Upaniṣad* (III.2 .13).

Bṛhad-āraṇyaka Upaniṣad

In the great debate organized by King Janaka of Videha, *Ārtabhāga* asks the sage *Yājñavalkya*: "When the speech (voice) of this dead person enters into fire, the breath into air, the eye into the sun, the mind into the moon, hearing into the quarters, the self into the ether, the hairs of the body into the herbs, the hairs on the head into the trees and the blood and the semen are deposited in water, what then becomes of this person ?".

Yājñavalkya takes the hand of *Ārtabhāga* and takes him to a secluded place away from the public gaze of the assembly and imparts to him the theory of Karma. He says that this cannot be discussed in pubic assembly.

"The two went away and deliberated. What they said was *karman* and what they praised was *karman*. Verily one becomes good by good action and bad by bad action. Therefore *Ārtabhāga* of the line of *Jaratkāru* kept silent" (*B.U.* III.2.13).

The very fact that *Yājñavalkya* takes away *Ārtabhāga* to a secluded place to discuss the theory shows that this is a new theory and that this cannot be discussed in public in the gathering of the priestly class because of its implications and the objections it may raise from the priestly class. This is a revolutionary theory alien to the main stream *Brāhmaṇical* concepts. Three points should be noted here :

(1) The Self on death is said to enter and get absorbed in ether. Transmigration of the soul is not suggested here. Metempsychosis is a later development and addition to the theory.
(2) What they spoke of and deliberated was action (karman).
(3) The dead person becomes good (*puṇya*) by good action and bad (*pāpaḥ*) by bad action. Here the good and bad actions – how are they qualified as good or bad ? Are these determined by the morally pure and impure motives behind the actions or are they termed good or bad depending on the good and bad observances of the traditional ritualistic religion or by both? The exposition is cryptic and leaves one confused.

Scholars are of the view that the theories of *karman* and rebirth have been taken over and absorbed in the *Upaniṣadic* thoughts over a period of time under the influence of the muni-*śramaṇic* cults coming down from the pre-Vedic non-*Āryan* tradition, from which Buddhism and Jainism sprang.

In the verse III.2.13 quoted above and again in the verse IV 5.13 *Bṛhad-āraṇyaka Upaniṣad* states that on death the Self vanishes in the ether. "When he has departed, there is no more (separate or particular) consciousness– " (*B.U.* IV. 5.13).

But in *B.U.* IV. 4.2, *Vijñānamayaḥ* soul is suggested as underlying the person. It has intelligence and the dying person becomes one with it when the life and the vital breaths depart. This is the transmigrating individual self. *Chāndogya Upaniṣad* also supports the view that the soul is of *Vijñānamayaḥ*.

At the time of death, this self or soul is said to depart with the subtle body comprising the vital breaths, mind and intellect, and with the impressions of the past experience and knowledge and with the results of his actions attached to it. As driven by the Law of *Karma*, it stretches out like a leech from the body and finds another body according to the sweet or bitter fruits of its past actions.

"Just as a leech (or caterpillar), when it has come to the end of a blade of grass, approaches (another blade) and draws itself together towards it, so does this self, after having thrown away this body and dispelled ignorance, approaches (another body), and draws itself together (for making the transition to another body)"(*B.U.* IV. 4.3).

"And as a goldsmith, taking a piece of gold turns it into another, newer and more beautiful shape, even so does this self, after having thrown away this body and dispelled its ignorance, make unto himself another, newer and more beautiful shape like that of the fathers or of the Gandharvas, or of the gods or of *Prajāpati* or of *Brahma* or of other beings"(*B.U.* IV. 4.4).

These passages bring out some important aspects of the theory of rebirth. It is suggested that the soul finds out its future body before it leaves the present one. Just as the leech draws itself and finds another blade of grass to feed on, in the same manner, the soul driven by the inner-controller casts away one body and finds another body according to the Law of Karma. The state of each existence of the soul is conditioned and determined by its knowledge (*vidyā*) and its conduct (*karma*) in the previous existence.

The idea here of the soul finding the new body contrasts sharply with the process of rebirth in Buddhism where the *karmic* force propels the rebirth consciousness to the new body. Even though *karmic* impressions and effects are being talked about here, the dynamism of their force is lacking and they are treated only as secondary, the supremacy assigned still to the self or the inner controller. This shows the borrowed nature of the theory of *karma* in the *Upaniṣads* and their adoption with a certain dilution to suit the Vedic tradition.

Another suggestion here is that every self or soul has the potential to reach Brahman and every birth is a further step in this ascendancy, It assumes that every birth knocks away part of the ignorance of the soul based on the experience undergone and in the next birth, it becomes a better being.

"——The object to which the mind is attached, the subtle self goes together with the deed, being attached to it alone. Exhausting the results of whatever works he did in this world, he comes again from that world to this world for fresh work. This is for the man who desires.

"But for the man who does not desire, he who is without desire, who is freed from desire, whose desire is satisfied, whose desire is the self, his breaths do not depart. Being Brahman, he goes to Brahman" (*B.U.* IV. 4.6).

The deeds and their effects get attached to the subtle self in the case of one who acts under the impulsion of desires. The one who has desires continues to be subject to rebirth.

One, who is impelled by desires, resorts to the sacrificial rituals, offerings and prayers for progeny, wealth, cattle, prosperity and fame in this world and for enjoyments in the heavenly worlds. His desires may be fulfilled and he may be born in the heavenly worlds to enjoy its pleasures. But the effects of these rituals and sacrifices will wear off and get exhausted. He will be reborn and come back to this world again for fresh work impelled by his desires. Thus the man afflicted by desire is always bound to the cycle of birth, death and rebirth. Not so for the man who is desireless. For him, there is no rebirth and he becomes one with Brahman. The soul is merged in Brahman.

"—— When all the desires that dwell in the heart are cast away, then does the mortal become immortal, then he attains Brahman here (in this very body). Just as the slough of a snake lies on an ant –hill, dead, cast-off, even so lies this body. But this disembodied, immortal life, is Brahman only, is light indeed, your majesty."—— (*B.U.* IV. 4.7).

The body of a desireless being is just like the slough cast off by a snake on an ant-hill, without any trace of evil. Such a desireless being becomes Brahman in this very life, in this very body.

Chāndogya Upaniṣad

Chāndogya Upaniṣad talks about two post-mortem paths for the departed soul in V. 10.

The enlightened souls who have meditated with faith and austerity and who have realized the Self within move along the 'path of gods' (*deva-yāna*) via heavenly stations, eventually to reach the world of *Brahma* (Brahman).

Those who have performed sacrificial rites and those who have led morally mixed lives, that is, doing works of public utility and almsgiving mixed with some demeritorious actions reach the moon by passing along the 'path of the fore-fathers' (*pitṛ-yāna*) and, after having experienced the fruits of their works in the heavenly realms, they return again according to the residue of their *karma.* The description of the return process is obscure, but it seems that the residual merit determines the kind of next birth.

Those whose conduct in the world has been good will attain a good birth ("good womb"), e.g. of a *brahmin, kṣatriya* or *vaiśya,* but those of bad conduct attain a bad womb, e.g of a dog, pig or *caṇḍāla.*

Depending on the "*karmic* residue", some others will be born as rice and barley, herbs and trees, as sesamum plants and beans, i.e. as edible vegetation, and some others as tiny creatures. Those who are born as edible vegetation have at least some prospects of moving up the chain of existence towards eventual liberation, i.e. one may assume the same form as the eater of one's vegetative form, taking on the appropriate embodiment after being emitted through semen in copulation. On the other hand, those who are reborn as tiny creatures have no such prospect and will be continually revolving in the cycle of birth and death. They have no chance of breaking the cycle. The idea here of a transmigrating soul taking the form of a vegetative plant and then passing on to a human form or so through the semen produced from the assimilation of the vegetative food seems to point to an obscure and strange development on the theory of karma and rebirth. The absence of well-developed theory in the *Upaniṣads* suggests its borrowed nature. Moreover, what is important for the *Upaniṣads* is the realisation of Self or knowledge or Brahman. The emphasis here is more on self-realisation rather than on the ethical nature of actions. For *Chāndogya Upaniṣad* reiterates in VIII.I.6 that final liberation from the cycle of birth and death is possible only for those who have discerned the Self within.

Śvetāśvatara Upaniṣad

The verse VI.4 in *Śvetāśvatara Upaniṣad* renders itself to different interpretations. Śaṅkara interprets this to mean that, if we dedicate all our works to *Īśvara,* we will not be subject to the Law of *Karma.*

"When a person, after having performed actions associated with the three qualities, surrenders them (the actions) to the Supreme, his association with them (the actions) is severed. He is also liberated from past actions. After having cut-off from the actions, he is liberated from them and attains Him" (S.U. VI.4).

Action without attachment and with dedication to the Supreme Lord is suggested here to break the Law of Karma. Supremacy of the Law of Karma is not upheld here, but other factors are brought in.

2. What Constitute the Transmigrating Self?

Sāṃkhya Theory Vs. Bṛhad-āraṇyaka Upaniṣad

What transmigrates is the buddhi (intellect), the individual counterpart of the cosmic seed *Mahat* i.e. the first evolute of *prakṛti* in the *Sāṃkhya* philosophy and *Vijñānamayaḥ* soul in the teaching of *Bṛhad-āraṇyaka Upaniṣad.* What endures death is this buddhi or soul conjoined with what is called subtle body (*liṅga śarīra*). It is the subtle body of each individual which identifies his or her particular series of existences linking one birth with the next, even though the ego identity is missing from one birth to the next. The moral accountability rests on the continuity of the subtle body even though the ego of future life is different from the ego of the present birth.

The *Bṛhad-āraṇyaka Upaniṣad*, while referring to the migrating self, speaks of its association with the five subtle elements, the senses, the mind and the intellect, and also refers to its being accompanied by the vital breaths and the impressions of the past experiences and knowledge as well as the results of its meritorious and demeritorious actions.

Of the twenty-three evolutes of *prakṛti*, as enumerated in *Sāṃkhya*, only the five gross elements are said to be dissolved after death. The remaining eighteen elements (intellect or *Mahat*, *ahaṃkāra*, mind, ten indriyas and five subtle elements), technically known as the subtle-body (*sūkṣma* or *liṅga śarīra*), persist even after death and pass away from the dying body to a new body.

The *Sāṃkhya* does not make separate mention of the vital breaths and the meritorious and demeritorious actions, since according to it the vital breaths are said to be operated by the three internal instruments (*antaḥkaraṇaḥ*), viz. the intellect, *ahaṃkāra* and mind, and all actions whether meritorious or demeritorious are said to be performed through the intellect assisted by the senses. Thus, they are supposed to be included within the eighteen elements constituting the subtle-body.

3. Underlying Principle Turning the Universe

Sacrificial Cult Vs Ethical Principle

The Vedic *Brāhmaṇas* impose and propagate a belief in the sacrificial cult as the inalienable mystery that influences the cosmic power and turns around the universe. Even though the *Upaniṣads* attempted to interiorize the whole process and shift the emphasis from the external rituals to the inner contemplation and meditation of the true significance and meaning of the sacrifices, they have not totally rejected the Vedic concept of sacrificial rituals bestowing health, wealth, happiness and heavenly rewards. Ethical aspects have no role in this concept.

On the other hand, the theory of *karman* upheld in the *śramaṇic* tradition is anchored in the firm belief in the operation of the moral principle turning around the universe. The morality of the motives behind our actions or the ethical nature of our actions is the underlying intrinsic universal principle which determines the evolution of the individual consciousnesses and, through them, the entire universe. Ethicization is the key element in the concept of *Karman.* As Paul Williams notes in his Buddhist Thought :

"It was the Buddha who declared that *karman* is intention, a mental event. In so doing, Gombrich comments, the Buddha "turned the brahmin ideology upside down and ethicized the universe. I do not see how one could exaggerate the importance of the Buddha's ethicisation of the world which I regard as a turning point in the history of civilization" (Gombrich 1996 : 51). Thus the Buddha turned attention from physical acts of cleansing the pollution resulting from '*bad karma*' – such as acts of physical ascetisim (as in practices of Jains) or the Brahmanic actions of purification, which typically involve washing or injesting 'the five products of the cow'– to 'inner purification', mental training—————————" (Buddhist Thought, p. 73).

Even those middle and later *Upaniṣads,* which have been greatly influenced by Buddhist ideas, have not repudiated the efficacy of the sacrifices in bringing about rewards in heaven as well as in this life. They only concede that the effects of these sacrifices are likely to wear off and the self performing them will return to the world after enjoying the fruits of their sacrificial acts in a heavenly existence. They uphold the efficacy of the sacrificial cult and its importance. This is amply demonstrated by the second boon granted to Naciketā in the famous episode with Yama in the *Kaṭha Upaniṣad.*

From the above, it will be seen that even though the theory of karman has been accepted in the *Upaniṣadic* philosophy and subsequent Hindu tradition, this co-exists uneasily with the Vedic legacy of sacrificial ritualistic practices and divine interventions which are alien to its concept. This has not been seamlessly incorporated in the Hindu thoughts.

CHAPTER 5

Theories on Brahman

1. Five Sheaths of Brahman *(Taittirīya Upaniṣad)*

In *Taittirīya Upaniṣad*, Brahman is considered as having five sheaths or as constituted of five selves. A hierarchy of these sheaths or selves has been recognized and spelt out (Figure 8).

At the lowest level is matter or body constituted of the essence of food. This is called physical self or physical sheath. This is also known as *Virāṭ* self composed of the five gross elements. This is the grossest and outermost sheath.

Higher than the physical self or bodily self is the *prāṇamayaḥ*, the vital self, consisting of the life-breath. This is also known as energy sheath, the gross manifestation of which in a human being is the breath. There are five vital breaths on which human biological functioning depends as we have already studied. Life-principle acts on the earth, produces food, eats food and develops into vegetable life, animal life and human life. Life-breath is the soul of the body.

Above life in the hierarchy and subtler than that is the mind. This is known as *manomayaḥ* or mental self. Mind acts on the life-forms and drives them, and as such, is the soul of the vital self. This state is shared by lower animals with men and is at the level of instincts, impulses and reflex actions.

Higher than the mind is the *Vijñāna* or intellectual faculty. This is called *Vijñānamayaḥ* or Intelligence self. Reasoning and analysis are the hallmarks of this state. Arts, science, mathematics, morals, poetry, philosophy and religion – all become possible only at this state. The intelligence self with its discriminative reasoning and logical powers is the soul of the mind and controls the mind.

TAITTIRĪYA UPANIṢAD

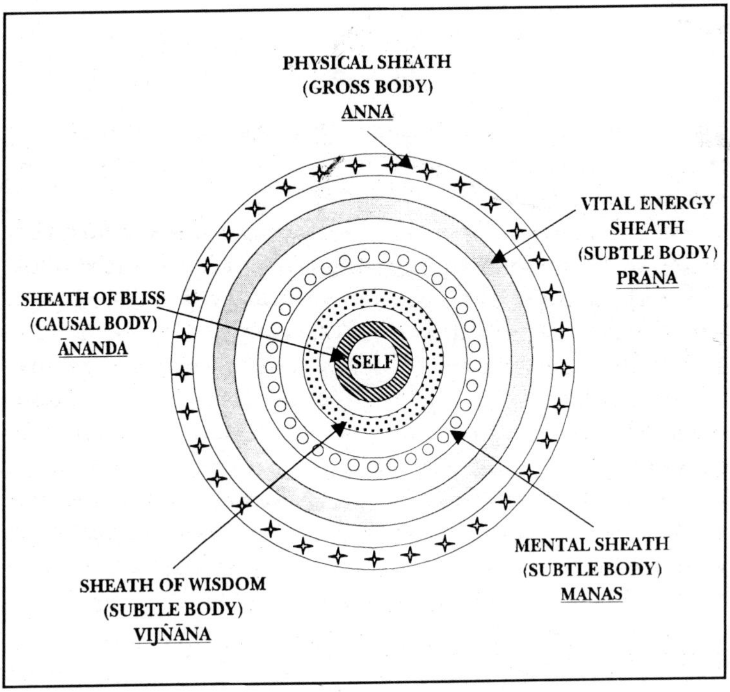

Fig. 8 The Five Sheaths or Kośas

Ultimate in the hierarchy of the selves constituting Brahman is the *Ānandamayaḥ* or the self of bliss. This is the state where bliss rules. The highest reality or the highest Brahman is identified with this *Ānandamayaḥ*.

Taittirīya Upaniṣad affirms that from nothingness came up Brahman as self-created (self-caused), as well-made (*sukṛtam*). *Tat* (That, Brahman) Itself (*svayam*) created (*akuruta*) Itself (*ātmānam*). That self-created Brahman is the essence of existence (the *rasaḥ*, the juice). This Brahman is nothing but bliss. *Taittirīya Upaniṣad* exclaims: "Who, indeed, could live, who, indeed, could breath, if there were not this Brahman (this bliss) in space (or in the secret place in the heart)?" (*T.U.* II.7.1)

"He knew that Brahman is bliss. For, truly, beings here are born from bliss, when born they live by bliss and into bliss when departing they enter" (*T.U.*III.6.1).

This Brahman or this bliss is the soul of the intelligence self (*Vijñānamayaḥ*) and in the ultimate analysis it is also the soul of *manomayaḥ* the soul of *prāṇamayaḥ* and the soul of *annamayaḥ*. Brahman is thus the fundamental root principle from which every thing evolves, on which everything rests and to which every thing returns according to his divine scheme of things. The evolution suggested is from top to down i.e. from the higher principle to the lower principles unlike in modern scientific theories.

The ultimate objective of every individual being, the *summum bonum* of life, is to attain this highest reality, this highest bliss that is in Brahman. The growth and development of the individual will not be complete unless this state is attained.

2. Seven Levels of Reality *(Kaṭha Upaniṣad)*

Whereas *Taittirīya Upaniṣad* treats Brahman or Reality as being constituted of five selves, *Kaṭha Upaniṣad* introduces two additional concepts of *ātmā-mahān* (the great self) and *avyakta* unmanifest (Figure 9).

Kaṭha Upaniṣad describes the hierarchy of the constituent principles of reality as below:

" Beyond the senses are the objects (of the senses) and beyond the objects is the mind, beyond the mind is the intelligence (buddhi) and beyond the intelligence is the great self (*ātmā-mahān*)" (*Kaṭha* I. 3.10).

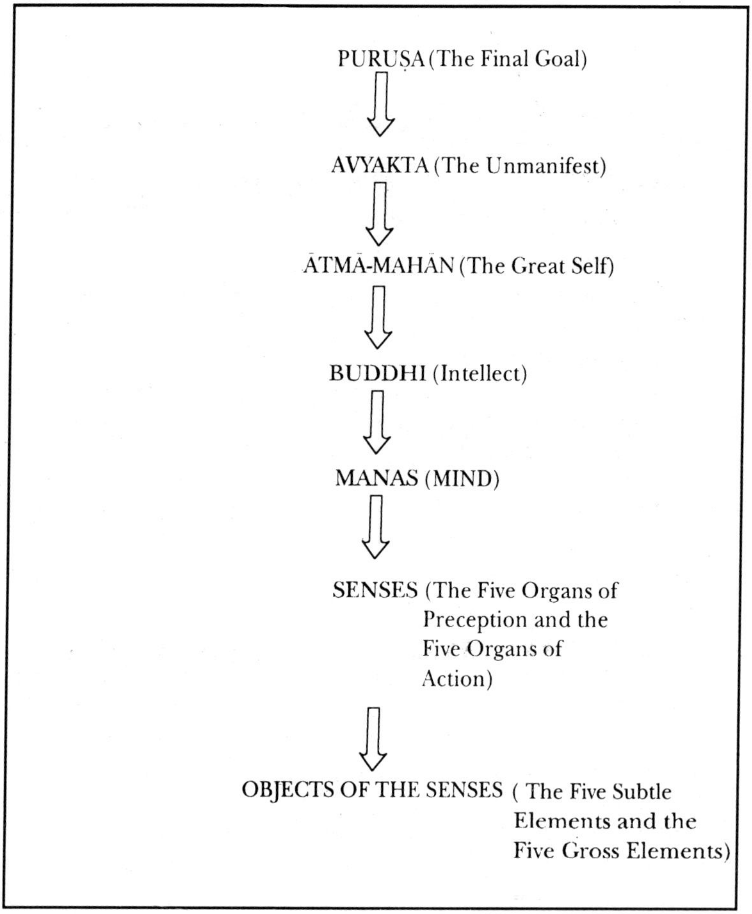

Fig. 9 Reality as per Kaṭha Upaniṣad

Beyond the great self (*ātmā-mahān*) is the unmanifest (*avyakta*); beyond the unmanifest is the spirit (*puruṣa*). Beyond the spirit, there is nothing. That is the end (of the journey); that is the final goal" (*Kaṭha* I.3.11).

The body that has been talked in the *Taittirīya Upaniṣad* as constituted of the essence of food is elaborated here as senses and objects of the senses. The senses are ten : five organs of perception and five organs of action. The objects of the senses are the five subtle elements and the five gross elements. These are the same as found in the *Sāṃkhya* theory of evolution of the universe.

Ātmā-mahān (the great self)

Ātmā -mahān (the great self) talked about here should not be confused with the *Ātman* which in the *Upaniṣad* terminology stands for the highest reality residing in the secret place of the heart of the individual and which is considered the same as Brahman behind the external universe. This highest reality (*Ātman* or *Brahman*) is identified by the word puruṣa or Spirit in the above passages in *Kaṭha Upaniṣad. Puruṣa, Ātman* and *Brahman* are synonymous terms and all denote the highest reality.

The *ātmā-mahān* here corresponds to the *Mahat* (buddhi or intellect), which, in the *Sāṃkhya* theory of evolution, is the first evolute from *prakṛti* when the latter has received the light of consciousness from *puruṣa* and begins its evolutionary spin.

The life-principle which was referred as *prāṇa* or breath in *Taittirīya Upaniṣad* is infused with more mystical connotations and more philosophical significance here, and elevated to a higher level above mind and intellect as a metaphysical entity called *ātmā-mahān.* This *ātmā-mahān* is the governing principle, ruler, lord or soul of the aggregate of body, senses, mind and intellect. This is the universal self, golden germ, *Hiraṇyagarbha* or the great soul of the universe at the macrocosmic level and the individual elemental self, soul or *Jīvātma* at the microcosmic level. This soul is the same one called as *prāṇātma* or *Vijñānātma* in the earlier *Upaniṣads* and *Prajñātma* (Intelligence Self) in *Kauṣītakī Upaniṣad.*

At the microcosmic level, he is the eater of the food and enjoyer of the objects. He is the particular individual self bound with a particular set or conglomeration of body, senses, mind and intellect and who is "affected by the bright or dark fruits of action, enters a good or an evil womb in the next birth so that his course is upward or downward according to his actions and wanders about affected by the pairs of opposites (pleasures and pains, joys and sorrows, heat and cold etc.)"

Avyakta ***(the Unmanifest)***

In *Sāṃkhya* theory, the principle of *Mahat* (the great one) is the first product of *prakṛti* when energized by *puruṣa*. It is the cosmic egg holding within it the universal soul and the causal laws of its development. At the microcosmic level, it is the egg containing within it both the individual soul and the potentialities of its development.

In *Kaṭha Upaniṣad*, the causal part has been segregated from the *'Mahat'* of *Sāṃkhya* and combined with a higher principle called '*avyakta*'. *Avyakta* denotes the causal phase of the highest Puruṣa associated with the material principle or the individual soul associated with body when names and forms are not yet distinguished but the potentiality of the universe and individual selves exists therein as in an egg or a seed. *Avyakta* is the higher principle holding within it the unmanifest *prakṛti* (energized by the *puruṣa*) and the universal laws of cause and effect which govern the evolution of the universe as well as the Law of Karma which determines the course of the lives of the individuals.

This *avyakta* directly evolves from *puruṣa* (Brahman) in *Kaṭha Upaniṣad* and has *puruṣa* as its soul and higher animating principle. It is the equivalent of prakṛti activated by the light of consciousness of *puruṣa* in *Sāṃkhya* philosophy. From out of *avyakta* emerge into manifestation all forms and all contents of the universe including *Hiraṇyagarbha* and *ātmā-mahāns*.

Whereas *Sāṃkhya* philosophy treats *prakṛti* and *puruṣa* as two separate eternal, uncaused, independent principles co-existing, all Upaniṣadic systems recognize only a single unitary principle – the highest *puruṣa* or Brahman – which has *prakṛti* as its body not separate and not different from it. The highest *puruṣa* (Brahman) has both the aspects of material and vital (life-force or consciousness) as two sides of the same coin.

This highest *puruṣa* is the end of the journey in search of reality and is the final and ultimate goal to be realized according to the *Kaṭha Upaniṣad*.

Even though there is no suggestion of *māyā* or illusion or unreality of the universe in the above passages in *Kaṭha Upaniṣad*, Śaṅkara treats the *avyakta* here as meaning the *māyā-śakti* of *Īśvara*. The theory of *māyā* will be studied later separately.

Buddhi and Ahaṃkāra

In *Sāṃkhya* theory, *buddhi* (intellect) is the first evolute from *prakṛti* as the individual or microcosmic counterpart of the cosmic state *Mahat*, and subsumes within it the principle of *ātmā-mahān* of the *Kaṭha*. Whereas in the *Kaṭha*, buddhi is the third evolute after *avyakta* and *ātmā-mahān*, it is included in the first evolute itself in the *Sāṃkhya* philosophy. In the *Kaṭha* the *ātmā-mahān* has intelligence as its adjunct, but in the *Sāṃkhya* intellect itself is the great soul being the first evolute.

Whereas *Sāṃkhya* treats *ahaṃkāra* or self-sense as a separate evolute from buddhi, in *Kaṭha Upaniṣad* it is subsumed in buddhi.

Avyakta and Puruṣa – Philosophical Questions

Even though the theory of karma finds mention in the earlier pre-Buddhist *Bṛhad-āraṇyaka* and *Chāndogya Upaniṣads*, it is for the first time that the concept of *avyakta* appears in the *Kaṭha Upaniṣad* as a separate constituent principle of the ultimate reality with the suggestion of the karmic seeds in it. What are the factors which determine the unfolding of this *avyakta* (the causal body)? Does this hold only the karmic seeds which determine the evolution of the individual self according to the moral law of karma or does it incorporate the over-riding command and will of the supreme *Puruṣa* also as well as the results of the sacrificial rituals carried out by the individual to bend the cosmic will to serve his purposes ? The *avyakta* postulated in the *Kaṭha Upaniṣad* seems to include all these factors because it is loyal to the tradition of Vedic religion and advocates sacrificial rituals and chanting of mantras accepting their efficacies in the turning-around and operation of the universe. In the *Kaṭha Upaniṣad*, as we have already seen, Yama teaches Naciketā the esoteric meaning of fire sacrifice and how it takes one to the heavens. As such, the *avyakta* described here is not purely a moralistic causal body determined by ethical principles. Even though it has been influenced by the *śramaṇic* and Buddhist thoughts, it is still a mixture of the various ideas including the legacies from the Vedic period.

Whether Brahman creates, supports and controls the individual selves and the universe or He evolves into them, as implied in the above *Upaniṣad* on the *Sāṃkhyan* lines, fundamental philosophical questions arise. Why does he create the universe with all these sufferings, sorrows, injustices and evil and what is the purpose of his creation? *Gauḍapāda* argues in his *Kārikā* :

"Creation is for the sake of enjoyment (or experience), so say some. Others say it is for the sake of sport. This again is the lordly nature of the divine, for what desire is there for the one who has obtained all wishes?" (*Gauḍapādīya-Kārikā*, First *Prakaraṇa*, verse 9).

Attributing enjoyment, sport or play to the divine is sacrilegious. *Brahma Sūtra* (*BS* 1.2.2) also accepts that Brahman can have no motive and hence no purpose of creation ; it is merely an overflowing of Brahman's essential fullness (*bhūman*). But this does not answer the basic questions. If *puruṣa* (=Brahman or *Ātman*) is considered a pure self-illumined consciousness, then it is a real conundrum why the *puruṣa* of such pure consciousness should first of all get deluded and enter into unjust and unequal creation or evolution and then aim for self-realisation.

As regards the sufferings, sorrows, injustices and evils of the world, attempts are made to explain them away as arising from "other factors" depending upon the actions of the individual selves in their former births. According to this view, God or Brahman merely allocates the *karmic* effects. If the *karmic* effects alone determine the course of the evolution of the individual self automatically as propounded by the Buddha ethicising the inner mechanism of the workings of the universe, then what is the necessity to postulate a Brahman or God ?

Brahman-pariṇāma theory also is beset with philosophical problems:

(1) How can Brahman, that is considered eternal and immutable, undergo transformation and still remain an unchanging reality?

(2) If it is stated that only part of Brahman is transformed, this goes against the unitary concept of Brahman.

Difficulties on these points have been recognized and that is why there has been a progressive development of thoughts in the later *Upaniṣads* towards the concepts of two selves, two Brahmans and *māyā* to explain away these inconsistencies. We have already seen the two selves theory propounded in the *Kaṭha*, *Muṇḍaka* and *Śvetāśvatara Upaniṣads.* We shall now study the further developments on the theories on Brahman and their culmination in the distinction of *para* (higher) Brahman and *apara* (lower) Brahman.

3. The Three States of Consciousness

The analysis of the different states of consciousness given in the *Upaniṣads* to gain an insight into the understanding of ultimate reality is a very significant contribution to the philosophical thoughts in India. From this analysis follow the most profound and subtlest of all teachings in the *Upaniṣads.*

The *Upaniṣadic* seers direct their search inward and analyse and dissect to find out what constitute the self and what the highest reality is. They delve deep within and analyse the three normative states of waking, dreaming and deep sleep in which we find ourselves normally. They come across a waking self, a dreaming self and a self in the deep sleep state (Figure 10). Analysing them, the seers conclude that the one self which is present in all the states is the highest one and has the highest reality. That self they identify with pure bliss.

Chāndogya Upaniṣad

Question is asked in this *Upaniṣad* : What is the Self (*Ātman* or Brahman)? What are the characteristic and distinguishing marks of him? *Prajāpati* describes the Self as the one:

"That is free from evil, free from old age, free from death, free from grief, free from hunger and thirst" (*C.U.* VIII. 7.1).

This definition we have already noted in the introduction. Everybody desires to attain such a state of happiness, bliss, free from grief, free from pains, free from death. Self is the one that is in such a state of bliss. *Prajāpati* teaches that one should know the Self, understand Him, realize Him and become one with Him to attain the same state of bliss He is in. Knower of Self obtains all worlds and all desires, attains the highest bliss.

To learn this secret knowledge of the Self, the gods send Indra and the demons Virocana to *Prajāpati.* They approach *Prajāpati* as disciples with offerings in their hands.

Prajāpati said to the two : "The person that is seen in the eye, that is the self. That is the immortal, the fearless. That is Brahman".

They asked "But, venerable Sir, he who is perceived in water and in mirror, who is he?".

Prajāpati replied : "The same one, indeed, is perceived in all these"(*C.U.* VIII.7.4).

By the person in the eye, *Prajāpati* meant the inner controller of the eye which gives the power of seeing to the eye. But, Indra

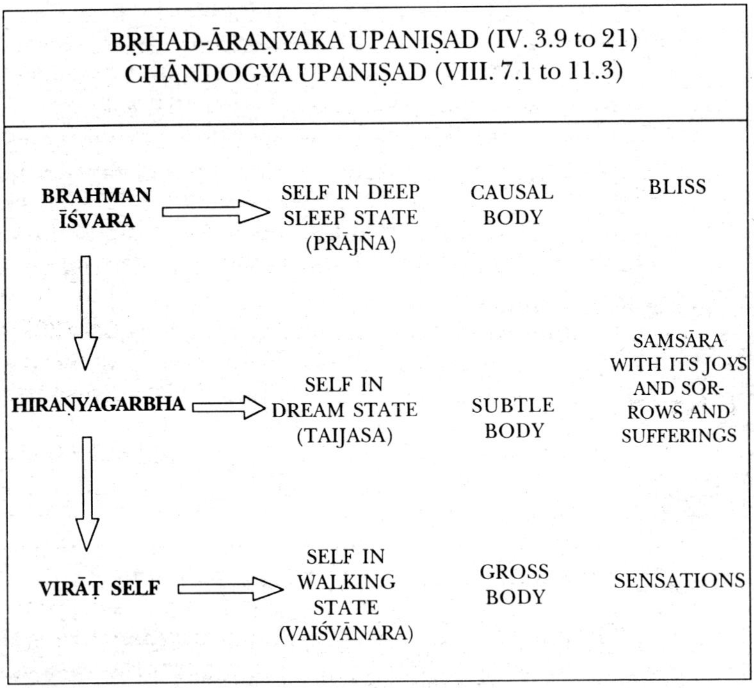

Fig. 10 Brahman as a Triad

and Virocana could not grasp the subtle truth. They mistakenly understand the image in the eye or the image of oneself in the water and in the mirror to be the self.

They find the image or the self in the pan of water well adorned when they are well-adorned, in the best clothes when they put on their best clothes, and tidy when they make themselves tidy. They mistake the self as image of the body.

Satisfied with this, Virocana goes back to the demons and declares the doctrine : "One's (bodily) self is to be made happy here, one's (bodily) self is to be served. He who makes his own self happy here and he who serves his own self, he obtains both the worlds, this world and the yonder" (*C.U.* VIII.8.4).

"Therefore even here they say of one who is not a giver, who has no faith, who does not offer sacrifices, that he is a demon, for this is the doctrine of the demons————" (*C.U.* VIII. 8.6).

From this emerges the doctrine of the demons that the self is nothing but body and sensual pleasures or bodily happiness is the ultimate happiness. There is nothing beyond.

On the other hand, Indra before reaching the gods reflects. "Even as this self (the bodily self) is well-adorned when this body is well-adorned, well-dressed when this body is well-dressed, tidy when the body is tidy, that self will also be blind when the body is blind, lame when the body is lame, crippled when the body is crippled. It perishes immediately when the body perishes. I see no good in this" (*C.U.* VIII. 9.1).

He returns to *Prajāpati* with his doubt and seeks clarification. *Prajāpati* concedes his point and tells him:

"He who moves about happy in a dream, he is the self, he is the immortal, the fearless. He is Brahman"(*C.U.* VIII 10.1).

With this knowledge, Indra returns satisfied. But even before reaching the gods, he sees this flaw in the above theory:

"Even though this self is not blind (when the body) is blind, is not lame (when the body) is lame, though he does not suffer defects from the defects of the body, though he is not slain (when the body) is slain, though he is not one-eyed (when the body) is one-eyed, yet it is as if they kill him, as if they unclothe him. He comes to experience as it were what is unpleasant, he even weeps as it were. I see no good in this"(*C.U.* VIII. 10.1 to 4).

Indra again comes back to *Prajāpati* with his misgiving. *Prajāpati* now tells him:

"When a man is asleep, composed, serene and knows no dream, this is the self————" (*C.U.* VIII. 11.1).

Indra seems to be satisfied with this theory. On his way back to the gods, he again reflects and finds flaw in this theory also.

"In truth this one does not know himself that 'I am he', nor indeed the things here. He has become one who has gone to annihilation. I see no good in this————" (*C. U.* VIII. 11.2).

Prajāpati agrees that such is the case and that the self has gone to total annihilation. But, he says that this is the highest state and that "there is nothing else besides this" (*C.U.* VIII. 11.3).

The bodily self or the consciousness associated with body and the dreaming (desiring) self associated with mind and *ahaṃkāra* (ego) have gone to total annihilation. These were the selves that were afflicted by desires and passions and were the prisoners of body and mind respectively. They were subject to hunger and thirst, subject to grief, subject to old age and subject to death and were not free from evil.

Indra was baffled because he had not realized the other self or the superconsciousness active underneath in the deep layers of *citta.* This other self remains hidden, in the secret place of the heart, supporting the life's biological functionings such as breath, circulation of blood, assimilation of food, growth etc and acting as the inner controller. It is beneath or beyond the normal conscious level and is "free from evil, free from old age, free from death, free from grief and free from hunger and thirst". This is the Self of highest reality ever present in all the three states.

Annihilation of the lower bodily self and dreaming (desiring) self that are at the normal conscious level and realisation of the highest self at the superconscious level constitute the highest state. There is nothing else besides this or beyond this state.

The sense of well-being and happiness experienced immediately on waking up from deep sleep gives a clue to the highest bliss in the state of extinction of the lower selves.

Chāndogya Upaniṣad thus treats Brahman as a triad with a bodily self, a dreaming (desiring) self and a self in deep sleep state. The last one is the inner controller ever present in all the states of waking, dreaming and sleeping. There is no state in which he is not there. Annihilation of the lower selves and realisation of the inner controller is the highest state to be achieved.

Bṛhad-āraṇyaka Upaniṣad

Bṛhad-āraṇyaka Upaniṣad also treats Brahman in a like manner as a triad.

It describes the dreaming self as below:

Dream Self

"———— When he goes to sleep, he takes along the material of this all embracing world, himself tears it apart, himself builds it up ; he dreams by his own brightness, by his own light. In that state, the person becomes self-illuminated" (*B.U.* IV 3.9).

"There are no chariots there, nor animals to be yoked to them, no roads but he creates (projects from himself) chariots, animals to be yoked to them and roads. There are no joys there, no pleasures, no delights, but he creates joys, pleasures and delights. There are no tanks there, no lotus pools, no rivers, but he creates tanks, lotus pools and rivers. He, indeed, is the agent (maker or creator)" (*B.U.* IV. 3.10).

"In the state of dream going up and down, the God makes many forms for himself, now as it were enjoying himself in the company of women or laughing or even beholding fearful sights" (*B.U.* IV. 3.13).

The god here is the ego-self or the mental-self. It builds its own worlds and enjoys or suffers.

In this dream state, the senses cease to function but the mind is active. The ego-self carries the impressions of senses gathered in the waking state and builds on them with the power of its own light. The point stressed in these passages is that the world of joys, pleasures, delights, pains and sorrows built by the ego-self is its own creation, projection or imagination, arising from the superimposition of its own desires. Desires are the root cause of this world of joys, sorrows and sufferings. There is nothing intrinsically good or bad, joyful or sorrowful in the external world. The joys and sorrows, the delights and pains experienced are only mental creations as in a dream, arising relative to the fulfilment or non-fulfilment of our desires superimposed on the external world. Our desires make up this world.

Self in Sound Sleep State

On the other hand, the state of the self in sound sleep is where "he desires no desires and sees no dream" (*B.U.* IV. 3.19).

"This, verily, is his form which is free from craving, free from evils, free from fear. As a man when in the embrace of his beloved wife knows nothing without or within, so the person when in the embrace of the intelligent self knows nothing without or within. This, verily, is his form in which his desire is fulfilled, in which the self is his desire, in which he is without desire, free from any sorrow" (*B.U.* IV 3.21).

The definition of the deep sleep state is very clear from these passages. " There he does not desire any desires, does not see any dreams." Desirelessness is the key distinguishing mark of the self in this state.

In *Chāndogya Upaniṣad* (*C.U.* VIII. 11.2) Indra was bewildered at the total annihilation of the selves in the deep sleep state. He could see only utter void or nothingess. But, *Bṛhad-āraṇyaka Upaniṣad* describes this state as comparable to the self-oblivion of earthly lovers in deep love and sexual intercourse where "they know nothing without or within". They become one with each other and lose their self-identity. Likewise, ego-self or mental-self loses its identity and becomes one with the inner controller or the supreme Self in the secret place of the heart within. *Subāla Upaniṣad* describes that in this state he merges in the supreme Self (*Īśvara* or Inner Controller) and becomes indistinguishable like water merged in water. *Bṛhad-āraṇyaka Upaniṣad* concludes that the characteristic feature of the self in this state is desirelessness, his only desire of becoming one with the supreme Self having been fulfilled. Tantric practices involving sexual union of the partners and other meditative techniques adopted by these practitioners for realisation of self and merger with the supreme Self (Brahman) derive their philosophical basis from the teaching in this passage (IV.3.21) of *Bṛhad-āraṇyaka Upaniṣad.*

"Verily, when there (in the state of deep sleep) he does not see, he is, verily, seeing though he does not see for there is no cessation of seeing of a seer, because of the imperishability (of the seer). There is not, however, a second, nothing else separate from him that he could see"(*B.U.* IV 3.3).

Likewise, there is no cessation of :

- the smelling of a smeller,
- the speaking of a speaker,
- the tasting of the taster,
- the hearing of a hearer,
- the thinking of thinker,
- the touching of the toucher and
- the knowing of the knower.

There is not a second, nothing else separate from him that he could see, smell, taste, hear or touch. There is nothing else separate from him to which he could speak, of which he could think. There is nothing else separate from him which he could know (*B.U.* IV. 3.24 to 30).

In this state, what remains is only the highest Self; there is no second ; there is no duality. This highest Self does not see or smell or taste or speak or hear or think or touch or know, for there is nothing separate from him. Yet he holds within himself the principles or powers of seeing, smelling, tasting, speaking, hearing, thinking, touching and knowing and the laws governing them. He is one with them. By his power of intelligence he holds them and controls them. This state of the highest Self is the most exalted blissful state. A particle of this very bliss is the support and anchor of all creatures.

Praśna Upaniṣad

Praśna Upaniṣad also describes that in the state of deep sleep the self has become one with the supreme God (*Īśvara*).

"The fires of *prāṇa* alone remain awake in this city. The house holder's fire is the out-breath. The (southern) sacrificial fire is the diffused breath. The in-breath is the oblation fire since it is taken from the house-holder's fire"(*Praśna* IV 3).

Southern sacrificial fire is the fire of the south used for offerings to the ancestors. According to *Praśna Upaniṣad,* a sacrifice or *yajña* of the life-spirit is going on in the deep sleep state. The vital breaths – *prāṇa, apāna, samāna, vyāna* and *udāna* – are symbolically identified with the fires used in the Vedic sacrifices. In this *yajña,* the life-spirit is merged in the Supreme *Īśvara* and its *yajña* is identical to the *yajña* described in *Gītā* as having been undertaken by *Īśvara* (Brahman) for the support and sustenance of the universe. This is His *yajña* as well as His *Dharma.* Such *yajña* is taking place at the microcosmic level in the deep sleep state for the support and sustenance of the individual.

4. Brahman of Four Quarters (Māṇḍūkya Upaniṣad)

The *Bṛhad-āraṇyaka* and *Chāndogya Upaniṣads* described the ultimate reality Brhaman as a triad consisting of three selves. In the *Māṇḍūkya Upaniṣad,* Brahman is described as one having four quarters (Figure11). The word used is *catuṣ-pāt* i.e. possessed of four quarters. *Pāt* may mean either a foot or a quarter (a denomination of a coin). Brahman constituted of

MĀṆḌŪKYA UPANIṢAD

BRAHMAN ↓	TURĪYA STATE (ĀTMAN)	INDESCRIBABLE	SMĀDHI
ĪŚVARA ↓	SELF IN DEEP SLEEP STATE (PRĀJÑA)	CAUSAL BODY	BLISS
HIRAṆYA-GARBHA ↓	SELF IN DREAM STATE (TAIJASA)	SUBTLE BODY	JOYS & SORROWS
VIRĀṬ SELF	SELF IN WAKING STATE (VAIŚVĀNARA)	GROSS BODY	SENSATIONS & PERCEPTIONS

Fig. 11 Brahman of Four Quarters or Four Selves

four quarters is a more appropriate description than Brahman with four feet (i.e. four-footed Brahman) as some would call it.

"Indeed, all this is Brahman; The Self (*Ātman*) is Brahman. This same self has four quarters"(*Mā.* U. 2).

Here, the three cardinal doctrines of the *Vedānta* – the universe is Brahman, the self is Brahman and there are four states of experience/existence of that self – are proclaimed.

"The first quarter is *Vaiśvānara,* whose sphere (of activity) is the waking state, who cognizes external objects, who has seven limbs and nineteen mouths and who enjoys (experiences) gross (material) objects"(*Mā* .U. 3).

This is the *Vaiśvānara* self or *Virāṭ* self (cosmic self) presented to us in the waking state. He possesses seven limbs and nineteen mouths as described below:

The seven limbs are :

- Heaven is his head,
- Sun is his eye,
- Air is his vital-force,
- Space is the middle part,
- Water is the bladder,
- Earth his two feet and
- *Āhavanīya* fire his mouth.

The nineteen mouths are :

- five organs of sense (hearing, touching, seeing, smelling and tasting),
- five organs of action (speech, grasping, locomotion, generation and excretion),
- five vital breaths,
- mind (*manas*),
- intellect (*buddhi*),
- the self-sense (*ahaṃkāra*) and
- consciousness (*citta*).

"The second quarter is *Taijasa,* whose sphere (of activity) is the dream state with consciousness of internal objects, who has seven limbs and nineteen mouths, and who is the enjoyer (experiencer) of subtle objects"(*Mā. U.* 4).

"Where one, being fast asleep, does not desire any enjoyable thing whatsoever and does not see any dream whatsoever, that is deep sleep. The third quarter is *Prajñā,* whose sphere (of activity) is the state of deep sleep, who is undifferentiated, just a unified mass of mere consciousness, who abounds in bliss, who is the enjoyer (experiencer) of bliss and who is the aperture (the doorway) to the experience (of the dream and waking states)" (*Mā.U.* 5).

"This one is the Lord of all ; this one is Omniscient ; this one is the inner controller (of all) ; this one is the womb of all ; this one is verily the origin and dissolution of all beings" (*Mā.U.* 6).

"The wise consider the Fourth (*Turīya*) to be that which is neither conscious of any internal world, nor conscious of any external world, nor conscious of both the worlds (together), nor a mass of consciousness, neither conscious nor unconscious ; which is unseen, unrelated, incomprehensible, indefinable (without any distinctive marks), unthinkable, indescribable ; whose valid proof consists in the single belief in the Self ; that into which the world is resolved (i.e. where all phenomena cease) ; the peaceful, the benign, the non-dual (*Śāntam-Śivam-Advaitam*). That is the Self (*Ātman*). That is to be known" (*Mā.U.* 7).

The first quarter of Brahman is the *Vaiśvānara* consciousness which cognizes the external world (*Viśva*) and identifies itself with the waking experience. The second is the *Taijasa*, the mental state, dream state with consciousness of an inner world, where the inner world of joys and sorrows, delights and sufferings, passions and desires, is experienced. This state is characterized by fantasies and mental fabrications and constructs. The third quarter is *Prājña*, the blissful state of serene, dreamless, sound sleep which is a desireless, sorrowless, undifferentiated mass of consciousness, where "one does not desire any pleasure whatsoever and does not see any dream whatsoever", where the waking self (consciousness) and the dreaming self (consciousness) have gone to total annihilation and what remains there is the inner-controller only regulating the various vital functions of the body at the sub-conscious level.

An analysis of the three states of experience reveals that basically waking and dream states are not much different from each other in as much as both are characterized by the superimposition of passions and desires, mental constructs and fabrications. In the waking state also we are dreaming, but in addition we are also acting with those dreams and desires and reaping the consequences. In the deep sleep state, there is no desire, no craving, no dream and no conceptual construct. The practitioner in Yoga meditates on the three states of consciousness and aims to simulate the conditions in the sound sleep state and identify himself with the inner-controller. In this process, he attains and enjoys the bliss which is the characteristic mark of the deep sleep state.

Whereas the *Bṛhad-āraṇyaka* and *Chāndogya Upaniṣads* have stopped their analyses at the third state of deep sleep with the suggestion that the inner controller (*Īśvara*) in this state is the highest Self (*Ātman*), the *Māṇḍūkya Upaniṣad* leap-frogs into a fourth state and postulates a still higher Self as the ultimate reality which exists both before the birth and after the death of the individual and at the cosmic level both before the creation and after the dissolution of the universe.The *Turīya* is a logical extension of the states of waking, dreaming and sleeping to be considered in any analysis of the various states of existence of reality and signifies the ultimate one obtaining after death or cosmic dissolution and before the next manifestation. In this state, the waking (*Virāṭ*) self, the dreaming (desiring elemental) self and the self in deep sleep (*Īśvara*) – all are withdrawn and all cease to exist. There is only the indescribable, indeterminate principle, Absolute unconditioned Brahman, in this fourth state according to *Māṇḍūkya Upaniṣad.* All phenomena cease here and the entire universe gets dissolved with all living beings. Only the true Self, the ultimate Brahman, shines here dreamless, sleepless, birthless and deathless. This highest Self is seen by the Yogins who have mastered the meditative techniques, entered into trances and developed the divine eye to have this vision of the ultimate reality.

This is the cessation of all plurality, cessation of all suffering, the quiescent, the divine and benign non-duality (*Śāntam-Śivam-Advaitam*). There is nothing whatsoever to perceive and cognize; there is neither cognition nor non-cognition, neither consciousness nor unconsciousness. All the negative descriptions given in *Mā .U.*7 point to the indefinable, indescribable and incomprehensible nature of the *Turīya.* This is akin to the state of nothingness or Neither Existence nor Non-existence as some Vedic sages have proclaimed or Nirvanic *śūnya* as the Buddhist philosophers have understood. But it is asserted in *Māṇḍūkya Upaniṣad* that a Self is seen in this state and this Self is the true Self that exists in all the states conceivable. It is maintained that this Self cannot be proved and realized by limited intellect of the ordinary mortals. It is beyond logical reasoning and enquiry. It has its *sāra,* valid proof, in the single belief in the Self (*eka-ātmapratyaya-sāra*). With faith and arduous practice alone, this highest Self (*Ātman*) can be realized.

"The fourth (*Turīya*) is partless (and) unrelated, (it is) the cessation of plurality, the appeased non-duality. The syllable OM is this Self. He who knows this enters the Self through his self". (*Mā.U.* 12).

The *Upaniṣad* identifies the letter 'A' of 'A - U - M ' (OM) with the waking state (*Vaiśvānara*), 'U' with the dream state (Taijasa) and 'M' with the deep sleep state (*Prājña*) (*Mā.*U. 9 to 11). The combined sound *AUM* or *OM* symbolizes the fourth, the *Turīya*, which is partless and which encompasses the three states of waking, dreaming and deep sleep just as *OM* encompasses the three letters. With the chanting of *OM*, the three states of consciousness are meditated upon and their natures, their inter-relationship and their ultimate rootedness in the all-encompassing unity of *Ātman* (Brahman) is realized inwardly. This is the symbolic meaning of meditation on *OM*. *OM* is the auspicious unity where all plurality ceases. Having known *OM* in this way, one attains identity with the Self immediately.

The concept of *Īśvara* (or the inner-controller) derived from an analysis of the deep sleep state is relegated to an inferior status in the *Māṇḍūkya Upaniṣad* because *Īśvara* here is still enwrapped in ignorance (*avidyā*) and subject to *Kāma*, the fundamental will to grow or create. As such, it has the seeds of evil and sin within it and is not free from their effects. This is the main criticism levelled against the Brahmanical concepts of creator God and *Īśvara* by the Buddhists whose philosophical thoughts were gaining ascendency then and influencing the cultural climate in the country. *Māṇḍūkya* concept of *Turīya* state seems to have arisen to free Brahman from the association with evil and sin and raise it to a pristine status of purity. The negative description of this state reminds one of the realm of absolute calmness and quietness, "the other shore" of *Nirvāṇa* in Buddhism. The influence of Buddha's teachings on the *Māṇḍūkya Upaniṣad* is undeniable in spite of its assertion of the existence of a Self (Brahman) in this highest state. The Brahman here which is devoid of the fundamental will to create or evolve and devoid of any defilement or imperfection is equatable with the *Nirvāṇa* in Buddhism. But when it is stated that this Brahman descends from its highest state of perfect purity and gives rise to the phenomenal world of evil and sufferings and miseries, it becomes an inscrutable mystery. There is always this philosophical problem of incongruity in such concepts of top-down evolution. The highest state is the ideal state to which one aspires and ascends. Any conception of the ideal descending and becoming defiled does not stand to logical reasoning.

When descended thus, this highest Self of *Turīya* is considered to be ever present in the other states also. But the precise relationship between this highest Self and *Īśvara* (the inner-controller) has not been clearly spelt out here although it is suggested that the former is the all encompassing ground and support of the other three states of existence. If it is ground and support, is it different from them? What is its nature? How does it support the others? The concept here seems to be akin to the one in the theory of two selves we have earlier studied. The highest Self may be considered as the witnessing Self. If it is only a witnessing Self, how does that which it witnesses come about?.

Even though non-duality is experienced in the serenity of deep sleep state (*Prājña*) as well as *Turīya*, the former is assigned an inferior status because it does not know of itself. It lacks the knowledge of itself. It is stated that *Prajñā* does not comprehend anything, neither himself nor others, neither truth nor falsehood. Self-awareness or consciousness of its own self is said to differentiate the fourth (*Turīya*) state from the third state of deep sleep. But, if self-awareness or consciousness is taken to be a characteristic of the *Turīya*, then this seems to contradict the descriptions in *Mā.* U.7 . The *Turīya* is the state or self after death and before birth of the universe; it is birthless, deathless, dreamless, sleepless. The Yogin aspires to attain this state. But, when the Yogin's self-awareness in his meditative state is equated with *Turīya*, then it is a superimposition of the quality of consciousness on the *Turīya* and a conceptual construct imposed on it.

Some scholars tend to equate the highest meditative state of the perfect Yogin with the *Turīya* and define *Turīya* in terms of this meditative state. This highest meditative state is not a normative state like those of waking, dreaming, deep sleep and post mortem dissolution and is a special state cultivated to apprehend reality after arduous practices and concentration. This is an acquired state where all the activities of the mind and intellect cease. This concept of cessation of perception. conception and volition as well as all duality of conceptual construction has been derived basically from the Buddhist teachings.

Some commentators detect a self-awareness or consciousness behind this cessation and identify the same with *Turīya*, the ultimate reality. "As no enquiry into its nature can be instituted without some description, its *svarūpa* or essential nature is said to be *sat* or being, *cit* or consciousness and *ānanda* or bliss. These are different phrases for the same being. Self-being, self-consciousness and self-delight are one" (Dr.Radhakrishnan, Basic Writings, p.128). In the ultimate analysis, all these teachings reduce to an assertion that self-consciousness of bliss is the highest reality. Truly speaking, the Yogin in this state is void of any conceptions as *Mā.U.* itself describes. But apprehending and asserting a self in this state is a superimposition on the void of this state and, as such, a fall from the perfect state.

Turīya, truly, is beyond all these conceptual constructs. Self-awareness cannot be said to be the attribute of the ultimate reality because it is not ever present and it is absent not only in the deep sleep state but also in other normative states experienced such as fainting and the existence as the embryo in the mother's womb. The common denomination or characteristic of all these states can only be described as void of conceptions. Therefore, the reality which exists in all these states can only be defined as void of conceptions and not as any self. The flowing nature of consciousness in the various states is overlooked and the bliss experienced in the meditative state is frozen and conceptually superimposed as the ever-existent reality. Self-awareness of bliss arises depending on causes and conditions. Even the highest meditative awareness is impermanent and it is only one particular state in a flowing or ever-changing consciousness; it comes and goes. Moreover, in the auspicious non-duality, how can there be a question of self-awareness when there is nothing else to be differentiated and no separate self to be aware of? When there is a not a second one or anything else separate from him, where is the question of self-consciousness to distinguish it from any other thing? Conceptual constructions on the self lead only to contradictions.

As Dr.Radhakrishnan points out, it is in the *Māṇḍūkya Upaniṣad* for the first time in the history of speculative thought that the distinction between Brahman as the Lord or *Īśvara* immanent in the individual as well as in the universe and Brahman as the absolute indeterminate principle has been suggested. Śaṅkara takes up the strands of thought in this *Upaniṣad* and also in *Paiṅgala Upaniṣad* and builds up his famous theories of *māyā*, *apara* Brahman and *para* Brahman.

5. The Four Selves of Brahman *(Paiṅgala Upaniṣad)*

Suggestion of *Māyā*

The concept of the four quarters or the four selves of Brahman outlined in *Māṇḍūkya Upaniṣad* is more fully developed and presented in *Paiṅgala Upaniṣad* adding also to it the suggestion of the theory of *māyā* or illusion.

"————At the beginning, all this, my dear, was Being alone. That is Brahman, the ever-free indeterminate, of the nature of Truth, Knowledge and Bliss (*Satyajñānānandam*), ever full, ancient (or eternal), one without a second" (*P.U.* I. 2).

"Even as in the mirage, the pearl-oyster, a log of wood, a piece of crystal and the like, there is (respectively) the manifestation of water, silver, the figure of a human being, streaks of light and the like, in that (Pure Being) is the root principle of all objectivity (*mūla-prakṛti*), possessed of the qualities of red, white and black, with the qualities in equipoise and incapable of being adequately expressed. When this is reflected in Brahman, it becomes the witness self"(*P.U.* I. 3).

Before the manifestation of the objective universe, in the beginning, there was only this Brahman as Pure Being or Pure Existence (*Sat*). The Absolute Brahman in the *Turīya* state, talked of as indescribable, ungraspable etc in *Māṇḍūkya Upaniṣad,* is described here to be of the nature of Truth, Knowledge and Bliss (*Satyajñānānandam*).

In this Pure Being was rooted the principle of all objectivity (*mūla-prakṛti*) or matter just as water is there in the mirage, silver in the pearl-oyster, streaks of light in a piece of crystal and figure of human being in a log of wood.

Of the four similes given, the first two suggest illusory perception and the last two creativity. Water is not actually there in the mirage. Pearl-oyster is mistaken as silver. What is there in the Pure Being is not known. It is mistaken just as we mistake mirage for water or pearl-oyster for silver. This has led to the interpretation of *mūla-prakṛti* as *māyā*, as illusion, as non-existent. On the other hand, the carving of human figure from out of the log of wood in the third analogy suggests creativity. Piece of crystal gives rise to streaks of light. Thus, even though the ideas of both illusion and creativity are suggested in the above passage, *mūla-prakṛti* as *māyā* or illusion prevails as a dominant view in the traditional interpretation. This concept of *māyā* aims at insulating Brahman from the evolution of *prakṛti* and the sufferings, sorrows, miseries and evils of the world, and thus safeguarding His integrity.

But, a deeper analysis of the verse P.U. I. 3 leads us also to the conclusion that the Highest Brahman himself is getting deluded in imagining the *mūla-prakṛti* where it is not there. Why and how the highest Brahman cognizes the *mūla-prakṛti* and becomes the witnessing self is not explained.

Another interpretation can be that Brahman imagines and creates *mūla-prakṛti* from out of nothing. His imagination becomes the actual existing *prakṛti.* His imagination or will is the unfailing one and *prakṛti* comes into existence as per His will. This shows his wonderful power. In this view, *māyā* is his wonderful power of bringing into existence *prakṛti* as his object or body from out of nothing.

But, the great intellectual powers and prowess of Śaṅkara have made the theory of *mūla-prakṛti* as an illusion (*māyā*) more appealing to the imagination and more popular.

Four Selves of Brahman

The scheme of evolution envisioned in this *Upaniṣad* (Figures 12 & 13) follows the *Sāṃkhya* theory generally. The existence is said here to be composed of four selves, of which the highest reality is the self of Brahman, the Pure Being. He descends into manifest existence and becomes the lower three selves through the inexplicable power of *māyā.*

Brahman, the Pure Being, has in the beginning *mūla-prakṛti* as his unreal body (objective principle). The idea of *mūla-prakṛti* here correspons to the impenetrable darkness or abyss of waters in the Hymn of Creation in the *Ṛg Veda.* This *mūla-prakṛti* is indescribable but spoken of as neither existent, nor non-existent, nor both existent and non-existent, in this *Upaniṣad.* The *mūla-prakṛti* here is said to possess the qualities of red (*rajas*), white (*sattva*) and black (*tamas*) initially in an equipoised or equilibrium condition and incapable of being adequately expressed. This is the same as in *Sāṃkhya* theory but with the difference that this *mūla-prakṛti* is the unreal body of Brahman, the Pure Being, (the Pure Consciousness) and has no separate existence as an independent eternal principle.

Sattva stands for intelligence, rhythm, pattern or order and goodness. *Rajas* stands for energy, activity and passion. *Tamas* is

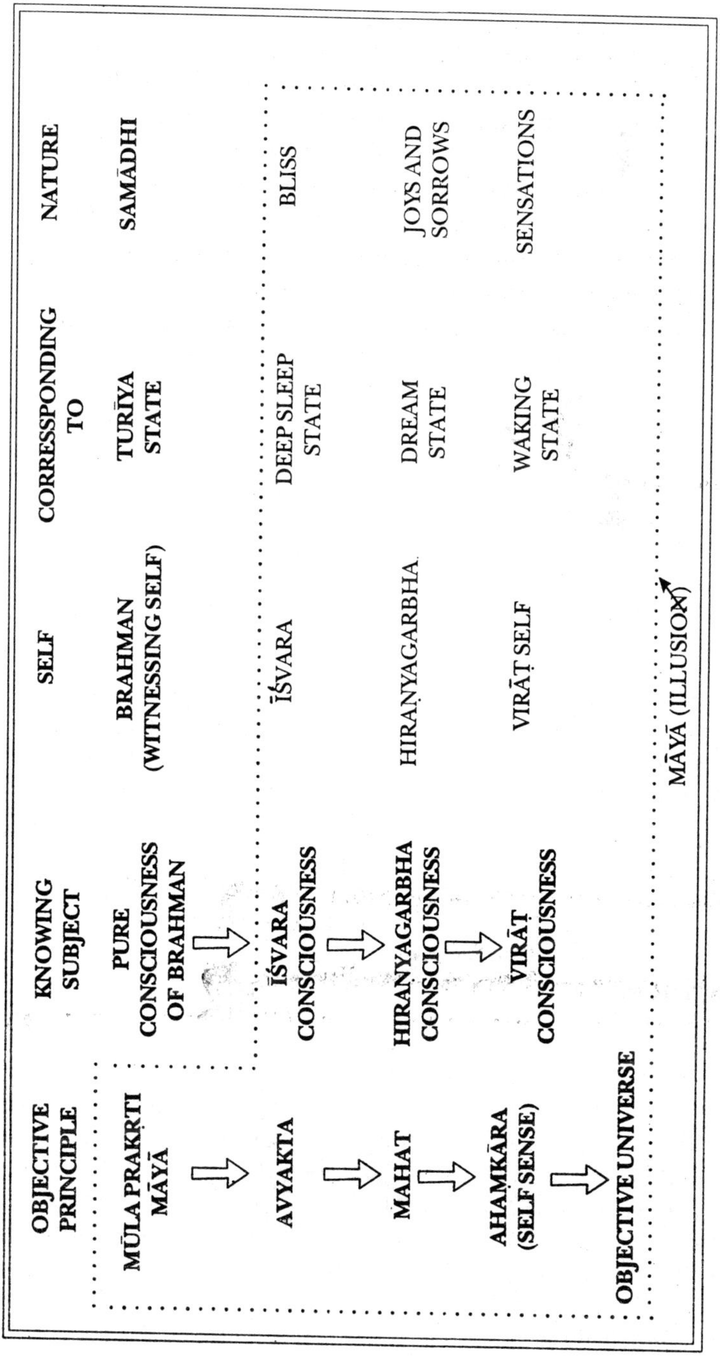

Fig. 12 Brahman of four selves (Paiṅgala Upaniṣad)

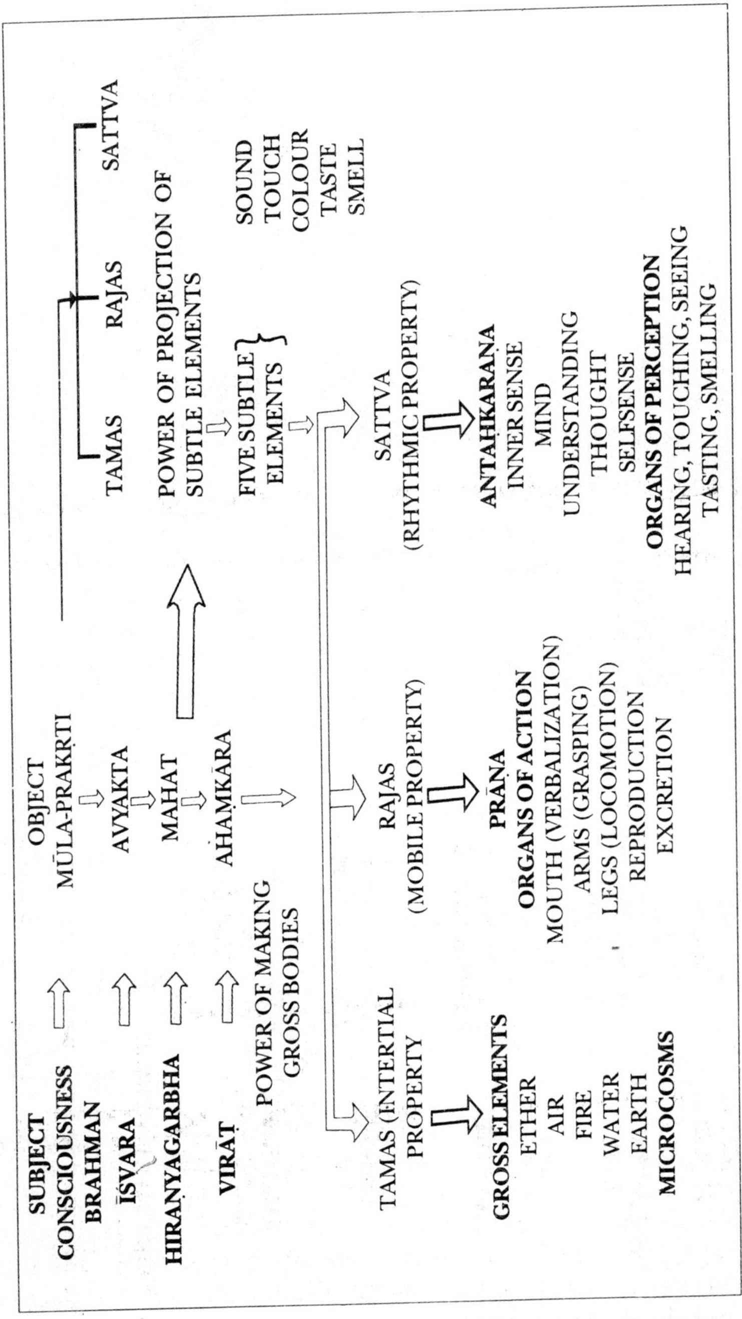

Fig. 13 Evolution of Mūla-Prakṛti (Paiṅgala Upaniṣad)

of the nature of inertia, ignorance and darkness. These are described as white, red and black respectively in this *Upaniṣad*. These three *guṇas* or forces in *mūla-prakṛti* are normally balancing each other and are in equilibrium i.e in an equipoised condition. As long as these *guṇas* are thus in equilibrium, there is no development-no evolution, no manifestation. *Mūla-prakṛti* by itself cannot give rise to subtle principles like life, mind etc. without the influence of consciousness.

When the Pure Consciousness of Brahman imagines or takes cognisance of the *mūla-prakṛti*, it is coloured and conditioned by the reflected image of *mūla-prakṛti* and becomes the witnessing consciousness. The witnessing consciousness as the subject takes the *mūla-prakṛti* as its object (body) and becomes the witnessing self. *Mūla-prakṛti* is thus animated with the light of consciousness of Brahman and spins into evolution. The first evolute is *avyakta* which has *Īśvara* consciousness as its subject and animating soul. Thus comes into existence the *Īśvara* Self with *avyakta* as its body. The Pure Consciousness of Brahman descends into or becomes this *Īśvara* consciousness which has *avyakta* (the unmanifest) as its body and animates it. The *avyakta* is the causal body. Since it has evolved from the *mūla-prakṛti* which is unreal and an illusion just as water in a mirage, the unmanifest *avyakta* is called '*māyā*' in this *Upaniṣad*. *Īśvara* as the Self has this *avyakta* or *māyā* under his control. He is the inner controller of *avyakta*, and the whole process of unfolding of the unmanifest and further evolution of *avyakta* are under his control. He becomes the first cause of creation, sustenance and dissolution of the world. He takes the form of the sprout of the world or the seed from which the world grows. He with his intelligence, rhythm (order, *ṛta*) and goodness, his laws of pattern and order, his laws of cause and effect and his law of Karma, controls the evolution and dissolution of the whole universe with all its beings. In him alone remains the entire universe like a piece of rolled-up cloth which is unfurled according to his will, his laws of cause and effect and Law of Karma (*Paiṅgala* I. 4).

The next evolute of *prakṛti* is *Mahat* (subtle body) which has *Hiraṇyagarbha* consciousness as its subject and the animating soul. The subject-object combination of *Hiraṇyagarbha* consciousness and the *Mahat* is *Hiraṇyagarbha* self. He animates *Mahat* and projects the inner world of mind and intellect, passions, desires and emotions. He is the dreaming self (*Taijasa*) talked about in the *Māṇḍūkya Upaniṣad*.

The next evolute is *ahaṃkāra* which has *Virāṭ* consciousness for its soul. From the *Virāṭ* self and *ahaṃkāra* arise the outer world of gross bodies that is the one experienced in the waking state.

Īśvara successively becomes *Hiraṇyagarbha* and *Virāṭ* to create the subtle bodies and gross bodies. In the act of creation, *Īśvara* embraces the quality of *tamas* and changes the subtle elements into gross ones through the power of making gross bodies dwelling in the *Virāṭ* Self. Embracing the mobile property (*rajas*) and rhythmic property (*sattva*), of the elements, He in turn creates the life-force with its five-fold functions and organs of action, and *antaḥkaraṇa* with its five-fold forms and organs of perception (Fig. 13). Thus come into existence the macrocosms of the outer worlds and the microcosms of the individual selves. They were not capable of moving and functioning without Him. "They were like a cart without intelligence." *Īśvara,* piercing through macrocosm and the caverns of the cranium of the individual bodies, entered them all. Thus entering them, He made them all sentient and became their driver and inner controller.

Paiṅgala Upaniṣad goes on to add that *Īśvara,* possessed of a particle of *māyā,* gets deluded on entering the several bodies by identifying itself with them and attains the state of the individual soul. By identification with the bodies, He attains the state of the doer and enjoyer, ever performing the functions of waking, dreaming, sleeping, fainting and dying and twirling around like a potter's wheel.

The individual soul, when the time comes for its body to die, gathers the subtle body comprising the vital breaths, mind and intellect together with the impressions of the past desires and conduct and departs to attain another body, in another birth and to reap the sweet and bitter fruits of its past actions. Thus, the individual soul is caught in the cycle of recurring births and deaths without any rest, like a worm caught within a whirlpool, till the desire for liberation arises through the ripening of the past virtuous conduct.

It may be seen from the above account of creation how the theory of *guṇas* of the *Sāṃkhyaites* has been weaved into its own scheme by *Paiṅgala Upaniṣad* incorporating also the concept of *māyā-śakti* or *Īśvara* as the inner controller of the entire evolution.

6. Comparison of the Ideas in Māṇḍūkya and Paiṅgala

In both *Maṇḍūkya* and *Paiṅgala Upaniṣads*, the existence is said to be constituted of four selves.

In *Paiṅgala Upaniṣad*, Brahman has been analysed at macrocosmic level of the entire universe whereas in the *Māṇḍūkya Upaniṣad* the exploration is at the microcosmic level of individual person. There is a correspondence and analogy between the four aspects of microcosm described in the latter and those of macrocosm in the former as shown below:

Waking bodily self	+	Dream Self	+	Self in Deep sleep state (*Prajñātma*, the inner controller)	⇒	Ātman
⇓		⇓		⇓		
Virāṭ Self	+	*Hiraṇyagarbha* Self	+	*Īśvara* (Inner Controller)	⇒	Brahman

As we have already seen, the conclusion of *Vedānta* unquestionably is that Brahman in the yonder space and the *Ātman* residing in the secret place of the heart of the individual person are identical, i.e. are one and the same because the universe and individual self are inter-related and interdependent.

The uniqueness of the teachings of *Māṇḍūkya Upaniṣad* and *Paiṅgala Upaniṣad* is that they soar beyond the level of the third state of self in deep sleep and *Īśvara* under the influence of Buddhist thoughts and identify the ultimate reality as *Turīya* (Brahman in the fourth state) or Brahman, the Pure Being (Pure Consciousness) unsullied by the cosmic will to expand or grow. Śaṅkara calls this Brahman of Pure Being as para Brahman (higher Brahman), and *Īśvara* (the inner controller in the third state) as apara Brahman (lower Brahman).

Both *Māṇḍūkya Upaniṣad* and *Paiṅgala Upaniṣad* identify and agree on the four selves of Brahman and their hierarchy. But there is no suggestion of *māyā* or illusion of the universe in *Māṇḍūkya Upaniṣad.* There is a suggestion of nothingness or non-existence in the *Turīya* state of Brahman. But this has the potential to give rise to the other three states. Just as the 10 paise, 25 paise and 50 paise coins are contained in the one rupee coin, the fourth state of highest reality contains the other three states. That is why, they are called the four quarters of Brahman in the *Māṇḍūkya Upaniṣad*, the quarters having the meaning as denominations. These are not negated as unreal whereas *Paiṅgala Upaniṣad* introduces the concept of *māyā* or illusion when it suggests that the *mūla-prakṛti* is in the Pure Being Brahman, just as water is in the mirage. Water in the mirage is an illusion. On the same analogy, it is suggested that *prakṛti* is an illusion.

In the philosophy in *Māṇḍūkya Upaniṣad*, the lower three selves arise from the all-encompassing ground and support (*Turīya*) and are dissolved in the *Turīya* whereas *Paiṅgala Upaniṣad* suggests that these are illusions. In the latter the highest Brahman himself is deluded and gives rise to the lower three selves as illusions (*māyā*).

Another point of difference is that *Māṇḍūkya Upaniṣad* describes the highest reality Brahman in the *Turīya* state as "not a mass of cognition, not cognitive, not non-cognitive" and indescribable. The state suggested here is more analogous to the concept of *śūnya* or nothingness in Buddhist thoughts.

On the other hand, *Paiṅgala Upaniṣad* defines the highest reality Brahman as Truth, Knowledge and Bliss (*Satyajñānānandam*). It is the ever existent Truth with nothing else to contradict it. When it is said to be Knowledge, that knowledge can only be knowledge or experience of its bliss or consciousness of its bliss for there is nothing else separate from it or second to it to know. As such, the truth or highest reality is this consciousness of bliss. Truth relates to the existence of bliss and knowledge to the consciousness of bliss.

There is a fall from the reality when any object or image of the object in the consciousness is taken cognisance of and identification/attachment with it starts because disturbance occurs in the blissful state due to the image of the object and attachment with it. Such a fall from reality or blissfulness takes place when the highest Brahman cognizes the *mūla-prakṛti* which is actually not there but exists only as an illusion just like water in a mirage. Thus, in the above account of *Paiṅgala Upaniṣad*, it is implied that the highest Brahman itself gets deluded and imagines or superimposes *mūla-prakṛti* where it is not there. But, the basic question why the highest Brahman deludes and descends into *Īśvara* consciousness imagining the *prakṛti*, remains unanswered.

7. The Two Brahmans

The *Maitrī Upaniṣad* also talks of two Brahmans as below:

"There are, assuredly, two forms of Brahman, the formed and the formless. Now that which is formed is unreal ; that which is the formless is the real ————————" (*Maitrī* VI 3).

Even though *Maitrī Upaniṣad* talks about the unreality of the formed Brahman, the dominant thrust of the teachings in the *Upaniṣads* is towards stressing the different degrees of reality rather than asserting the unreality of the universe.

The basic reason for *Maitrī Upaniṣad* calling the formed Brahman with his manifested world as unreal is because they are constantly changing. They are impermanent, incessantly undergoing change, not remaining the same any two moments and invariably leading to sufferings, sorrows, decay, destruction and death. Formless Brahman is considered the ever existing, absolute, unchanging reality.

The same *Upaniṣad* further describes the highest reality Brahman as that beyond time, beyond sound, beyond breath, beyond death, beyond the conditioned (objectified) consciousness and beyond all conditions of existence.

"There are verily two forms of Brahman, time and the timeless. That which is prior to the sun is the timeless, without parts. But that begins with (i.e. has a beginning from) the sun is time, which has parts————————" (*Maitrī* VI 15).

"And thus it has been said elsewhere; There are, verily, two Brahmans to be meditated upon, sound and non-sound, By sound alone is the non-sound revealed. Now here the sound is *AUM*. Moving upward by it, one comes to ascend in the non-sound. So (one says) this is the way, this is immortality, this is complete union and also tranquillity. And now as the spider moves upward by the thread, obtains free space, thus assuredly, indeed the meditator moving upward by the syllable *AUM* obtains independence————————.

"Having passed beyond this variously characterized (sound), they disappear (become merged) in the Supreme, the non-sound, the unmanifest Brahman. There they are uncharacterised and indistinguishable like the various juices that have reached the condition of honey. For thus it has been said, "There are two Brahmans to be known, the sound Brahman and what is higher.

Those who know the sound Brahman get to the higher Brhaman" (*Maitrī* VI. 22).

"And thus it has been said elsewhere : " What is (called) the sound is the syllable *AUM*. That which is its end is tranquil, soundless, fearless, sorrowless, blissful, satisfied, steadfast, unmoving, immortal, unshaking, enduring called *Viṣṇu*; for obtaining what is higher than everything (final release), let him reverence these two". For thus is it said, "He who is both higher and lower, that God known by the name of *AUM* is soundless and void of being too. Therefore, let one concentrate on (the crown) of the head" (*Maitrī* VI. 23).

The concept of time arises only from the relative movement of the earth with respect to the sun. It has parts like year, half-year, month, weeks and days. In time all things arise and all things end. This *Upaniṣad* says that time cooks all things. This time itself which cooks all things is considered the great self, that is the manifested form of Brahman. The higher Brahman is the non-time in which time itself is cooked or matured. This non-time is earlier than the birth of suns, stars, planets and earth. It is without parts and it is the highest Brahman.

Likewise, sound is the lower Brahman and non-sound is the higher Brahman; breath is the lower Brahman and non-breath the higher Brahman. The lower Brahman is the sound in syllable *AUM* and the higher Brahman is the non-sound, tranquillity at the end of the chanting of *AUM*. The higher Brahman at the end is tranquil, soundless, fearless, sorrowless, blissful, steadfast, unmoving, immortal unshaking, enduring. The *Upaniṣad* also describes this as soundless and void of being. In describing the highest reality as void of being, this *Upaniṣad* moves closer to the concept of *śūnyatā* in Buddhism.

In the *Māṇḍūkya Upaniṣad*, significance of the chanting of *mantra OM* lies in the understanding and inwared realisation of the combined sound '*A-U-M*' as symbolizing the ultimate rootedness of the three selves (waking, dreaming and deep sleep) in the all encompassing unity of Brahman. On the other hand, in the *Maitrī Upaniṣad*, the higher Brahman is identified with the non-sound at the end of the chanting of *OM*. Here the transcendence and void are being emphaiszed.

The essence of the teaching in *Maitrī Upaniṣad* is that the highest state of Brahman is the state of unqualified understanding (unqualified consciousness) where the mind is completely dissolved without any trace of the concept of space, time, sound, breath or any object.

8. The Radiant Supreme

The *Subāla Upaniṣad* passes beyond even the *Turīya* state of the *Māṇḍūkya* and describes the supreme state as one in which there is neither existence, nor non-existence, nor both existence and non-existence (Figure 14).

"In the beginning this was non-existent. He who knows Brahman as unborn, uncaused, unestablished (in any thing else), devoid of sound, devoid of touch, devoid of form, devoid of taste, devoid of smell, imperishable, not dense, not prodigious, originless, as one's own self, he sorrows not.——————— ." (*Subāla* III.1).

Subāla Upaniṣad sums up the supreme state of Brahman (*Ātman*) as the one in which all other states of waking, dreaming, deep sleep and *Turīya* have been burnt. It is beyond all these states and there the Self (*Ātman*) has burnt not only the gross and subtle elements but also the *prāṇa* along with other vital breaths, the *Mahat tattva*, the unmanifest (*avyakta*) and the Imperishable. Death becomes one with the radiant supreme. There is only non-being covered by Death. In the supreme, there is neither existence nor non-existence nor both existence and non-existence (*Subāla* XV.1). We are asked to go to the state in the beginning when there was only *asat* and even the consciousness of Brahman was not there. Death or desire arose and from this developed the Imperishable in *Turīya* and the rest in order. This comes back to the initial proposition in *B.U.* I. 2.1 & 2.2 (Figure 3).

This doctrine becomes indistinguishable from the concept of *śūnyatā* in Buddhism. The influence of Buddhist thoughts is clearly seen in these later *Upaniṣads – Māṇḍūkya, Maitrī, Paiṅgala* and *Subāla Upaniṣads.*

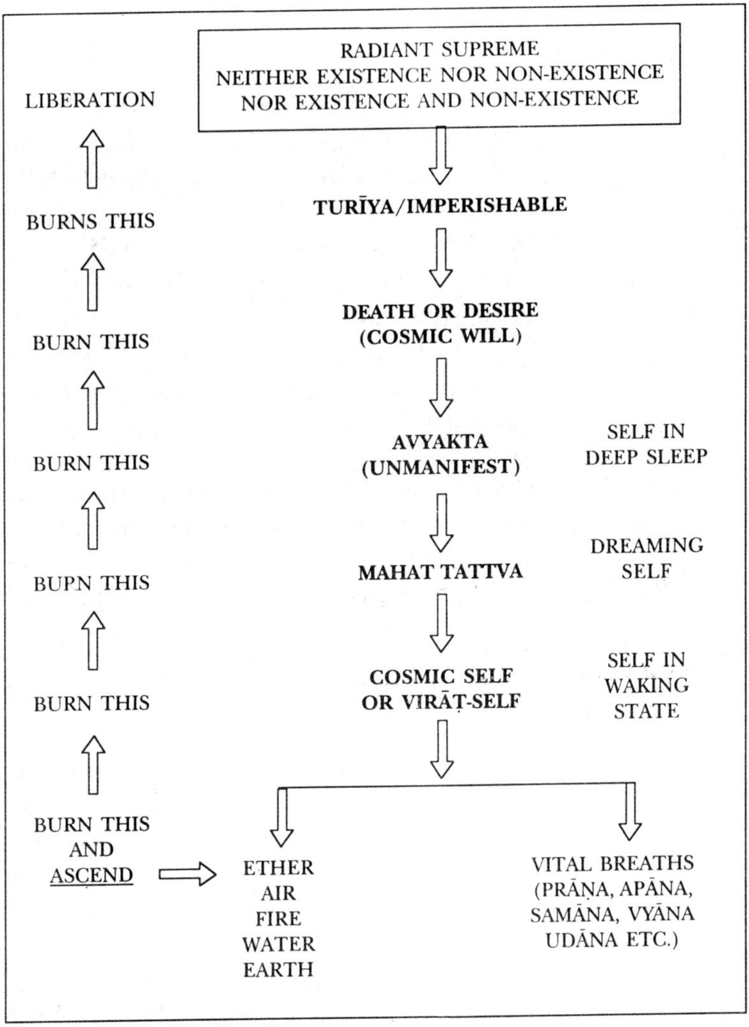

Fig. 14 Subāla Upaniṣad XV.1

9. Summary

In the ultimate analysis, we find that the philosophical theories of the *Upaniṣads* on the Brahman may be reduced in essence to the following six models:

- Model 1 - Brahman as a triad or constituted of three selves (*B.U* & *C.U*) (Figure 10).
- Model 2 - Brahman with five sheaths (*kośas*) or constituted of five selves (*Taittirīya*) (Figure 8).
- Model 3 - *Puruṣa* of *Kaṭha Upaniṣad* (Reality with seven hierarchical levels (Figure 9).
- Model 4 - Brahman constituted of four selves including the one in *Turīya* state of cosmic dissolution and withdrawal (*Māṇḍūkya*) (Figure 11).
- Model 5 - Same as Model 4 but with the suggestion of *māyā* introduced (*Paiṅgala*) (Figure 12).
- Model 6 - Radiant Supreme in a state even beyond the *Turīya* – Neither Existence, Nor Non-Existence, Nor Existence And Non-Existence – *Śūnya* (*Subāla Upaniṣad* (Figure 14)

We see a progressive development of thoughts in the *Upaniṣads* and how they are approaching the concept of *śūnya* propounded in Buddhism which we shall be taking up for study a little later. The idea here is that the aspirant selects appropriate model for meditation and spiritual upliftment.

CHAPTER 6

Liberation (Life Eternal)

1. Ultimate Goal

The ultimate goal of the Vedic *Āryan* culture was longevity in this life and immortality in a heavenly realm after death. Their lives centred around the rituals and sacrifices to achieve these. The entire creation, subsistence and destruction of the universe was seen in terms of the primordiality of the sacrificial act. In the *Puruṣa-sūkta* (*Ṛg Veda* X. 90), the universe is said to have been created through the sacrifice of the cosmic person *Puruṣa* and his self-dismemberment. This original sacrifice contained the norms for all subsequent sacrifices and maintenance of world-order.

It was through the potency of the sacrificial fire alone that the performer of the rites was supposed to gain secular welfare, progeny, wealth and a blessed life in the company of gods in heaven after death. Difference in the quality of the sacrifice was supposed to account for the difference in the state of the after-life and different sacrifices were believed to lead to the worlds of the different gods. Some sacrifices were for the sake of *devaloka* and some for *pitṛloka* (the world of the ancestors). Even the gods were supposed to have gained their immortality through sacrifices and they further stand in need of being fed by the sacrifices of the humans.

The highest goal was the attainment of heaven and enjoyment of heavenly pleasures in the company of gods and beautiful maidens. Prolongation of life in this world with all its pleasures and life in heaven after death were the aims. The whole outlook of the *Vedas* and *Brāhmaṇas* was pleasure-loving and world-affirming. The world-renouncing thoughts of the *munis* and forest-dwellers, which had been the legacies of the pre-*Āryan* non-Vedic tradition prevalent in India, were alien to the culture and practices of *Vedas* and *Brāhmaṇas.* In the pre-*Upaniṣadic* literature, we find only disparaging references to the *munis* and forest-dwelling mendicants who had renounced the world.

With the intermingling of races and cultures, the world-renouncing ideals of these *śramaṇic* communities have greatly influenced the thoughts of the *Upaniṣadic* sages. They have also come to realize the irrelevance and futility of the soul-less rituals performed mechanically and the vileness of the abhorrent animal sacrifices. No doubt Buddhism which is an off-shoot of the *śramaṇic* tradition has played a great part in the reformation of these practices and ideas. The *Upaniṣadic* sages have not revolted against the practices of the sacrificial religion of the priestly class as Buddha has done. In *Kaṭha Upaniṣad,* as we have seen earlier in our study, Yama teaches Naciketā how to lay the sacrificial fire which will lead to heavenly abode and enjoyments therein. Even in some later *Upaniṣads* like *Maitrī,* which have been influenced by Buddhist thoughts, the importance of sacrifices and rituals have not been undermined.

"———— For those who do not perform *agnihotra* sacrifice, who do not build up the fire, who are ignorant, who do not meditate, the remembering of the ethereal (heavenly) place of Brahman is obstructed. Therefore, that fire should be worshipped with oblations, should be built with bricks, is to be praised, is to be meditated upon" (*Maitrī* VI.34).

The *Upaniṣads* have remained loyal to the Vedic tradition and affirm that the rituals and sacrifices prescribed in the *Vedas* bring about secular welfare as well as *Brahmā*-world and heavenly enjoyments. But these are regarded as inferior *karma* because they are impelled by desires and selfish motives. Such results brought out by the due performance of the rituals and sacrifices as the secular welfare and heavenly rewards are short-lived and impermanent. They perish with the withering away of the effects of the sacrifices. These are not worthy of desire. The only desire that is worth desiring is the Self (*Ātman*) and this alone will lead to liberation.

"As here on earth the world which is earned by work perishes, even so there the world which is earned by merit (derived from the performance of sacrifices) perishes. Those who depart hence without having found here the Self (*Ātman*) and those real desires, for them there is no freedom in all the worlds. But those who depart hence, having found here the Self and those real desires – for them in all worlds there is freedom" (*C.U.* VIII. I. 6).

"Continuing diversely in the midst of ignorance, the unenlightened, on performing the rituals, think that they have attained their goal. Since they do not understand the truth due to the influence of attachment and desires, therefore, they sink down wretched and are deprived of heaven on the exhaustion of the results of *karma*" (M.U. I. 2.9).

"The deluded fools, believing the rites inculcated by the *Vedas* and *Smṛtis* to be the highest, do not understand the other thing (that leads to) liberation. Having enjoyed the fruits of actions in the high place of heaven, they enter again this world or a still inferior one"(*M.U.* I. 2.10).

The important point stressed is that the rituals and sacrifices cannot wash away the past misdeeds. Even if these rituals take them to heaven, this sojourn is short lived and they return again to the world to reap the bitter fruits of their misdeeds.

"But those who practise austerity (tapas) and meditation (*śraddha*) in the forest, the tranquil knowers who live the life of a mendicant, the learned who have their senses under control-these men depart, freed from sin, by the path of the sun to where lives that Puruṣa, the immortal and the imperishable" (M.U. I. 2.11).

Those who live in the forests and practise tapas and meditation, having conquered their desires and brought their senses under control, reach the eternal imperishable Puruṣa through the path extolled as the path of the sun or the path of the gods (*devayāna*). They do not return to this world. The same truth is stressed in *Chāndogya Upaniṣad* also in the passages V. 10.1 to 10.8.

Whereas the mendicants who follow the path of meditation and renunciation reach union with the highest reality Brahman and is not born again in this world, the followers of the ceremonial code who revel in rituals and sacrifices are said to reach only upto the world of *Brahmā* from where they will be thrown back for rebirth in this world after the exhaustion of the merits earned by them. Their path is an inferior path and is described as the path of the moon or path of the ancestors (*pitṛyāna*).

Those who seek for the Self in all the moving and unmoving through *tapasya* (austerity, control of the senses), *brahmacarya,* faith and meditation – they conquer the sun by proceeding along the Northern Course. This is the resort of all that lives and this is the highest goal, for from this they do not come back to this world again. This is the *devayāna,* path of the gods. This is free from fear, not subject to the fear of waxing and waning like moon. This one is the supreme goal for the meditators as well as for the men who combine meditation with rites ; for from this they do not return like others who perform rites alone. That is the stopping or rebirth (*Praśna* I.10).

Thus, we see that the rituals have not been rejected by the *Upaniṣads*; but combining with *tapasyā* and meditation, a spirit of reform has been ushered in. They have also reinterpreted the significance and inner meaning of the sacrifices. The trend in the *Upaniṣads* is progressively towards an emphasis on the contemplation and interiorisation of the inner meaning (*artha*) of sacrifice. The significance of ritual came to be understood in an increasingly symbolic sense. In the *Puruṣa-sūkta* (*Ṛg Veda* X. 90), creation of the universe came about through the self-sacrifice and self-dismemberment of the cosmic person *Puruṣa.* The significance here is the self-sacrifice for the sake of the universe. In this, the symbolism of self-sacrifice came to be recognized and an intrinsic relationship established between the individual as sacrificer and the universe as the actualisation of the sacrifice itself. Inward realisation arises that the betterment of the individual self or the universe is thus achieved not so much through the external performance of the ritual as through the practice of certain forms of contemplation and meditation and 'self-sacrifice'. This leads to the enquiry into the question of true nature of the individual self.

Richard King succinctly summarizes :

"Here we have a clear change of emphasis in relation to the earlier Vedic cult of the sacrifice. It is not action (*karman*) which leads to salvation. Action leads to a corresponding reaction in this world. In the *Upaniṣads* this is not usually seen as a desirable consequence. The goal is the attainment of knowledge, a mystical gnosis of one's true self, the permanent essence of conscious existence-beyond the incessant round of rebirths. It is in the *Upaniṣads,* then, that we find the establishment of a new spiritual goal, that of *mokṣa* – liberation or salvation from rebirth. Salvation no longer consisted in being established in a heavenly realm somewhat similar to life on earth, but in an awareness that one's own true nature is beyond the fluctuations of rebirth. Liberation (*mokṣa*) is the realisation of Truth (*satya*), truth being that which is (*sat*), was and forever will be. This reflects the cosmogonic interest of the *Vedānta* scriptures. Reality is that which always is i.e. that which exists before, during, and after the created realm of names and forms (*nāma-rūpa*)" (*Early Advaita Vedānta and Buddhism,* p.55).

Thus, the ultimate goal in the *Upaniṣads* emerges as *mokṣa*-liberation from rebirth and redeath, and establishment in the highest reality. Deliverance is a state of permanent union with the highest Self. This is immortality, *amaratvam* (life eternal).

2. Liberation in *Sāṃkhya* Philosophy

The *Upaniṣadic* thoughts have been greatly influenced by the parallel *Sāṃkhya* philosophy. *Sāṃkhya* helps to clarify the thoughts.

The bondage in the *saṃsāric* cycle of birth and death according the *Sāṃkhya* is due to the false identification of *Puruṣa* with the intellect, mind and other evolutes of *prakṛti* (the unconscious principle) and its failure to distinguish and separate itself from *prakṛti*. All activities, changes, thoughts, feelings, pains and pleasures pertain to the psycho-physical organism (the body-mind complex, the evolutes of *prakṛti*) and not to the self or *Puruṣa* who is quite distinct and separate from the body, senses, mind, intellect and ego. The intellect is responsible for all actions and the experiences of the phenomenal world and for the pains and miseries that result from the actions. *Puruṣa* ignorantly identifies itself with the intellect and wrongly thinks that it experiences pain and misery as the intellect does. *Puruṣa* forgets its original purpose of coming closer to *prakṛti*, the purpose being to realize itself as distinct and separate from *prakṛti*. Instead of discriminating and distinguishing itself from the unconscious principle *prakṛti*, it entangles itself with *prakṛti* and its evolutes. The moment it remembers its original purpose and discriminates itself from the manifested world and the evolutes of *prakṛti*, it realizes its true nature of pure consciousness and gains freedom from the bondage of *prakṛti* and its evolutes.

Liberation is the attainment of correct discriminative knowledge and realisation of the true nature of *Puruṣa* as distinct and separate from *prakṛti*. In actuality, pure consciousness of *Puruṣa*, is subject to neither bondage nor liberation. The concepts of bondage and liberation, pain and suffering-all arise from ignorance and false identification.

Intellect plays an important part in tightening or releasing the perceived bondage of *Puruṣa*. Intellect, when coloured in sāttvic character, becomes pure and helps to release, and when coloured in rājasic and tāmasic characters, tightens the bondage of *Puruṣa*. All the actions and experiences are the modifications of *prakṛti* and intellect only which the *Puruṣa* takes upon itself. When *sattva guṇa* predominates, intellect gives rise to virtue, knowledge, discrimination and dispassion, and the process of release begins. The distinction of *puruṣa* and *prakṛti* becomes apparent in the intellect, and the *puruṣa* and *prakṛti* are emancipated from each other. Therefore, the fundamental prerequisite for attaining liberation is the cultivation and nurture of *sattva guṇa.*

Through the practices of virtue and yogic disciplines with repeated affirmations of non-identification with the body, senses or mind (such as for instance, ' I am not the experiencer', 'I am not the doer ', ' Whatever is going on is in *prakṛti* '), one polishes one's mind and intellect and removes the impurities that impede the rise of correct discriminative knowledge. With the removal of these impediments, one gains freedom from all confusions and false identifications and thus one attains the knowledge of the true Self. Then the Self becomes disinterested in seeing *prakṛti* and *prakṛti* becomes disinterested in showing herself because she has been seen and her purpose has been fulfilled. *Prakṛti* and *Puruṣa* are both infinite and all pervading and are therefore eternally together, like two sides of the same coin ; but when their purposes are fulfilled, the process of manifestation ceases.

In this condition, the perfected Yogī lives in the body, in the realm of *prakṛti,* but the spirit has mastered the body, namely the sensual and other enslaving propensities of *prakṛti.* The ideal in the *Sāṃkhya* system is the attainment of the state of *sthitaprajña* with pure, steady mind and intellect, active in the world but rising above the worldly, with an unwavering, unflickering intellect like a steady lamp in a windless spot. The qualities of spirit (*Puruṣa*) – wisdom, kindness, serenity, forbearance etc. – radiate outwards from him. This is the state of '*kaivalya*' (aloneness) attained even in this life.

In *Sāṃkhya* philosophy, there are two kinds of liberation : *jīvana-mukti* and *videha-mukti.* The former is the liberation attained in one's life-time. In this kind of liberation, a person continues his existence in this world as a liberated being until he casts off his body. He continues his journey through worldly life just as the potter's wheel continues to rotate due to its previously generated momentum. When all the *saṃskāras* – the impressions of past actions-are exhausted, then he casts off his body and is said to enter *videha-mukti,* which is liberation after death.

3. Liberation in the *Upaniṣads*

Bṛhad-āraṇyaka Upaniṣad

Yājñavalkya plans to retire to the forests renouncing the state of the house-holder and wants to make a final settlement between his two wives - *Maitreyī* and *Kātyāyanī.*

Maitreyiī, who is spiritually disposed, asks *Yājñavalkya* : If, indeed, Venerable Sir, this whole earth filled with wealth were mine, would I be immortal through that ?" Her goal is to attain spiritual perfection and immortality (*amaratvam*).

Yājñavalkya replies that there is no hope of attaining immortality through wealth. Maitreyī requests to be enlightened on the way to achieve immortality. *Yājñavalkya* instructs her that the way to immortality is only through the realization of the Self within oneself and within all beings.

All these worlds, these gods (divine powers), these beings are this Self and are not different from the Self. Everything is dear for the sake of the Self that lies hidden within. This Self should be seen, heard of, reflected on and meditated upon. "Verily, by the seeing of, by the hearing of, by the thinking of, by the realization of the Self, all this is known"(*B.U.* II. 4.5).

"As a lump of salt thrown in water becomes dissolved in water and there would not be any of it to seize forth as it were, but wherever one may take it, is salty indeed, so, verily, this great being (Self), infinite, limitless, consists of nothing but knowledge (*Vijñāna*, consciousness)————"(*B.U.* II. 4.12).

All the worlds and beings are composed of the gross and subtle elements. They arise from out of these elements and vanish away into them. When the individual soul realizes the supreme Self and merges in it, there is no more knowledge.

Maitreyī is bewildered when *Yājñavalkya* tells that there is no more knowledge when the individual soul has merged in the supreme Self. *Yājñavalkya* clarifies:

"For where there is duality as it were, there one smells another, there one sees another, there one hears another, there one speaks to another, there one thinks of another, there one understands another. Where, verily everything has become the Self, then by what and whom should one smell, then by what and whom should one see, then by what and whom should one hear, then by what and to whom should one speak, then by what and on whom should one think, then by what and whom should one understand? By what should one know that by which all this is known? By what my dear, should one know the knower?"(*B.U.* II. 4.14).

Attaining such non-dual state is immortality. After imparting these instructions, *Yājñavalkya* goes away to the forest.

"———— When all the desires that dwell in the heart are cast away, then does the moral become immortal, then he attains Brahman here in this very body————" (*B.U.* IV. 4.7).

"Knowing that immortal Brahman, I am immortal" (*B.U.* IV. 4.17).

Bṛhad-āraṇyaka Upaniṣad also prescribes renunciation, child-like innocence and meditation to attain this state (B.U. III. 5.1).

According to the above passages in *Bṛhad-āraṇyaka Upaniṣad,* immortality is merger or union with Brahman without any trace of duality. This union is achieved by casting away all desires and becoming self-less. With the renunciation of all desires vanishes the false-notion of a separate independent self different from Brahman. There is nothing else apart from Brahman. This realisation is the attainment of immortality (life-eternal).

What is talked about in these passages of *Bṛhad-āraṇyaka Upaniṣad* is impersonal immortality where the soul achieves oneness with the Absolute Brahman, unconditioned. Adepts interpret this as illumined consciousness and not oblivion of consciousness as the bewildered Maitreyī exclaims.

Chāndogya Upaniṣad

"There are three branches of duty (*dharma*) – sacrifice (*yajña*), study and alms-giving. *Tapas* (austerity), indeed, is the first. The second is the pursuit of sacred wisdom dwelling in the house of the teacher. Absolute control of body in the house of the teacher is the third. All these attain to the worlds of the virtuous (*puṇya-loka*). He who stands firm in Brahman attains life-eternal (*C.U.* II. 23.1).

Yajña (sacrifice) is given a new meaning here. It is the *tapas* (austerities) coupled with intense concentration and meditation on Brahman. Instead of the sacrificial rites of the *Vedas* and *Brāhmaṇas,* triple *dharmas* of *tapas,* study of sacred books and absolute self-control are prescribed here for attaining *puṇya-loka* and life-eternal.

Kaṭha Upaniṣad

"One becomes freed from the jaws of death by knowing that which is soundless, touchless, colourless, undiminishing and also tasteless, odourless, eternal, without beginning and without end, beyond *Mahat* the great and ever constant" (*Kaṭha* I. 3.15).

"When the five senses of knowledge together with the mind cease (from their normal activities) and the intellect itself does not stir, that they say is the highest state"(*Kaṭha* II. 3.10).

"When all the knots that fetter here the heart are cut asunder, then a mortal becomes immortal. This alone is the teaching (of all *Upaniṣads*)" (*Kaṭha* II 3.15).

This summarizes the teachings of all *Upaniṣads.* When the wise man with his rare discriminating intellect knows what is permanent and what is impermanent, he does not run after the transient sensual pleasures which only plunge him into the snares of the wide-spread death, but turns his eyes inward seeking the eternal indwelling Self within. When the wisdom dawns and the false views arising from ignorance such as ' I am this body', 'This wealth is mine' and concomitant desires are eradicated, one realizes that he indeed is Brahman, everything is Brahman and there is nothing but Brahman, the one eternal. When all the knots of ignorance and desires that bind the heart are cut asunder, his heart expands and envelops the entire universe with love and compassion. All the senses and the mind cease from their activities and intellect also does not stir. All these vanish and what remains is only the objectless, motionless consciousness merged in Brahman just as the wave that has subsided. He becomes one with Brahman. This is called the highest state wherein the aspirant attains life-eternal i.e. immortality even while in the body. He lives in Brahman.

Even though knowledge of Brahman is talked about here, cessation of all mental acitivities is suggested in this *Upaniṣad* for the first time reminding the concept of no-mind and void of conceptions in Buddhism.

Muṇḍaka Upaniṣad

In *Muṇḍaka Upaniṣad,* two states of liberation have been mentioned : supreme equality with the Lord and impersonal absorption in the highest Brahman.

"When a seer sees the creator of golden hue, the Lord, the *Puruṣa,* the source of *Brahmā,* then being a knower, shaking off good and evil and free from stain, he attains supreme equality with the Lord"(*M.U.* III.1.3).

Impersonal absorption into "All itself" (*M.U.* III. 2.5) or "the Supreme Immutable Being" (*M.U.* III. 2.7) has been suggested in other passages:

"Just as the flowing rivers disappear in the ocean casting off name and shape, even so, the knower, freed from name and shape, attains to the divine *Puruṣa,* higher than the high" (*M.U.* III. 2.8).

It all depends on what one identifies as the highest reality according to his understanding. The former i.e. the equality with the supreme Lord refers to the identification with the *Īśvara* (the inner controller) whereas the latter refers to the merger in the Absolute Brahman of the fourth (*Turīya*) state. Equality suggests separate existence of the individual self in the realm of *Īśvara.*

Maitrī Upaniṣad

In Buddhism, *Nirvāṇa* is understood as the blowing out or extinction of the fires of lust, hatred and delusion and also sense of self and anything belonging to self. Likewise, *Maitrī Upaniṣad* characterizes liberation as the extinction of mind's activities using the same oft-repeated analogy of extinction of fire cited in Buddhism. According to it, the mind is the cause of the bondage as well as liberation; mind bound to objects is bondage and mind free from objects is liberation.

"——— Even as fire without fuel becomes extinct in its own place, even so thought, by the cessation of activity, becomes extinct in its own source. Even in a mind which seeks the truth and has quieted down in its own place, there arise false ideas due to past acts when deluded by the objects of senses. One's own thought indeed, is *saṃsāra* ; let a man cleanse it by effort,—————.

"The mind, it is said, is of two kinds, pure and impure, impure from contact with desire and pure when freed from desire. By freeing mind from sloth and distraction and making it motionless, he becomes delivered from his mind (reaches mindlessness), then that is the supreme state. So long should the mind be restrained in the heart till it reaches its end (i.e. mindlessness), that is knowledge, that is liberation.

"All else is but extensions of the knots that bind us to this life. The happiness of a mind whose stains are washed away by concentration and who has entered the self cannot be described by words. It can be grasped by the inner organ only. One cannot distinguish water in water, fire in fire or ether in ether, even so he whose mind has entered in the Self, he is released completely.

"Mind, in truth, is the cause of bondage and liberation for mankind; for it is bondage if it is bound to objects ; freedom from objects, that is called liberation.————" (*Maitrī* VI. 34).

Mind that has become absolutely pure without any trace of desire or thought vibrations, objectless, steady, undistracted and motionless, and that has merged in the *Ātman* (Self) indistinguishably just as water is indistinguishable in water, fire in fire or ether in ether – that is liberation. Becoming merged in Brahman, it is birthless and deathless and it has entered life-eternal. It has attained *amaratva*, immortality.

Paiṅgala Upaniṣad (Chapter IV)

Paiṅgala Upaniṣad defines bondage as the persistence of the sense of 'I am', 'This is mine' and such egoistical thoughts and feelings. Liberation is the absence of these egotistical thoughts and feelings.

Selfishness or looking upon the body and the world as one's own, as means to one's enjoyment, causes bondage. The surest way to liberation is the conviction that 'I am Brahman', 'I am not this body and I am not the desires arising from the body', 'I am not the enjoyer chasing the sensual pleasures that are transient', '"I am indeed the Brahman, the eternal, undying Self that is within me and also within all beings', 'There is nothing else apart from Brahman'. Once these ideas become ingrained in the mind and the mind becomes inseparable from these ideas to the exclusion of any egotistical thoughts, then the functionings of the mind cease and it becomes a void. Thereby, the individual gets liberated and merges in Brahman without any trace of duality (*Paiṅgala* IV 9, 19 to 21).

Remaining aloof, yet not aloof, remaining in the body, yet not of the body, the innermost self of the seeker becomes the all pervading Brahman.

The seeker after Brahman, after becoming one with Brahman, becomes the self of all beings and perceives that he is the all, the transcendent, the blissful (*Paiṅgala* IV. 3 & 9).

Just as water poured into water, milk poured into milk or ghee into ghee becomes one without differentiation, even so the individual soul and the Supreme Self become one, that is, of non-dual form (*Paiṅgala* IV 11).

The state of liberation is described not as that of a fish in water but as that of a dew drop or river water that has entered the sea and lost its separate identity (Dr.Radhakrishnan).

The liberated soul retains his body till his previously commenced *karma* remains unspent. Until the *karma* is fully spent he carries his body like a snake with the slough on. He, though possessed of the body, wanders about homeless like the moon on the sky (*Paiṅgala* IV. 4).

When his *karmas* are spent and when the time comes, he casts off his body either in a place of pilgrimage or in the cottage of a dog-flesh eater (since both these places are same to him) and attains aloneness (*kaivalyam*). He scatters away his vital breaths and attains aloneness (*kaivalyam*).

After the knower of Brahman has run his appointed course of life and dies, his body should be cast away as an offering to the birds and the like to appease their hunger or else it may be buried. Burial is prescribed only for the one who has become a monk and not for others.

No pollution is to be observed by the blood relations, no rituals to be performed, no oblations in the form of balls of cooked rice to be made, no offerings of water to be given ; nor any other rituals on new moon or other days should be adopted for the departed knower or mendicant who has become Brahman.

Even as there is no cooking of food that has already been cooked, there is no cremation of the body of a knower of Brahman which has already been burnt in the fire of austerity. For one whose body has already been consumed by the fire of knowledge, there is no need for the performance of *śraddha* ceremonies or any other obsequies.

It is only so long as the seeker does not attain knowledge of the real that endless ceremonies, observances of purity, prayers, likewise performance of sacrifices and visits to places of pilgrimage are prescribed by the scriptures. All these are not ends in themselves. They are means to the realisation of the eternal.

As the space in the pot gets merged in the all-pervading space when the limiting adjuncts of the pot are broken, even so the liberated individual is merged in the universal Self.

Kaivalya Upaniṣad

"He is all, what has been and what shall be. He is eternal. By knowing him, one conquers death. There is no other way to liberation" (*Kaivalya* 9).

"By seeing the self in all beings and all beings in the self, one goes to Brahman, not by any other cause"(*Kaivalya* 10).

There is no other way to liberation except by recognizing the Self (*Ātman*) and seeing the Self in all beings and all beings in the Self.

4. Identification with Reality

The bondage in the *Upaniṣadic* view is identification with the lower selves – the waking self (associated with the body) and the dreaming self (associated with the mind and desires). In the ultimate analysis, both these selves are the same, both being the conceptual constructs of the mind with the only difference that in the former the conceptual constructs are based on bodily sensations while in the latter these constructs are purely imaginations without any physical objects being there actually. Both are truly the superimpositions of desires and passions. As such, both these have no inherent reality. These are the ever-changing formations, impermanent, leading only to sufferings and sorrows. Denying and negating these, the higher the one ascends in the hierarchy of reality, the greater the one gains happiness and bliss.

The earlier *Upaniṣads* like *Bṛhad-āraṇyaka* and *Chāndogya* treat the self in the sound sleep state or *Īśvara* as the highest reality. When the aspirant or Yogin tries to identify with *Īśvara*, what are the characteristics and attributes of *Īśvara* which he recognizes and merges in? *Īśvara* is the inner controller which concept is invariably linked to power – this Brahman is power. He is regarded as omnipotent, omnipresent and omniscient. He who knows Brahman knows and controls the universe. He becomes the almighty; he becomes the universe. He rules over others, is not controlled by others, is not dependent on others and is self-dependent and almighty. This sort of concepts will only engender in the aspirant an arrogance of absolutism, an arrogance of permanence, uniqueness and sovereignty over others. The goal of identifying Brahman and becoming one with Brahman – is this goal based on such concepts of *Īśvara*? Such concepts of almighty Brahman are the hangovers of the earlier Brahmanic ideals which have been reinterpreted by later *Upaniṣads*, no doubt under the Buddhist influence. Unfortunately, the *Upaniṣadic* teachings, not having been systematically worked out on strict logical basis, lead to different interpretations. The aspirant has to be clear on the conceptual identification basis to work out an appropriate spiritual practice.

The *karmic* formations arising according to the Law of Karma have been recognized explicitly as a separate constituent principle of reality only in the later *Upaniṣads* like the *Kaṭha*. These formations are identified with *avyakta* which is again equated with *Īśvara* as his evolution and as part of his divine will. These *karmic* formations have to be burnt away to avoid rebirth and attain life eternal. How these *karmic* formations will be burnt away have not been unambiguously explained in the *Upaniṣadic* teachings. Desireless actions in this birth may not add to the *karmic* burden. But how will the past accumulations be wiped out?. It is understood that these melt away on identification and union with Brahman. That means, the knowledge of Brahman eradicates these formations. It is presumed here that the knowledge of Brahman has this magical power just as magical power was assumed for the sacrificial power in the Vedic knowledge. But the seeker after Truth has to analyse and understand whether the realisation of the ultimate Brahman becomes the cause of the eradication of *avyakta* (*karmic* formations) or it is the effect realized after wiping out all *karmic* residues. After all, it should be borne in mind, the *avyakta* is the veil or sheath covering the ultimate reality. The stress should be on exploring and exposing the unconscious deep within and burning away all ingrained and deeprooted propensities and *karmic* formations.

The concept of liberation and the ideas concerning the characteristic marks of liberation will differ depending on which of the status of reality one identifies with and merges in. Any new aspirant will have to meditate on all these teachings, deliberate and find out the truth for himself, so that he may formulate appropriate spiritual practices to identify and merge himself in the highest reality.

The *Upaniṣadic* teachings on the life-eternal (*amaratvam*) lend themselves to different interpretations. Some readings seem to suggest separate existence of the soul and its amaratva whereas liberation would not be possible without the total annihilation of the notion of a separate soul. This is nothing but a carry-over of the lingering desire for heaven in the *Vedas*.

CHAPTER 7

Moral Preparation for Spiritual Life

1. The Three Principal Virtues (B.U. V. 2.1. to 2.3)

Three principal virtues of self-control (*dāmyata*), giving (*dāna*) and compassion (*dayadhvam*) are taught in these passages of *Bṛhad-āraṇyaka Upaniṣad* (V 2.1. to 2.3).

The children of *Prajāpati* are classified here as gods, men and demons according to the predominant qualities that characterize them. After completing their studies under *Prajāpati* as students of sacred knowledge, they approach him individually for final instructions.

To the gods, *Prajāpati* gives the instruction of '*da*'. They understand this as '*dāmyata*', 'control yourselves'. Gods are those who are all full of virtues but given to indulgence in sensual pleasures. To them, the instruction is to practise self-control.

When the men approach *Prajāpati*, the same syllable '*da*' is uttered as the instruction. The men understand this as '*dāna*'. Greediness characterizes men. They are asked to cultivate the virtue of *dāna* – giving (offering) and eradicate greediness in them.

To the demons also, the same syllable '*da*' is given as the final instruction by *Prajāpati*. Demons are those given to cruelty. For them, the antidote is *dayā* – compassion, forbearance.

Thus, the three virtues of *dāmyata* (self-control), *dāna* (giving) and *dayā* (compassion) are prescribed to cleanse the evil tendencies in all.

2. Duties to be Performed (T.U.)

The duties to be performed are emphasized in *Taittirīya Upaniṣad* verse I. 9.1.

> Righteousness and learning and teaching are to be practised.
>
> Truth (*satyam*) and learning and teaching are to be practised.
>
> *Tapas* (austerity) and learning and teaching are to be practised.
>
> Control of the outer organs (*dama*) and learning and teaching are to be practised.
>
> Control of the inner organs (*śama*) and learning and teaching are to be practised.
>
> The fires are to be kept up and learning and teaching are to be followed.
>
> The *agnihotra* sacrifice is to be performed and learning and teaching are to be practised.
>
> Guests are to be adored and learning and teaching are to be practised.
>
> Social good conduct is to be maintained and learning and teaching are to be carried on.
>
> Progeny is to be begotten and learning and teaching are to be carried on.
>
> Procreation and learning and teaching are to be carried on.
>
> A grandson is to be raised and learning and teaching are to be carried on.
>
> Truth, *Tapas*, learning and teaching are to be practised.

Although truth, *tapas*, learning and teaching were mentioned earlier, they are emphasized again to show their importance. Learning and teaching are mentioned in all the contexts in order to imply that these two are to be practised diligently even by one who is engaged in other duties.

3. Final Teachings to the Departing Students (T.U. I. 11.1 to 6)

Having completed the teachings of the *Veda*, the *guru* gives the following instructions as a farewell sermon to the departing students in the *Taittirīya Upaniṣad* (I. 11. 1 to 6).

> Speak the truth.
>
> Practise virtue.
>
> Let there be no neglect of your daily reading.
>
> Do not cut-off the thread of the off-spring.
>
> Let there be no neglect of truth.
>
> Let there be no neglect of virtue.
>
> Let there be no neglect of welfare.
>
> Let there be no neglect of prosperity.
>
> Let there be no neglect of study and teaching.
>
> Let there be no neglect of duties to the gods and the fathers.

Next the student is enjoined to respect and honour the mother, the father, the teacher and the guest as the veritable gods.

> Your superiors should be respected.
>
> Offerings of gifts should be given:
>
> - with faith
> - with modesty
> - with fear
> - with sympathy
> - in plenty

In case of any doubt on the deeds or conduct or when spoken ill of, in such matters behave yourself emulating the *Brāhmaṇas* who are competent to judge, devoted to good deeds, not led by others, not harsh lovers of virtue. Behave as they behave.

This is the command. This is the teaching. This is the secret doctrine of *Veda*.

4. Oneness of Self—(Īśa and Kaivalya)

"He who sees all beings in his own self and his own self in all beings, feels no hatred by virtue of that realization" (*Īśa* 6).

"When to the man of realization, all beings have, verily, become one with his own self, then what delusion and what sorrow can there be for that seer of oneness ?" (*Īśa* 7).

"By seeing the Self in all beings and all beings in the Self, one goes to Brahman, not by any other cause" (*Kaivalya* 10).

The virtues of non-hatred, *ahiṃsā* and non-injury to others flow logically from these mantras. Where is the question of hatred in the heart of one who has realized that all beings are his own self and that *Īśa* the Lord, pervades every being and is immanent in all that moves in this world? All are Brahman. Injury to any being is an injury to the Lord and also to your own self. The fundamental principles of ethics are derived from these mantras. Since every being is your own self, you would not like to do to others what you would not like others to do to you. Diversity you see is a creation of your mind arising from your desires and as such is false. The basic truth is the unity and oneness of the life-force.

Sorrow and delusion afflict only the ignorant man who does not perceive the seed of selfish desires impelling him to action and as such, sees conflict of interests and diversity; but not to the man who realizes the absolute oneness of the Self in all, oneness of the Self pervading all like space.

For such a person, the entire universe is Brahman and he lives in Brahman-Consciousness. He finds all beings in himself and himself in all beings. His heart is filled with love and compassion for all. He is free from all passions, desires and emotions such as hatred, jealousy, anger and so on.

CHAPTER 8

Path to Liberation (Life Eternal)

1. Bṛhad-āraṇyaka Upaniṣad

We have already seen the teaching of *Yājñavalkya* to his wife Maitreyī in the *Bṛhad-āraṇyaka Upaniṣad* that the way to immortality is only through the realisation of the Self (*Ātman*) within oneself and within all beings. There is no hope of attaining immortality through wealth or rituals or sacrifices.

All these worlds, these gods (divine powers) and all the beings that we come across are this Self and are not different from the Self. Everything is dear for the sake of the Self that lies hidden within. Here *Yājñavalkya* declares that everything that is valued is so treasured not because of itself but because of the *Ātman* within.

" ————Verily, O Maitreyī, it is the Self that should be seen, heard of, reflected on and meditated upon. Verily, by the seeing of, by the hearing of, by the thinking of, by the understanding of the Self – all this is known" (*B.U.* II. 4.5).

After listening to the instructions, reflection and meditation are recommended. Yājñavalkya instructs Maitreyī that the *Ātman* should be looked into, reflected on and meditated upon. The contemplative focus advised here is for the intuitive apprehension of *Ātman.*

2. Chāndogya Upaniṣad

C.U. in Verse VII 23.1 points the source of happiness, the source of bliss.

"The infinite is happiness. There is no happiness in anything small(finite). Only the infinite is happiness. But one must desire to understand the infinite.——————" (*C.U.* VII. 23.1).

"Where one sees nothing else, hears nothing else, understands nothing else, that is the infinite. But where one sees something else, hears something else, understands something else, that is the small (the finite). Verily, the infinite is the same as the immortal, the finite is the same as the mortal. "Venerable Sir, on what is the infinite established ?" "On its own greatness or not even on greatness" (*C.U.* VII. 24.1).

In the finite, there can be no happiness. It only produces craving which ultimately becomes the seed of sorrow. Hence, transcend the finite and merge in the infinite without any notion of the duality or separatedness of the self and the Brahman. The infinite is the highest Brahman which is pure bliss. This is the ultimate non-dual state where nothing else is there except the pure consciousness of Brahman. On what this infinite is established is an imponderable metaphysical question to which whatever reply is given will be inadequate and self-contradictory. It will be interesting to note the doubt here whether the infinite Brahman is self-established or established in nothingness. Suggestion of *śūnyatā* may be detected here.

3. Kaṭha Upaniṣad

The Path of Goodness

We have earlier studied the famous discourse of Yama to Naciketās in the *Kaṭha Upaniṣad* imparting to him the knowledge of the immortality of soul.

In that episode in the *Kaṭha Upaniṣad*, when the boy Naciketā asks Yama to enlighten him on the secret of life after death, Yama first tries to persuade him not to insist on answer to this question, saying that it is extremely profound and that even the gods do not know precisely. Instead he offers Naciketā all conceivable earthly pleasures, wealth and kingdom beyond compare. But Naciketā rejects all these, saying that these are transient and ephemeral, existing briefly and gone next moment leaving only the miseries and pains behind. Of what avail are these things as long as these are evanescent and the world is ruled by death? How can we enjoy these when the fear of death and impermanence stalk us? Naciketā is intent upon acquiring the sacred knowledge of salvation. Yama is pleased seeing his eagerness for the wisdom, and tells:

"Thou, O Naciketā, hast rejected after examining the desires that are pleasant and seem to be pleasing. Thou hast not taken to the way of wealth where many mortals sink to ruin" (*Kaṭha* I. 2.6).

"The small-minded go after outward pleasures. They walk into the snare of widespread death. The wise, however, recognizing life-eternal do not seek the stable among things which are unstable here"(*Kaṭha* II. 1.2).

The path of goodness is different from the path of pursuing hedonistic pleasures. The latter will lead the individual soul astray from the goal of apprehending Brahman and attaining *amaratvam.* The inevitable result of running after the sensual pleasures is the bondage to the wheel of life and death and the continued subjugation to the evils and miseries of the world according to the Law of Karma. It is *avidyā* or ignorance which impels one in this path of sensual enjoyments whereas it is wisdom that leads one in the path of goodness to reach the ultimate goal of uniting with Brahman.

Undistracted by the transient pleasures and the lure of wealth and kingdom, Naciketā chose to tread the path of wisdom and received as his third boon from Yama the secret knowledge of the deathlessness of soul and path to immortality.

The above episode and dialogue between Naciketā and Yama in the *Kaṭha Upaniṣad* illustrate the first step in the quest for truth and immortality. That is to discriminate the path of goodness from the path of sense enjoyments and reject the later so that the ultimate goal of realizing Brahman can be achieved.

"Not he who has not desisted from evil ways, not he who is not tranquil, not he who has not a concentrated mind, not even he whose mind is not composed, can reach the Self through right knowledge" (*Kaṭha* I. 2.24).

This verse emphasizes the moral conduct that is necessary to lead to the spiritual life and realisation of the Self. The spiritual life is based on moral and ethical foundation and causally linked to the purity of the conduct. No spiritual life or realisation of Truth is possible without this moral basis. Adherence to ethical values only can lead to the concentration, tranquillity and serenity of the mind which is pre-requisite for apprehension of the indwelling Self. Only the pure in heart shall see the Self.

Such passages or teachings as above emphasizing the importance of moral and ethical foundation fort the spiritual life are few and far between in the vast corpus of the *Upaniṣadic* literature. These passages remind one of the Buddha's teachings in The Dhammapada in the following verses:-

"Choose the path that leads to *Nirvāṇa*; avoid the road to profit and pleasure. Remember this always, O disciples, and strive always for wisdom"(Dh.75).

"Don't run after pleasure and neglect the practice of meditation. If you forget the goal of life and get caught in the pleasures of the world, You will come to envy those who put meditation first" (Dh. 209).

Restraint of the Sense Faculties-Parable of the Chariot

Liberation from the repeated cycle of birth and death is to be attained through the restraint of the sense-faculties from evil ways and by following the path of goodness. This truth is brought out and illustrated through the analogy of chariot in the *Kaṭha Upaniṣad.*

"Know the (individual) Self as the lord of the chariot and the body (*śarīram*), verily, as the chariot. Know the intellect (*buddhi*) as the charioteer and the mind (*manas*), verily, as the reins" (*Kaṭha* I. 3.3).

"The senses (*indriya*), they call, the horses; the senses having been imagined as horses, know the objects (*viṣaya*) of the senses as the paths (they range over). The Self associated with the body, the senses and mind – the wise man declare – is the enjoyer"(*Kaṭha* I 3.4).

Here, the body is compared to the chariot and the indwelling Self (*Ātman*) to the Lord of the chariot who is on journery. The senses are compared to the horses yoked to the chariot and the mind to the reins. Intellect is the charioteer commandeering the chariot. The senses like horoses have to be reined in by the calm and pure mind and guided properly in the correct path by the discriminating intellect in order to take the indwelling soul to the goal.

"He who has a discriminating intellect as his charioteer and who has under control the reins of the mind – he reaches the end of the journey, that supreme abode of the all-pervading Brahman" (*Kaṭha* I. 3.9).

Liberation is achieved by controlling the body-mind complex and through the realisation that the true essence of existence is not this ephemeral passing complex, but rather the *Ātman* which travels within it. Rather than roaming around searching for ephemeral satisfactions like a chariot without a master controlling its reins, one should endeavour to control the 'vehicle' of one's experiences, through the yogic control of the senses. One should endeavour to realize one's status as the ' Lord of the chariot ' (*rathin*).

We find the analogy of horses to describe the wild senses in the Buddha's *Dhammapada.*

"Even the gods envy the saints, whose senses obey them like well-trained horses and who are free from pride. Patient like the earth, they stand like a threshold. They are pure like a lake without mud, and free from the cycle of birth and death" (*Dh.* 94 & 95).

"As a well-trained horse needs no whip, a well-trained mind needs no prodding from the world to be good. Be like a well-trained horse, swift and spirited, and go beyond sorrow through faith, meditation, and energetic practice of the *Dharma*" (Dh. 143 & 144).

The influence of the Buddhist theories of inner moral laws determining the evolutions of the individual consciousnesses (*vijñānas*) and universe and the ethicisation of the evolutions is clearly seen in the *Kaṭha Upaniṣad* in the above passages even though at some places the same *Kaṭha Upaniṣad* upholds the efficacies of the sacrificial rituals also. The latter may be a sort of concession to the Vedic tradition to which it retains its loyalty.

Yogic Control of the Senses

As we have already seen, the *Kaṭha Upaniṣad* has postulated a hierarchy of principles constituting Brahman – senses, mind, intellect, *ātmā-mahān, avyakta* and *puruṣa.* "Beyond *puruṣa,* there is nothing. That is the end of the journey. That is the final goal" (*Kaṭha* I. 3.10 & 11).

Thus, *puruṣa* is the highest reality and the others are having different levels or grades of reality. The teaching is to contemplate and meditate on these principles and ascend the hierarchy of the constituent principles to reach the highest reality. The lower ephemeral principles have to be controlled and transcended to reach the highest goal.

The wise-one passes beyond the senses by merging them in the mind, passes beyond the mind by merging it in the intellect, passes beyond the intellect by merging it in the *ātmā-mahān* (or the life-force), passes beyond the life-force by merging it in the *avyakta* and finally passes beyond *avyakta* also and merges in *the Supreme puruṣa.*

"The discriminating man should merge the (organ of) speech into the mind; he should merge that (mind) into the intelligent self; he should merge the intelligent self into the great self (*ātmā-mahān*); he should merge the great self into the transquil Self" (*Kaṭha* I 3.13).

"Arise, awake and learn by approaching the adorable teachers (who know the Self). Sharp as the edge of a razor and hard to cross, difficult to tread, is this path (so) declare the sages" (*Kaṭha* I 3.14).

"The Self is without sound without touch and without form, undecaying; is likewise, without taste, eternal, without smell, without beginning, without end, beyond the great, abiding ; by discerning that, one is freed from the jaws of death" (*Kaṭha* I 3.15).

This is the path of contemplation of the philosophical truths and meditation and ascension to the highest reality taught in the *Kaṭha Upaniṣad.* This is the path of yogic control of the senses. Success in this path requires proper sense-control and self-discipline. This path is described as sharp as the razor's edge, difficult to tread. Dedication, faith and perseverance and absolute surrender to the will of the supreme are the essential elements in this path.

"When the five knowledges (senses) together with the mind cease (from their normal activities) and the intellect itself does not stir, that, they say, is the highest state" (*Kaṭha* II 3.10).

"This, they consider to be Yoga, the steady control of the senses. Then one becomes undistracted, for Yoga comes and goes" (*Kaṭha* II. 3.11).

When the five forms of sense knowledge along with the mind stand still and the intellect stirs not, that, they say, is the highest state. In this exalted state, the individual ego self with its desires and dreaming mind gets completely dissolved and what remains is the consciousness, unconditioned, objectless and motionless, like a still lake in perfect peace and serenity. This is merger in Brahman and Yoga.

Single-minded concentration and undistracted attention are necessary for Yoga. Constant practice and persistent efforts will be required to keep the mind free from any fluctuation and steady as the light of a candle in a windless place. Mind is liable to fluctuation and concentration in Yoga will come and vanish if it is not steadied by proper practice and purity of heart. In perfect Yoga, the mind should be free from any objects of desire and should be motionless, still, quiescent, without any trace of images of objects and disturbing thoughts. With this Yoga, one becomes Brahman and experiences pure bliss.

What *Kaṭha Upaniṣad* talks of *yoga* as coming and going, *Kena Upaniṣad* illustrates through analogies and states that vision of Brahman arises like a flash of lightning or winking of the eye (*Kena* IV. 4).

The two analogies of flash of lightning and the winking of the eye suggest the sudden glimpse into Brahman. By persistent practice of *yoga* and purity of heart, this flash of a glimpse into the reality has to be made a permanent realisation.

4. Muṇḍaka Upaniṣad

Muṇḍaka Upaniṣad emphasizes on the practices of truth, *tapas,* right knowledge and *brahmacarya* for attaining the Self.

"The bright and pure Self within the body, attainable through the constant practice of truth, *tapas* (austerity), right knowledge and *brahmacarya* (chastity, continence)-Him the ascetics with their sustained effort and with their imperfections eradicated through constant practice of these virtues behold."(*M.U.* III. 1.5).

"Truth alone wins (*Satyam eva jayate*), not untruth. By truth is laid out the path leading to the gods (*devayāna*) by which the desireless sages ascend to where exists the supreme treasure attainable only through truth"(*M.U.* III. 1.6).

"He is not grasped by the eye nor even by speech nor by other sense-organs, nor by austerity nor by work; but when one's (intellectual) nature is purified by the light of knowledge, then alone he, by meditation, sees Him who is an indivisible whole without parts"(*M.U.* III.1.8).

Though the intellect in all beings is intrinsically able to make the Self known, still being polluted by such blemishes as attachment to external objects etc, it becomes non-transparent and impure, and does not, like a stained mirror or muddied water, make the reality of the Self known, though it is ever at hand. When the intellect becomes purified by the light of *Vedāntic* knowledge and by the removal of the pollution caused by the dirt of attachment, desire, anger and delusion, the enlightened one sees the *Ātman* through meditation i.e. intense contemplation with single-pointed concentration.

Intense meditation with mind and intellect purified by the *Vedāntic* knowledge and spiritual disciplines such as adherence to truth, *ahiṃsā* and *brahmacarya* will lead to the realisation of *Ātman* (Brahman). Yoga is the system of practices recommended to control the modifications of the mind and unfold its great power for realizing Brahman.

5. Maitrī Upaniṣad

Knowledge, Tapas and Meditation

Maitrī emphasizes that by knowledge, by *tapas* and by meditation is Brahman apprehended. This is the traid by which the rider of the chariot goes beyond the *Brahmā* (the lower, *Hiraṇyagarbha*) and ascends to the state of supreme divinity above the gods (*Maitrī* IV.4.).

That which is *Sat,* that which is eternally existent, is Brahman. *Brahma-Vidyā* is the knowledge of this *Sat* (this Self) and knowledge of the philosophical truths revealed in the scriptures.

Tapas is the door leading to Brahman. *Tapas* is the fire that burns away the evils of desires and passions and purifies the body, mind and intellect. *Tapas* is derived from the root, *tap,* i.e. to burn. Negatively it is cleansing our soul of all that is sinful and imperfect. Positively it is building up of all that is good and holy. In the history of religion, the practice of *tapas* or bodily austerities has been looked upon as the chief means for attaining spiritual ends. The privations of food and drink, of sleep and clothing, of exposure to heat and cold, are labours undertaken to wear down the body and strengthen the spiritual resolve to attain the highest goal.

Practice of *tapas* is considered the essential pre-requisite for gaining success in the knowledge of the Self and also in the perfection of one's own duty and works. "By austerity(*tapas*) goodness is obtained and from goodness is understanding reached and from the understanding is the Self obtained, and he who obtains the Self does not return"(*Maitrī* IV. 3).

The next of the triad by which Brahman is apprehended is meditation. Meditation on the *mantra* '*AUM*' is recommended.

'*A*' is the *Virāṭ* Self (Self in the waking state), '*U*' is the *Hiraṇyagarbha* Self(dreaming Self) and '*M*' is the *Īśvara* Self(Self in the sound-sleep state)-*AUM.* Contemplate and withdraw the *Virāṭ* Self into the *Hiraṇyagarbha* Self, *Hiraṇyagarbha* into *Īśvara* and *Īśvara* into the ultimate soundless Brahman, the silence at the end of *AUM.* Pass on from sound to soundless Brahman, pass on from time to time-less Brahman, pass on from formed Brahman to formless Brahman, pass on from breath to non-breath, pass on from *sat* to *asat*, pass on from existence to non-existence, pass on from conditioned consciousness to unconditioned i.e. objectless and motionless consciousness.

"That, which is at the end of the syllable *AUM*, is tranquil, soundless, fearless, sorrowless, blissful, satisfied, steadfast, unmoving, immortal, unshaking and enduring" (*Maitrī* VI. 23).

Know and worship Brahman with this triad – knowledge, *tapas* and meditation – and attain complete merger with the Brahman of undecaying and immeasurable bliss.

Best form to Meditate Upon

To the question which one is the best form to meditate upon-whether fire, air, sun, time, whatever it is, breath, food, *Brahmā*, *Rudra*, *Viṣṇu*-the answer is given.

"These are but the chief forms of the Supreme, the immortal, the bodiless Brahman. To whichever one a man is devoted here, in the world of that deity he rejoices. For it has been said, 'Verily, this whole world is Brahman. Verily, these which are its chief forms, one meditates upon, worships and discards. For with these, one moves higher and higher in the worlds. And, when all things perish in universal dissolution, he attains unity with the *Puruṣa*, yea, with the *Puruṣa*" (*Maitrī* IV. 6).

The different concepts of Brahman, the Supreme, are supports for contemplation and meditation. By the worship of these deities which are nothing but the chief manifestations of Brahman, one rises to higher levels of consciousness. As one rises higher and higher, the lower levels of reality will be discarded. At the end of this world, at the time of universal dissolution, *Virāṭ* Self, *Hiraṇyagarbha* and *Īśvara* – all lapse into the Absolute Brahman. Then, he attains unity with the *Puruṣa*. Till then, it is suggested here that the individuality of the soul is retained.

Six-fold Yoga

"This is the rule for achieving this oneness with Brahman.

- control of breath,
- withdrawal of the senses,
- meditation,
- concentration,
- contemplative enquiry and
- absorption.

"This is said to be the six-fold yoga.

"When, by this yoga, he beholds the gold-coloured maker, the lord, the *puruṣa*, the *Brahma* source, then the sage, shaking of good and evil, makes everything into oneness in the supreme indestructible.

"For thus has it been said 'As beasts and birds do not resort to a burning mountain, so sins do not find shelter in those who know Brahman" (*Maitrī* VI. 18).

The Yoga praxis in *Maitrī* comes close to the meditation on emptiness in Buddhism.

When a knower has restrained his mind from the external, when his breath has put to rest objects of sense, let him then remain void of conceptions. Since the living individual who is named the breathing spirit has arisen here from what is not the breathing spirit, therefore let the breathing spirit merge his breathing spirit in the non-breathing spirit (*Maitrī* VI. 19).

There is yet a higher concentration than this. By pressing the tip of the tongue down the palate, by restraining voice, mind and breath, one sees Brahman through contemplative thought. When, by suppression of the mind, he sees through the self, he sees the shining self, more subtle than the subtle. Then he becomes selfless merged in the infinite, immeasurable, in that which is without origin or without end. This is the mark of liberation, the highest mystery (*Maitrī* VI. 20).

There are, verily two Brahmans to be meditated upon, sound and non-sound. By sound alone is the non-sound revealed. Now here the sound is *AUM*. Moving upward by it, one comes to ascend in the non-sound. This is the way, this is immortality, this is complete union and also tranquillity. And now as the spider moves upward by the thread, obtains free space, thus assuredly, indeed the mediater moving upward by the sound *AUM* obtains independence.

Other expounders of the sound as Brahman teach :

"By closing the ears with the thumbs, they hear the sound of the space within the heart. There is the sevenfold comparison of it -like rivers, a bell, a brass vessel, a wheel, the croaking of frogs, rain, as when one speaks in a still place. Having passed beyond this variously characterized sound, they pass on to the non-sound and become merged in the supreme, the non-sound, the unmanifest Brahman. There they are uncharacterized and indistinguishable like the various juices that have reached the condition of honey. For thus has it been said: 'There are two

Brahmans to be known, the sound Brahman and what is higher. Those who know the sound Brahman get to the higher Brahman'" (*Maitrī* VI. 22).

"Controlling of breath, withdrawal of senses from the objects, dissolution of mind and abandonment of all conditions of existence – this is designated as Yoga" (*Maitrī* VI. 24 and 25).

Verily, freedom from desire is, as it were, the highest prize from the choicest treasure. For a person who is made up of all desires, who has the marks of determination, conception and self-love is bound. In thinking, 'I am he', 'this is mine', he binds himself with himself (waking self and dreaming self) as a bird in a snare. He who is the opposite of that is liberated. Therefore, stand free from determination, free from conception, free from self-love. This is the mark of liberation. This is the path, the opening door to Brahman (*Maitrī* VI. 30).

6. Paiṅgala Upaniṣad (Chapters III & IV)

The first stage of enlightenment is the hearing of the noble teachings : 'That art thou', 'I am Brahman' etc. from those well-versed in the *Upaniṣads* and who are the seers of Brahman.

The second stage is the reflection, the investigation into the import of these noble teachings and enquiry into the meaning of what is heard and different interpretations of these teachings.

The third stage is meditation i.e. fixing up of thought with one-pointed attention solely on the object attained through hearing and reflection such as ' That art thou', 'I am Brahman', 'All are Brahman' and 'There is nothing else apart from Brahman'. With the thought absorbed only in the object meditated upon, giving up the distinction of the meditator and the act of meditation, the mind absolutely motionless like a steady lamp in a windness spot, unflickering, one attains the highest enlightenment.

Even as the sun shines with all his splendour on the dissolution of clouds, likewise the Self manifests itself in this condition with the veil of *avidyā* (ignorance) removed.

Through this meditation, the numberless previous karmas accumulated during the beginningless cycles of birth and death attain their dissolution. Thence, through the power of practice, a stream of nectar showers always from a thousand directions. Therefore, the adepts in Yoga call this highest enlightenment as the cloud of virtue. When the nets of dispositions-good and bad-are dissolved without any residue, when the accumulated deeds (virtuous and vecious, are completely destroyed to the very roots, the past and future alike, owing to the removal of all impediments, there arises the direct and immediate perception of Brahman (*ātma-darśana* or *samādhi*), as of the amalaka fruit on the palm of the hand. Then, the knower of Brahman becomes one with Brahman, liberated while in this life (while alive in this body).

With a purified mind, with a purified consciousness, full of forbearance, his heart is fully established in the supreme Self. His body attains the state of quiescence and his mind scintillating with the intellect becomes void of its functionings.

What is the use of milk to one satiated with nectar? Even so, what is the use of the study of the *Vedas* for one who has realized the Self? Remaining aloof, yet not aloof, remaining in the body, yet not of the body, the innermost self becomes the all pervading Brahman. After purifying the heart, thinking of Brahman the perfect, the Yogin perceives that he is the all, the transcendent, blissful. He becomes one with the supreme Self (Brahman) without differentiation just as water poured into water, milk poured into milk and ghee poured into ghee.

The seeker after reality (Truth), after becoming one with the ultimate reality Brahman, becomes the self of all beings. He sees all beings in himself and himself in all beings.

There is the pitfall of the aspirant getting attached to the union with the third state of Brahman i.e. *Īśvara* with wrong notions of almightiness and omnipotence and going astray in the path. This should be guarded against and the aspirant should aim to transcend the same and reach the highest level.

7. Subāla Upaniṣad

Subāla (III.1) suggests the six means of : truthfulness, charity, *tapas*, fasting, chastity of mind and body and complete indifference to worldly objects (renunciation of all objects which do not help in the attainment of the knowledge of the Self) for 'becoming Brahman, remaining as Brahman alone'. One should also attend to the following three: self-control, charity and compassion and cultivatation of the characteristics of a child.

" - - - - - - - He should not be afraid of death. Even if cut asunder, he should not get angry, he should not quake. He should be like a rock and even if cut asunder, he should not get angry, he should not quake. He should be like the sky and should not get angry, should not quake. He should stand by the truth, for verily, this truth is the Self, ——————In the Supreme there is neither existence nor non-existence nor existence and non-existence. This is the doctrine leading to liberation. This is the doctrine of the *Veda*. This is the doctrine of the *Veda*" (*Subāla* XIII. 1).

8. Doctrine of Divine Grace

Divine grace is suggested in some *Upaniṣads* for realisation of the supreme Self.

"This Self cannot be known through much study, nor through the intellectual power, nor even through much hearing. He is to be attained through the Self alone that the aspirant prays to. To such a one the Self reveals His own nature"(*Kaṭha* I.2.23).

The Self cannot be attained through the scriptural study and knowledge, not through the power of the intellect, not through hearing from the masters of Vedic knowledge. To a desireless man who seeks for the Self alone, the Self reveals of its own accord through its grace.

The same mantra occurs in *Muṇḍaka Upaniṣad* also(*M.U.* III. 2.3). Through intense seeking and prayer alone, one can attain the knowledge of the Self. When this knowledge dawns through the divine grace of the Self, the Self stands revealed just like the things in darkness get revealed when the light flashes on. The *Ātman* reveals its true character to one who seeks it ardently and exclusively.

This doctrine will appeal to the mind imbued with religious faith.

Part III
BUDDHISM

CHAPTER 9

Early Buddhism

1. The Buddha

Our search now leads us to the teachings of the Buddha. In the history of mankind, Gautama Buddha stands as the rarest and finest example of man who has attained the highest possible state of perfection and purity in his life. The honorific title "Buddha" is used to denote his awakening, his enlightenment. He is the one "who has awakened fully to the final truth of things, and thus freed, liberated, himself once and for all from all forms of suffering. He is also the one who, out of supreme compassion, has taught others the way to attain liberation themselves. Buddhas are not born that way and they are certainly not thought to be eternal gods (or God). Once (many life times ago) they were just like you and me. They strove through their own efforts, and became Buddhas. A Buddha is superior to the rest of us because he 'knows it how it is.' We, on the other hand, wallow in confusion, in ignorance. Thus we are unhappy and suffer" (Paul Williams, Buddhist Thought, p.1).

His life is his message and his message is his life. He showed to mankind by his example the hidden potentialities and creative power within man and proved that perfect enlightenment, Buddhahood, is within the reach of everybody who devoutly makes strenuous single-pointed, concentrated efforts. He taught that man can gain his salvation and freedom from suffering by his own exertions and efforts without depending on any supernatural agency or God and the mediating priests and without resorting to any rituals and sacrifices of the Vedic religion. He revolted against the evil practices of animal sacrifices to curry the favour of the gods and the degrading caste system imposed by the Vedic culture. For him, all life is sacred and all beings are equal. He preached to the ego-centric world the noble ideals of all encompassing loving kindness, compassion and selfless service.

He is a unique religious teacher who does not demand from his disciples unquestioning faith or belief in his teachings. He is the one teacher who will not be satisfied unless his statements are put to the test of reason, analysed rationally and comprehended. He is a thorough-going rationalist totally opposed to blind faiths or beliefs not based on reasoning.

An acquaintance with his life story is not essential for an understanding of his teachings. The authenticity of the life account that has come down to us may also be questioned. But this will throw some light on his life and teachings for the benefit of the new seekers.

The Four Sights that Altered the Course of His Life

Siddartha Gautama (that was his name before he became enlightened and known as the Buddha) was born in a family of the *śākya* clan in the kingdom of *Śākya* (modern Nepal) in the foothills of the Himalayas. The conventionally accepted date for his birth is 566 BCE. He lived a full life of about eighty years.

He was a young man of such deep sensitivity and delicate disposition that he was moved by the sufferings and sorrows he saw around him in the world. The story of Buddha is well-known. The efforts of his father, the ruler of *Śākya* kingdom in Nepal, to bring him up in a cloistered and luxurious environment shut-off from the miseries of the world and to make him a subsequent ruler of his kingdom, failed. Four major incidents, which he happened to witness, changed the course of his luxurious life and his destiny.

On one occasion, he saw a shrivelled old man worn-out with swollen veins and broken back bending on a staff and trembling. On another occasion, he saw a sick man writhing in pain, overcome by fever, exhausted and helpless. On the third occasion, he saw a dead man being carried on a bier with people wailing and lamenting behind. On the fourth occasion, he came across an ascetic standing on the road quiet and tranquil, full of peace and grace.

The first three sights shocked and tormented his tender heart. He saw the universal problem of misery in individual instances. He felt the miseries to which the humanity is subjected: birth, disease, old age, decay, death and destruction. On reflecting on old age, he realized that he was also subject to old age and not free from old age, and his elation in youth completely disappeared. On reflecting on sickness, he realized that he was also subject to sickness and not free from sickness and his elation in health completely disappeared. On reflecting on death, he realized that he was also subject to death and not free from death, and his elation in life completely disappeared.

Thus, facing reality, he underwent a vicarious experience of the sufferings of mankind and tried to understand the nature of things, as they are actually and not as they appear to be. As Paul Williams points out: " This theme of seeing things one way and their really being another way is the thread running throughout the first part of the life-story of the Buddha. It is not surprising that this thread is the theme of Buddhism, for the whole story of the Buddha exemplifies what Buddhism is all about." *(Buddhist Thought,* p. 29).

Moved by those experiences of the cases of old age, sickness and death and reflecting on their implications, he groped for ways to end the sufferings of the humanity. The fourth sight of the ascetic, standing tranquil and peaceful, gave him hope. This sight of the renunciate and the ideas generated by it inspired him ultimately to quit his regal chambers leaving his beautiful wife and infant son. This was at his twenty-ninth year.

Renunciation and Wanderings an Search of the Truth

(*Majjhima Nikāya* , Vol.I, *Ariya-Pariyesana Sutta* No. 26/The Buddha-Dhamma by Nārada Thera, Chapter III)

Siddhartha renounced his position, wealth and the kingdom he was to inherit. "He had his head and beard shaved and, wearing yellow garments, went forth from home to the homeless state". He ventured out into the world as a wandering mendicant, "a seeker after what is good, searching for the unsurpassed, peaceful state, most excellent."

Siddhartha wandered from teacher to teacher, and from monastery to monastery, in search of the highest knowledge that would lead to the cessation of suffering and usher in peace and tranquillity. Nothing he found satisfied him.

From the teacher *Ālāra Kālāma,* he learnt the doctrine of 'The Realm of Nothingness' and strove hard with faith, energy, concentration and wisdom. Striving thus, he attained that state, 'The Realm of Nothingness'. But, this did not satisfy him. He thought:-

"This teaching does not lead me to disgust, detachment, cessation, tranquillity, intuition, enlightenment and *Nibbāna,* but only to the attainment of "The Realm of Nothingness". And so, disciples, dissatisfied with this doctrine, I took my departure content therewith no longer."

Then, he went to the teacher *Uddaka Rāmaputta* and learnt from him the doctrine of "The Realm-of-Neither-Perception-Nor-Non-perception". He mastered the technique learnt from *Uddaka Rāmaputta* and attained that state "The Realm-of-Neither-Perception-Nor-Non-perception". But, this also did not satisfy him. To continue the story in his own words:-

"This doctrine does not lead me to disgust, detachment, cessation, tranquillity, intuition, enlightenment and *Nibbāna*, but only to the attainment of 'The Realm-of-Neither-Perception-Nor-Non-perception". And so, O disciples, dissatisfied with this doctrine also, I departed thence content therewith no longer".

Practice of Austerities and Self- Mortificatin
(Majjhima Nikāya, Vol I, Mahā Saccaka Sutta, No. 36)

Thereafter, he in accordance with the belief that the mind becomes elevated by extreme disciplinary austerities, practised self-mortification and self-torture relentlessly for seven years.

He followed the self-control methods of clenching the teeth, pressing the tongue against the palate and striving to control the mind and hold down, subdue, and destroy immoral thoughts with moral thoughts. He also practised the non-breathing exercises as means to control the mind. He changed the methods and starved his body also by abstaining from food or taking very little.

"Accordingly, I checked inhalation and exhalation from mouth, nostrils and ears. And, as I stopped breathing from mouth, nostrils and ears, the (imprisoned) airs beat upon my skull most violently. Just as if a strong man were to bore one's skull with a sharp drill, even so did the airs beat my skull with great violence as I stopped breathing. Even though such painful sensations arose in me, they did not at all affect my mind .——.

"Nevertheless, my energy was strenuous and indomitable. Established and unperturbed was my mindfulness. Despite which my body was fatigued and not calmed as a result of that painful endeavour, being overpowered by exertion. ——————.

"Thereupon, the deities who saw me thus said : "The ascetic Gotama is dead" ; some said : "the ascetic Gotama is not dead yet, but is dying". Whilst some others said : "The ascetic Gotama is neither dead nor is dying, but an Arahant is the ascetic Gotama. Such is the way in which an Arahant abides !"

Yet, in spite of all these strenuous efforts, the goal was in no way near at sight. He decided to change the method and practise abstinence from food.

"As I took such a small quantity of solid and liquid food, my body became extremely emaciated ——————.

"And I, intending to touch my belly's skin, would instead seize my backbone. When I intended to touch my backbone, I would instead seize my belly's skin. So was I that, owing to lack of sufficient food, my belly's skin clung to the backbone, and I, on going to pass excreta or urine, would in that very spot stumble and fall down, for want of food. And I had to stroke my limbs in order to revive my body. Lo, as I did so, the rotten roots of my body's hairs fell from my body owing to lack of sustenance".

Thus, Gotama strenuously and resolutely practised all forms of severe austerities and fasting. "Adding vigil after vigil and penance after penance", he made superhuman efforts for seven long years. The more he tormented his body, the farther his goal receded from him. Ultimately, he realized the utter futility of these bitter difficult austerities and self-mortification, and discovered the middle path (*Majjhima-Paṭipadā*) of avoiding the two extremes of self-mortification and self-indulgence. The former weakens one's body and intellect and the latter retards one's moral progress. He realized that neither extreme indulgence in sensual gratification nor severe asceticism is conducive for higher knowledge. The middle path, which yields sight, knowledge, which tends to peace, higher wisdom, enlightenment and Nibbāna, has subsequently been incorporated as one of the salient elements of his doctrines.

Enlightenment and Discovery of Truth

Discovering the middle path, he gave up his painful penances and extreme austerities and began to nourish his body sparingly with coarse food to revive his lost strength.

At that time, five disciples were attending on him, thinking that whatever truth ascetic Gotama would comprehend would be imparted to them. But when Gotama began to partake of coarse food such as boiled rice, the five disciples got disappointed at this change of method and deserted him saying that ascetic Gotama had become luxurious, had ceased from striving and had turned to a life of comfort.

Gotama continued his *tapas* adhering to the middle path, with mind firmly rooted in determination and concentration to find the highest truth and wisdom. He was sitting and meditating deeply under a banyan tree at Uruvelā (near Gayā) on the banks of the Neranjara river. There arose in him the recollection of the First Ecstasy he experienced as a young prince in his native place by concentrating on 'inhalation and exhalation'. That First Ecstasy was "born of seclusion, free from lust and immoral states, accompanied by reflection and investigation and associated with joy and happiness". Could this be the path to Enlightenment ! Yes, he realized that this is the path to Enlightenment.

With this realisation, he concentrated with unflinching vigour. With his mind thus concentrated and one-pointed, he attained to the First Ecstasy (*Jhāna*) "which is born of aloofness from pleasures of the senses, which is accompanied by reflection and investigation and which is rapturous and joyful".

Then, stilling the mind from reflection and investigation, he passed on to the Second Ecstasy "which is devoid of reflection and investigation, which is born of concentration and which is rapturous and peaceful". Then, separating himself from the rapture and rising above it, he entered into and abided in the Third Ecstasy "which is characterized by peace, and perfect equanimity (even-mindedness)".

"By getting rid of joy, by getting rid of suffering, by the dying down of my former pleasures and sorrows, I entered into and abided in the Fourth *Jhāna* which has neither suffering nor joy, and is entirely purified by perfect equanimity and mindfulness.

"With the mind thus composed, quite purified, quite clarified without blemish, without defilement, grown soft and pliable, fixed, immovable, I directed my mind to the knowledge and recollection of former habitations——————————"(*Vinaya -Piṭaka* III, 3 - 6)

The Fourth *Jhāna* is a state of profound stillness and peace in which the mind remains rooted in perfect equanimity and single- pointed concentration. It becomes like a polished mirror, radiantly pure, which is capable of reflecting the truth of the things as they are. This seems to have been the state from which the Buddha went on to attainment. The above discourse in *Vinaya-Piṭaka* describes how he experienced the gradual awakening of the threefold higher knowledge in three successive watches of the night and had a direct knowledge and insight into things as they were, as they are and as they will be. With the eye of wisdom thus developed, he had direct extra-ordinary perception (para-normal perception) of the following threefold higher knowledge:-

(1) Retrocognitive knowledge or Reminiscences of previous births.

(2) Clairvoyance or knowledge of the disappearance (decease) and reappearance of beings.

(3) Knowledge of the destruction of defiling impulses (corruptions).

Through the retrocognitive knowledge he gained in the first watch of the night, he could recall the great many cycles of his previous births and his manifold past experiences. He recalled the modes and details of his varied lot in his former existences.

With the second knowledge gained in the middle watch of the night and the attendant "clairvoyant vision, purified and supernormal, I perceived beings disappearing from one state of existence and reappearing in another. I beheld the base and the noble, the beautiful and the ugly, the happy and the miserable, and beings passing according to their deeds. I know that these good individuals, by evil deeds, words and thoughts, ——— after the dissolution of their bodies and after death, had been born in sorrowful, miserable and woeful states. I knew that these good individuals, by good deeds, words and thoughts ——after dissolution of their bodies and after death, had been born in happy celestial worlds. Thus with clairvoyant vision, I beheld the disappearing and reappearing of beings".

The third knowledge, he gained in the last watch of the night, is the highest form of knowledge in which Buddha is claimed to have been endowed with the eye of wisdom and to have apprehended with it the Four Noble Truths of Suffering, the Cause of Suffering, the Cessation of Suffering and the Path leading to the Cessation of Suffering. By means of it, he comprehended the nature of defilements (corruptions), their cause, their cessation and the path leading to their cessation. The truth of dependent nature of all things dawned on him (the doctrine of dependent origination). Thus he became enlightened as to the true nature of things with these flashes of higher knowledges. Then follows the account of his liberation.

"As long as, O Bhikkhus, the absolute true intuitive knowledge regarding these Four Noble Truths ——————— was not perfectly clear to me, so long I did not acknowledge, in this world together with gods, *Maras* and *Brahmās,* amongst the hosts of ascetics and priests, gods and men, that I had gained the incomparable, Supreme Enlightenment. When, O Bhikkhus, the absolute true intuitive knowledge regarding these Four Noble Truths————became perfectly clear to me, then only did I acknowledge in this world together with gods, *Maras* and *Brahmās*, amongst the hosts of ascetics and priests, gods and men, that I had gained the incomparable, Supreme Enlightenment".

"Thus cognising, thus perceiving, my mind was delivered from the Corruption of sensual craving, delivered from the corruption of craving for Existence (i.e. the desire to be born), delivered from the corruption of ignorance. Being delivered, I knew, 'Delivered am I', and I realized, 'Rebirth has ended; fulfilled the Holy Life; done what was to be done ; there is none other beyond this life."

"Ignorance was dispelled and wisdom arose; darkness vanished and light arose"(*Mahā Saccaka Sutta, Majjhima Nikāya*-No. 36).

With the mind thus pure and with the arising of the threefold higher knowledge culminating in the knowledge of dependent origination and the Four Noble Truths, he had the inner realisation that he had burnt away all ignorance and *karmic* formations. With the removal of the causes leading to rebirth, he became aware of the extinction of the *karmic* forces and the extinction of his rebirth. Such was his deliverance and such was his liberation.

"And there arose in me the knowledge and insight : 'Unshakeable is the deliverance of my mind, this is my last birth, and now there is no existence again'."

With his knowledge of dependent origination, he realized the contingent nature and selflessness in everything. He became totally selfless apprehending neither any self in him nor anything belonging to his self (i.e. without any notion of 'I' or 'mine') and completed the remainder of his life in his physical body without producing any more karma which would cause him to be reborn.

Important to note in this account of the process of getting enlightened and liberated is the fact that there is no indication of any intervention of superhuman divine powers or any union with a transcendent Absolute Being. "Quite by myself, you see, have I the *Dharma* won."

Decision to Teach the Dhamma

As he was engaged in solitary meditation, the following thought occurred to him:

"This *Dhamma* which I have realized is indeed profound, difficult to understand, tranquil, exalted, not within the sphere of logic, subtle and to be understood by the wise. These beings are attached to desires, cling to desires and delight in desires. To those who are to attached to desires, cling to desires and delight in desires, this causally connected 'Dependent Origination' is a matter which is difficult to perceive. And this *Nibbāna*, the quietude of all activities, the renunciation of all passions, the destruction of craving, the dispassion, and the cessation is also a matter which is not easily perceptible. If I too were to preach this *Dhamma*, the others would not understand me."

Thus reflecting, his mind turned to inaction and not to the preaching of the *Dhamma*.

The legend has it that *Brahmā Sahampatī* (from the *Brahmā* realm), knowing with his mind the thoughts of the Blessed One, feared that the world would perish without the teachings of the Blessed One and appeared before him and pleaded with him to expound the *Dhamma*.

"There are beings with little dust in their eyes who, not hearing the *Dhamma*, will fall away. There will be those who will understand the *Dhamma*."

Thereupon the Blessed One surveyed the world with his Buddha vision. He saw beings with little and much dust in their eyes, with keen and dull intellect, with good and bad characteristics, beings who are easy and difficult to be taught and few others who live perceiving the dangers of evil and of a future life.

Out of compassion for the human beings, Buddha agreed to impart his experiences to others and teach them the way to salvation and freedom from suffering.

He thought about his earlier five disciples who had been administering to him when he was striving after the highest truth and who left him when he changed his method to the middle path avoiding the extremely severe penances and fasting. He wondered how it would be if he were to preach the *Dhamma* to them first. He left Uruvelā and set out for Benares to look for his earlier disciples. He arrived in due course at the Deer Park in Isipatana near Benares where he met them.

He addressed them:

"Give ear, O Bhikkhus ! Immortality has been attained. I shall instruct and teach the *Dhamma*. If you act according to my instructions, you will before long realize, by your own intuitive wisdom, and live attaining in this life itself, that supreme consummation of the Holy Life, for the sake of which sons of noble families rightly leave the household for the homeless"(*Mahāvagga - Majjhima Nikāya* No.26).

Merv Fowler writes:

"So the Buddha did not attain final *parinirvāṇa* (*Parinibbāna* in *Pāli* language) but completed the remainder of his life in his physical body without producing any more *karma* which would cause him to be reborn. His purpose now would be to teach the *Dharma* (*Dhamma* in *Pāli*) and, in making this decision, there was evident a radical shift from the individualistic and elitist striving for *mokṣa* of Brahmanical Hinduism; it was a turning towards humankind (with the possible exception of women !), regardless of class"(*Buddhism,* p. 19).

His first sermon is known by the name of "*Dhammacakka-Pavattana*", that is "Setting in Motion the Wheel of *Dhamma* or Law". It also means "The Establishment of Wisdom." According to the commentators, *'Dhamma'* here means (Truth, Ideal or Religion) and *'cakka'* means establishment. It is also called as: 'The Wheel of Righteousness' or 'The Kingdom of Righteousness' metaphorically.

In ancient times, traditionally it was held that the foundation for establishing a kingdom to be ruled by a *cakra-vartin* (Turning the Wheel), an emperor, would be laid by his throwing a wheel into the air. The golden wheel thus thrown would go around in the sky and come back to the original place in seven days. The area covered around by the motion of the wheel would determine the sphere of the *cakra-vartin*'s kingdom. Likewise, "*Dhammacakka-Pavattana*" here could mean the laying of the "foundation of Kingdom of Truth".

The first sermon of the Buddha was addressed to his first five disciples at the Deer Park in Isipatana, near Benares. This *Dhammacakka Sutta* (Discourse) is the most favourite sermon of the Buddhists. In this, Buddha expounded the fundamental principles of his *Dhamma*: The Four Noble Truths and The Noble Eightfold Path. These and related teachings became the Buddha's Middle Path, the path to *Nirvāṇa* (*Nibbāna* in *Pāli*).

Spreading the Message of Love and Peace

After his enlightenment, Buddha travelled far and wide with indefatigable energy as a wandering monk to preach his *Dhamma* and to spread the message of all-enveloping loving kindness, compassion, peace and *Nibbāna* (*Nirvāṇa*). His theory of *anātman* (no-self) directly negating and opposing the *Upaniṣadic* concept of *ātman* (self) and the utter selflessness he displayed in his life and in his activities charmed the masses. His *Dhamma* (religion) spread rapidly and his disciples grew in large numbers.

He organized the Buddhist order of monks and nuns which grew into a powerful vibrant religious movement. According to the traditional account, the first sixty monks whom the Buddha had converted and ordained were despatched to spread the message of *Dhamma* with the following exhortation:

"Freed am I, O Bhikkhus, from all bonds whether divine or human. You, too, O Bhikkhus, are freed from all bonds whether divine or human.

"Go forth, O Bhikkhus, for the good of the many, for the happiness of the many, out of compassion for the world, for the good, for the benefit and for the happiness of gods and men. Let not two go by one way. Preach, O Bhikkhus, the *Dhamma*, excellent in the beginning, excellent in the middle, excellent in the end, both in the spirit and the letter. Proclaim the Holy Life, altogether perfect and pure.

"There are beings with little dust in their eyes, who not hearing the *Dhamma* will fall away. There will be those who will understand the *Dhamma*.

"I, too, O Bhikkhus, will go to Uruvelā, to Senanigama, in order to preach the *Dhamma*" (*Mahāvagga*).

He did not want his disciples to lead the lives of social recluses like the ascetics in the Hindu faith. He moulded them into missionary torch-bearers of his *Dhamma*. His religion became a serious rival to Hinduism which was bound to the Vedic practices of rituals and sacrifices rather than the moral and ethical conducts and which was being exploited by the Brahmanical priestly class to further their own vested interests. Obnoxious animal practices, degrading caste system and exploitation of women as chattels rather than as human beings were the bane of Brahmanical religion against which Buddha waged a relentless battle.

Practising what he preached, resting barely for one or two hours in the night, wandering from place to place, permeating the whole world with thoughts of loving kindness, he worked incessantly for the good and happiness of all, even upto his last moment. As Vivekānanda describes, he was the finest example of a *Karma-Yogī*.

The inexorable law of death overtook him in the form of a meal with *sukaramaddava* which, according to some, is a tender boar meat, or a kind of mushroom in some other account. After partaking this meal served with reverence and love by a blacksmith named Cunda, the Buddha developed a serious sickness (dysentery) with severe pains and succumbed to the same. According to some other accounts, he recovered from this, but later died of natural causes.

Popular accounts describing his death state that the Buddha has passed into *parinibbāna* (*Pāli*). This meant "fully passed away", "fully blown out" or "fully extinct", as, according to the early Buddhist tradition, the Buddha or an Arahant has no re-existence after his death. No residue of *karmic* forces remained to cause his rebirth.

2. Buddhist Scriptures

Like all the great teachers of ancient India, the Buddha taught through discourses and dialogues and for a long time his teachings were transmitted orally from generation to generation through the memory and word of mouth of his disciples and followers.

Sometime after the passing away of the Buddha, the elders of the Buddhist order assembled to recapitulate his doctrines and teachings and compile them for the benefit of posterity. Venerable *Upāli* recited the *Vinaya* (monastic rules of discipline and code of conduct to be followed) and venerable *Ānanda*, the life-long attendant of the Buddha, who had the special privilege of hearing all his discourses, recited the master's teachings on the *Dhamma*, the *Sutta*. These renderings were debated and a definitive version agreed upon as authoritative canonical teaching (though it seems not entirely unanimously). Scholars opine that the compilations in this first Buddhist council may have formed the basis for the subsequent development and growth of the *Pāli* Canon in three major scriptures called Tipitakas, which term means "the three baskets of knowledge." These are: *Vinaya Piṭaka*, *Sutta Piṭaka* and *Abhidhamma Piṭaka*.

The *Sutta Piṭaka* or the basket of sermons is the earliest and the most important collection of Buddha's teachings and contains his utterances, discourses and dialogues on the doctrines of the *Dhamma*, ethics, morality and spirituality. This comprises five sections:

Dīgha Nikāya (Collection of long discourses)
Majjhima Nikāya (Collection of medium-length discourses)
Saṃyutta Nikāya (Collection of kindred sayings i.e thematically-grouped discourses)
Aṅguttara Nikāya (Collection of discourses arranged in accordance with number)
Khuddaka Nikāya (Smaller collections as well as *Dhammapada* and *Jātakas*)

Dhammapada is a very important Buddhist scripture for lay Buddhists and is a collection of 423 memorable verses preaching in a nutshell the Buddhist way of life.

The *Vinaya Piṭaka* mainly deals with the rules and regulations for the order of monks (*bhikkhus*) and nuns (*bhikkhunis*). It details the code of conduct to be followed by the monks and nuns in their daily lives and also sets down the methods for settling disputes in the monastic order and disciplining the offenders.

The *Abhidhamma* ("Higher *Dharma*") *Piṭaka* is regarded as a later development and contains expositions on the philosophical and metaphysical aspects of the Buddha's teachings. The prefix '*Abhi*' means either 'higher' or 'about'. Therefore, *Abhidhamma* would mean "Higher *Dhamma*" or "further discourse on *Dhamma*". While *Dhamma* is the general teaching of the Buddha, the *Abhidhamma* is a special philosophical and metaphysical discourse providing deeper insights into the Buddha's general teachings.

At the time of the first and second Buddhist councils (483 BCE and C383 BCE respectively), probably only the two *Piṭakas* – *Sutta* and *Vinaya* – were recognized. *Abhidhamma* probably came to be recognized as one of the *Piṭakas* only in the third Buddhist council (250 BCE) held during the reign of the illustrious emperor Aśoka to resolve the dispute between the sectarian groups *Sthavirās* (Orthodox Elders) and *Sarvāstivādins.* This dispute is the precursor to the development of *Mahāyāna* Buddhism.

Only two complete *Abhidhamma* canonical collections are now avilable: the *Theravāda Abhidhamma* in the *Pāli* canon and the *Sarvāstivāda* (Vaibhāṣika) *Abhidharma* that survives mainly in Chinese translation. The expression '*Theravāda*' means 'Doctrine of the Elders' while '*Sarvāstivāda*' means 'Doctrine of those who hold that All Exist'. In the *Theravāda Pāli* canon, the *Abhidhamma Piṭaka* is attributed directly to the Buddha himself with the possible exception of one book (the *Kathāvatthu*) which is said to be the work of Moggaliputtatissa and which clearly relates to doctrinal disputes that arose long after the death of the Buddha. On the other hand, all the seven books of the *Sarvāstivāda Abhidharma* are attributed to various elders other than the Buddha, but the claim is that those elders were compilers rather than authors in as much as they assembled the books from material scattered throughout the canon.

Both these *Abhidharma* canonical collections consist of seven books, but they teach quite different doctrines. On the other hand, the *Sutta* and *Vinaya* collections of the two schools have striking similarities. This indicates that their *Sutta* and *Vinaya* have a common origin, which is not the case with regard to the later work, the *Abhidharma* collections.

The *Pāli* canon, that has come down to us with its Tipatakas, represents the *Hīnayāna* sect of Buddhism particularly the *Theravāda* school. Not everyone who attended the First Council at Rajagaha agreed that what had been recited there was the authentic word of the Buddha. Dissident groups have preserved and handed down their own versions of what the Buddha had taught. *Mahāyāna* Buddhists think that the *Pāli* canon is the product of cloistered monks who have distorted the true teachings of the Buddha and they claim that much of the teachings preserved by the other disciples and later written down in Sanskrit are the authentic versions. *Mahāyāna* sect is based on these literatures that have come down in Sanskrit. Because of all these we cannot say with certainty what precisely are the teachings of the Buddha in his own words. But, in as much as they have a common origin , central core principles illuminating all of them and binding them all to a common Buddhist tradition can be identified. The present scholarship on Buddhism is of the view generally that the *Sutta Piṭaka* consisting of the five *Nikāyas* may be taken as the true embodiment of the principal teachings of the Buddha.

Unlike Hinduism, Buddhism does not claim any divine revelation and hence 'infallible' authority for its canonical scriptures. Everyone is advised to exercise his rational judgement and decide for himself the path to be traversed for attaining salvation.

3. The Four Noble Truths

The Four Noble Truths of which the Buddha gained knowledge and insight in the wake of his Enlightenment are :

(1) There is suffering (*Dukkha*)
(2) There is a cause of suffering (*samudaya*, the root cause of *Dukkha*). That is, the suffering does not happen randomly, haphazardly or accidentally; it is caused. It arises according to the inexorable moral laws of cause and effect.
(3) There is cessation of suffering (*Nirodha*, the end of *Dukkha*)
(4) There is the path leading to the cessation of suffering (*Magga*, the way to destroy *Dukkha*)

The First Noble Truth : Dukkha (Duḥkha in Sanskrit)

This is the opposite of *sukha*, the term *sukha* having the meaning of being at ease, comfortable and happy. The very life is characterized by the omnipresence of *dukkha*. The Buddhists recognize three types of *dukkha*. The first one is the physical pain and misery to which all sentient beings are subject. The second type is the mental agony and anguish the human beings pass through when their desires are not fulfilled or undesirable things happen to them. The third type is the *duḥkha* they invariably experience because of the impermanence and evanescent nature of things they cling to, including their own selves and what they consider their belongings. This is the *duḥkha* of change and the inevitability of dependence on other things i.e. being conditioned and affected by other things.

As the Buddha described in his first sermon: "Birth is suffering, decay is suffering, disease is suffering, death is suffering, to be united with the unloved is suffering, to be separated from the loved is suffering, not to get what one craves for is suffering; in brief, the five aggregates of attachment are suffering."

Whatever is born is subject to disease, decay, old age and death as the Buddha realized when he witnessed the sights that inspired him to embark on his remarkable quest for Truth. Not only disease, decay, old age and death, but also despair at not getting what is desired, frustrations, failures and dejections are all sources of suffering. Buddha analyses deeper and concludes that the five aggregates to which we get attached are suffering.

We are normally blind to the basic fact of our impermanence. "Day after day we continue to live our lives as if we will walk this planet at least for a couple of centuries, if not for all eternity." We invariably cling to the ideas of self ('I') and 'mine'. The Buddha pricks these bubbles and shows their evanescence and emptiness. He proves that there is no self, no 'I', no mine". This is his basic theory of '*Anattā* ' (no *ātmā*, no self). According to him, what we consider as our "self" is nothing but a process of coming together of the five heaps of *rūpa* (matter or form), *vedanā* (sensations), *saññа* (perceptions) *sankhārā*(volitions) and *Vijñāna* (consciousness) according to causes and conditions, which are in a flux and which are continually changing. Buddha reduces the so-called being or self as nothing but an aggregate or coming-together of these five heaps (*skandhas*). These five heaps are in a state of constant flux. Without realizing the continually changing nature of these heaps, one gets attached to them and mistake them to be permanent. Therefore, when these heaps undergo change which they must, frustrations, disappointments and sufferings inevitably follow. Thus, these five aggregates of attachment are *duḥkha.*

As Merv Fowler comments:

"The acceptance that *duḥkha* permeates the whole of existence is not to affirm that there can be no place for happiness. Indeed, the many different forms happiness can take are clearly set out in the *Aṅguttara Nikāya,* while in the *Majjhima Nikāya* (both these early *Pāli* texts contain collections of the Buddha's original discourses), the Buddha praises the blissful equaminity experienced in the high spiritual state of *dhyāna.* However, all these states of happiness, which include physical and mental happiness, as well as the joy experienced in family life, sense pleasures and even *dhyāna,* have one thing in common-impermanence. It is this common factor, especially the failure to recognize this commonality, which makes all things *duḥkha.*" (*Buddhism,* p.41).

In the ultimate analysis, the world we make up and all the sufferings we endure are due to the craving for sensual-pleasures and attachments to what constitute the self and the sense-objects. In short, all that is born of attachment is misery. Craving for transitory worldly objects leads to a long chain of suffering. For instance, craving for wealth impels a man to resort to any means, fair or foul, and he has no mental peace. Even when he obtains it, he still suffers for he must take pains to guard it. He is still assailed by the fear of losing it. All the sensual enjoyments that the human beings long for and strive to obtain are absolutely ephemeral; they are only a prelude to pain. They end in exhaustion, disappointment and dejection.

The Second Noble Truth : Cause of Suffering

The Buddha propounds a theory of causal law to explain the suffering and calls this *paṭicca-samuppāda* (*pratītya-samutpāda* in Sanskrit) or the theory of Dependent Origination.

According to this theory, for everything, there is a cause. There is an invariable law linking the cause and effect. Depending upon the cause, the effect arises and in turn, the latter becomes the cause of another effect. This impersonal lawlike nature of causation is well demonstrated in its standard formula found in early Buddhist sources : "This existing, that exists; this arising that arises; this not existing that does not exist; this ceasing, that ceases" (Gethin 1998:141). The existence of *duḥkha* also depends upon some cause. This is explained as below in an early formulation of the scheme of dependent origination in the *Mahātaṇhā-sankhaya Sutta* (the 'Greater Discourse on the Destruction of Craving').

> "A child is born and grows up
>
> On seeing a visible form with the eye,
>
> On hearing a sound with the ear,
>
> On smelling an odour with the nose,
>
> On tasting a flavour with the tongue,
>
> On touching a tangible with the body,
>
> On cognizing an idea with the mind,
>
> (Note: These indicate the eighteen *dhātus* of sense, object, and the resultant consciousness for each of the six senses)
>
> He lusts after it if it is likable
>
> Or has ill-will towards it if it is dislikable
>
> (That is, dependent upon ignorance of its true nature, he produces greed and hatred).
>
> ---
>
> ---
>
> Engaged as he is in favouring and opposing,

> when he feels any feeling, whether pleasant or painful or neither-pleasant-nor painful,
>
> he relishes that feeling, affirms and accepts it.
>
> Relishing arises in him when he does that.
>
> Now any relishing of those feelings is clinging.
>
> With his clinging as a condition, being ;
>
> With being as a condition, birth ;
>
> With birth as a condition, ageing and death come to be, and also sorrow and lamentation, pain, grief and despair.
>
> That is how there is an origin to this whole aggregate mass of suffering."
>
> (Trans. In *Ñāṇamoli* 1992 : 251 ff)

As Paul Williams explains further on this *Sutta* :

"This, in a practical sense, is how suffering comes about. It comes about through *causes.* Thus, through reversing the causes, the suffering can be ended. And the text continues by telling us that perhaps a Buddha may appear in the world. Someone might hear the *Dhamma* and eventually become a monk. Through following seriously the Buddha's path as a monk he might so develop his ability in mindfulness and meditative absorption that he learns to cut his lust after sensory experiences. Thus each link in the above list ceases through the cessation of the previous link:

> with the cessation of his relishing, cessation of clinging;
>
> with the cessation of clinging, cessation of being;
>
> with the cessation of being, cessation of birth;
>
> with the cessation of birth, ageing and death cease, and also sorrow and lamentation pain, grief and despair ;
>
> that is how there is a cessation to this whole aggregate mass of suffering."
>
> (*Buddhist Thought,* p.65)

In the *Mahānidāna Sutta* (the "Greater Discourse on Causes"), the scheme of dependent origination is amplified and ignorance (*Pāli:avijjā*; Sanskrit : *avidyā*) introduced as the fundamental factor behind craving and hence the final explanation conceptually for *duḥkha* and the cycle of rebirth, the root of *saṃsāra.* The doctrine of dependent origination is elaborated thus:

Dependent on ignorance (*avijjā*) arise volitions/ formations (*Pāli: Saṅkhārā*; Sanskrit; *Saṃskāra*)

Dependent on volitions/formations arises Rebirth Consciousness (*Viññāṇa : Pāli ; Vijñāna :* Sanskrit) .

Dependent on Rebirth Consciousness arise mind-and-body (*Nāma-rūpa*)

Dependent on mind-body arise the six senses (Ṣaḷayātana)

Dependent on the six senses arises sense-contact (*Phassa* : *Pāli* ; *Sparśa* : Sanskrit)

Dependent on the sense-contact arises feeling (*Vedanā*)

Dependent on the feeling arises craving (*Taṇhā* : *Pāli ; Tṛṣṇā ;* Sanskrit)

Dependent on the craving arises clinging (or grasping : *Upādāna*)

Dependent on clinging arises becoming (*Bhāva*)

Dependent on becoming arises birth (*Jāti*)

Dependent on birth arise old age and death (*Jarā-maraṇa*)
(*Saṃyutta Nikāya* II : 12 : 1)

This theory of dependent origination is symbolically represented as the Wheel of Becoming (*Bhāvacakra*). This is called the Twelve Limbed Wheel of Causation and Becoming (Figure 15). This demonstrates that the evolution of being or life is cyclical with no beginning and no end. Life is thus a beginningless or endless cycle.

Let us first understand the causal relationship among the following limbs of the above Wheel of Becoming: (Re)-Birth Consciousness-Mind and Body – Six senses – Sense Contact-Feeling (or perception) – Craving – Clinging – Becoming (Limbs 3 to 10 of the wheel).

Birth and growth of the mind-body organisam result from the preceding limb or cause, that is the birth or rebirth consciousness. What is that subtle agency that descends into the embryo in the mother's womb and that causes the development and growth of the mind-body complex? That is the blind will to be born, to live and expand, that is the birth or rebirth consciousness (*Vijñāna*) according to the Buddha. Without this will as the underlying cause, the multiplication of the cells in the embryo is not possible and if there is no

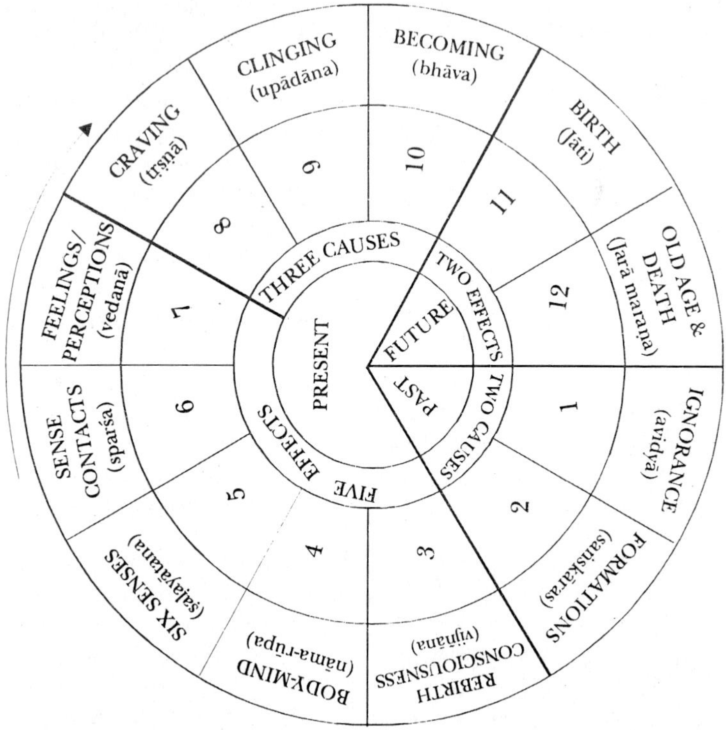

Fig. 15 Buddhist Wheel of Life

multiplication of cells there will be no growth in the embryo and no development of the mind-body organism.

The mind-body organism evolves into the six organs of cognition i.e. the five senses and the mind. The senses come into contact with the external objects and this contact gives rise to sensation (feeling) – pleasant, unpleasant or neutral (indifferent). The pleasant sensation leads to the craving for such pleasure – inducing objects which in turn gives rise to clinging to such pleasures and such objects. If the sensation is unpleasant, he develops disliking and hatred for such sensations and the corresponding objects, and if the sensation is neutral he develops uncertainty and delusion. The net result of all is the arising of the consciousness of self and self-interest, the false theory of individuality, the discrimination of subject and object, the discrimination of self and others and the amoral instinctual drives of self-aggrandizement at the cost and injury to the interests of others. These produce the three primary afflictions (*kleśa*) (also called the three primary root poisons): lust (craving, attachment), hatred and delusion.

Craving leads to attachment or clinging. Buddha enumerates four types of clinging:

- Clinging to the objects of sense desire
- Clinging to views and ideas
- Clinging to precepts and vows
- Clinging to the doctrine of self

Clinging to these and the various afflictions of mental states arising therefrom, the *Vijñāna* (consciousness) acts. According to the Buddha, all actions sprout from consciousness. Every action done, in addition to resulting in some phenomenon in the external world, rebounds and affects and modifies the internal consciousness itself according to the Law of Karma. Thus there is action impelled by the will in the consciousness, which results in a phenomenon in the external world. Reaction immediately follows with the phenomenon impinging on the consciousness and modifying it. The modified consciousness again acts and the cycle repeats. This is the becoming or evolving of consciousness, the becoming or unfolding of life. This tenth limb of 'Becoming' is the most crucial in the understanding of Buddhist philosophy.

To summarize, the analysis of the limbs 3 to 10 in the Wheel of Becoming reveals that the *Vijñāna* descends into the embryo in the mother's womb and develops the mind-body organism which gives rise to the six senses, sense-contacts, feelings and perceptions, craving, clinging and further becoming of *Vijñāna*- all in a causally determined relationship. As we have already seen, Buddha affirms that there is no separate unchanging reality or self underlying this process of becoming. The so-called self, the idea of 'I', is a mere figment of the imagination with nothing real or permanent to correspond to it. What we understand as 'self' is also nothing but the process of coming together and functioning together of the five heaps or aggregates: form, sensation, perception, volition and consciousness. The coming together and functioning together of these five aggregates are determined by causes and conditions as per the Wheel of Becoming.

The five aggregates of the individual life are :

Aggregate	**Constituents**
Form (Matter)	Five elements (earth, water, fire, air and ether), five sense objects, body and senses.
Sensations (Feelings)	Pleasure, pain and indifferent (neither pleasure nor pain) associated with the five senses.
Perceptions (Conceptions)	All images, words and concepts used to recognize, identify and interpret sensations and to organize experience.
Volitions	Desires, hates, delusions and many other emotions and instinctual impulses (i.e. mental states totalling 50 in number).
Consciousness	Sensations, perceptions and volitions arise in a consciousness which in later *Yogācāra* philosophy is devided eight-fold as below: The five primary *Vijñānas* (Consciousnesses associated with the five senses and the corresponding sense objects) *Mano-Vijñāna* (minding/mental consciousness). *Klista-manas* (defiled *manas* or intellectual discriminating consciousness). *Ālayavijñāna* (All-seed or store consciousness).

The aggregate of form (matter) includes the body with its sense organs. The second aggregate is that of sensations or feelings which arise with sense contacts when the sense organs interact with external objects. The third aggregate is that of perceptions which recognize, identify and interpret the sensations. The fourth aggregate is the aggregate of fifty volitional activities such as lust, hatred, delusion, arrogance, pride, envy, deception and so on. The false view of individuality and a self or *ātman* is also included in this aggregate. These are all karma-producing activities because of the volitions or moral intentions behind them. According to the Buddha, *Kamma* (*Karma*) in the ultimate sense is good or bad volition (intention) and the nature of this intention determines the "becoming".

The last aggregate is the aggregate of consciousness which includes the all-seed (*sarva-bījaka*) consciousness as described by the Buddha in the *Saṃdhinirmocana-Sūtra* in addition to the five sense consciousnesses and the mental and intellectual consciousnesses.

> *Ādāna-Vijñāna* is highly profound and subtle ;
>
> It is the All-seed-consciousness (*sarva-bījaka*), and is like a violent current.
>
> I do not reveal it to common men,
>
> Lest they imagine it to be *ātman*
>
> (*Saṃdhinirmocana-Sūtra*)

This gives rise to the previous aggregates and in turn it is also affected by them. The tenth limb, 'Becoming', in the Wheel of Life represents the becoming or evolving of this all-seed consciousness.

Driven by craving and the attendant clinging, the so-called 'I' or self, which is composed of the above five aggregates, engages in the *karma*-producing volitional activities. All actions, according to Buddhism, are ultimately mental and sprout from the seeds in the consciousness. But these have their repercussions and retributions meted out according to the moral Law of Karma and they leave their imprints on the aggregate of consciousness in the form of new seeds which in due time will sprout and give their fruits.

> "According to the seed that is sown,
>
> So is the fruit ye reap therefrom,
>
> Doer of good will gather good,
>
> Doer of evil, evil reaps,
>
> Sown is the seed, and thou shall taste

The fruit thereof."

(*Saṃyutta Nikāya,* Vol. I, p. 227)

Thus arise the *karmic* formations in the aggregate of consciousness that drive the Wheel of Becoming or the Wheel of Life. In the ultimate analysis, this tenth limb 'Becoming' represents the whole life wherein deeds are done and *karmic* formations are accumulated which bear their fruits in this life itself or the next lives. The limbs third to nine give the causal links to this 'Becoming' in the present life. As a conceptual abstration, the causes of 'Becoming' may be summarized and indicated as 'Ignorance' and '*karmic* formations of volitions' to represent the past life concisely. These are conceived as the first and second limbs of the Wheel of Life.

On deeper analysis, ignorance of the real nature of things as they actually are i.e. ignorance of the transitoriness and ephemeral nature of things, ignorance of the law of change and the Law of Karma, in short, ignorance of the Four Noble Truths, is discerned to be the fundamental factor behind craving and clinging, which turns out to be the ultimate cause of suffering and the cycle of birth and death. As Paul Williams points out, ignorance is not a first cause in Buddhism in the sense of some concrete thing that chronologically started the whole *saṃsāra.* It is simply a conceptual explanation for suffering and the cycle of *saṃsāra.* (Buddhist Thought, p.46).

The rebirth consciousness is the 'blind will to become' as conditioned and determined by ignorance (*avidyā*) and *karmic* formations (*Saṃskāra*).

Just as ignorance and *karmic* formations represent the past life in a concise manner as the first two limbs of the Wheel of Life, the last two limbs-'birth' and 'old age and death'-represent the future life and complete the wheel. This is the grand conception of the Wheel of Becoming or the Wheel of Life.

The core tenets of Buddhism have already come to be identified in the foregoing analysis. These stand in stark contrast to the teachings in the *Upaniṣads.*

The *Upaniṣads* postulate *ātman* (Brahman) as the ultimate underlying and unchanging reality and talk of its characteristics as '*Sat*' (Self-extant, ever-existent Truth), '*Cit*' (Consciousness) and '*Ānanda*' (bliss). On the other hand, for Buddha, the hallmarks of existence are anityam (impermanence), *anattā* (no-self, no *ātman*) and *dukkha* (suffering). These are the 'three signs' of Buddhism as they are called.

Against the Brahmanical theory of 'permanent ever-existent being' (*Sat*), Buddha holds that nothing in this world has an abiding permanent self or innermost self-essence. Nothing is self-created, self-maintained and self-abiding. Dependent origination is the key principle of existence according to the Buddha. Everything is dependent on some other thing or things. Buddha does not subscribe to the theory or belief in a first cause or primordial creator God. To speak of a creator God, existing outside and entirely independent of his creation, upon whom his creation, is entirely dependent, is logically untenable according to Buddhism.

Buddha denies the immortality of the soul or self. According to the Buddha, the notion of self is a false conceptual construction. There is no permanent, unchanging self. What we call a self is nothing but the process of coming together and functioning together of the five heaps, the five *skandhas* (aggregates), brought together by causes and conditions. All these aggregates are constantly in a state of flux. All existence is temporary and transitory. Nothing will remain the same for two consecutive moments.

Since the world has no abiding substance and no enduring permanence, suffering is inevitable. Even the bliss experienced in the deep meditative states is not permanent. Contrary to popular view, Buddhism is not pessimism. It aims to be only realistic in understanding things as they actually are and working out solutions for overcoming the ills of the world. Buddha is neither a pessimist nor an optimist but a realist. He dons the mantle of a physician to diagnose the ills afflicting the world and their causes correctly and prescribe cures. He is the healing physician.

Against the principle of Pure Consciousness (*Cit*) studied as the unchanging reality in the *Upaniṣads,* Buddha posits his theory of *Vijñāna* which is the 'blind will to live and to become' conditioned and determined by ignorance (*avidyā)* and *karmic* formations (*Saṃskāras*). For Buddha, ignorance is the ignorance of the Four Noble Truths ; it is the non-knowledge of the things as they truly are, or of oneself as one really is. It is the illusion of a permanent unchanging self in one and attachment to the concept of self and its possessions which is the fountain-head of all evils and injustices in the world. On the other hand, ignorance in the *Upaniṣads* is the ignorance of the knowledge of the Self or *Ātman.* Realisation of the Self is said to be the sole means of overcoming the ignorance which binds mankind to the *saṃsāric* wheel of bondage, whereas the Buddha teaches that the knowledge and practices based on the Four Noble Truths alone will be the antidotes to ignorance and means to liberation.

The ultimate goal in the *Upaniṣadic* thoughts is Life Eternal, immortality (*amaratvam*). But, the Buddha considers this as an object of craving. The *Dhammacakkapavattana Sutta* describes craving: "It is this craving which produces rebirth, accompanied by passionate clinging, welcoming this and that (life). It is the craving for sensual pleasures, craving for existence and craving for non-existence". Thus, craving is here described to include not just cravings for sensory pleasures, but also craving for continued existence (eternal life) and craving for complete cessation (non-existence), a complete end to it all. The Buddha teaches the Middle Path of avoiding the extremes.

Profound philosophical truth is encapsulated and presented in the tenth limb 'Becoming (*Bhāva*)' in the Buddhist Wheel of Life. The whole process of becoming which results from the *karma*-producing volitional activities is governed by moral principles (laws) according to the Buddha. As Gombrich comments, it is for the first time in the history of civilisation that the Buddha has fully ethicized the whole process of becoming and, with it, the turning around and evolution of the universe. His formulation has totally overturned the Brahmanical concept of sacrificial rituals and mantras with their magical potencies influencing and determining the cosmic order and the workings of the universe.

The causal scheme of existential elements derived from the Buddhist concept of Wheel of Life is compared with a typical philosophical scheme in the *Upaniṣadic* thought that has evolved in the course of its long history and that is exemplified in the evolution and hierarchy of the constituent principles as enunciated in the *Kaṭha Upaniṣad* (Figure 16). The '*avyakta*' in the scheme of the *Kaṭha Upaniṣad* corresponds to the limb of 'Becoming' in the Buddhist philosophy. In this 'Becoming', the *Vijñāna* (the fundamental blind will) sprouts into karma-producing activities, conditioned and caused by craving and the accompanying clinging that have their root cause in ignorance (*avidyā*). The moral intentions of this blind will determine the reactions and the further evolution of the will and, with it, the world it creates according to the universal principle of Law of Karma. As against this, *avyakta* of the *Upaniṣad* is interpreted and spoken of as the '*māyā-śakti*' of *Īśvara*. The evolution here is

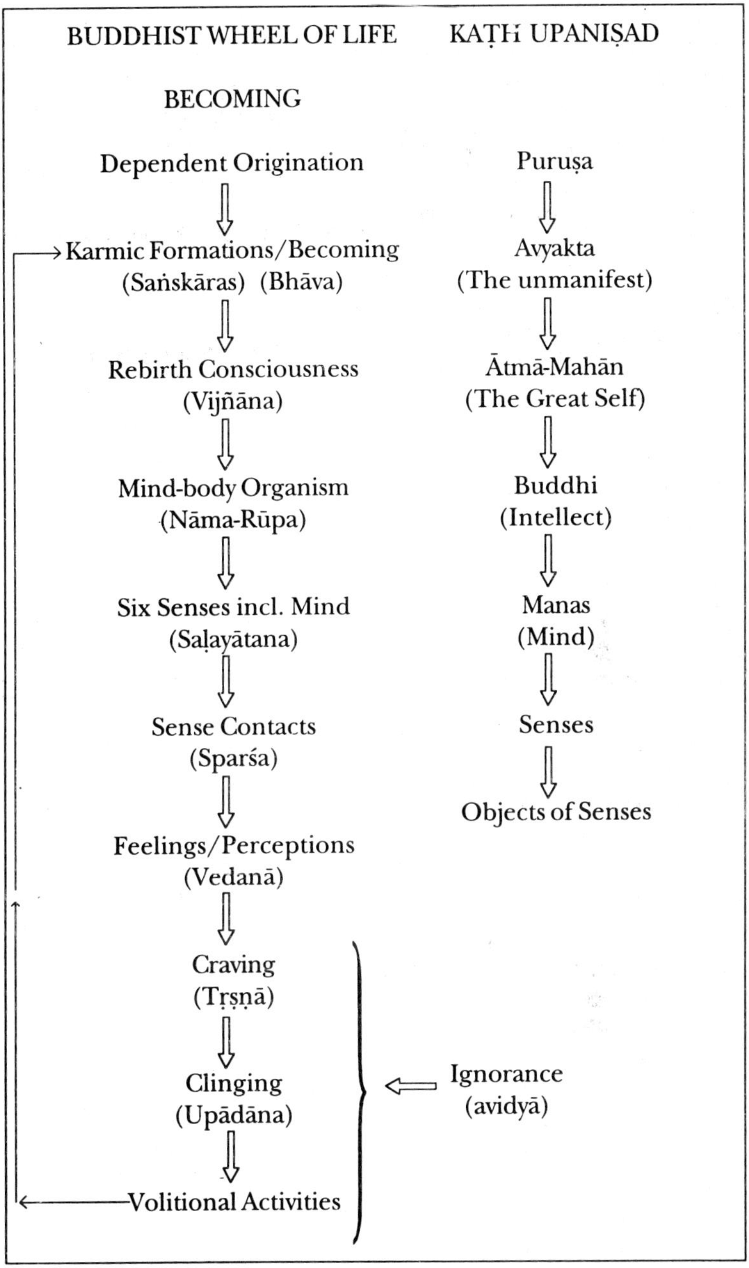

Fig. 16 Comparison with Kaṭha Upaniṣad

top-driven and *Īśvara* always acts from above. The relationship between the *Īśvara* and the higher principle *puruṣa* is ambiguous. The distinction between *puruṣa* and *Īśvara* seems to have arisen in the *Upaniṣads* only with a view to insulate the higher *puruṣa* i.e *para* Brahman from the imperfections of *Īśvara* and his creation.

The *avyakta* reduces to be an amalgam of different concepts and ideas which are contradictory to each other. First is the idea that *Īśvara* as the supreme Lord creates, supports, controls and destroys the individual self and the universe. The second idea is that, in the creation of the world, He is dependent on other factors like *guṇas* in addition to his own divine will. The third idea is that He is not the creator, He is not the doer, but only the operator of Law of Karma and dispenser of rewards and punishments for the actions done by the individual self. The fourth idea is that in his role as the dispenser of justice or as the cause of the evolution of *avyakta*, his divine will is influenced by the sacrifices and prayers of the individual self. This is a carry-over of the earlier blind faith in the Brahmanical rituals. All these ideas and faiths co-exist uneasily in the concept of *avyakta*.

The *Dhamma*, the Eternal Law, the body of eternal, immutable and invariable laws of cause and effect, is represented by the doctrine of Dependent Origination (i.e. the causal genesis of things) in Buddhism. According to the Buddha, one who sees dependent origination sees *Dhamma* and who sees *Dhamma* sees dependent origination. This is the cornerstone of the Buddha's philosophy and this is the principle that governs the world of "becoming". There are moral and spiritual laws as well as physical laws. But, it is on the former, the moral and spiritual laws, that the Buddha lays emphasis. For him, *Dhamma*, the impersonal force, that determines each according to his deeds as the moral retribution, is supreme.

Ignorance of this *Dhamma*, the Eternal Law, is the cause of *saṃsāric* 'becoming' and attendant sufferings whereas the knowledge of the operation of this Eternal Law (encapsulated in the Four Noble Truths) leads to the sorrowless and the most perfect, pure and peaceful state of *Nibbāna*. There is no spirituality without morality. This is the highest knowledge in Buddhism whereas the *Upaniṣads* consider the knowledge of *ātman* or Brahman (*Puruṣa*) as the highest. Even though the Law of Karma is talked about in the *Upaniṣads*, but it is as one of the different elements determining *avyakta*. The predominant and overwhelming emphasis in the *Upaniṣads* is on the realisation or apprehension of *Ātman* (Brahman) rather than on the ethical and moral principles.

Buddhism does not believe in the promises of rewards and threats of punishments from a creator God who is all-knowing and all-seeing, an onipotent God "who resides somewhere up there; who created us imperfectly, yet for reasons best known to himself, punishes us for our imperfections". According to the Buddhists, the concept of a creator God is logically untenable. The problem arises as to how to reconcile the sufferings, sorrows, pains, evils and injustices in the world without compromising the integrity and the benevolent supreme qualities of the omnipotent God or *Īśvara.* Buddha rejects the idea of creator God. There is also no place in the Buddhist scheme for the higher principle *'Puruṣa'* (Higher Brahman) of the *Upaniṣads.* The laws of cause and effect and the Law of Karma are the only universal principles the Buddhists recognize. These are spontaneous in operation.

Buddha also denies the efficacy of the sacrifices and prayers in altering the individual's destiny. He teaches that man is the author of his own destiny and that without self-efforts on mind-culture and ethical perfection through the Noble Eightfold Path, salvation will not be possible.

The *Ātmā-Mahān,* the self in the individual body, postulated in the *Kaṭha Upaniṣad,* corresponds to the ever-changing all-seed consciousness *Vijñāna* in the Buddhist philosophy. This is the consciousness which is always evolving and passes as the rebirth consciousness at the end of the present life to descend into a new embryo. Here there is no transmigration of a permanent unchanging soul or self with its subtle body as in the Hindu philosophy, but only a flow of continually changing consciousness driven into a new birth by *kamma.* In this Buddhist concept, each unit of consciousness is a packet of will or mind energy and consists of three phases-genesis, development and dissolution. One unit of consciousness perishes only to give birth to another. The subsequent thought-unit or will is neither absolutely the same as its predecessor (since its composition is not identical), nor entirely another, being the same continuity of *Kammic* energy.

In the *Milinda Pañha* and *Visuddhi Magga,* the Venerable Nagasena and the Venerable Buddhaghosa have employed several similes to illustrate that nothing permanent transmigrates from one life to another.

The simile of the flame is very striking. This life is a flame. Rebirth is the transmission of this flame from one group to another. The flame of life is continuous although there is an apparent break at so-called death.

King Milinda questions :

"Venerable Nagasena, does rebirth take place without anything transmigrating ?"

"Yes. O King. Rebirth takes place without anything transmigrating."

"Give me an illustration, Venerable Sir."

"Suppose, O King, a man were to light a light from another light, pray, would the one light have passed over to the other light?'

"Nay indeed Venerable Sir."

"In exactly the same way O King, does rebirth take place without anything transmigrating."

"Give another illustration."

"Do you remember, O King, having learnt, when you were a boy, some verse or other from your teacher of poetry?"

"Yes Venerable Sir."

"Pray, O King, did the verse pass over to you from your teacher ?".

"Nay, indeed, Venerable Sir."

"In exactly the same way, O King, does rebirth take place without anything transmigrating."

Dr. Ānandā Coomaraswamy in his book "Buddha and the Gospel of Buddhism" (p.106) illustrates this process taking the example of billiard balls as an analogy :-

"If, for instance, another ball is rolled against the last stationary ball, the moving ball will stop and the stationary ball will move on. The first moving ball does not pass over, it remains behind, it dies. But it is undeniably the movement of that ball, its momentum, its *Kamma* and not any newly created movement, which is reborn in or transmitted to the foremost ball."

The Third Noble Truth : *Cessation of Suffering*

The Buddha's Third Noble Truth affirms that suffering in life can be voluntarily brought under control and eradicated through self-efforts. The Buddha has diagnosed the cause of suffering. He prescribes the cure also. If the cause is removed, the effect, suffering, comes to an end naturally. The cause of becoming and suffering has been diagnosed as the craving and the accompanying clinging which have their roots and origin in ignorance (*avidyā*). When this ignorance is turned into knowledge which sees things as they really are – *anityam, asukham* and *anattā*-and, seeing their true nature, one lets go the craving and clinging, then the life-flux is diverted into the realm of *Nirvāṇa* (*Nibbāna:Pāli*) and the suffering ceases.

"Through the total fading away and extinction of craving (*taṇhā*), clinging (*upādāna*) is extinguished ; through the extinction of clinging, the process of becoming (*bhāva*) is extinguished; through the extinction of the process of becoming, rebirth (*Jāti*) is extinguished and through the extinction of rebirth, decay, death, sorrow, lamentation, suffering, grief and despair are extinguished. Thus comes about the extinction of this whole mass of suffering" (S.II.72).

Thus does the cessation of this entire aggregate of suffering result and is the life-flux diverted into *Nibbāna-Dhātu.* The method for removing the ignorance and gaining the wisdom to enter into *Nibbāna* (*Nirvāṇa* or Buddhahood) is the subject matter of Buddha's Fourth Noble Truth.

The Fourth Noble Truth: The Path *(Magga : Pāli ; Mārga : Sanskrit)*

Nirvāṇa is the complete and permanent cessation of all types of suffering. The Buddha gives a complete and systematic guide for attaining this state of *Nirvāṇa,* total extinction of suffering. The ethical and mind-culture system developed and bequeathed by him to the mankind as the guide to *Nirvāṇa* is unsurpassed or even unparalleled in any philosophical or religious tradition. It is the Noble Eightfold Path, avoiding the two extremes of sensual enjoyment ("which is base, vulgar, worldly, ignoble and profitless") and self-mortification ("which is painful, ignoble and profitless").

It is an eightfold composite path like a wheel with eight spokes. Its spokes are :

Right view.
Right resolve/intention.
Right speech.
Right action/morality and conduct.
Right livelihood.
Right effort.
Right mindfulness.
Right concentration.

Just as all the eight spokes of a wheel should be in position to make the wheel complete and enable it to roll on, in the same manner, all the elements of the Noble Eightfold Path should be practised simultaneously to complete the *Dharma* Wheel.

'Right' in the above enumeration of the Path has been used in the sense of 'correct', 'perfect' and 'just'.

Right View

Ignorance, which is the root cause of suffering, is basically misunderstanding, wrong view or lack of knowledge of the true nature of things and true nature of self. Therefore, Buddha first of all prescribes 'Right View' as the antidote to ignorance.

Right view is seeing things as they actually are: *anityam, asukham* and *anattā*. Analysing every aspect of the inner or other experience, the Buddha shows that it is all impermanent, sorrowful and selfless (*anattā*). Every cognisable element, whether internal or external, gross or subtle, is said to have these three characteristics. They are applicable, without exception, to 'everything that is seen, heard, reflected, contemplated' (*M.I.*136).

"When, O monks, the monk sees the impermanent corporeality (form), feeling, perception, volitions, and consciousness as impermanent (subject to suffering and without a self), in that case he is possessed of the right view."(*S.*III.51).

"Material shape (form) and the other *skandhas* are impermanent ; what is impermanent is suffering ; what is suffering (sorrowful) is not self ; what is not self-that is not mine, that I am not, that is not my self. This should be seen by means of right wisdom as it really is" (*Vinaya Piṭaka* I. 14).

"The instructed disciple of the Ariyans beholds of material shape (form) and the other *skandhas* as : "This is not mine, this am I not, this is not my self." So that when the material shape and so on change and become otherwise, there arise not for him grief, sorrow, suffering, lamentation and despair"(*S.* III. 19 etc.).

Because of ignorance and wrong views, we not only crave and cling to the things, but also further construct false views about them conditioned by our cravings and impulses. The view we form of the things, the judgement we make and the value we attach, in short, the world we form-are all conditioned by our personal needs, purposes, lusts and cravings. These in turn give rise to the various afflictions and defilements such as hatred, anger, pride, conceit etc. The view of things we form is not the right view of things as they are, but with subjective attributes and qualities. There is no absolute truth in them. That is why, the Buddha calls them illusory and compares them to a lump of foam, a water-bubble, a mirage, trunk of a plantain-tree and an illusion or dream.

All these things are to be rightly understood and also the truth of the Four Noble Truths realized inwardly.

Right Intention/Resolve

Mere knowledge or understanding is not sufficient to free one from the conflagration of suffering. The truth should be firmly established in the mind through constant reflection, awareness and resolve to assimilate and realize the same in the deepest possible manner so that they become the core of the personality. Right resolve means firm determination to reform one's life in the light of the truth and the right views. This includes cultivation of thoughts free from lust, thoughts free from ill-will (hatred) i.e. thoughts of loving kindness (*Mettā*), and thoughts free from cruelty i.e. compassion (*karuṇā*).

As Dhammapada (1.1) says, what we are today is the result of our intentions of yesterday and our intentions of today will decide our tomorrow. Our life condition is determined by the intentions of our mind. For the Buddha, intention is karma. If a man speaks or acts with an impure intention, *duḥkha* follows him as the wheel of the cart follows the beast that draws the cart.

Right Speech and Right Conduct

Right resolve must be co-ordinated with right speech and right conduct for the attainment of the goal.

The *Sammādiṭṭhi Sutta* reads as follows:- "Right view, right view, they say, friend. How is the noble disciple possessed of the right view?" (*M.I.*46). "When, friends, the noble disciple understands unrighteous action and the root of unrighteous action, the righteous action and the root of righteous action, then he is possessed of the right view"(*M.I.* 46-47).

With regard to the question as to what constitute the righteous and unrighteous actions and their respective roots, it is pointed out that greed, hatred and delusion are the roots of all unrighteous actions and their opposites are the roots of righteous actions.

The bodily, verbal and mental actions, righteous and unrighteous, arising from their respective roots are enumerated as below:-

A)	**Unrighteous bodily actions**	A)	**Righteous bodily actions**
1.	Destruction of life	1.	To abstain from the destruction of life
2.	Stealing	2.	To abstain from stealing
3.	Sexual misconduct	3.	To abstain from sexual misconduct
B)	**Unrighteous verbal actions**	**B)**	**Righteous Verbal actions**
4.	Speaking falsehood	4.	To abstain from speaking falsehood
5.	Slandering	5.	To abstain from slandering
6.	Speaking harsh words	6.	To abstain from speaking harsh words
7.	Talking frivolously	7.	To abstain from talking frivolously
C)	**Unrighteous mental actions**	C)	**Righteous mental actions**
8.	Covetousness	8.	Absence of covetousness
9.	Ill-will	9.	Absence of ill will
10.	Wrong view	10.	Correct view

Right conduct includes the five vows to practise: non-violence, truthfulness, non-stealing, non-sensuality (celibacy) and non-possessiveness (or, according to some scriptures, non-intoxication).

Non-violence or non-injury has been prescribed as the cardinal virtue to be practised in the Buddhist code of conduct. In the course of prescribing the virtue of non-injury, Buddha speaks of treating all creatures like oneself, promoting happiness to all and refraining from doing any harm to any living creature. The *raison d'etre* of treating all creatures like oneself, according to Buddhism, is just the empirical fact that all living beings like ourselves have a natural liking for life and happiness, and they hate pain and death. On the basis of this empirically observed common trait of their nature, Buddha lays down the ethical principle of non-injury or non-violence, and directs one to treat all beings like oneself. He says : "All tremble at punishment, all fear death ——to all, life is dear. Comparing others with oneself, one should neither kill nor cause to kill" (*Dh.*129 & 130).

Right Livelihood

One must earn a living to meet the essential needs of the body to keep it in a healthy condition. Buddha emphasizes the importance of the right (honest) livelihood that does not harm or interfere with other's lives and does not disturb social harmony.

The following five trades are forbidden, even for lay Buddhists (leave alone monks and nuns), as unrighteous forms of livelihood:

(i) selling arms;
(ii) selling human beings;
(iii) selling flesh i.e. breeding animals to sell for slaughter;
(iv) selling intoxicating drinks ; and
(v) selling poison.

Right Effort

While a person is trying to live a reformed life through right views, right intentions, right speech, right conduct and right livelihood, he still has to deal with his deeply rooted *Saṃskāras* that produce negative thoughts. Constant effort to uproot old negative thoughts and to prevent new ones from arising is very important in the path to *Nirvāṇa.* First one has to clean the mind and then immediately fill it with positive thoughts. This process is called right effort or constant endeavour to maintain moral as well as spiritual progress by banishing negative thoughts and assimilating positive ones. Right effort is directed at the mind (the will) at the sub-conscious level and aims at transforming the consciousness at the root.

"These are the four right efforts: an aspirant generates desire, endeavours, stirs up vigour, exerts his mind and strives that:

(i) evil unwholesome mental states that have not arisen should not arise (i.e control them from arising),
(ii) evil unwholesome mental states that have arisen should be gotten rid of,

(iii) wholesome mental states that have not arisen should arise (i.e. develop them to arise) and

(iv) wholesome mental states that have arisen should be maintained, preserved, increased, matured, developed and brought to completion."

(*Dīgha Nikāya* III. 221)

Right Mindfulness

'Right mindfulness' is the constant mindfulness, awareness, reflection and deep-inquiry into the nature of the body, the feelings, the mind and the various physical and mental states so that total comprehension of the true nature of these mental as well as physical phenomena arises and a spirit of detachment develops to let them go and become free. The efforts are directed here to achieve cultivation of the points of mindfulness, produce those points of mindfulness as yet undeveloped and strengthen, perpetuate and extend the points of mindfulness once they have been developed.

Four applications of mindfulness to be practised have been described beautifully in *Majjhima Nikāya* (I.55-63). An extract of the same is given below.

In contemplating the body in the body, the monk arouses mindfulness and constant awareness of whatever he does and whatever happens to his body. When he breaths in, he contemplates that he is breathing in. When he breaths out, he contemplates that he is breathing out. Whether he is breathing in a long or a short breath, he comprehends that he is breathing in a long or a short breath. Similarly when he is breathing out. Whatever he is doing, whether walking, standing still, sitting down or lying down, he comprehends and is fully mindful that he is doing so.

He reflects and visualizes the body as encased in skin-covered bone structure with full of various impurities inside and as composed of the four primary elements : earth, water, air and fire (solidity/extension, fluidity/cohesion, motion and heat). Just as a skilled cattle-butcher displays a slaughtered cow or goat for selling meat, even so the monk dissects mentally his own body and examines the same part by part dispassionately. He might also visualize a body lying in various stages of decomposition in a cemetery. Thus, he abides in meditation contemplating the body in the body and lives mentally separate from the body and independently of body, not grasping or clinging to anything in the world.

Then, how does a monk abide in concentration contemplating the feelings in feelings? When he is experiencing a pleasant or a painful feeling or one that is neither painful nor pleasant, he comprehends that he is feeling so. Likewise he examines and comprehends what feeling he is passing through at every moment. He views his own feelings objectively as if he is separate from them.

Then he examines his mind and comprehends whether it has passion, hatred or confusion, whether it is distracted or collected, whether it is concentrated, whether it is free and so on. It is thus that a monk lives contemplating the mind in the mind.

And how does a monk live contemplating mental states in mental states?

In the first place, he does so from the point of view of the five defilements or hindrances/impediments. He examines and comprehends whatever defilement he is passing through-whether of sensual desire, hatred, sloth and torpor, excitement/depression or delusion. He contemplates these mental factors (which impede wisdom) as and when they arise and understands the root causes of their emergence and analyses why they have arisen and how they have arisen and what their effects will be. He analyses dispassionately and understands these passions as they are i.e. understands the *dhammatā* of these passions, their dependent nature and their emptiness or hollowness, substancessness.

In the second place, he lives contemplating mental states in mental states from the point of view of the five heaps or the aggregates constituting his self. He comprehends :

"Such is the material form, such is its arising and such is its decaying?" He thinks and comprehends likewise of feelings (sensations), perceptions, volitions/impulses and consciousness.

Thirdly, he contemplates mental states in mental states from the point of view of the six inward-outward sense-fields He comprehends the eye and the physical forms, the ear and the sounds, nose and smells, tongue and tastes and body and tactile sensations (touch) and analyses the corresponding defilements/fetters brought on by each combination.

Fourthly, he contemplates mental states in mental states from the point of view of the seven limbs of enlightenment. He comprehends when any of these seven-limbs-mindfulness, investigation of mental states, vigour, tranquillity, rapture, concentration, even-mindedness – is present and he also comprehends when any of them is absent. He makes conscious efforts to arouse and cultivate the seven limbs of enlightenment that had not arisen before and to develop and promote them that have already arisen.

Fifthly, a monk lives contemplating mental states in mental states from the point of view of the Four Noble Truths :

> There is suffering.
> There is a cause of suffering.
> There is cessation of suffering.
> There is a way leading to the cessation of suffering.

Thus contemplating the body in the body, the feelings in the feelings, the mind in the mind and the mental states in the mental states, the monk abides and lives mentally separating himself from the body, the feelings, the mind and the mental states and keeping himself independent of each of these and not grasping or clinging to anything in the world. Such is the way he avoids attachment, hatred and delusion. He fares along independently of and not grasping anything in the world.

In contemplating these mental factors and passions and watching their flow, one becomes aware of their fleeting nature (thought patterns arising and falling), aware of their impermanence and aware of letting them go. In watching this way, one perceives them as they are and abandons any notion that they might be worth craving, as capable of providing lasting happiness or as an object of attachment as one's true Self. In knowing, seeing the body, the feelings, the mind and the physical and mental processes as they are, one begins to erode any basis for craving and uproot the forces that lead to suffering and rebirth.

In the *Upaniṣadic* philosophy, we have seen how the seers endeavour to generate intuitive knowledge of Self (*ātman* or Brahman) in the students by asking them to meditate on the *Mahāvākyas* like 'Thou Art That', 'I am Brahman' etc. But Buddha does not believe in the existence of such a permanent unchanging Self and he recognizes only the 'blind will to become' (*Vijñāna*) which grows and manifests as the body, the feelings, the mind and the mental as well as physical phenomena and which is intent only on self-preservation, self interest and self-aggrandizement, moment to moment, without any consideration for others and their interests. In this process, it accumulates the Kammic burden and rolls on from one life to another, to another and so on and on. The Buddha's teaching on Right Mindfulness is to enable us to see this blind will nakedly as it is and expose the same for what it is. When it is nakedly seen like this through the applications of Right Mindfulness, it becomes a purified consciousness. With the practices of Right Mindfulness, the *karmic* formations also fade away. This is the way to liberation and this is liberation.

The underlying principle is to analyse every phenomenon (mental or physical), every passion, and comprehend why it has arisen, how it has arisen and what its effect will be. This is the diagnosis and prognosis of the passions and emotions. The endeavour should be to analyse dispassionately and understand them as they are i.e. understood the *dhammata* (true nature) of these passions and emotions, their dependent nature and their emptiness or hollowness. Once the *dhammata* of these passions and emotions is understood, they lose their force and automatically transform themselves into virtues.

The later day Spinoza has aptly summarized this truth in the following statement in his 'Ethics' :-

"A passion ceases to be a passion and becomes a virtue as soon as one forms a clear distinct and adequate idea of it. The mind is subject to passions and hence suffers in proportion to the number of inadequate ideas which it has".

The emphasis in the *Upaniṣads* is to see the unchanging ever-existent Self (*ātman*) within whereas in Buddhism the thrust is to view nakedly the ever-changing blind will within oneself for what it is, through Right Effort and Right Mindfulness, and burn away the *karmic* formations and the deep-rooted habits, addictions, passions, prejudices and obsessions.

Right Concentration

Right concentration is equanimity and single-pointedness, a state of profound stillness and peace, with the mind radiantly pure like a cleansed mirror capable of reflecting the higher truths as para-normal vision. According to Buddhist accounts, there are four stages of progress in the perfection of this meditation and concentration and these are described as the four *Jhānas* (Sanskrit:*dhyāna*) or ecstasies (absorptions). These *Jhānas* are said to take the meditator outside, as it were, the desire realm (*kāmadhātu*) in which we humans normally live and elevate him to the realm of pure form (*rūpa-dhātu*). Hence these are called *rūpa-Jhāna*.

Four *rūpa-Jhānas* :-

The first *Jhāna* is characterized by reflection (applied thought), investigation (examination/enquiry), joy, peace and single-pointedness of mind. Here, reflection and investigation predominate. The practitioner concentrates his or her pure and unruffled mind on reasoning and investigation regarding the Four Noble Truths and the Eightfold Path. Here the practitioner enjoys the pure thinking involved.

The second *Jhāna* has just joy, peace and one-pointedness of mind since in this stage all doubts and confusions of the practitioner are completely dispelled and his mind is firmly established in the Four Noble Truths and the Eightfold Path. Here, in this stage, the practitioner passes beyond reflection and investigation, and his ability in meditative practice becomes so refined that consciously applied thought and examination are no longer needed in order to place the mind on the object of meditation. This is the stage of duality in which the practitioner is the enjoyer, and joy, peace and internal tranquillity born of meditation are considered to be the objects of his enjoyment.

The third *Jhāna* lacks even this joy which can become a disturbance to the final quest and has only peace and one-pointedness. In this stage, the practitioner, by intense and deep meditation, transcends joy also and enjoys only peace and tranquillity of one-pointedness. Here, with this enjoyment of peace, the feeling or awareness of his physical existence remains.

Ultimately, there does come a stage of mind in which the feeling of bodily existence and the enjoyment of peace also cease. This is the fourth *Jhāna* or ecstasy in which only the tranquillity of one-pointedness remains and the adept now sees the uninterrupted mind (consciousness) without any disturbance. This is a state of profound stillness and peace, in which the mind rests with unshakeable one-pointedness and equanimity, and breathing has calmed to the point of stopping. Buddha seems to have attained enlightenment and gained the paranormal vision and insight into the higher knowledges from such a state of radiant purity.

With the intense *Jhāna* of the fourth stage emerges, as a natural sequence, the insight into the reality of existences as they actually are and not as they appear to be, and enlightenment follows. The Buddha came face-to-face with reality and realized the Four Noble Truths. He became freed from the cycle of 'becoming' with the inward realisation of all *karmic* residues having been burnt away and the extinction of the outflows. His mind was freed from the outflows of : craving for sensual pleasures, craving for becoming, and ignorance. He attained absolute and perfect freedom.

Four *Brahmā Vihāras* (Divine Abidings/ Immeasurables) :-

Gombrich and Paul Williams suggest that meditation on the Four *Brahmā Vihāras* or the 'Four Unlimiteds' (Immeasurables) is "possibly originally thought of as one sufficient means for attaining enlightenment itself" (Paul Williams: Buddhist Thought, p. 83).

The Four *Brahmā Vihāras* are the four sublime states of mind:

- All-pervading loving kindness (*Mettā : Pāli ; Maitrī :* Sanskrit) with the pervasive wish: " May all sentient beings be well and happy."
- All-pervading compassion (*karuṇā*) with the pervasive wish: "May all sentient beings be free from suffering."
- All-pervading sympathetic joy (*muditā*)-delight at the happiness of others.
- All-pervading equanimity – calmness and serenity with no sense of self or ego (*Pāli : upekkhā* ; Sanskrit : *upekṣā*)

The practitioner abides in the four *Brahmā Vihāras,* radiating and suffusing the four quarters of the world, in all directions, above, below, in every way, with the thoughts of loving kindness, compassion, sympathetic joy and equanimity that are far-reaching, wide-spread, immeasurable, without enmity, without ill-will.

He realizes the larger oneness of life and recognises himself in all. He is filled with love beyond measure for the whole world. His loving-kindness, selfless-love, non-possessive love extends to encompass all forms of sentient beings as *karuṇā,* compassion. His heart bleeds at the sufferings of others and goes out to their help. His *karuṇā* melts down all the barriers of separatedness. It leads, also, to *muditā,* a sharing in other's happiness, a joy in other's joy, the renunciation of envy and malice. Finally, having shared in the emotions of others, he enters into a condition of serene detachment, *upekṣā.* He responds to the world neither with attachment nor with aversion (Ranjit Hoskote: Four Ways of Embracing the World).

The cornerstone of the practice is found in the Buddha's teaching in the fifteenth chapter of Dhammapada, the Verses on Joy:

"Let us live in joy, never hating those who hate us. Let us live in freedom, without hatred even among those who hate" (*Dh.* 197).

For the Buddha, joy lies, not in returning hate with hate, but in responding to hate with love. "Hatred can never put an end to hatred; love alone can. This is an unalterable law" (*Dh.* 5).

A little reflection will show why the above practice based on the Four *Brahmā Vihāras* should be considered as the single sufficient means for attaining liberation. For, all the *karmic* residues one accumulates in life have their origin, source and cause in the false theory of individuality and in the hatred, anger, cruelty, covetousness, pride, envy and such other unwholesome acts which one inflicts on others out of self-interest and self-aggrandizement. The antidotes for these negative emotions and the *karmic* residues they form are the four *Brahmā Vihāras*. They only can burn away these *karmic* residues and lead one to liberation. That is why the four *Brahmā Vihāras* have been given such a great importance in Buddhism.

Five *arūpa-Jhānas* :-

Buddha has bequeathed to us a thorough and incisive analytical treatise on different hierarchical levels of happiness and bliss, which is unparalleled in philosophical thoughts. This treatise is literally a search-light in the service of any aspirant who is in search of truth or reality.

In the *Bahuvedaniya Sutta* (No.57, *Majjhima Nikāya*), Buddha enumerates ten grades of happiness beginning at the lowest with the gross material pleasures, which result from the pleasant stimulations of the five senses. We call the experience of these as happiness; but this is merely the gratification of some sensual desire. No sooner is the desired thing gained than it begins to be scorned and he craves for yet other varied pleasures. Insatiate are all desires and sorrowful they become ultimately.

The man deriving pleasure out of sense-object contact has been compared to a leper who is scratching his wound and heating it over a fire and deriving momentary pleasure thereby, which ultimately worsens his wound and augments his trouble all the more (*M.* I. 507). The same is also suggested by the analogy of a dog lustily gnawing at a fleshless piece of bone, and gaining ultimately nothing but pain and suffering (*M.* I. 364).

Then comes in the hierarchy of happiness the four ecstasies or *rūpa-Jhānas* achieved step-by-step through meditative concentration. Buddha takes us higher and higher in the meditative practices. Thus, as one ascends higher and higher in these spiritual practices, the so called happiness becomes more and more exalted, sublime and subtle so much so that it is scarcely recognizable as happiness by the man of the world. One in the first *Jhāna* experiences a spiritual happiness which is absolutely independent of the five senses. This happiness is gained by discarding the desire for the pleasures of the senses. In the fourth *Jhāna,* however, even this type of happiness is discarded as coarse and unprofitable, and equanimity (*upekkhā*) or stillness of mind is termed happiness.

Even the fourth ecstasy is not considered the highest happiness by Buddha because it is still mental. There is happiness more sublime and exalted raising one into formless realms with the gradual deepening of the concentration (*samādhi*).

"Here a bhikkhu, passing entirely beyond the perception of form with the disappearance of sense reaction, freed from attention to perceptions of diversity, thinks: 'INFINITY IS SPACE' – and lives abiding in the Realm of Infinite Space.

"Nevertheless, if this were declared the highest happiness – I do not grant it. There is happiness more sublime than that.

"Here a bhikkhu - transcending entirely the Realm of Infinite Space, thinks: 'INFINITE IS CONSCIOUSNESS' – and lives abiding in the Realm of Infinite Consciousness.

"And yet should this be declared the highest happiness – I do not grant it. There is higher happiness.

"Here a bhikkhu transcending the Realm of Infinite Consciousness thinks: 'THERE IS NOTHING WHATSOEVER'- and lives abiding in the Realm of Nothingness" (*śūnya*).

"And still were this declared the highest happiness – I do not grant it. There is happiness more exalted.

"Here a bhikkhu passing entirely beyond the Realm of Nothingness lives abiding in the 'REALM OF NEITHER PERCEPTION NOR NON-PERCEPTION.' This is the other happiness which is more exalted and sublime than that.

"Yet whoso should declare: "This is the highest bliss and pleasure which beings may experience " – I do not grant him that;

and for what reason? Because there is yet another happiness which is more exalted and sublime than that.

"------ Here a bhikkhu utterly transcending the Realm of Neither Perception Nor Non-Perception lives, having attained to the "CESSATION OF SENSATION AND PERCEPTION". This, *Ānanda*, is the other happiness which is more exalted and sublime than that" ('The Blessing', No. 4, pp 129 – 132).

Of all the ten grades of happiness, this is the highest and the most sublime with the consciousness associated with the sensations and perceptions of even happiness also transcended. This state is in other words known as '*Nirodha samāpatti*', i.e. experiencing *Nibbāna* in this life itself.

It may be asked: "How can that state be called highest happiness when there is no consciousness to experience it ? ".

In conventional terms, Buddha says : *Nibbāna* is the highest bliss. It is bliss supreme because it is not a kind of happiness that is experienced by the senses, mind or intellect. In this highest state which transcends everything conceivable, there is not even the consciousness of bliss. This is the highest bliss because it transcends even the feeling of bliss. As *Śāriputra* exclaims : "This precisely, O friend, is bliss that there is no feeling " (A. IV. 415). This is *Nibbāna.*

In the ultimate analysis, *Nibbāna* is not only the negation and extinction of the craving for worldly pleasures, the negation and extinction of the attachment, hatred and delusion, the negation and extinction of the conceit of 'I-ness' and 'mine-ness', the negation of enjoyable objects, the negation of sensation, the negation of perception, and the negation of volitions, but also the negation of consciousness i.e. the blind will to become and enjoy.

Even the highest state of meditative consciousness, either abiding in emptiness or in the realm of Neither-Perception-Nor-Nonperception, is not considered the most exalted and the most sublime by the Buddha because according to him this is also impermanent and passes away when one comes out of meditation. This is relegated to a lower category and Buddhist inner exploration goes deeper and deeper. The most exalted and the most sublime state transcends everything conceivable and there is not even the consciousness of bliss valued highermost in every *Upaniṣadic* thought.

Here Buddha exhorts his disciples to view nakedly the *Vijñāna*, the blind will to become and the accretion of *karmic* formations over it, which condition it. In the mindfulness and meditation, the defiling impulses conditioning the *Vijñāna* should be exposed and laid bare. Liberation or *Nirvāṇa* is all about "the arising of the knowledge of the destruction of these defiling impulses" and the inner realisation of the burning away of the *karmic* formations. Idea of self is the root cause of the defiling impulses and the *karmic* formations and this idea of 'I' or 'mine' should be eradicated and the *Vijñāna* made like the stump of a palm tree unable to grow. Delve deep into the state when you were a speck or a worm in your mother's womb and realize what was there then? What was the condition of the *Vijñāna* then and how it was growing? Were there a sense of self, ideas of 'I' and 'mine' then? Become aware of the defiling impulses and *karmic* formations which had accrued because of your clingings to the self. Burn them and transform your *Vijñāna* from the will to live to the will to love which is the only antidote to all your *karmic* defilements. This is the cessation of the *Vijñāna*, the cessation of further becoming of *Vijñāna*.

Here in the pinnacle of right mindfulness and right concentration, the fundamental *Vijñāna* i.e. the will to live is transformed into the will to love, love only without selfish desires and clingings, utterly selfless as the Buddha's life after his attainment of the supreme wisdom and enlightenment exemplifies. This *Nibbāna* is ultimately the extinction of self and the rootedness and abiding in the four *Brahma Vihāras*.

4. Meditative Practices

The Noble Eightfold Path described in the foregoing is normally divided under three major heads as below:

***Pañña* (Wisdom)**
Right view
Right resolve/intention
***Śīla* (Ethical conduct)**
Right speech
Right action/conduct
Right livelihood
***Samādhi* (Meditation/Concentration)**
Right effort
Right mindfulness
Right concentration

According to Buddhism, the highest knowledge (*Paññā*) leading to final deliverance *(vimutti)* is to be attained through meditation (*samādhi*) which in its turn requires prior purification of mind by means of moral virtuous conduct and discipline (*śīla*). One is first said to cultivate moral virtue, then enter into concentration through which he acquires knowledge and insight and having attained perfect knowledge, he is finally released. Thus, the virtuous life is a prerequisite for attaining true wisdom.

In this virtuous and holy path, the meditative practices are aimed at cleansing and purifying the mind to enable it to see the things as they truly are (*Yathābhūta-darśana*) without the veil of ignorance and also at transforming it to bring to an end the forces generating suffering and rebirth, and thereby attain liberation.

In the Buddhist meditative practices, we discern two distinctive approaches. The first one is to calm down and still the mind. One then uses the still, calm, mind to investigate how things really are and realize the truth. Calming the mind is called 'calming (meditation)'- *Śamatha.* Discovering with a calm mind how things are really is called 'insight (meditation)'-*Vipaśyanā,* of which Right Mindfulness and Right Concentration are essential elements. At least some degree of calming is considered necessary to insight meditation. When calming and insight are linked, the mind has the strength and orientation really to break through to a deep transformative understanding of how things truly are.

Calming Meditation

Calming meditation aims to still the mind. In order to bring about the desired state of mental calm, the meditator starts by learning to focus the mind, narrowing down its attention so that he or she becomes simply aware of uninterrupted mind or consciousness free from any disturbance. In other words, he or she concentrates and focusses to improve the ability to monitor the mind and use it effectively to concentrate on something and develop unerring/unfailing control of emotions and reactions. To aid concentration, forty different possible objects of concentration have been specified in the literature such as the *Visuddhimagga* ('Path of Purification') of the *Theravādin Buddhaghoṣa.* In the consummated practice finally, the concentration is focussed on the mind itself without any conceptual image ; it is meditation on the uninterrupted, still mind (consciousness) itself.

Objects of concentration

They are :

- the ten *kasiṇas* (devices)
- the ten impurities
- the ten reflections
- the four immeasurables or divine abodes (*Brahma Vihāras*)
- the one perception
- the one analysis
- the four formless states (*arūpa* realms)

The ten *kasiṇas* (devices) are namely :

the earth *kasiṇa*
the water *kasiṇa*
the fire *kasiṇa*
the air *kasiṇa*
the blue *kasiṇa*
the yellow *kasiṇa*
the red *kasiṇa*
the white *kasiṇa*
the light *kasiṇa*
the space *kasiṇa*

The ten impurities are namely :

a bloated corpse
a discoloured corpse
a festering corpse
a dissected corpse
a gnawed-to-pieces corpse
a scattered-in-pieces corpse
a mutilated and scattered-in-pieces corpse
a bloody corpse
a worm-infested corpse
a skeleton corpse

The ten reflections or deep thoughts may be :

Reflection on the Buddha (Virtues of Buddha)
Reflection on the doctrine (*Dhamma*)
Reflection on the Sangha
Reflection on Virtue
Reflection on liberality
Reflection on devas
Reflection on Peace

Reflection on Death
Mindfulness regarding the body
Mindfulness regarding the respiration (breath)

The four 'immeasurables' or *Brahmavihāras* are :

All-pervading loving kindness (*Maitrī*)
All-pervading compassion (*karuṇā*).
All-pervading sympathetic joy (*muditā*)
All-pervading equanimity (*upekṣā*)

The one perception is :

the perception of the loathsomeness of material food

The one analysis is :

the analysis of the four elements (*pṛthvī*-earth, *āpo*-water, *vāyu*-air and *teja*-heat)

The four formless states (*arūpa* realms) are :

The Realm of the Infinity of Space
The Realm of the Infinity of Consciousness
The Realm of Nothingness
The Realm of Neither-Perception-Nor-Non-Perception

Selection depending upon temperament

Objects are recommended to be selected for concentration from among the above depending on the temperament or nature of the individual practitioner.

Objects suitable for those of lustful temperament are:

The ten impurities
Mindfulness regarding the body

The best way to control the lustful thoughts is to view the body as a corpse in various stages of composition and finally, with all the flesh fallen away, concentrate on the body as a bleached skeleton shining with light.

Objects suitable for those of irritable temperament (dominated by hatred) are:

The four "*Brahma Vihāras*"
The four coloured *kasiṇa* circles

Objects suitable for those of illusive temperament i.e, those who are dominated by delusion and whose mind is inclined to instability) and also those of discursive temperament are:

Mindfulness regarding respiration (breathing)

Objects suitable for those of devotional temperament are :

The first six reflections

Objects suitable for those of intellectual temparament are :

Reflections on Peace and Death

The perception of the loathsomeness of material food

The one analysis of four elements

The following objects are generally suitable for all practitioners :

Reflection on the Buddha

Reflection on Death

Mindfulness regarding the body

Mindfulness regarding breathing

Meditation on loving-kindness

The four 'Immeasurables' (*Brahma Vihāras*) have been particularly recommended as objects of concentration for those whose personality is dominated by hatred among the three root poisons. But possibly these were originally thought of as one efficacious and sufficient means for attaining enlightenment itself, as already discussed.

Preliminaries to be observed

Before he really embarks upon the practice of *samādhi,* the aspirant should give a careful consideration to the subject of contemplation and choose the one most suited to his character and temperament. He should also decide the best time for meditation and retire to a quiet place to engage in meditation.

The posture is important for facilitating concentration. The posture generally recommended is the triangular cross-legged position with the body maintained erect. The practitioner sits placing the right foot on the left thigh and the left foot on the right thigh and at right angles to each other. If this posture is found difficult to maintain, a half-position may be adopted with only the right foot on the left thigh or the left foot on the right thigh. Convenience or ease to concentrate shall determine the posture. The whole body shall be at ease and well-balanced.

The left hand should be placed on the right hand. The neck should be straightened so that the nose is in a perpendicular line with the navel. Before the practice, bad air from the lungs should be breathed out slowly through mouth and then closing the mouth, fresh air should be inhaled through the nose. The tongue should rest against the upper palate.

The aspirant who is keen on practising *samādhi* should endeavour his best to control the passions he is obsessed with, even at their inception. Right Mindfulness is the way to the control of the passions. The negative passions and emotions should be countered by applying mindfulness with the following techniques as recommended in *Majjhima Nikāya, Sutta* 20 :-

- Dwelling and concentrating on idea of an opposite nature e.g. love as against hatred
- Reflecting upon the causes that led to the arising of the passions and analysing their evil effects and consequences.
- Avoiding and neglecting them or becoming wholly inattentive to them.
- Applying mental strength and force to overcome the evil thoughts i.e. with clenched teeth and pressed tongue, to coerce and constrain the mind to overcome the evil thoughts

(The Buddha-Dhamma by Nārada Thera, p.282/283)

He makes a persistent effort to focus his mind and eye on the selected physical object like *kasiṇa*, or mind alone in the case of a mental object such as loving-kindness, virtues of the Buddha etc. to the entire exclusion of all other thoughts.

Meditation on some virtue like compassion, it may be remarked, possesses the specific advantage of building up that particular virtue in the character of the individual.

Calming Meditation

Whilst meditating, one may intelligently repeat the words-if there be a special formula or key words of selected Buddhist teachings, since they act constantly to evoke the idea they represent and condition the mind positively. They also act as an aid to concentration.

One may also take up Buddha's teachings as objects of meditation, reflect on them, investigate them and assimilate them. He attentively meditates on the Buddha's teachings on the workings of the inner consciousness. Then he passes on to probe and meditate on the inner stream of the meditating consciousness. When one practises correctly and diligently in this way he becomes calm and stable, achieves unfailing control of emotions and reactions and attains physical and mental ease with mind itself surfacing as the sole object of focus without any disturbing waves or objects of images i.e. mind becoming uninterrupted mind. Here the mind itself sees the mind without any thought waves or bubbles. Thus, this is the calming meditation (*Śamatha*) with the concentrated focus on the uninterrupted mind (consciousness) itself, made still like a stready lamp or a calm lake in a windless place. The consciousness of mind seeing the uninterrupted mind is also transcended ultimately.

The calming meditation encompasses the four *rūpa-Jhānas* and four *arūpa-jhānas* as well as meditation on the four *Brahma Vihāras* which we have already studied. Reflection and investigation predominate in the first *rūpa-jhāna* (ecstasy) and the practitioner transcends them and ascends progressively to the subsequent stages of the *rūpa-jhānas* with the mental states of joy, peace and one-pointedness of mind getting more and more refined and transcended step by step. In the fourth *rūpa-jhāna*, he attains the blissful state of immersion in the uninterrupted mind, extremely tranquil, still and silent. In this single-pointed and concentrated gaze, with all the defilements and afflictions of the mind having been burnt away, he sees only the pure mind and immerses in the emptiness of the same.

Ascending further into the realms of the four *arūpa-jhānas*, he reaches the ultimate goal of cessation of suffering i.e. *Nirvāṇa*. With the combined operation of calming meditation and insight meditation, the unconscious depths of the mind are explored and the lurking propensities and latent tendencies of the mind and the *karmic* formations are destroyed. The will energy propelling the mind is seen nakedly as it is, and is transformed into a supermundane consciousness thoroughly purified.

The calming meditation also involves immersion in four kinds of tranquillity – one in each of the four immeasurables (*Brahma Vihāras*): all-pervading immeasurable loving kindness, compassion, sympathetic joy and equanimity. The transformation of consciousness becomes complete with the immersion in these immeasurables.

Insight Meditation

The attainments resulting from the calming meditation are temporary. The defiling impulses and passions that are only temporarily inhibited by the calming meditation may burst forth quite unexpectedly at any time. It is the perfection of insight

(*Paññā*) or wisdom, the third and the final stage (after *sīla* and *samādhi*), that enables the aspirant to annihilate completely the defiling impulses and the passions that are only temporarily suppressed by the *samādhi* practice, and attain final release (*vimutti*).

The insight meditation is on how things are there actually and truly without distortion. This is taken up with the physical and mental ease attained through calming meditation as a basis. The basic difference between calming meditation and insight meditation is that the object of focus and concentration in the former is the mind devoid of any conceptual images i.e the uninterrupted mind itself whereas in the latter it is the mind with conceptual images. The mental states and the Buddhist principles and teachings are the objects of meditation here. Insight meditation also involves investigation into the real nature and truth of things and contemplation to attain higher wisdom, detachment and ultimate liberation. Calming meditation and insight meditation are then combined to culminate in single-pointed concentration and *samādhi* characterized by cessation of all sensations, perceptions and mental activities. The calming meditation and insight meditation are complementary to each other – the calm, ease and tranquillity of the former enabling deeper penetration of insight meditation and the deeper insight thus gained contributing to the further refinement and purification of the calm mind to result ultimately in seeing the underlying will energy as it is and stilling and transforming the same.

The adepts have developed and prescribed different models for insight meditation. The model of "seven purifications" described in *Buddhaghoṣa's Visuddhimagga* (chapters 18-22) is considered here.

1. Purification by proper moral conduct (*sīla*)
2. Developing serenity and calmness (*śamatha*)
3. Purification of View :-

Here the aspirant cultivates 'Purity of Vision' in order to see things as they really are. He reflects, examines and enquires what constitute the so-called self, 'I' and 'mine'. He realizes that there is not any permanent unchanging self underlying his experiences. There are only experiences and there is no 'experiencer', only actions and no 'actor'. He has a correct, purified, unperverted vision of the self. The so-called self is nothing but the process of coming together and functioning together of five heaps or five aggregates of corporeality (form), sensations, perceptions, volitions and consciousness (*Vijñāna*), depending on causes and conditions. The object of meditation here is the whole mind-body complex and its functioning. Look everywhere for your real self. You soon discover that there is no fixed and permanent identity within yourself, no independent point of subjectivity. There is only a continuous and ever-changing flow of the five aggregates depending on causes and conditions. You just happen to be there relatively. This discovery becomes the insight into selflessness, the doorway to liberation. The insight meditation increases the ability to cease identifying with cognitions, thoughts and emotions and instead realizing that what seems like an absolute 'I' is only a temporary conceptual construct, a relative fabrication. False theory of individuality and self is thus negated and the utter selflessness (*anattā*) of everything is realized through this insight meditation. Whereas the *Upaniṣads* and other scriptures of Hinduism talk of gaining insight into the vision of a permanent unchanging self underlying the personality, Buddhism emphasizes the selflessness in everything. Here the insight is into the selflessness which becomes the object of realisation.

4. Purification by overcoming doubt :-

Next he turns his insight into the causes and conditions which give rise to the process of coming together and functioning together of the five aggregates. He realizes that everything wordly is conditioned by some cause or causes, past or present and that his existence is due to past ignorance, craving, clinging, *Kamma* and physical food of the present life. On account of these five causes, this personality has arisen, and as the past activities have conditioned the present, so the present will condition the future. Meditating thus, he transcends all doubts with regard to the past, present and future. This is the purification through overcoming doubt. He understands the force of *Kamma* and sees how the limb of "becoming" in the Wheel of Life unfolds according to an impersonal law-like causality. He sees the dependent origination of everything and he sees *Dhamma.*

5. Purification by distinguishing between the right path and the wrong path:-

Thereupon he contemplates that all conditioned things are transient (*anityam*), subject to suffering (*duḥkha*) and devoid of an abiding self or soul (*anattā*). He sees these three ruling principles in every existence. He realizes that life is a mere flow, a process, a continuous flux of changing stages. Neither in heaven nor on earth does he find any genuine happiness, for every form of pleasure is only a prelude to pain. What is transient is therefore painful, and where change and sorrow prevail, there cannot be a permanent self.

At this stage, the aspirant may enter into the trance state of first *jhāna* and falsely think that he has attained sainthood. Soon he realizes his misconceptions and endeavours to distinguish what is the right path and what is the wrong path.

6. Purification of vision in the knowledge of progress :-

Perceiving the right path, he resumes his meditation and gains the following nine kinds of insight :-

- Arising of conditioned things (dependently caused).
- Passing away of conditioned things (dependently caused).
- Dissolution of things. He perceives that the five *skandhas* constituting his personality are in a state of constant flux, not remaining the same for any two consecutive moments.
- Knowledge that all dissolving things are fearful. The whole world appears to him like a pit of burning embers, a source of danger.
- Reflection on the wretchedness and vanity of the fearful and wicked world.
- Feeling of disgust for the world.
- Wish to escape from the clutches of the fearful and wicked world.
- Meditation again on the three characteristics of the world:
- Equaminity with neither attachment nor aversion for any worldly object.

He attains a state of deep equanimity and concentration

7. Final purification - Purity of vision :-

After attaining the state of perfect equanimity and one-pointedness, (i.e. concentration on the uninterrupted, calm, still mind or consciousness), the aspirant delves deep within the consciousness and keeps on developing insight into the defiling impulses within and will-power to eradicate the same.

He becomes a "stream-winner" (*sotāpanna* : *Pāli* ; *srotāpanna*: Sanskrit) (i.e. he enters the stream intent on reaching the other shore of *Nirvāṇa*, liberation) by breaking the first three of the ten fetters, namely, the false view of individuality (self), doubt and clinging to precepts and vows and adherence to wrongful rites and ceremonies. He is destined to enlightenment and he will be reborn at the most seven times before becoming enlightened.

With the distant glimpse of *Nibbāna* he has gained, the aspirant strives further and makes further progress in the path to *Nibbāna*. Perfecting his insight into the destruction of the defiling impulses, he weakens the next two fetters – sensual desire and aversion-and becomes an 'once-returner' (*sakadāgāmin* : *Pāli*; *sakṛdāgāmin* : Sanskrit) who will be reborn as a human-being on this earth only once in case he does not attain *Nibbāna* in this life itself. This is the second stage of sainthood he has attained. He has not yet completely eradicated the thoughts of lust and anger; at times he may be assailed by them.

On completely eradicating the five fetters, one becomes a 'Never-Returner' (*anāgāmin*) and on death, is reborn in one of the highest planes of the pure form realm of Brahmās or Higher Beings. He will never be reborn as a human again on this earth. He will attain enlightenment from 'that pure abode'. Even this *anāgāmin* has not so far transcended his 'will-to-become' and therefore he is reborn in the Pure Abode.

On destroying the remaining five fetters, namely : lust for life in Realms of Form and in Formless Realms, pride/conceit, agitation (restlessness) and ignorance (*avidyā*), he attains '*Arhantship*', the last stage of sainthood. He realizes that he has lived the holy life, accomplished what should be accomplished, rebirth has ended and there is no other birth beyond this.

It is said that the *anāgāmin* and the *arahants* who have adopted the *Śamatha* path i.e. calming meditation and developed concentration and acquired different kinds of *jhānas* (ecstacies), could experience the bliss of *Nibbāna* in this life itself. This, in *Pāli*, is called the *Nirodha samāpatti*. In the bhikku who experiences the ecstasy of this *Nirodha samāpatti*, vitality persists, heat abides and the faculties are clear although respiration, sensation and perception are stilled and quiescent. This is the cessation of perception and conception. According to early Buddhism, this is the highest form of happiness that could be experienced in this life as we have already studied earlier.

5. Theory of *Anattā* (No-self)

The theory of *Anattā* (no-self or soullessness) is central to the teachings of the Buddha. Without a proper appreciation and realisation of the truth of this core teaching, the rest of his teachings and the path shown by him to reach the goal of permanent cessation of *duḥkha* cannot be truly understood, for his teachings are logically well-knit into a coherent system of philosophy and way of life. Selflessness is the liberating truth, realisation of which sets one free. Therefore, it is proposed to examine this theory in some more depth even at the risk of repetition.

Once the Buddha took a bit of cowdung in his hand and spoke to the monks :

"If, O monks, even that much of permanent, ever-lasting, eternal, changeless self-hood, identically abiding for ever, could be found, then living of a life of purity for the complete eradication of suffering would not be feasible" (*S*.III. 144).

Even a trace of the idea of self remaining in the mind is bound to affect the purity of the holy life. The holy life will be complete, perfect and pure only when this idea of self is totally obliterated from the mind and utter selflessness is reached.

According to the Buddha, this idea of self, 'I', is a false conceptual construct of the mind. There are only flows of experiences as continuous streams : experiences of form, experiences of sensations, experiences of perceptions, experiences of volitions and experiences of consciousnesses. In the ultimate analysis, consciousness only is experiencing all these forms, sensations, perceptions and volitions, and it flows as a stream comprising various units of consciousness. Consciousness as the 'blind will-to-become' evolves into the body-mind complex as unconscious unfolding (blossoming) of the will and with the mind it develops, it feels, thinks and wills further. It constructs its means for livelihood and in effect it constructs the world of its existence. (Even the five basic elements on which we depend for our existences – earth, water, fire, air and ether-flow from consciousness. The modern science has broken the barriers between matter, mind and energy. We cannot say that these elements have no consciousness of their own. We miss the truth when we restrict the idea of consciousness to its narrow cognitive aspect i.e. the aspects of knowing and understanding and exclude the broader aspects of will and energy from its definition).

Without digressing, let us come back to the flow of consciousness. The whole life is the continuous evolving and becoming of this consciousness according to the *Kamma* as we have already seen. Becoming is because of *Kamma.* The existence or this life of the stream of consciousness is determined and conditioned by past ignorance, craving, clinging, *Kamma* and the nourishment.

However much we delve deep within our being, we find nothing else excepting these streams of forms, sensations, perceptions, volitions and consciousness. As later day philosopher Hume has summed up, we find only thought and not any thinker behind it, only consciousness and not any identifiable person behind the consciousness. What we normally call a self is nothing but a composite of the five aggregates or streams of experiences bound together by the five causes of past ignorance, craving, clinging, *Kamma* and the nourishment. For conventional purposes, for purposes of day-to-day life and transactions, this conceptual construct of self is required. The Buddha does not deny this. What he denies is that there is a permanent, ever lasting, eternal self underlying or sustaining this construct. A changing self or changing consciousness is recognized for conventional purposes. But if an eternal self is suggested as underlying these experiences, then that is a false theory altogether.

The Buddha has expounded his famous theory of *anattā* in his second discourse to the five bhikkhus (*Anattalakkhaṇa Sutta,* "Discourse on the Definition of Not-Self"; *Mahāvagga Saṃyutta Nikāya* III).

"The body (*rūpa*), O bhikkhus, is not self (*rūpam bhikkhave anattā*) i.e. it is self-less, no self behind it. If, O bhikkhus, there were in this a soul or self, then this body would not be subject to afflictions (ills) and it could be had of body: "Let my body be thus ; let my body be not thus". And it is because the body is selfless, it is subject to afflictions and it cannot be had of body i.e. no possibility exists for ordering the body : "Let my body be thus ; let my body be not thus".

In like manner,
Sensation is not self ----------------
Perception is not self ---------------
Volitions are not self ----------------
Consciousness (*Vijñāna*) is not self -------

The logical reasoning the Buddha adduces for proving his theory of *anattā* is that if Self be there, then it would not lead to afflictions for Self should exercise total control of the body, sensations, perceptions, volitions and consciousness according to definition and keep them free from afflictions. A real Self would be happy since it would be aware of itself, it would not change and it would not depend on anything else. But the fact of experience is different. The facts of impermanence and sufferings prove the theory of *anattā*. Thus Buddha directly attacks and rejects the *Upaniṣadic* concept of Self or *ātman* as a permanent eternally existing principle within the being, as the inner controller and as blissful. If an eternal immutable self exists within as the inner controller, then why are there these impermanence and sufferings and why is the Self not able to control and maintain the constituents (of which it is the Self) to be permanent and blissful? If other factors are determining the conditions of the constituents, then the Self is not the self of these constituents. The concept of Self is thus self-contradictory.

The Buddha concludes that neither the five aggregates of form, sensations, perceptions, volitions and consciousness taken severally or jointly constitute the Self of being nor is there any separate abiding permanent Self underlying and supporting them.

The *Pāli* Canon is full of references where Buddha analysing the total personality of man into the five ingredients as above explains that there is nothing permanent and blissful in them, and establishes the point that it is wrong to cling to anything and to have the conceit of 'I' in any or all of them. He is frequently found to proceed by asking his disciples whether corporeality(*rūpa*) is permanent or impermanent (*M*.I. 232-233 ; *S*.III.88,118) and on the reply that it is impermanent, he further asks whether that which is impermanent is to be regarded as sorrowful or blissful. To this the natural reply is that it is sorrowful. Then he asks : "Is it proper to look upon that which is impermanent, sorrowful and changeable as 'this is mine, I am this or this is my self?', and then the obvious reply comes as certainly not, Lord."

By applying the same formula with regard to the rest of the constituents, he finally shows the absurdity of the conceit of the 'I' and 'mine' and remarks: 'I'(self) and mine (anything belonging to the self), not being truly and really discovered, is it not, monks, a perfectly foolish doctrine to hold the point of view, "this is the world, this is the self ; permanent, abiding, eternal, immutable shall I be after death, in eternal identity shall

I persist?". This is, briefly speaking, the way in which Buddha tries to remove the erroneous notion of the 'I' or self.

It is important to note that the characteristic of soul-lessness (*anattā*) is unsparingly applied even to consciousness (*Vijñāna*) which in the *Upaniṣads* is considered to be an eternal and immutable element. This question of the applicability of the soullessness in relation to consciousness is very pointedly raised in the *Saṃyutta Nikāya* (IV. 166-168), and a definite positive answer is given with the illustration of the voidness of a plantain tree.

"Just as with regard to this body, it has in diverse ways been stated, explained and shown by the Exalted One that this body is non-self (*anattā*), is it possible in the same way to describe, teach, state, set forth, make plain, analyse and expound in relation to the consciusness also that "this consciousness is not-self"? (*S*.IV.166).

"-------- it is surely possible in the same way to describe — ——— that "this consciousness also is non-self" (*S*.IV.166).

"Suppose ——————— a man in need of the heart of the wood, in search of the heart of the wood, looking for the heart of the wood, should roaming about enter a forest taking a sharp axe. There he sees a mighty plantain-trunk, straight up, new grown and of towering height. He cuts it down at the root. Having cut it down at the root, he chops it off at the top. Having done so, he thoroughly peels out the skin. But he would not find there even the pith, not to speak of the heart of the wood. Even so —— a monk beholds no self or anything belonging to the self in the sixfold group of contact" (*S*.IV. 168).

Exactly the same analogy of the essenceless plantain tree is given by Buddha when he, in his discussion with Saccaka, explains to the latter the utter voidness or soul-lessness of all the five aggregates (*M*.I. 233). He calls this world as the empty world saying it is empty because it is empty of the self and empty of anything belonging to the self (*S*. IV.174-5).

It is made quite clear that this false conceit of 'I' or the self arises only on account of our vain clinging to the fivefold aggregate of personality, and, therefore, it must be completely shaken off in order to lead a really holy life and attain the state of the absolute cessation of suffering. This conceit of 'I' is considered so detrimental to the religious quest that it is singled out as the one which must be abandoned at all costs.

It is only by shaking off all conceit of 'I' in this conscious body as well as in all external objects that one becomes thoroughly free from all clinging and thereby attains unfettered salvation. The monk Kappa asks Buddha : "Pray, Lord, how should one know, how should one see, so that in this body together with the consciousness, as well as in all objects external to it, the mind has gone away from all conceit of 'I' and 'mine', gone away from egotism, gone beyond all distinctions, is calmed and wholly released?" (*S.* III. 170).

To this Buddha replies: "Whatever corporeality, Kappa, be it past, present or future ——— you behold thus: "This is not mine, this not I, this is not my self". So knowing things objectively as they are by perfect insight, one, having forsaken clinging, is free (Similarly with regard to the other four aggregates). Thus knowing, thus seeing Kappa———, the mind has gone away from all conceit of 'I' and 'mine', gone away from egotism, gone away from all distinctions, is calmed and wholly released"(*S.*III.170).

Since this conceit of 'I' is the result of attachment or lust for the five aggregates and consequent grasping of them or clinging to them, Buddha exhorts monks as follows : "Whatsoever desire, attachment, lust, craving ———there be monks, concerning corporeality, do ye abandon that. Thus will that corporeality be abandoned, cut down at the root, made like the stump of a palm tree, unable to grow in future. (Similarly with regard to other aggregates)" (*S.*III. 161-2). If in relation to corporeality one is not free from attachment, desire, love, thirst, fever and craving, there arise in him the sorrow, lamentation, grief, woe and despair(similarly in relation to other aggregates)——— but one who is free from them, in him they do not arise" (*S.*III. 107).

It is made quite clear by Buddha that the conceit of the 'I' or the self is possible only in and through the five aggregates of the personality. He clearly says : "Any ascetic or *Brahmin* who variously conceives of the self, all of them conceive the five groups of grasping or any one of them (as the self)"(*S.*III. 46). The way in which the conceit of the 'I' or self arises in its various forms is described as follows: "There is, O monks, an uninstructed worldling who has not seen the noble one, who has no knowledge of the noble doctrine, no training in the noble doctrine-he regards corporeality as the self or the self as possessing corporeality or the corporeality as being within the self, or the self as within the corporeality (Similarly with regard to the rest of the *skandhas*). Seeing in this manner he forms the notion 'I am' (*S.*III. 46).

"Just the opposite is said to be the case with regard to the 'instructed noble disciple', (*S.*III. 114, 165) who does not regard corporeality as the self or the self as possessing corporeality, or corporeality as being within the self or the self as within the corporeality (similarly with regard to the rest of the *skandhas*) and accordingly he does not grasp corporeality, does not cling to corporeality and does not hold (the view) that "this is my self". (Similarly with regard to the other four *skandhas*) (*S.*III. 115).

6. Theory of *Kamma*

As we have already studied, the whole life is the "becoming" of *Vijñāna* (consciousness) according to the Law of *Kamma.* Past ignorance, craving, clinging and *Kamma* determine the course of the existence.

"By karma revolves the world, by karma revolves mankind. Like the nail holding the rolling chariot wheel, beings are held by karma"(*Sn.*120).

"Beings, O monks, are responsible for their deeds, are heirs to deeds, having deeds for matrix, deeds for kin, deeds for refuge. Whatsoever deed they do, be it good or evil, they become its heir"(*A.V.* 288).

It is therefore proclaimed in the Dhammapada : "Neither in the sky nor in the mid-ocean, nor by entering the mountain cave can be found a place in the universe where, having stationed, one may escape one's evil deeds" (*Dh.* 127).

This theory of *karma* (*Kamma* in *Pāli*) alone can offer a satisfactory explanation of the inequality that baffles us in life.

Inequality and *Kamma*

On one occasion, a certain young man named Subha approached Buddha, and questioned why and wherefore it was that among human beings there are low and high states. (*Cullakamma Vibhanga Sutta-Majjhima Nikāya* No.135).

'For', said he, "we find amongst mankind the short-lived and the long-lived, the sickly and the healthy, the ill-looking and the good-looking, the uninfluential and the influential, the poor and the rich, the low-born and the high-born, the ignorant and the intelligent."

Buddha briefly replied : "Every living being has *Kamma* as its own, its inheritance, its cause, its kinsman, its refuge. *Kamma* is that which differentiates all living beings into low and high states."

Depending on this difference in *Kamma* appears the difference in the birth of beings, high and low, base and exalted, happy and miserable. Depending on the difference in *Kamma* appears the difference in the individual features of beings as beautiful and ugly, high-born or low-born, well-built or deformed. Depending on difference in *Kamma* appears the difference in the worldly conditions of beings as gain and loss, fame and disgrace, blame and praise, happiness and misery.

The inequalities and incongruities are facts of life and these perplex the enquiring minds. The wicked and the crooked prosper in life whereas the virtuous and pious suffer, dogged by ill-luck and misery. Why should innocent children be born blind, deaf or with infirmities ? How are we to account for these? Are they due to blind chance or accident?"

Buddha outright rejects blind chance or accident as the explanation for these inequalities and incongruities in life. According to him, nothing in the world happens by blind chance or accident. Everything is conditioned and depends on some cause or other. If blind chance or accident rules the world and the laws of cause and effect have no place in the happenings in the world, then there is no possibility of knowledge and leading a moral and holy life to achieve liberation. As such, the theory of blind chance or accident cannot provide a satisfactory answer to the problem of inequality.

It cannot also be said that the inequality is due to the fiat of an omnipotent, omnipresent and omniscient God. How can the injustice, inequality, pain, misery crime, poverty and the existence of evil be reconciled with the concepts of all-wise, all-merciful, all-good and all-powerful God?

Can it be said that the inequality and variation are due to heredity and environment? No doubt they are partly instrumental; but surely they cannot explain the subtle distinctions in the psychological, intellectual and moral capabilities we come across in the individual beings and particularly in the twins. We come across twins born of the same parents, under the same conditons of time and environment, one of whom is an angel and the other a demon, though their physical forms closely resemble each other. Likewise, the births of child prodigies, geniuses and perfected holy ones cannot be explained and accounted for by heredity alone. The case of Mahatma Gandhi and his wayward eldest son will illustrate the point regarding the inadequacy of the hereditary theory to account for these abnormalities and variations. Thus, we find that heredity and environment fail to provide convincing answers to the problems of inequality, variation and incongruity in life. These theories should be supplemented by the doctrine of *Kamma* and rebirth for an adequate explanation of these puzzling problems.

As proof of their belief in the cycles of birth, death and rebirth, the Buddhists cite the experience of Buddha himself and the supermundane (paranormal) knowledge which enabled him to perceive the past and future lives of his own and also other beings. As further proof, they cite the instances of other highly developed perfect ones like Kṛṣṇa, Mahāvīra and Christ and pose the question: "Can they be the product of a single existence ?"

Further, the anamoly we find in this world where the virtuous persons are very often unfortunate and vicious persons prosperous, is indeed a strong argument in favour of past and future lives.

We are born into the state created by ourselves. If, in spite of our virtue, we are destined to lead an unfortunate life, it is due to our own past evil *Kamma*. If, in spite of our wickedness, we are prosperous, it is also due to our good *Kamma* of the past. The present deeds will, however, have their due consequences at the earliest possible opportunity. We ourselves are responsible for our own deeds, happiness and misery. We create our own heavens or build our own hells. We are the architects of our own fate. In short, we ourselves are our own *Kamma*.

Buddhism believes that the effect of *Kamma* which gives rise to the relinking (rebirth) consciousness (*Vijñāna*) exhibits a tendency to select the appropriate germ for the *Vijñāna* to descend upon and commence a new life and work out its *Kamma*.

Buddhism does not subscribe to the belief in fatalism. It is based on the central principle of *pratītya-samutpāda* or Dependent Origination which is only akin to determinism and not fatalism. The causes determine the effects. Buddhism does not believe that only particular causes will be effective at any particular time. Different causes owing to the different earlier *Kammas* may come into play and determine the effects at any particular time. Thus, the theory leaves room for free will to assert and select an appropriate good deed or abstain from a bad deed and to organize the way of life most conducive for the attainment of *Nibbāna* .

What is *Kamma*?

Kamma-literally means 'action'. But in Buddhism it is invested with deeper meaning and stands for good or bad volition.

Buddha says: "I declare, O Bhikkhus, that Volition is *Kamma*. Having willed, one acts by body, speech and thought."

Volition is conscious choice, intention and decision. There is no *Kamma* where there is no consciousness and no intention. Any action which is unintentional is not a *Kamma* for *Kamma* depends on the will or volition that is involved in the doing. Thus, mind is the most important factor in the working of *Kamma*. All our actions, words and thoughts are coloured by the mind or consciousness we experience at such particular moments.

"When the mind is unguarded, bodily action is unguarded, speech also is unguarded, thought also is unguarded. When the mind is guarded, bodily action is guarded, speech also is guarded and thought also is guarded."

> "Our life is shaped by our mind; We become what we think.
> If one speaks or acts with an evil mind, pain follows one as the wheel (follows) the hoof of the ox.
> If one speaks or acts with a good mind, happiness follows one as the shadow that never departs."
> (*Dh.* 1 & 2)

Just as every being is accompanied by his/her shadow, every volitional activity (*Kamma*) is accompanied by its due effect (*vipāka*) which arises quite automatically without the intervention of any external agency, determined solely by the moral or immoral nature of the *Kamma*. Volition is action and *vipāka* is its fruit, its reaction according to the Law of *Kamma*.

According to *Abhidhamma*, *Kamma* is classified as below:-

- Ten types of immoral consciousness (Evil *Kamma*)
- Twelve types of moral consciousness (Good *Kamma*) which pertain to the Sentient Realm
- Five types of moral consciousness (Good *Kamma*) which may ripen in the Realms of Form
- Four types of moral consciousness (Good *Kamma*) which may ripen in the Formless Realms.

The volitional activities of the supermundane consciousness are not regarded as *Kamma* since they tend to eradicate passions that condition rebirth and since they do not cause rebirth. In the supermundane consciousness, wisdom (*Pañña*) is predominant, whilst in the ordinary types of consciousness volition is predominant.

Evil *Kamma* (Immoral Consciousness)

There are ten evil *Kammas* which are caused by deed, word and thought.

Three are caused by deed:

- Killing
- Stealing
- Unchastity(sexual misconduct)

Four are caused by word

- Lying
- Slandering
- Harsh speech
- Frivolous talk

Three are caused by thought:

- Covetousness
- Ill-will
- False view

Killing is the most heinous crime. Destruction of any living being including the animals is the most condemned evil *Kamma*. Plant life is excluded from the concept of killing because there is no transmission of stimuli or sensation of pain through nerves in the plants and no blood-letting.

Gravity of the crime of killing depends on the goodness and the size of the being killed. In the case of killing of a virtuous person or a big animal, it is more heinous than killing in the case of vicious person or a small animal. Nevertheless all killings are condemned because they entail suffering.

Beings are said to be in miserable states on account of their evil *Kamma*. The following four miserable states or the worlds of "becoming" (rebirth) according to the *Kamma* have been described in Buddhism :

The woeful world of hell
The animal world
The world of *petas* or ghosts
The world of demons (*asuras*)

Metaphorically, these stand for the lower levels of existence we normally wallow in. The first is the miserable hellish existence dominated by pains and destruction. The second is the animal-like existence where we are driven by amoral instincts and impulses. Here self-preservation and self-aggrandizement prevail with no consideration for others. The third is the existence or state characterized by insatiable hunger and craving (*Taṇhā*) for food, wealth, enjoyable things, sex, power, success and so on. This is the existence dominated by greed and hunger, like *petas* and ghosts. We also pass through the fourth world of *asuras* with our hatred, anger, violence, pride and envy.

Good *Kamma* (Moral consciousness)

Good *Kammas* arising out of moral consciousness are classified into three categories as below:-

- Good *Kamma* which may ripen in rebirth in the realm of sentient existence i.e. the realm of human beings and higher perfected beings. (*Kāmaloka*)
- Good *Kamma* which may ripen in the Realms of Form. (*rūpaloka*)
- Good *Kamma* which may ripen in the Formless Realms. (*arūpaloka*)

Good *Kammas* entail rebirths ini *Kāmaloka, rūpaloka* and *arūpaloka* depending on their moral natures. *Kāmaloka* includes the realm of human beings and also the six celestial realms. The meditational and spiritual practices are understood to lead to the heavenly *rūpaloka* and *arūpaloka* depending upon their degrees of purity and progressive levels of attainment (Figure 17).

Good *Kamma* which will Ripen in Rebirth as Sentient Beings in Kāmaloka

The twelve moral actions which will result in rebirth in sentient existence as human beings and perfected beings are the following:

Generosity	Morality
Meditation	Reverence
Service	Transference of merit
Rejoicing in other's merit	Praising other's good works
Hearing *dhamma* and expounding *dhamma*	Taking the Three Refuges
Mindfulness	

		GOOD KAMMA / MEDITATION	WORLD OF BECOMING
IV		CESSATION OF BECOMING (NIRODHA - SAMĀPATTI)	ARAHANTS
III	ARŪPA SAMĀPATTI	NEITHER PERCEPTION NOR NON-PERCEPTION NOTHINGNESS (ŚŪNYA) INFINITE CONSCIOUSNESS INFINITE SPACE	HEVEN WITHOUT FORM (ARŪPA LOKA) FOUR LEVELS
II	RŪPA SAMĀPATTI	FOURTH ECSTASY (JHĀNA) THIRD ECSTASY (JHĀNA) SECOND ECSTASY (JHĀNA) FIRST ECSTASY (JHĀNA)	HEAVEN WITH FORM (RŪPA LOKA) SIXTEEN LEVELS
I		GOOD KAMMAS	WORLD OF SENTIENT BEINGS (KĀMA LOKA) HUMAN/CELESTIAL (SIX LEVELS)

Fig. 17 Worlds Attainable by Good Kamma

The realm of human beings involves both happiness and sorrow. It provides opportunities for the human beings to improve and perfect their virtues and attain higher states of existence.

The *Kāmaloka* includes the six celestial realms also which are the abodes of gods or *devas*. The gods are superior classes of beings higher than the human beings in the hierarchy of existences. Like human beings they are also subject to birth and death and are not eternal even though they are more evolved and possess some higher powers.

Good *Kamma* That May Ripen in the Realms of Form *(Rūpaloka)*

The attainments of the four *jhānas* (i.e. meditative absorptions or ecstasies) in this life may lead to rebirths in the Realms of Form (*rūpaloka*) as gods or *Brahmas* (Higher Beings)

Four classes of Brahmās are talked of in *Theravāda* Buddhism corresponding to the four *jhānas.* Brahmās within the form realm are said to have only two senses-sight and hearing.

Good *Kamma* that May Ripen in the Formless Realms *(Arūpaloka)*

Formless meditative attainments *(arūpa-jhānas)* in this life may lead to rebirths as Brahmās (Higher Beings) in the Formless Realms.

The Brahmās of the formless realm are of four types, corresponding to the hierarchy of the four formless meditative attainments (*samāpatti*): (i) infinite space; (ii) infinite consciousness; (iii) nothingness, and (iv) neither perception nor non-perception. This last is also referred to as the 'peak of existence'. Brahmās within the formless realm have just consciousness ; and so long as they are in that rebirth and have not attained enlightenment, they presumably enjoy uninterruptedly the appropriate meditative ecstacy.

Heavenly births in *Brahmā* realms are here said to be attained by good *Kamma.* This stands in stark contrast to the Vedic religion which maintains that heavenly rewards are assured by sacrificial rituals.

Nirvāṇa transcends all these heavenly realms which are considered part of *saṃsāra.* It is not located at any particular place ; but it is simply not *saṃsāra.* Buddhist tradition holds that it is not necessary to pass through all the realms and planes to attain *Nirvāṇa. Nirvāṇa* can be attained only from the human realm or a god realm above the human. Fourth *jhāna* is said to be the springboard for one to attain *Nirvāṇa.* Once this *jhāna* is consummated, there is no more return to the lower realms of *saṃsāra.*

Who does *Kamma* and Who Reaps the Fruits?

If there is not any permanent entity or soul underlying this aggregate of corporeality (form), sensation, perception, volition and consciousness, then who is the doer of *Kamma*? Who reaps the fruit of *Kamma*?

> Says the Venerable *Buddhaghoṣa* in the Visuddhi Magga:-
> "No doer is there who does the deed
> Nor is there one who reaps the fruit ;
> Constituent parts alone roll on."

Volition or will is itself the doer. The resultant consciousness that arises as its *vipāka* with the feeling of misery or happiness is itself the reaper of the fruits of *Kamma.* Volition is the sower and the feeling is the reaper. *Kamma* arises from the flow of the five skandas (corporeality, sensation, perception, volition and consciousness) depending on causes and conditions.

"Where, Reverend Sir, is *Kamma* ?" questions King Milinda, addressing the Venerable *Nāgasena.*

"O *Mahārāja*", says the Venerable *Nāgasena,* "*Kamma* is not said to be stored somewhere in this fleeting consciousness or in any other part of the body. But dependent on mind and matter, it rests manifesting itself at the opportune moment, just as mangoes are not said to be stored in the mango tree, but dependent on the mango tree, they lie springing up in due season."

Just as wind or fire is not stored in any particular place, even so volition or *Kamma* force is not stored anywhere within or without this body. *Kamma* is the packet of will energy that flows from one existence to another, continuously changing and getting modified by reaction influence (*vipāka*).

Free-Will

In spite of its emphasis on the theory of Dependent Origination and the deterministic nature of its philosophy, Buddhism recognizes free will and lays stress on one's own effort to lead a religious and holy life and achieve emancipation.

Although it is stated that neither in heaven, nor in the recesses of a cave, there is any place in the world hiding where one could escape evil *Kamma*, yet one is not bound to pay all the past arrears of one's *Kamma*. In such case no escape is possible. One can do good *Kamma* which may become a counteractive *Kamma* or destructive *Kamma* to offset the force of an earlier evil *Kamma*. One is neither the master nor the slave of the *Kamma*. Even a most vicious person can by his own efforts become the most virtuous person. We are always 'becoming' something and that something depends on our own actions. We may at any moment change for the better or for the worse.

Buddha is not categorical that a man must reap according to his deeds; in that case, there is no religious life nor is an opportunity afforded for the entire extinction of sorrow (*duḥkha*). He only says that what a man reaps is according to his deeds, in which case, there is religious life and an opportunity is afforded for correcting the mis-deeds and changing one for the better.

Even the most sinful person should not be discouraged or despised on account of his evil nature. We must have compassion on him for we must have also been in that same position at a certain stage. As we have changed for the better he may also change perhaps sooner than ourselves. Who can say what good *Kamma* he has in store for him? Who knows his potential goodness? Buddhism teaches that every one has the potential to become a Buddha.

This doctrine of *Kamma* opens up the possibilities of consolation, hope, self-reliance and moral courage to mankind. A Buddhist faces the misfortunes, sufferings and sorrows with a strength of mind and fortitude. He consoles himself with the thought that they are the results of his own doings. He knows that he reaps what he only has sown. But he also knows at the same time that he can alter the destiny by sowing good deeds. The future is entirely in his hands. *Kamma* enables him to shape his future as he wills.

The law of *Kamma* explains the problem of suffering, the mystery of the so-called fate and above all the inequality of mankind.

When the wicked are found successful in life, while the virtuous meet with ill-luck and are thrown to the lot of a miserable life, a Buddhist would neither accuse any one of injustice nor blame the world for its unjust ways, since he knows that they are only reaping what they have sown earlier. The virtuous are thereby not discouraged because they are convinced that their good acts will have their due effects in some future life though not in the present.

We ourselves are responsible for our happiness and misery. We are the architects of our own fate. We are our own destroyers. We build our own heavens. We build our own hells.

Says the Buddha:

"Man's merits and the sins he here hath wrought.
That is the thing he owns, that takes he hence,
That dogs his steps, like shadows in pursuit
Hence let him make good store for life elsewhere
Sure platform in some other future world,
Rewards of virtue on good beings wait."

(Kindred Sayings - Vol I, Page 98)

Process of Rebirth

The process of rebirth described in Buddhism differs from the traditional description of transmigration of soul in the *Upaniṣads* and *Saṃkhya* since it rejects the concept of a permanent and abiding self in man. The *Bṛhad-āraṇyaka* talks about the permanent unchanging Self within transmigrating to a new body in association with the five subtle elements, the senses, the mind and the intellect and also accompanied by the vital breaths and the impressions of the meritorious and demeritorious actions (*B.U.* IV. 4.5). Here the eternal Self transmigrates with the subtle body modified according to the *karmic* formations. But, Buddha, having rejected the concept of a permanent and changeless self in man, explains the process of rebirth differently.

The life is the 'becoming' or 'evolving' of *Vijñāna* (consciousness) only, propelled by the *Kammic* energy. As we have already seen in our study of the Wheel of Life, the consciousness is always in a state of flux and constantly changing depending upon its *Kamma* and the retributive energy that shapes it further. Each unit of consciousness perishes giving birth to another and while perishing gives up its whole energy or all the imprints it received, to its successor. Each successive consciousness therefore consists of the potentialities of all its predecessors and something more. Each unit of consciousness is a packet of energy which is constantly changing according to the Law of *Kamma*. At death, with the disintegration of the body, the final consciousness becomes the Relinking (Rebirth) Consciousness which driven by the Kammic energy finds an appropriate sperm and ovum cell combination for it to work out its future life. The Relinking Consciousness then becomes the sub-conscious state to sprout into new body-mind complex. This has all the *karmic* formations of the earlier stream.

The Relinking Consciousness, the last state of the consciousness of the dying creature with its Kammic residue, the Buddha calls '*gandhabba*'. This is said to vitalize the combination of the sperm and ovum of the parents and give rise to a new existence. Thus, accounting for the event of rebirth, Buddha says: "Where, monks, three are found in combination, there a seed of life is planted. Thus, if a father and mother come together, but it is not the mother's period and the being to be born (*gandhabba*) is not present, then no seed of life is planted. Or, if a father and mother come together and it is the mother's period, but the being to be born (*gandhabba*) is not present, then again no seed of life is planted. But, when, monks, a father and mother come together and it is the mother's period and the being to be born (*gandhabba*) is also present, then by the combined agency of these three, a seed of life is planted" (*M.I.* 265 - 6).

Scholars differ in their interpretation of the term '*gandhabba*'. Some scholars tend to read into it the affirmation of the traditional concept of the subtle-body. Mrs. Rhys Davids, the renowned Buddhist scholar, sees in this theory of *gandhabba* the advent of the soul, self of man, encased in the invisible subtle-body. Buddha has accepted the concept of self for conventional purposes, but has totally rejected the idea of self remaining changeless. No eternal, immutable entity called self or *Ātman* is recognized by him. He subscribes neither to the eternalistic view of a permanent and changeless Self nor to nihilism. He recognizes only a flux or stream of consciousness as is clear from *Majjhima Nikāya* (II.262) which calls *Vijñāna* as '*saṃvattanika Vijñāna*' i.e. the consciousness that evolves into the next world. Therefore, it would only be appropriate to identify '*gandhabba*' with the Relinking Consciousness that is part of the flowing stream of continually evolving, continually changing consciousness, as has been interpreted by the southern school of Ceylon Buddhists. In this view, the Relinking Consciousness is the seed consciousness which is pregnant with the potentialities of the Kammic energies of all the preceding units of consciousness.

(*Early Buddhism and the Bhagavadgītā* by K.N. Upadhyaya, p.373-375)

Thus, this stream of consciousness flows on ad infinitum. At death the consciousness perishes only to give birth to another in a subsequent birth. This renewed consciousness inherits all the past experiences.

"This new being which is the present manifestation of the stream of *Kamma*-energy is not the same as, and has no identity with, the previous one in its line, the aggregate that makes up its composition being different from, and having no identity with those that make up the being of its predecessor. And yet it is not an entirely different being, since it has the same stream of *Kamma*-energy, though modified perchance just by having shown itself in that last manifestation which is now making its presence known in the sense perceptible world as the new being"(*Śīlācāra*).

It may be noted that, whereas the relinking consciousness here is propelled by the Kammic force into a sperm-ovum combination, in the *Upaniṣadic* view the indwelling Self draws itself to another body accompanied by the modified subtle body (*B.U.* IV. 4.3)

The question arises : Is Buddha's theory of *Anattā* (soullessness or selflessness) then a nihilistic doctrine?

Buddha has always maintained that the truth can be discovered by avoiding the extremes and adopting the middle path *(Majjhimā-Paṭipadā)*. In his time, there were the two extreme views-the view of eternalists that the soul exists for ever and the contrary view of the annihilationists that nothing exists. Buddha avoided both these metaphysical extremes by preaching the doctrine of universal change and perpetual flux. Buddha clearly dissociated himself from both the extreme views.

When the wanderer Vacchagotta pointedly asks Buddha whether the self is or the self is not, Buddha refrains from answering and remains silent. After the wanderer's departure when Ānanda asks Buddha about the reason for his silence, he says that in case of his affirming the former, Vacchagotta would have taken him to mean that he accepted the view of eternalists and in case of his affirming the latter, Vacchagotta would have confused it with annihilationism (*S.*IV.400).

" Whoever maintains the view that the soul is identical with the body, holds that with the destruction of the soul, the body is destroyed and with the destruction of the body, the soul is destroyed. The view of him who holds thus is known as annihilationism on account of holding that the being is destroyed.

------. In the second instance, whoever maintains the view that the soul is different from the body, holds that the body is destroyed here itself but the soul passes off at will like a bird out of the cage. The view of him who holds thus is known as eternalism on account of holding the view that the soul has passed from this world to another" (S.II. 63).

Buddha has avoided both the extreme views by adopting the theory of universal change and perpetual flux. It is an ever-changing flow following the laws of dependent origination i.e. depending on causes and conditions.

What is it that is Reborn?

If there is not any permanent soul or self that transmigrates, and starts a new life, then what is it that is reborn?

This question is asked by King Milinda in *Milinda Pañha* :

"Venerable *Nāgasena*, what is it that is born into the next existence?."

"O King, it is mind and body that is born into the next existence."

"Is it the same mind and body that is born into the next existence?"

"O King, it is not the same mind and body that is born into the next existence; but with this mind and body, O King, one does a deed – it may be good or it may be evil. By reason of this deed, another mind and body is born into the next existence."

The new body and mind sprout from the Relinking Consciousness. Both body and mind are manifestations of energy as the modern scientific theories prove conclusively. Modern scientists now define matter only in terms of waves lacking fixed boundaries and changing continually.Buddha has foretold this truth some 2600 years ago. Buddha has declared that the *paramāṇu* of matter considered indivisible is nothing but a manifestation of particular inter-related forces and qualities which he called *paramatthas* i.e. essentials of matter. These paramatthas are :

Pṛthvī - Element of extension or occupation of space.

Āpo - Element of cohesion which binds the scattered atoms of matter.

Tejo - Element of heat and cold which have the. power of maturing bodies or the vitalizing energy.

Vāyo Element of motion

Heat and motion in the material realm correspond respectively to consciousness and *Kamma* in the mental.

The four elements are the fundamental units of matter and are invariably combined with the four derivatives – namely, colour (*vaṇṇa*), taste (*rasa*), nutritiive essence (*oja*) and odour (*gandha*). The four elements and the derivatives are inseparable and interrelated, but one element may preponderate over another, as for instance, the element of extension preponderates in earth, cohesion in water, heat in fire and motion in air.

Thus, matter is composed of these forces and qualities which are in a state of constant flux. This is the first aggregate of corporeality or form (*rūpa*), the first constituent of the personality of human being.

Buddha considers mind as a complex compound of fleeting mental states. Fifty-two such mental states are recognized. Sensation is one and perception another. The remaining fifty mental states are collectively called volitions (*Saṅkhāras*). These immaterial states have corresponding consciousnesses. Thus, the personality of the human being consists of an aggregate of sensations, an aggregate of perceptions, an aggregate of volitions and an aggregate of consciousnesses in addition to the aggregate of corporeality or form. What we call self of the human being is nothing but a conglomerate of these five aggregates brought together and functioning together according to causes and conditions. This functioning together as a flow of life is basically 'becoming' or evolving of consciousness (*Vijñāna*) according to the Law of *Kamma*, as we have already seen.

The flow of life is thus because of the ever-changing nature and 'becoming' of the consciousness. Each unit of consciousness consists of three phases – genesis, development and dissolution. One unit of consciousness perishes only to give birth to another. The subsequent thought-unit is neither absolutely the same as its predecessor – since its composition is not identical – nor entirely another, being the same continuity of *Kamma* energy.

Consciousness constantly flows on like a river. No state once gone ever recurs; nor is it absolutely identical with what goes before. These states constantly change not remaining for two consecutive moments the same. This is the theory of momentariness, also called the theory of flux or ceaseless flux

(*Santanavāda*). It is applicable to mind and matter alike for both are momentary. Two classical similes are normally cited to illustrate the doctrine of universal momentariness : that of the stream of river and that of a flame of a lamp. This theory of momentariness has been most pithily expressed by Heraclitus in the following words : "You cannot bathe twice in the same river."

There is no unchanging consciousness but only a continuous flow of mental thoughts. The apparent continuity of flow is mistaken for an unchanging consciousness, soul or *Ātmā.*

"The so-called being is like a flash of lightning that is resolved into a succession of sparks that follow upon one another with such rapidity that the human retina cannot perceive them separately, nor can the uninstructed conceive of such succession of separate sparks" (Dhalke) (The Buddha-Dhamma by Nārada Thera, p. 222).

Buddhism does not totally deny the existence of a personality in an empirical sense for conventional practical purposes. It only denies the personality in the ultimate sense because of its transient and ever-changing nature. The Kammic force of each individual binds the psycho-physical elements together. "This uninterrupted flux or continuity of psycho-physical phenomenon, which is conditioned by *Kamma* and not limited only to the present life, but having its source in the beginnignless past and its continuation in the future – is the Buddhist substitute for the immortal soul or Self in the *Upaniṣadic* philosophy"(The Buddha-Dhamma by Nārada Thera, p. 223).

Moral Resonsibility

Strictly speaking, the term 'rebirth' is not applicable in Buddhist philosophy since there is no permanent being-the same one which is taking birth again. Buddhism recognizes only a series of births of psycho-physical phenomena flowing in succession just like a river with intermittent breaks of so-called death and the series extend on and on until wisdom dawns resulting in salvation or *Nibbāna.* Technically speaking, it is another being that takes birth after death of an individual and not the same individual in the Buddhist account.

Is it one who does the act in this birth and another who reaps its results in the other birth? Then, this is not fair retribution as Kutadanta exclaims in his conversation with Buddha. The momentary consciousness which performs an action vanishes without reaping its fruit and another momentary consciousness reaps the fruit of an action it never performed. This is open to the criticism that this undermines the ethical theory of *Kamma* and moral responsibility.

Buddhists answer these charges stating that the one who reaps is neither absolutely the same as nor absolutely different from, the one who sows. In the Visuddhi Magga, the Venerable *Buddhaghoṣa* emphasizes the point that the successor is neither the same nor different from the predecessor. It is a continuous process of becoming. The preceding link in the chain does not perish before transmitting its content to the succeeding link and so the continuity is never broken. The successor bears all the burden of the predecessor. The Law of *Kamma*, being an impersonal force, makes action possible without an agent and transmigration without a transmigrating soul.

To illustrate their theory of continuous process and becoming, Buddhists quote the two analogies of butterfly and flame of a lamp.

The butterfly was first an egg and then it became a caterpillar. Later it developed ito a chrysalis and finally evolved into a butterfly. This process occurs in the course of one life-time. The butterfly is neither the same as, nor totally different from, the caterpillar. Here also there is a flux of life or a continuity of process of becoming.

Similarly, in the case of a lamp, the flame of the first watch of the night is not identical with that of the last watch, but continues burning. In the same way, there is a continuity of life-each succeeding state depending upon the preceding one.

Buddhists maintain that there is nothing permanent, there is no soul, but there is moral responsibility because there is a continuity. Identity is set aside and is substituted by a continuity.

A child, for instance, becomes a man; yet the latter is neither absolutely the same as the former nor totally different, since the cells that formed his body in manhood have undergone a complete change. This constant change applies not only to body but also to mind. In the latter, the change is more marked. Nevertheless, the individual as a man is responsible for whatever he did in his childhood. The most important point here is the continuity and not the identity.

The Venerable Nāgasena illustrates the point by another analogy in his dialogue with King Milinda.

"O King, it is as if a man were to take away another man's mangoes, and the owner of the mangoes were to seize him, and show him to the king and say, "Sire, this man hath taken away my mangoes" and the other were to say, "Sire, I did not take away this man's mangoes. The mangoes which this man planted were different from those which I took away. I am not liable for punishment". Pray, O King, would the man be liable for punishment?"

"Assuredly, Venerable Sir, would he be liable for punishment."

"For what reason?"

"Because, in spite of what he might say, he would be liable for punishment for the reason that the last mangoes derived from the first mangoes."

"In exactly the same way, O King, with this mind and body one does a deed-it may be good or it may be bad-and by reason of this deed another mind and body is born into the next existence. Therefore is one not freed from one's evil deeds" (*Buddhism* in Translations by Warren, p. 234/235).

The above proves that, for moral responsibility, identity is not considered necessary.

In the case of next birth after death of the physical vehicle in the previous one, there is no memory. The successor does not remember his actions in the previous birth, but he will suffer for his evil deeds. Buddhism maintains that memory is also not essential in assessing moral responsibility.

If, for instance, a person were to commit a crime and by sudden loss of memory he were to forget the incident, would he not be responsible for his act? His forgetfulness would surely be immaterial for the operation of the laws of the country.

In the same manner, the consideration of loss of memory in the successive birth is immaterial for the operation of the law of *Kamma.* When a man suffers in this birth for his evil deeds in the previous one of which he is unaware, it is not as if he is being punished for his evil deeds. Whatever pain or happiness we experience is the inevitable consequence of a past act. There are no considerations of rewards and punishments in Buddhism. Buddhists talk only in terms of cause and effect.

"The fact that a person does not remember his evil deeds in the past birth is no hindrance for the impersonal and inevitable operation of the Kammic law. It is this knowledge of the inevitability of the consequences of *Kamma* in the course of one's life in *saṃsāra* that shows the holy path and shapes the life and conduct of a Buddhist" (*The Buddha-Dhamma* by Nārada Thera, p. 227).

Kammic Descent and Kammic Ascent

Buddhists believe that there is possibility of Kammic descent as well as Kammic ascent.

In the course of our wanderings in *saṃsāra*, we gather various experiences, do different deeds, receive manifold impressions, acquire diverse characteristics. The different natures we thus acquire lie dormant within us and the unspent natures may at unexpected moments, rise to the surface, "in disconcerting strength", and reveal our latent Kammic tendencies.

One's past, however, is not always a true index to one's future. For we are creating fresh *Kamma* every moment. In one sense, we are truly what we were, and we will be what we are. But in another sense, we are not what we were, and we will not be what we are. Who was a criminal yesterday may become a saint to-day; who is to-day a holy man may turn out to be a wretched sinner tomorrow.

Now we sow the seeds of our future and create our own hell or our own heaven. This present thought-moment conditions our second thought-moment. The subsequent birth, too, according to Buddhist philosophy, is determined by the last thought-moment we experience in this life. Just as in the course of one's life, one thought-moment perishes giving up all its potentialities to its successor, even so the last thought-moment of this life perishes giving up all the acquired characteristics and natures to the succeeding moment in the subsequent birth.

Now, if the dying person cherishes a base desire or idea or experiences a thought or does an act which befits only an animal, his evil *Kamma* will condition him a birth in animal form. The Kammic force which manifested itself in the form of a man will then manifest itself in the form of an animal. It must not be misunderstood by this that all his past good Kammic tendencies are lost. They also lie in a dormant state seeking an opportunity to rise to the surface. It is such a good *Kamma* that will later effect a birth as a human being.

Just as there is the possibility for a Kammic descent for one bound in the so-called evolutionary scale of beings, so also there is the possibility for the contrary, a Kammic ascent.

7. Nibbāna

The ultimate goal of the holy life according to Buddhism is the attainment of salvation or the Eternal Peace of *Nibbāna.* Buddha clearly states : "The purpose of this holy life does not consist in acquiring alms, honour and fame, nor in attaining virtue, concentration or the knowledge and insight. That unshakable deliverance of the heart-that, indeed, monk, is the object of the holy life, that is its essence, that is its goal"(*M.*I. 197).

Reflecting on the positive and negative aspects of life, Buddha concludes that there must exist a sorrowless and birthless *Nibbāna* which is opposed to a sorrowful and changing *saṃsāra* .

"Even as, although misery is,
Yet happiness is also found ;
So, though indeed existence is,
A non-existence should be sought.

"Even as, although there may be heat,
Yet grateful cold is also found
So, though the three-fold fire exists,
Likewise *Nirvāṇa* should be sought

"Even as, although there evil is,
That which is good is also found ;
So, though it is true that birth exists,
That which is not-birth should be sought."

(Warren, Buddhism in Translations, p.6)

Eradication of Craving is *Nibbāna*

The *Pāli* word *Nibbāna* (*Nirvāṇa* in Sanskrit) is composed of '*Ni*' and '*Vana*'. '*Ni*' implies 'negation' or 'extinction' and '*vana*' means 'weaving' or 'craving'. Thus, etymologically, *Nirvāṇa* means negation or extinction of craving which acts as a cord connecting one life with another.

As long as one is bound up by craving, one accumulates fresh *Kammic* forces which must materialise in one form or other in the eternal cycle of birth and death. When all forms of craving are extirpated, *Kammic* forces cease to operate, and one attains *Nibbāna,* escaping the cycle of birth and death.

The Buddhist conception of *Nibbāna* is this escape from the ever-recurring cycle of life and death with the extinction of the fire of craving. Thus it is said : "It is the eradication of craving which is known as *Nibbāna*" (*S.*I. 39).

"By destroying craving with root, one being free from hunger attains the perfect *Nibbāna*" (*S.*III.26).

"It is due to desire that man is bound and it is by surmounting (the self-same) desire that he is liberated" (*S.*I. 40).

It is this extinction of suffering which is taught by Buddha in the third Noble Truth as follows:- "What, monks, is the Noble Truth of extinction of suffering? It is the complete fading away and extinction of this craving, its forsaking and abandonment, freedom and emancipation from it" (*D.*II. 310).

Nibbāna is the Destruction of Attachment, Hatred and Delusion

It is this desire or craving which manifests itself in three forms viz. lust or attachment, hatred and delusion. According to Buddhism, from feeling results the craving. Now this feeling is said to be of three kinds-pleasant, unpleasant and neither pleasant nor unpleasant-which respectively tend to produce attachment, hatred and delusion. It is said: "To the pleasant feeling, the inclination to attachment adheres, to the unpleasant one, the inclination to hatred, and to the feeling neither pleasant nor unpleasant, the inclination to delusion" (*M.*I. 303). At times, *Nibbāna* is described as the destruction of this tripartite division of craving. "*Nibbāna,* they say, friend *Śāriputra,* what now means *Nibbāna,* friend?" (*S.*IV.251, 261). "That which is the destruction of attachment, friend, the destruction of hatred, the destruction of delusion, that is called *Nibbāna.*"

Nibbāna is the Destruction of the Conceit of 'I'-ness

Yet another way of describing *Nibbāna* is as the destruction of the conceit of 'I'-ness. The root cause of all our craving and consequent suffering is ignorance. This ignorance consists in the lack of proper knowledge about the five aggregates and the consequent clinging to them which gives rise to the conceit of 'I'-ness. With the rise of proper knowledge about self and about the impermanent, sorrowful and soulless nature of the five aggregates constituting the self and with insight into things as they are, clinging to them is destroyed, conceit of 'I'-ness is destroyed and ignorance is destroyed.

"Whatever corporeality, be it past, present or future, ——— you should behold thus, "this is not mine, this not I, this not my self." So seeing things as they are, through proper insight, one being free from clinging is thoroughly released (Similarly with regard to the other aggregates)" (S.III. 170).

Is it A State of Nothingness or Annihilation

Thus, *Nibbāna* is variously described as the destruction of craving, destruction of attachment, destruction of hatred, destruction of delusion and destructionof the conceit of 'I'-ness. All these are only negative descriptions. These do not answer the basic questions that arise: (1) "What then are we when freed from these defilements, hindrances and limitations?" (2) "If corporeality, sensations, perceptions, volitions, consciousness-if any of these or any combination of these is not mine, is not I, is not my self, then what am I? Am I a nothing or something other than these?"

In the absence of clearly spelt-out answers on these and considering such explicit statements of Buddha that "it is all empty, void or non-self" (*S.*IV.174-5), some traditions and some scholars tend to treat *Nibbāna* as a state of nothingness or utter annihilation.

The analogy of the extinction of fire most frequently used to describe *Nibbāna* and the idea of being 'blown off' arising out of another etymological derivation of the term *Nibbāna* lend credence to this nihilistic interpretation.

The passage of the *Sutta-nipāta* reads as follows:- "Just as the flame of a lamp struck by a gust of wind disappears and cannot be traced, so also does a perfect saint freed from name and form disappear without leaving any trace" (*Sn.* 195). *Nirvāṇa* in *Hīnayāna* school of Buddhism is described using this metaphor of "blown out lamp". The ideal saint iin this school is the Arahant who has simply "blown" himself out of existence by annihilating all cravings and clingings.

But, the other more commonly used metaphor is that of extinguishing of the fire by the exhaustion of the fuel and being not fed with fresh fuel. Thus, Buddha himself explains the state of *Nibbāna* as follows :-"The fire which blazed on account of the fuel of grass and wood comes to be reckoned as 'gone out' (*nibbuto*), since it had consumed the fuel and was not fed with more fuel, so also the *Tathāgata* . . . . . .being freed from the marks of corporeality,. . . . . . feeling. . . . . . perception. . . . . volition and consciousness becomes deep, incomprehensible and unfathomable" (*M.*II. 487-8). It is this metaphor which largely governs the early Buddhist concept of *Nibbāna.*

But, it may be seen that the meaning conveyed by both the metaphors is very much the same, i.e. the going out of a lamp or fire, the fire of craving. The world is said to be in flames and it is the fuel of craving which keeps it ablaze (S.II. 85-87).

So the *Nibbāna* consists in the extinguishing of the fire of craving, the fire of lust, hatred and delusion, and the fire of the conceit 'I'-ness. It is a state where all these fires are "blown out". When these fires are extinguished, what is it that remains? Is it a state of mere extinction of these fires and utter annihilation as the *Hīnayānists* interpret or is there any positive entity in the state of *Nibbāna* ?.

Positive Epithets of *Nibbāna*

It is true that, in *Pāli* Canon, *Nibbāna* has been described mostly in negative terms. Some positive expressions have also been used in *Pāli* Canon as below:

"This is the *Nibbāna*, the uncompounded, the ultimate, free from defilements, the truth, the further shore, the subtle, very difficult to see, the unfading, the stable, the undecaying, the ineffable, the undifferentiated, the peaceful, the deathless, the excellent, the good, the security, the destruction of craving, the wonderful, the marvellous, free from ill, the harmless, the passionless, the purity, the release, the non-attachment, the island, the cave, the protection, the refuge and the goal, which the well-accomplished One has taught"(*Saṃyutta Nikāya* S.IV. 373).

Nibbāna is essentially supra-mundane and is considered inexplicable in terms of logic (*D*.I. 12). It is said to be an object of direct reaiisation and verification by the wise (*M*.I. 37).

The fact that *Nibbāna* has been taught as an object to be realized, that is, as one of the *Vatthu dhammas*, is adduced by some of the scholars to prove that it is not a state of nothingness (*śūnya*), even though in some passages, while speaking of the different modes of existence, Buddha talks of the 'Realm of Nothingness'. These scholars contend that, if *Nibbāna* is a state of Nothingness, Buddha would not have described it in such glowing epithets as Supreme, Highest, Refuge, Safety, Indestructible etc.

The above descriptions of *Nibbāna* and the positive epithets used in *Saṃyutta Nikāya* for *Nibbāna* have led many scholars, who energetically denounce the annihilationist view of *Nibbāna*, to go to the other extreme and give an eternalistic interpretation to it. George Grimm observes that "after having freed himself from every kind of sensation, he (i.e. the liberated saint) has not become nothing........but he has remained what he is from all eternity" (The Doctrine of the Buddha, p. 251). Radhakrishnan also pronounces the same view. He says: "*Nirvāṇa* is not a lapse into a void but only a negation of the flux and a positive return of the self to itself" (*Indian Philosophy*. Vol. I. p. 386).

But, both these extreme interpretations are contrary to the declared position of Buddha who proclaims the middle path avoiding both the extremes. Buddha has said: "This world, Kaccana, usually leans upon a duality : upon(the belief in) existence or non-existence————Avoiding these two extremes, the *Tathāgata* shows the doctrine in the middle." (*S*.II. 17)

Both the positive and negative descriptions of *Nibbāna* only seem to suggest the indescribable, the incomprehensible and the uncharacterisable nature of *Nibbāna*. In his very first utterance after the attainment of his unshakable salvation, Buddha speaks of his attainment as "profound, difficult to see, difficult to comprehend, tranquil, subtle, beyond reason, excellent and realisable by the wise"(*M*.I. 167).

Nibbāna is Unborn and Unoriginated

As a dialectical proposition, it is true that *Nibbāna* is conceived as an antithesis to Existence, that is, as Non-existence. It becomes Non-birth as an antithesis to Birth.

In the *Udana* and *Itivuttaka,* Buddha refers to *Nibbāna* as follows:-

"There is, O bhikkhus, an unborn, unoriginated, not-made and non-conditioned. If, O bhikkhus, there were not this unborn, unoriginated, unmade and non-conditioned, an escape to the born, originated, made and conditioned would not be possible here. As there is, O bhikkhus, an unborn, unoriginated, unmade and unconditioned, an escape to the born, originated, made and conditioned is possible."

Nibbāna is here described as not-conditioned by any cause and as birthless, decayless and deathless. It is neither a cause nor an effect. It passes beyond the laws of cause and effect. *Nibbāna,* being non-conditioned and having not arisen from a cause, is, in contradistinction to phenomenal existence, eternal, desirable and happy.

Says the Itivuttaka:

"The born, become, produced, compounded, made,
And thus not lasting, but of birth-and-death,

An aggregate, a nest of sickness, brittle,
A thing by food supported, come to be,-
'T were no fit thing to take delight in such,
The escape therefrom, the real, beyond the sphere
Of reason, lasting, unborn, unproduced,
The sorrowless, the stainless path that ends
The things of woe, the peace from worries-bliss ".
(Woodward – "As It Was Said" – p.142)

Thus, *Nibbāna* has been described here neither as a mere extinction of fires and sorrows nor a state of nothingness. It has here been described as a positive state of bliss.

Nibbāna - The Highest Goal

We have earlier studied the ten grades of happiness as described by the Buddha in a hierarchically ascending order. At the pinnacle of this hierarchical order is the most sublime state of cessation of all sensations, all perceptions and all voltions, that is, cessation of the evolution and becoming of *Vijñāna* (consciousness). In this analysis, *Nibbāna* is not only

the negation of cravings for worldly pleasures,
the negation of lust, hatred and delusion,
the negation of the conceit of Self and 'I'-ness and
mine-ness,
the negation of corporeal worldly objects,
the negation of sensations,
the negation of perceptions and
the negation of volitions,

<u>but also</u>

the negation of becoming of *Vijñāna* (Figure 18).

Negative descriptions point only to the means of achieving the final stage and the ultimate goal that is *Nibbāna.*

In this highest state transcending everything conceivable, there is not even the consciousness of bliss. This is the highest bliss because it transcends even the feeling of bliss, the consciousness of bliss and the consciousness of self. It is the state of utter selflessness.

Here all the defiling impulses causing *karmic* formations have been destroyed, all the *karmic* residues have also been burnt away and the aspirant realizes that all that to be accomplished as the fruit of the holy life has been accomplished and there is no

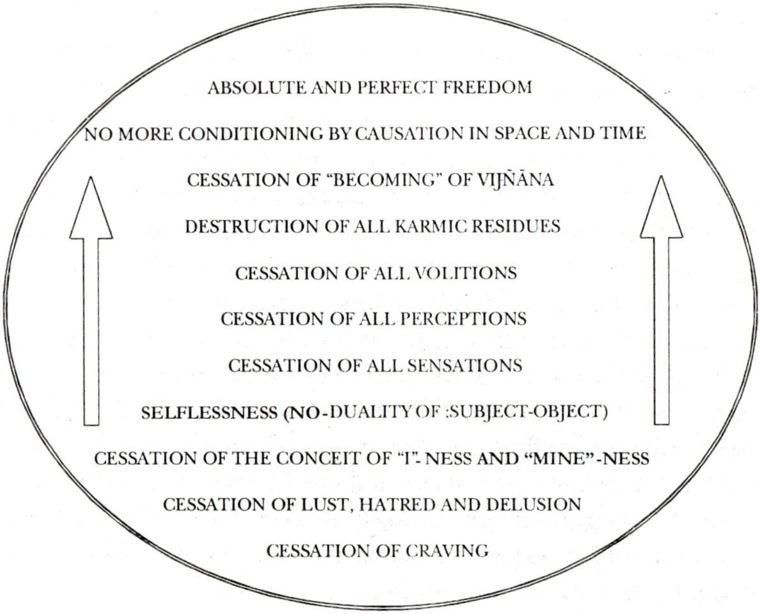

Fig. 18 Nirvāṇa

more rebirth for him. The evolution and becoming of his conscious-ness has stopped, never more to be conditioned by causation in space and time, because the *karmic* residues have been extirpated. He is now utterly selfless and perfectly and absolutely free. Two alternative possibilities are recognized for him in Buddhism. One is: "He will not be reborn." The second is : "He will willingly and volitionally take rebirth again for the benefit of all sentient beings driven solely by compassion (*karuṇā*) for them. Early Buddhism adopts the first stand whereas *Mahāyāna* Buddhism opts for the second with its concept of bodhisattva.

The concept of *Nibbāna* in Early Buddhism has been summed up in the *Udāna* in the following words:-

"There is, O monks, a domain where there is no earth, no water, no fire, no wind, no sphere of infinite space, no sphere of infinite consciousness, no sphere of nothingness, no sphere of neither awareness nor non-awareness ; there is not this world, there is not another world, there is no sun or moon. I do not call this coming or going, nor standing, nor dying, nor being reborn; it is without support, without occurrence, without object. Just this is the end of suffering".

(Trans. in Gethin's "The Foundations of Buddhism" 1998 : 76-7)

It may be interesting to compare this with the *Turīya* state described in the *Māṇḍūkya Upaniṣad.* Both describe the highest state as devoid of internal as well as external objects of cognition and as neither awareness nor non-awareness (neither cognitive nor non-cognitive). *Turīya* is the state of or equivalent of the state of Absolute Brahman or *ātman* after cosmic dissolution with the cosmic will to create having been withdrawn. The state of consciousness experienced in deep meditative concentration (trance) is equated with that state of cessation of cosmic will to create. Buddhist *Nibbāna* is the highest state of perfection characterized by the cessation of 'becoming' of *Vijñāna.* Thus, it is seen that the concept of *Turīya* in the *Māṇḍūkya Upaniṣad* is akin to *Nibbāna.* The influence of Buddhism on *Mā. U* is obvious.

Some scholars and notably Hindu philosophers like Dr. Radhakrishnan tend to read an affirmation of the *Upaniṣadic* view of Absolute reality or Brahman in Buddha's saying in the above passage in *Udāna.* They also quote the following passage in *Udāna* as another example in support of their view:

"If there were not this unborn, not-become, not-made, not-compounded, then an escape to the born, become, made, compounded would not be possible here".

Unlike the *Upaniṣads,* Buddhism is very clear on what it understands by the term 'Consciousness' (*Vijñāna*). It is the *Vijñāna* that is evolving. The epithets 'unborn', 'not-become', 'not-made' in the above passage of *Udāna* have been interpreted to indicate a 'true self' like the *ātman* or Brahman of the *Upaniṣads.* This is a distortion of Buddha's teaching because Buddha is very categorical in his assertion that there is no eternal and changeless self and that what we call life is the evolving of consciousness. *Anattā* or selflessness is the core and fundamental teaching on which his whole philosophy is anchored. This selflessness or emptiness (i.e. nothing exists of itself and by itself uncaused, i.e. everything is dependently originated based on causes and conditions) is the ultimate truth for him. This is the true nature of things as they are. This true nature, the dependent nature or selflessness, is the ultimate truth and this nature is uncaused and unborn. The fact of experience is that 'it is like that', 'it is suchness'. Apart from this nature, there is no such thing or reality in experience that is uncaused, unborn.

If you talk of Brahman or *ātman* as the reality and as the cause of everything, then the logical question is : what is the cause of Brahman? For causation as a principle cannot be assumed to start only at a particular point in time. Further this also contradicts dependent origination which is an undeniable fact of experience. If Brahman or Arman is talked of as uncaused, unborn, then it is an assumption first contrary to the facts of experience and then assertion to that effect is made. It is not a self-evident truth. On the other hand, the teaching of Buddha that selflessness (emptiness) is a ruling principle in every thing and it is uncaused, is a self-evident truth. What the above *Udāna* passages describe as unborn, not-become, not-made, not-compounded, neither coming nor going, neither standing nor dying etc. are about selflessness or emptiness (nature of things) and not about an Absolute (for such an Absolute Reality as a thing is logically untenable).

Emptiness is, in the ultimate analysis, the stopping of *karma* and eradication of all defilements. Without becoming selfless and empty, one cannot eradicate all defilements that cause rebirth and *saṃsāra.* Thus, without selflessness, there could be no escape from *saṃsāra* of birth and becoming. Further, as

Nāgārjuna proves with his incisive logic, if every thing is not empty and selfless, passage from *saṃsāra* to *Nirvāṇa* would not be possible. This point will become more clear when we consider the Madhyamaka philosophy of Nāgārjuna later.

The *Upaniṣadic* ideas of consciousness and identification of the same with the Absolute reality are ridden with contradictions. In fact, some *Upaniṣads* concede these and lean towards the concept of emptiness taught by the Buddha in as much as they point out that reality is 'not this', 'not this' (neti, neti), all in negative terms. Another shortcoming of *Upaniṣadic* philosophy is that it concentrates only on the realisation of the Self as the ultimate goal and as if this realisation is the panacea for all ills. Destruction of the defilements and extermination of the *karmic* residues are least talked about in the *Upaniṣads.* For the Buddha these are the real concerns and these only bring about *Nirvāṇa* and not the love of any 'self' which is an imaginary concept and which is as unreal as the daughter of a barren women. Buddha considers this concept of self as another object of attachment and as such a hindrance to the holy life.

Kilesa-Parinibbāna and Khanda-Parinibbāna

As to the question whether *Nibbāna* is attainable in one's life-time, Buddha says yes. He speaks of *Nibbāna* as "realisable in this life, immediate and inviting to come and see" (D.II.93,217,218; M.I. 265).

On the attainment of *Arahantship*, the saint experiences the complete extinction of impurities and so the state is called *kilesa-parinibbāna* (*Dh.* A.I.286 ; IV.194). This is the complete cessation of all passions and defilements(*Kilesa : Pāli* ; *Kleśa* : Sanskrit). As the body of the liberated saint (*Arahant*) constituted of the five aggregates still remains, this life-time liberation is also known as '*sa-upādi-sesa-nibbāna*' (*Dh.* A.II.163) in contradistinction to '*an-upādi-sesa-nibbāna*' or '*khanda-parinibbāna*'. These, in fact, are not two different kinds of *Nibbāna* but the very same *Nibbāna* receiving two names according to when it is experienced : before or after death.

> "These two *Nibbāna*-states are shown by him
> Who seeth, who is such and unattached,
> One state is that in this same life possessed
> With base remaining, tho' becoming's stream
> Be cut-off. While the state without a base

Belongeth to the future, wherein all
Becomings utterly do come to cease,
They who, by knowing this state uncompounded,
Have heart's release, by cutting off the stream.
They who have reached the core of *dhamma*, glad
To end, - such have abandoned all becomings."
(Itivuttaka- p. 38; Woodword-*As It Was Said* - p. 143)

The attainment of *Nibbāna* in this life itself suggests that it does not mean denial of all existence, denial of life. In this sense, it is not life-negating but negation of all subsequent becomings.

What Happens to the Liberated Saint after Death? Whether He Exists or does not Exist?

What happens to the arahant after his *Parinibbāna*, after physical dissolution of his body?

As a flame, blown to and fro by the wind, goes out and cannot be registered, even so, says Buddha, an *arahant*, set free from mind and matter, has disappeared and cannot be registered. This is illustrated by the Buddha in the interesting dialogue with Vacchagotta on this question (*Majjhima Nikāya, Aggivacchagotta Sutta* No. 72).

Vacchagotta, a wandering ascetic, approached Buddha and questioned : "But, Gotama, where is the bhikkhu, who is delivered of mind, reborn?"

Buddha replies "Vaccha, to say that he is reborn would not fit the case."

"Then, Gotama, he is not reborn."

"Vaccha, to say that he is not reborn would not fit the case."

"Then, Gotama, he is both reborn and not reborn."

"Vaccha, to say that he is both reborn and not reborn would not fit the case."

Vaccha was baffled on hearing these seemingly preposterous answers, and, in his confusion, exclaimed :

"Gotama, I am at a loss what to think in this matter, and I have become greatly confused."

"Enough, O Vaccha ! Be not at a loss what to think in this matter, and be not greatly confused. Profound, O Vaccha, is this doctrine, recondite and difficult of comprehension, good, excellent and not to be reached by mere reasoning. Subtle and intelligible only to the wise ; and it is a hard doctrine for you to learn, who belong to another sect, to another faith, to another persuasion, to another discipline and who sit at the feet of another teacher. Therefore, Vaccha, I shall now question you, and do you make answer as may seem to you good. What think you, Vaccha ? Suppose a fire were to burn in front of you, would you be aware that a fire was burning in front of you?"

"Gotama, if a fire were to burn in front of me, I should be aware that a fire was burning in front of me."

"But suppose, Vaccha, some one were to ask you, 'On what does this fire that is burning in front of you depend? What would you answer, Vaccha?"

"I would answer, Gotama, "It is on fuel of grass that this fire burning in front of me depends."

"But, Vaccha, if the fire in front of you were to become extinct, would you be aware that the fire in front of you has become extinct?"

"Gotama, if the fire in front of me were to become extinct, I should be aware that the fire in front of me has become extinct".

"But, Vaccha, if someone were to ask you, 'In which direction has that fire gone, East or West, North or South?' What would you say, Vaccha?

"The question would not fit the case, Gotama, For the fire depended on fuel, grass and wood, and when that fuel has all gone, and it can get no other, being thus without nutriment, it is said to be extinct."

"In exactly the same way Vaccha, all forms, sensations, perceptions, mental activities and consciousness have been abandoned, uprooted, made like a palmyrah stump, become non-existent and not liable to spring up in future.

"The Saint, O Vaccha, who has been released from what are styled the five aggregates, is deep, immeasurable, like the mighty ocean. To say that he is reborn would not fit the case. To say that he is not reborn would not fit the case. To say that he is neither reborn nor not reborn would not fit the case."

One cannot say that the arahant is reborn, as all passions that condition rebirth are eradicated, nor can one say that the arahant is annihilated, for there is nothing to annihilate.

If the corporeality whereby one seeking to know the arahant (*Tathāgata*) were to cognize him, that corporeality of the *Tathāgata* has been abandoned, cut off from the root, made unable to grow, rendered incapable of future becoming like an uprooted palm tree. So in relation to the *Tathāgata* who is free from the mark of corporeality, it does not fit the case to say that he is born ———— not born, born as well as not-born———— and neither born nor not-born. Similarly with regard to feeling, perception, volitions and consciousness (*M.I.* 487-8).

This illustration clarifies why all the four alternatives about the existence or non-existence of the *Tathāgata* were set aside. Just as it is inappropriate or meaningless to speak of the direction of fire which being free from the fuel has gone out, so also it is inappropriate or meangingless to speak of the existence or non-existence of the *Tathāgata* who being free from all the cognizable marks has become indeterminable.

CHAPTER 10

Abhidhamma

The Buddhist teachings we have so far studied are derived basically from the *Sutta Piṭaka* and the *Vinaya Piṭaka* of *Pāli* Canon. The third *Piṭaka–Abhidhamma*–contains detailed analyses and expositions of profound philosophical and metaphysical contents of the Buddha's teachings. The prefix '*Abhi*' has the meaning of 'further' or 'about'. Therefore, *Abhidhamma* (*Pāli* ; Sanskrit : *Abhidharma*) would mean 'The Higher or Special *Dharma*' or "The Higher Discourse on *Dharma*".

The development of *Abhidhamma* has been as an aid to insight meditation and understand things as they truly are. The main topics of the teachings in the *Sūtras* (*Sutta*) are taken here, analysed, elaborated and explained to aid insight meditation. The so-called being is microscopically analysed and the psycho-physical component parts constituting the same are minutely described for a correct understanding of them and for removing false views leading to craving and clinging. *Abhidhamma* has been developed as a truth system to serve as antidote to ignorance that is the root cause of craving and clinging.

It appeared that there was a Self but on analysis it was found to reduce to only a flow of the five aggregates or *skandhas*–namely, corporeality or form, sensation, perception, volition and consciousness. What we call the Self is nothing but a conglomerate of these five aggregates brought about depending on causes and conditions and is just an artificial unity constructed by mind for pragmatic purposes. As the Buddhist thoughts on insight meditation to probe and investigate deepened further, it was found that even these five aggregates are mental constructs which can be analysed and dissolved further into component elements. This analysis rapidly came to embrace not just the psycho-physical aggregates of a conscious being but also to include all things in the universe. These elements were called '*dharmas*' (*Pāli* : *dhammas*).

In the *Abhidharmic* philosophy, the word '*dharma*' stands for reality, Fact, Element or Phenomenon as a factor of experience. The *dharmas,* in this philosophy, form the psychophysical building blocks of the world as experienced by us and as such are the 'constituent elements'.

The *Abhidhamma* aims at classification and codification of the *dharmas* and provides a canonical list for the practitioners to contemplate or meditate upon and to analyse and have insight into the things as they truly are. Such meditative practices and such analysis and insight into the things and the discernment of the ultimate constituents of experience (*dharmas*) are said to be the means for the purification of the mind and the life-stream. Right Mindfulness of the Noble Eightfold Path flows from such analysis and insight.

Abhidharma-kośa (I.3) of Vasubandhu states: "Whereas the world erroneously falls into the flood of becoming by reason of defilement (*kleśa*) and whereas there is no access to the taming of defilement without the discernment of *dharmas,* therefore for the purpose of discerning the *dharmas,* it is said that the *Abhidharma* was declared by the teacher (The Buddha)".

Only two *Abhidharma* canonical collections have survived: the *Theravāda Abhidhamma* in the *Pāli* Canon and the *Sarvāstivāda* (*Vaibhāṣika Abhidharma*) that survives mainly in Chinese translation.

1. The *Theravāda Abhidhamma*

The *Theravāda Abhidhamma* produced a list of eight-two classes of *dhammas* of which eighty-one are said to be conditioned (*saṃskṛta* : Sanskrit ; *samkhata* : *Pāli*) i.e. the direct result of causes). The last one, *Nibbāna,* is unconditioned (*asaṃskṛta* / *asamkhata*).

The eighty-one conditioned *dhammas* are classified and grouped under the following categories:

Material or physical form (*rūpa*)
Consciousness (*citta* = *vinnana* ; Sanskrit : *vijñāna*)
Mental associates (*cetasikas* ; Sanskrit : *caitasikas*)

Material form consists of twenty-eight *dhammas* and consciousness one *dhamma.* The category of mental associates has the following sub-divisions:

- Wholesome mental associates (25 *dhammas*).

Non-greed, non-hatred, non-delusion, faith, mindfulness, compassion and so on.

- Unwholesome mental associates (14 *dhammas*) Wrong views etc.
- Morally-neutral mental associates (13 *dhammas*) These are morally neutral and gain their moral colouring from the other *dhammas* that occur along with them. Out of these, the following seven *dhammas* are common to all mental 'occasions': contact, feeling, perception, volition, mental life, concentration and attention.

As Paul Williams comments, this is not abstract philosophy purely of intellectual interest. The purpose is finding the path to liberation. The monk engaged in insight meditation will dwell quietly and in concentration, observing the arising and falling of *dhammas*, their flows, to see how things really are and to cut out the sense of Self. He will also know which mental factors conduce to positive, wholesome, mental occasions, and will thus know how to 'cease to do evil and learn to do good' (Buddhist Thought, p. 91).

Of course, its concern is not limited only to the practical issues of how to lessen attachment, but also to find things how they are truly. The *dhammas* (excluding, of course, *Nibbāna*) are evanescent events, linked by an impersonal causal law. That is how it truly is.

In such *Abhidhammic* analysis, the *dhammas* are the ultimate and irreducible elements of our experience, "the primary existents found as the terminating points of the process of analytical probing"(*dravyasat*). The doctrine that the *dharmas* have their own intrinsic nature, own-existence (*svabhāva*), is not found in the *Theravāda Abhidhamma* of the *Pāli* Canon. But this notion of *svabhāva* of *dharmas* has been taken in and finds mention in the later texts of the *Theravāda* school. It is developed explicitly in the *Patisambhidhamagga* where it says that "a *dharma*'s *svabhāva* is its individual essence" (Richard King, Early *Advaita* Vedānta and Buddhism, p. 94/95).

The practice of insight itself came to be seen as penetration into the *svabhāva* of *dharmas.* Momentariness of the *dharmas* was of course recognized ; but despite their evanescence, they were considered real entities each defined by their own characteristics(*svalakṣaṇa*). But the *dharmas* themselves were not understood as having ultimate substantial existence (*paramārtha dravyasat*) of their own. The understanding here seems to be that the *dharmas* and the things constituted of the *dharmas* are present there as 'given' or as 'manifested' ; but are not existent always as independent, self-producing, self-subsisting entities.

It is in the interpretation and understanding of the *svabhāva* of *dharmas* (existence of *dharmas*) that doctrinal dispute arose in the Third Council of Buddhists called at *Pāṭaliputrā* during the seventeenth year of *Aśoka*'s rule. The dispute was over the question of the existence of *dharmas* in the three periods – past, present and future. The *Sarvāstivādins* (those who held the doctrine that all exist) argued that the *dharmas* exist in all the three time periods. This amounted to an affirmation of the eternality of the *dharmas* and, as such, contravened the basic Buddhist principles of no-self (*anattā*) and universal impermanence (*anityam*). This group was expelled for holding false (non-Buddhist) views on metaphysical questions.

Those who opposed the *Sarvāstivāda* were known as '*Sthaviravādins*' ('Docrtine of the Elders') who declared themselves to be Distinctionists' (*Vibhajyavādins*–those who make distinctions). These *Sthaviravādins* accepted that *dharmas* exist in the present but denied that they exist in the future. As regards the past, they made a distinction between a wholesome or unwholesome intention that has already issued its *karmic* fruit and as such could no longer be said to exist, and that which has not yet issued its fruit and as such, should be held to exist still. The traditional *Theravādin* position on this issue of *dharmas* in the three times is that only the present *dharma* exists (see *Kathāvatthu* 1 : 6).

In India as a whole in classical times, the *Sarvāstivāda* appears to have been by far the most important and influential of the *Abhidharmic* traditions, although it has not survived to the present day as an independent school. The *Sarvāstivāda* is discussed below.

2. The *Sarvāstivāda* (The Realistic School)

Sarvāstivāda Texts

The principal *Abhidharma* text of this school is *Kātyāyanīputra's Jñāna-prasthāna* (Source of Knowledge), also called the *Aṣṭa-grantha* (Eight Books), probably compiled as early as 200 BCE. The subsequent works of the school seem to have been a special exegesis on *Jñāna- prasthāna* and are designated as Six *Pādas* (Legs).

Then probably in the second century A.D., a great and minute commentary named *Vibhāṣā Śāstra* was compiled on *Kātyāyanīputra*'s work (*Pārśva*'s *Mahāvibhāṣā*). The word '*Vibhāṣā*' means an extensive annotation or various opinions, and this title indicates that many opinions of the time were gathered and criticized in detail and that some optional ones were selected and recorded. The chief object of the *Vibhāṣā* commentary was to transmit the correct exposition of the *Abhidharma* School which has since then come to be called *Vaibhāṣika* School.

Then there appeared a compendium of the *Abhidharma* doctrine called *Abhidharma-hṛdaya* (Heart of the Higher *dharmas*) by Dharmottara and a commentary on it called "*Saṃyukta-abhidharma-hṛdaya* " by Dharmatrata.

Then followed the key literature of this school "*Abhidharma-kośa-kārikā*" and "*Abhidharma-kośa Śāstra* (Commentray)" by Vasubandhu (C. 420-500 A.D).

Classification of *Dharmas/Dharmic List*

Sarvāstivāda school treats the self or the personality of the individual (pudgala) as empty in conformity with the basic Buddhist *anātman* (no-self) theory; but considers the five *skandhas* (form, sensation, perception, volition and consciousness) constituting the personality as existing real and not empty. Their philosophical position is summarized as : "self is empty but the *dharmas* exist" (*Pudgala-nairātmya dharma-ātmya*). Each one of the five *skandhas* is called a *dharma* i.e. an elemental factor of experience or being.

In Buddhism there is no actor apart from action, no percipient apart from perception; therefore, no conscious subject behind consciousness. Mind is simply a transitory state of consciousness of an object. There is no permanent conscious subject. All reality is considered to have only momentary existence for no fabric of body remains the same for two consecutive moments as the modern physicists would say.

By analysing the things experienced and selecting out the elemental aspects that make up the universe, *Sarvāstivādins* have established seventy-five (75) *dharmas* or elemental factors. They consider these *dharmas* as existing and real. Their name '*Sarvāsti*' (all (*dharmas*) exist) indicates their basic philosophical point and shows their strong realistic tendency.

All elements of the universe have been minutely analysed by Vasubandhu and systematically classified and arranged in his

Abhidharma-kośa. His dharmic list contains seventy — five (75) *dharmas* considered as the ultimate substantial constituents of reality (*paramārtha dravyasat*).

Asaṃskṛta Dharmas (Unconditioned *Dharmas*)

Three of these *dharmas* are *asaṃskṛta,* that is, uncompounded or casually unconditioned (i.e., not conditioned by causes, unchanging and immovable). They are :

(i) Space (*ākāśa*) that is all pervasive and unhindered. It gives no hindrance and itself penetrates through any hindrance freely. It manifests no change. It is unaffected by changes taking place within it just as it is unmarked by the flight of birds.

(ii) Liberation – *apratisaṃkhyā-nirodha* (cessation of *saṃskṛta dharmas* or liberation due to absence of causal factors i.e. liberation attained not through discriminative knowledge).

(iii) Liberation – *pratisaṃkhyā-nirodha* (Cessation of *saṃskṛta dharmas,* attained through discriminative knowledge which burns away the formative forces leading to rebirth).

Saṃskṛta Dharmas (Conditioned)

The remaining seventy-two (72) *dharmas* are all compounded (*saṃskṛta*). They are causally conditioned/determined, and destined to change, non-eternal (*anitya*), momentary (*kṣaṇika*), mundane (*laukika*) and predominantly impure. These *saṃskṛta dharmas* are classified and grouped under the following categories:-

(i) Forms (*rūpaṇī*)

(ii) Consciousness (*citta*)

(iii) Concomitant mental functions or mental associates (*caitasika* or *citta – saṃprayukta – saṃskāra*)

(iv) Independent *dharmas* – Elements Neither Physical Form Nor Mental (*citta – viprayukta – saṃskāra*)

Forms *(Rūpa, 11 Dharmas)*

This group consists of practically all that we call matter. Of the eleven *dharmas,* the first five are sense-organs and the next five are sense-objects.

The four gross elements – earth, water, fire and air – are not considered separately but subsumed in sense-objects.

The eleventh is the one peculiar to this school :"form-element not manifested" outwardly (*avijñapti-rūpa*). When we intend to act, the mental function itself is called will (*cetanā*). In Buddhism it is called will-action. When it is expressed in words, it becomes word-action and when expressed in physical action by body, it is body-action. These actions : will-action, word-action and body-action, whether they are morally good, bad or neutral, when they issue forth, produce and leave an abiding imprint or impression (*vāsanā*) in the sub-conscious which will decide the later will-action and existence. The present action flows from the past will and its imprint determines the future will. The imprints bear the latent energy and are then called unmanifested action (*avijñapti-karma*) which will bear fruit later. These are considered the unmanifested 'form–elements–not yet manifested'.

Consciousness (Citta, 1 *dharma*)

Through this is one, it naturally functions in five ways corresponding to the five sense-organs.

Concomitant Mental Functions (*Caitasika, 46 dharmas*)

This category of mental associates is given the most importance and attention by this school and on this account, it seems quite reasonable to designae the school as a psychological school of Buddhism.

The mental associates themselves are again sub-divided and grouped under the following heads :-

General functions or 'Universals' (*Mahābhūmika*, 10 *dharmas*):-

Mahābhūmika means of the universal ground. The ground here is the consciousness. Whenever the consciousness (mind) functions, the universals such as perception, idea, will etc, always appear concomitantly.

General functions of good or 'Moral Universals' (*Kuśala Mahābhūmika*, 10 *dharmas*) :-

These are the morally good functions such as belief, non-injury, non-greediness etc.

General foul functions (*Kleśa-Mahābhūmika*, 6 *dharmas*) :-

These are the ones tainted with earthly desire or passion (*kleśa*) such as ignorance, indolence, non-belief etc.

General functions of evil (*Akuśala-Mahābhūmika*, 2 *dharmas*) :-

These are the concomitants with all evil thoughts.

Minor functions of defilement (*Upakleśa-bhūmika*, 10 *dharmas*) :-

These arise from ordinary passionate character. They always accompany evil mind and also the neutral mind which hinders the noble path such as anger, envy, enmity, deceit etc. These are to be eliminated gradually by the way of self-culture (*bhāvanā-mārga*), not abruptly by the way of insight (*darśana-mārga*).

Indeterminate functions (*Aniyata*-bhūmika,8 *dharmas*) :-

Those which cannot be classified as belonging to any of the above functions are covered in this e.g refelction, investigation, repentance etc.

Elements Neither Physical Forms nor Mental Associates (14 dharmas):-

Among the elements conditioned by causes, there are those which have no connection with form or mind. They are neither matter nor mind and are included in the canonical list as independent *dharmas*.

- Acquisition (*prāpti*) is the power that binds an acquired object to the one who acquires it.
- Non-acquisition (*aprāpti*) is the power that separates an object from being possessed by one.
- Communionship (similarity-*sabhāgatā*) is the power that causes a species or class of beings to have similar forms of life.
- The three *dharmas*–fruition in thoughtless heaven, thought less ecstasy and annihilation trance (nirodha-*samāpatti*)–are the ecstasies or the realms of happiness attainable by progressive meditation.
- The other eight *dharmas* relate to the life (vital power) and speech.

Sarvāstivāda – Theory

In the Hindu *Vedas*, we come across a plethora of gods conceived as the powers behind the various forces of nature and as the various aspects or manifestations of reality. In the *abhidhammic* schools of Buddhism, we see a number of *dharmas* postulated as the ultimate irreducible and elemental factors of experience. These make up the world of our experience and constitute the fundamental aspects of reality. The canonical list of *dharmas* compiled by the *abhidharmists* aims to be exhaustive and cover all factors one is bound to experience in reality. There is no experience beyond the *dharmas* in this list. Each *dharma* is conceived as having an innate inherent self-nature (*svabhāva*) of its own and a durable essence (i.e. substantive reality).

Sarvāstivāda drew a systematic distinction between the way *dharmas* exist and the way the composite entities like you, me, tables or chairs that are constructed out of *dharmas* exist. The *dharmas* are the primary existents that are found as the terminating points of the process of analytical probing or analysis to find what is actually there and thus are irreducible simples. On the other hand, the composite entities are conglomerations of *dharmas* brought together by causes and conditions and, as such, are constructed out of primary existents. They are thus 'secondary' or 'conceptual existents' (*prajñaptisat*) and are lacking in 'own-existence' (*niḥsvabhāva*) whereas the *dharmas* constituting them are considered to have their 'own-existence'.

Sarvāstivāda school treats the self or the personality of the individual human being as 'secondary existent' and empty (*śūnya*) of own-existence. This is in conformity with the basic *anattā* (no-self) theory; but in keeping with the above definition, the five *skandhas* (form, sensation, perception, volition and consciousness) constituting the personality are considered as existing real and not empty in this school. Their philosophical position is summarized as : 'self is empty but the *dharmas* exist' (*pudgala-nairātmya dharma-ātmya*).

If *dharmas* can be abstracted from out of experience and established as existing and real attributing substantial existences to these theoretical notions, the self can also be spoken of as existing and real idealistically in like manner. But they hold on to the basic Buddhist tenet of: 'Void (empty) of abiding self'. Whether or not he anticipated the pitfall of being involved in the admission of Self, Vasubandhu devoted the whole ninth chapter of his '*Abhidharma-kośa*' to the refutation of the *Ātman* theory (Junjiro Takakusu: The Essentials of The Buddhist Philosophy, p. 66).

The strong realistic tendency of this school may seem to be a great deviation from original Buddhism. But in so far as they are maintaining the original formula: *anattā* (no-self), *anityam* (impermanence) and *asukham* (suffering) except *Nirvāṇa*", we cannot regard their philosophy as an entire deviation.

They adhere to the theory of momentariness. When they talk of *dharmas* as existing and real, what they actually mean is a theoretical existence as an abstract experiential factor, with a possibility of experience in reality ; it is a conceptual existence, but not an ever-existent one ; but is a momentary existence or a continuity of separate momentary existences.

All 'entities' are conglomerations (*saṅghāta*) of various evanescent *dharmas* which appearing and then disappearing in quick succession, create the illusion of a unified and persisting entity. *Dharmas* are thus the ultimate momentary (*kṣaṇika*) 'building blocks' of all entities and the occurrences of the evanescent *dharmas* to produce any entity are brought about by the coming together of a cluster of causes and conditions and the formative forces (*saṃskāras*) of volitions. The change in the entity here comes about because of the successive flow of the evanescent *dharmas* arising and decaying in quick succession. Change is the destruction of one moment and the arising of the next and the *dharma* is destroyed in the same place where it was produced (*Abhidharma-kośa Bhāṣya* IV.2). "It becomes extinguished at the very moment of birth". This doctrine is at the very foundation of the *Sarvāstivāda* teaching. A compounded *dharma* lasts for only a moment (*kṣaṇa*) and then ceases to be. It is replaced by another. No change of substance occurs but merely a succession of evanescent occurrences. Formative forces (*saṃskāras*) are said to cause these occurrences and give rise to the entities.

Thus, for the *Sarvāstivādins*, the *dharmas* are impermanent and evanescent in their manifestation, but still possess their *svabhāva* (own-nature) as ultimate abstract existential factors which exist throughout the three temporal spheres of past, present and future. As we have already seen, this is the doctrine which caused serious dissensions in the Third Buddhist Council and resulted in the expulsion of *Sarvāstivādins*.

The *Sarvāstivādins* argued that the *dharmas* exist at all times because something simply non-existent could not serve as a basis for knowledge (i.e. you cannot have knowledge of nothing, that is, something that does not exist) and also because without this presupposition the temporal gulf between action and fruition in the *kārmic* process cannot be explained.

Past actions have a result in the present and in the future; therefore those *dharmas* must in some sense 'be' (in a latent and non-functioning form). In this theory, two aspects of the *dharmas* are recognized : 'What-it-is-ness' and 'what-it-does'. *Svabhāva* is the 'what-it-is-ness' of the *dharma*, that enables one to cognize and speak about it. It is in this sense that each past or future *dharma* exists. The *Sarvāstivādin* wants to suggest that because a past *dharma* has this sort of existence, there is no-longer any paradox in a result occurring of something that is past. But in addition to existing this way, each *dharma* has also an aspect of 'what-it-does'. The *dharma*'s not yet doing what is does is what makes it a future *dharma.* Its doing what it does when the appropriate causes and conditions come together makes it a present *dharma,* and its ceasing to do what it does when the causes and conditins cease is what renders it a past *dharma.* This 'doing-what-it-does' is instantaneous, momentary. Thus any *dharma*'s being present is momentary (For more on this, please refer Paul Williams, Buddhist Thought, p. 115).

This distinction of 'what-it-is-ness' and 'what-it-does' is not accepted by Vasubandhu himself who argues, from the *Sautrāntika* point of view, that to exist is to be causally efficient. For Vasubandhu, then to 'exist' is to function ; thus, a *dharma* cannot be said to exist outside its own phenomenal manifestation. *Karman* is explained in terms of the transformation of a given consciousness stream rather than as the actualization of an existent but previously latent cause (Richard King, Early *Advaita Vedānta* and Buddhism, p.103/104).

The *Sarvāstivāda* calssification of *dharmas* is basically an abstraction of ultimate irreducible factors from the occurrences in experience and treating them as supporting elemental factors of experience (*dhr. dharma,* that supports experience). But, take any *dharma* and we find that it has no separate independent existence. For instance, perception is not perception *per se,* but perception of something. What *Sarvāstivāda* does is a theoretical abstraction of a factor and assigning a name to it. In the final analysis, every *dharma* is also only a flow of experiences which is designated by a name for conventional worldly purposes. By postulating ultimate substantial primary existence (*paramārtha dravyasat*) to these *dharmas* and assigning a durable own-existence and nature (self-nature, *svabhāva*) to each, the *Sarvāstivādins* have made them into ultimate immutable and unchanging realities. This view not only contravenes the basic Buddhist tenets of impermanence (*anityam*) and selflessness (*anattā*) of all *dharmas,* but also ends up in a paradoxical conclusion that even the seventy-two *saṃskṛta* (compounded) *dharmas* in their canonical list are unchanging and uncompounded (*asaṃskṛta*). This anamoly in the theory is seized upon and vehemently critisized by the *Mahāyānists* and the theory rejected.

By analysing the doctrine of momentariness which takes as axiomatic that no *dharma* occurs in two consecutive moments, Nāgārjuna proves that no *dharma* can occur at all because each moment is segmentable into several sub-moments which again into sub-sub-moments and so on ad infinitum (Richard Robinson, Early Mādhyamika in India and China, p. 44). Thus, for Nāgārjuna, *dharmas* are indistinguishable from one another and have no beginning or end limits. They are ungraspable like space and they also have no foundation or support like space. Since they have no beginning or end points, they lack any fundamental boundaries or any distinguishing marks (*svalakṣaṇa*). Consequently one can never pin-point when or where one *dharma* ends and another begins.

Prāpti and *Aprāpti*

These are the two unique *Sarvāstivāda* doctrines which became topics of intense debate with other schools. *Prāpti* is 'possession' or 'acquisition'. It is the power that binds the *karmic* result of an action (with a wholesome or unwholesome intention) to the particular psychophysical continuum which had that intention and which committed that action. The *prāpti* of having had that intention is here said to continue in that psychophysical stream till the appropriate *karmic* result matures and issues forth. Thus, in addition to the original intention itself, this further dharma, *prāpti* (possession), is said to occur. This was postulated by the *Sarvāstivādins* to account for the *karmic* connection between successive thoughts, words and deeds, and their consequences till they mature and also to distinguish between an ordinary mortal and an enlightened person.

Ordinary person has a possession of the negative taints (passions/defilements) whereas an enlightened noble one has the *prāptis* of virtuous natures resulting from his spiritual practices. In the case of the enlightened noble one, not only has the possession of negative taints been completely removed, but there is also a different dharma present called *aprāpti* (non-possession) which keeps the negative taints from ever appearing again.

Both *prāpti* and *aprāpti* were rejected as unnecessary by rival schools like *Sautrāntika*.

3. *Sautrāntika*

Sarvāstivāda is a naïve realistic school postulating a plurality of *dharmas* as existing. Reality is split into seventy-five discrete elements called *dharmas* which exist only momentarily temporally speaking. This school flourished in Kashmir and Gandhara. The studies in Gandhara centre gave rise to a splinter group known as *Sautrāntikas* who rejected the *Sarvāstivāda* theory of existence of *dharmas* in the three time periods which, they thought, would make them permanent and, as such, would be unbuddhistic. According to *Sautrāntikas*, only the present *dharma* exists. The past does not exist, because it is no more, and the future *dharma* is not real, because it has not yet come into existence. The future *dharma* may materialize only if appropriate conditions develop to manifest it. However, the *Sautrāntikas* are otherwise basically in agreement with the *Sarvāṣtivāda* (*Vaibhāṣika*) classification of *dharmas* but with critical abridgement to conform to the teachings in the Sanskrit *āgamas* (*Sūtras*) as interpreted by them.

The *Sautrāntikas* did not accept the claim of *Abhidharma Piṭaka* as the authentic words of the Buddha. The name "*Sautrāntika*" indicates that this school takes the *Sūtras* (the Sanskrit *āgamas*) as the valid authority (*pramāṇa*) and not the later treatises such as *Abhidhamma Piṭaka.*

They are generally in agreement with the *Sarvāstivādins* as regards the reality of the *skandhas* which nevertheless do not constitute a unified and persistent personality(*pudgala*) or a permanent changeless Self. They subscribe to the *pudgala-nairātmya* view. According to them, consciousness (*vijñāna*) is in a constant state of transformation or evolution (*pariṇāma*) and thus can never be said to constitute a persisting individual entity(*pudgala*); rather it is the succession of discrete, yet causally connected mental states or energies.

They deny the existence of separate *dharmas* assigned as '*prāpt*' and '*aprāpti*' ('possession' and 'non-possession') by the *Vaibhāṣikas* to account for the presence or absence of specific natures in a given stream of consciousness. For the *Vaibhāṣikas*, *prāpti* is the cause that originates specific natures in a given stream of consciousness by virtue of which the Noble One is differentiated from the average person. The Noble One has the *prāptis* of certain natures resulting from meditative attainment, which the average person does not have. But, the *Sautrāntikas* do not assign separate realities to these states of possession or non-possession of specific natures arguing that the differentiation between the two is merely the question of having destroyed or not destroyed the defilements. Likewise, they also deny the existence of *Nirvāṇa* and *ākāśa* as separate entities (*dharmas*), for, according to them, these are merely the names (*prajñapti*) for the non-existence (*abhāva*) or cessation (*nirodha*) of the *saṃskṛta dharmas* (conditioned *dharmas*).

As we have already seen, the *Sautrāntikas* do not also accept the theory that the past *dharma* still exists, which was originally postulated as existents by the *Sarvāstivāda* scholars to account for causal continuity between a past action and its subsequent fruition at a later date. Instead, the *Sautrāntikas* explain that any *karman* immediately produces its impression or reaction on the stream of consciousness which is thus continually modified according to the moral intention of the *karman.* Thus, moment to moment, the stream of consciousness is modified depending on the *karman.* The modification is thought of as seeding or perfuming the stream of consciousness. The influence of wicked or unwholesome intention is like perfuming i.e. there is no additional thing, but the stream is now imbued with a different fragrance. Thus, the seed consciousness, the modified stream of consciousness, is perfumed and holds the effect as a new fragrance. Some *Sautrāntikas* have suggested that there is a subtle level of consciousness in which this occurs.

CHAPTER 11

Prajñāpāramitā

1. Revival of *Anātman* Teaching

Prajñāpāramitā Sūtras, which are the roots of *Mahāyāna* development, attack the *dharma* theories of *Sarvāstivādins* and *Sautrāntikas* and their naive realism which assigns permanent ever-existent self-natures to the *dharmas* experienced. However, they accept the *abhidharma* technique of reduction; but they see no level at which this reductionist process can conceivably be terminated. For them, correct position is no position in this reduction process and *dharmas* do not occur at all. The *dharmas* do not arise (*an-utpāda*) because in the ultimate analysis they have no essential being or self-nature of their own and do not exist.

Prajñāpāramitā movement is characterized by their rejection of *abhidharmic* ideas first on the philosophical grounds that the self-nature ascribed by these theories to the *dharmas* implies the existence of an unchanging reality and this contradicts the basic Buddhist tenets of *anitya* (impermanence) and *anātma* (no self-nature, no self-origination, no self-dependence). Further this group objects to the meditative practices of contemplating on the *dharmas* as realities since according to them this technique leads to attachment and clinging to self, that is, attachment and clinging to the 'selfness' of *dharmas* and becomes an obstructive hindrance to total liberation. Their attitude is uncompromising adherence to the core Buddhist doctrines of 'selflessness' and 'dependent origination' (i.e. no self-orginated or no self-established entity). They lay emphasis on the concept of *śūnya* (emptiness of self-nature).

Their philosophical position is a reaffirmation of and a re-emphasis on the basic Buddhist teachings of *anātman* (no-self) and emptiness which expresses the substanceless of things and negation of the self or independent nature of things. Since all things arise depending on conditions and causes, nothing in this world is self-established or self-dependent. Hence, nothing possesses any substantive reality i.e., ever-remaining existence as a permanent unchanging substance with a self-nature of its own. *Śūnya* (emptiness) signifies this selflessness and substancelessness. Thus, it is a negation of 'self' and 'substance' and an affirmation of the dependent origination.

Thus, contrasting with the *Sarvāstivādin*'s theory of "Self is empty but things (*dharmas*) exist", *Prajñāpāramitā* movement maintains that 'self and things are both empty'. This is expressed by the phrase '*pudgala-dharma-nairātmya*' and the term *śūnyatā* signifies the *nairātmya* of both *pudgala* and *dharmas.* In their philosophy, *śūnyatā* is synonymous with '*nairātmya*' which is a negation of substantive existence. In this manner, the *anātman* was first an expression of the negation of a self with its characteristics of egoism and self-interest and then the negation of the universal self when the meaning of *ātman* was expanded to include the reality of a fundamental and universal *Ātman.* Thus, *anātman* theory became an expression of the emptiness of the whole world in the *Prajñāpāramitā* philosophy.

2. *Prajñāpāramitā* Literatures

There is a large number of versions of *Prajñāpāramitā* such as the *Mahāprajñāpāramitā*, the *Aṣṭasāhasrikā-Prajñāpāramitā* and the larger and smaller *Prajñāpāramitā-hṛdaya.*

The earliest version appears to be the *Aṣṭasāhasrikā Prajñāpāramitā* (the 'Eight-thousand Verse Perfection of Wisdom). Edward Conze considers *Ratnaguṇasaṃcayagāthā* as the earliest form of the text. This is the verse summary from which *Aṣṭasāhasrikā* might have been expanded. The *Pañcaviṃśatisāhasrikā* (Twenty-five Thousand Verse), also extremely important, is probably later than the above.

One of the most popular *Prajñāpāramitā* texts is the famous *Vajracchedikā Sūtra* (the 'Diamond' or 'Diamond Cutter', otherwise known as the "Three-hundred Verses") which Edward Conze takes as an example of a later summary *Sūtra.*

As Paul Williams states, the *Prajñāpāramitā Sūtras* are not systematic philosophical or doctrinal treatises. They are inspired teachings clearly with a message-the message of a *Dharma* – preacher rather than the message of a philosopher or doctrinal theorist (*Buddhist Thought,* p. 132). The expositions of

Madhyamaka philosophy and the bodhisattva practices which developed later are rooted in these sermons.

3. Perfection of Wisdom (*Prajñā*)

In conventional usage, *Prajñā* may refer to intellectual analysis. But, here, it is used primarily to denote ultimate wisdom, knowledge of reality, seeing truly how things actually are in contrast to the way they appear to be. This is the deep meditative insight into the true nature of things, seeing directly how they are (a *darśana*). The insight in the *abhidharma* practices was the discernment of the *dharmas* as the ultimate primary existents (*dravyasat*) in reality in contradistinction to their conceptual nature and their momentariness. The *Prajñā* there referred to the analysis and discrimination of the *dharmas* and contemplation on their momentariness. According to *Prajñāpāramitā* masters, that *Prajñā*, that wisdom of abhidharmists is imperfect and that has to be perfected. Perfection of that wisdom comes from the realisation of the emptiness of all *dharmas.* Here the insight is into the emptiness of *dharmas.* This is the *Prajñāpāramitā* (i.e.'wisdom perfected' or 'wisdom that has gone beyond'); this is the ultimate wisdom that alone can lead to *Nirvāṇa.*

The *Prajñāpāramitā* also prescribes perfections to be practised and mastered in the path to *Nirvāṇa*. These perfections relate to: giving (*dāna*), morality (*śīla*), patience (*kṣānti*), effort (*vīrya*) and meditative concentration (*dhyāna*) in addition to the perfection of wisdom (*Prajñā*). These *pāramitās* can be perfect only when they are underpinned and sustained by perfection of wisdom; that is, when insight into emptiness and selflessness of thing illumines and guides these *pāramitās.* All these *pāramitās* are enjoined to be dedicated to supreme enlightenment without any perception of self and others and without any perception of duality. Insight into emptiness of self is the key factor in all these perceptions.

4. Emptiness (*Śūnyatā*)

Early Buddhism was categorical in its assertion of selflessness of all things. According to the Buddha, none of the five *skandhas* – corporeality (form), sensation, perception, volition, and consciousness – can be considered as self of being or as being possessed by the self of being or as being within the self or as containing the self. However much we delve deep within our being, no permanent changeless self is ever truly found. Buddha proves definitely through so many analogies, especially through the analogy of the plantain tree, that after stripping oneself layer after layer of these five *skandhas*, nothing as essence or self is found, and it is all substanceless, essenceless, selfless, empty, void or non-self. We find nothing else except the flow of the stream of the five *skandhas*. The idea of 'self', 'I' or 'mine' is a false construct of the mind which is the root of ignorance, craving, clinging and consequent suffering.

The abhidharmists held to the view of personality of individual human being (*pudgala*) or self of being as a conceptual construct and accordingly, as empty of own-existence i.e., as selfless, substanceless. For them, all conceptual existents like chairs, tables, forests, you, and me are empty of own-existence. But they identified various classes of *dharmas* as primary existents (*dravyasat*) by analysing all psychophysical phenomena into final irreducible factors, and considered these *dharmas* as having their own self-existence. But deeper analysis reveals that these also have only conceptual or theoretical existence, not real existence at all times. Therefore, the *Abhidharmic* philosophy of '*Pudgala-nairātmya Dharma-ātmya*' has been changed and perfected to '*Pudgala-Dharma-nairātmya*' ('the selflessness of person and things') by the *Prajñāpāramitā* masters.

Thus, the *Prajñāpāramitā* movement extends the concept of *nairātmya* or *śūnya* (emptiness) not only to *Pudgala* but also to all *dharmas*. In their philosophical understanding, everything is 'empty like a magical illusion'. In other words, absolutely all things have the same status as persons, tables, chairs and forests. They are all conceptual constructs and as such, cannot be vested with own-existence. To think that *dharmas* have primary existence (own-existence) is to grasp and cling and 'cling to' is to miss enlightenment. The means to enlightenment is cessation of grasping and clinging even to the most subtle sources of attachment. This ceasing to grasp and cling comes about only by realizing the true nature of even the most subtle sources of attachment and see them as empty and as mere conceptual fabrications.

No basis is ever found for apprehension of any *dharma* as an ever-existent reality. This understanding of the lack of basis for apprehension of *dharmas* as ever-existent reality and the insight into the emptiness of *dharmas* are called the 'Perfection of Wisdom'. This emptiness is the object of meditation for the practitioner to aid him in the abandonment of attachment to things and cutting away the grasping at the roots. He merges in emptiness "where there is no perception, no appellation, no conceptual construction or conventional expression". There one speaks of 'Perfect Wisdom' (*Aṣṭasāhasrikā* VII. 177). *Śūnyatā* (emptiness) together with the signless (*animitta*) and the wishlessness (*apraṇihita*) are said to be the three doors to deliverance.

In *Śatasāhasrikā* (XLV. F. 119), the emptiness and Perfect Wisdom are likened to infinite space (*ākāśa*) that contains the multitude of things in its vacuity and that is left unmarked by the happening of anything within it. Just as the flight of a bird through the open space does not leave any mark, the emptiness and perfect wisdom are unmarked by anything. They have no beginning or end limits (*koṭis*). Just as *ākāśa* is unsupported, they are also unsupported by anything. They have no foundation or support. Further, *Śatasāhasrikā* states that it is because of 'I-making' and 'mine-making' i.e. because of the mental constructs and discriminations of 'I' and 'mine', duality of subject and object, the beings run and wander about in birth-and-death.

"It is surely in this sense that one conceives of beings as defiled. In so far as they indulge in I-making and mine-making, insofar as they take hold of things (i.e. are attached to things), they are defiled. In so far, however, as they do not take hold of things, in so far they are considered as purified, and do not run about and wander in birth-and-death."(*Śatasāhasrikā* XLV, F.119).

When one resorts to emptiness, characterized as blissful and as the quietude of all discursive ideas, all the discursive ideas which are a net of thought constructions disappear. When discursive ideas have disappeared, discrimination comes to rest, and with it all *karmas* and defilements and all kinds of rebirth. Hence emptiness is called *Nirvāṇa*, as it brings to rest (*Nirvāṇa*) all discursive ideas.

5. Knowledge of the Five *Skandhas* in Perfect Wisdom

In *Mahāprajñāpāramitā* (trsl. Hsuan–tsang, fasc. 532, ch. 29 (1),

Buddha describes the true knowledge of the five *skandhas* gained by a Boddhisattva *Mahāsattva* in his deep practice of the perfection of wisdom as regards their marks, their origin – and – extinction and their Suchness.

In his deep perfection of wisdom, the Bodhisattva *Mahāsattva* realizes that:

- form is nothing but holes and cracks, and is indeed like a mass of bubbles, with a nature that has no hardness or solidity.
- sensations (feelings) are like a boil or an arrow, swiftly arising and swiftly vanishing, and are indeed like floating foam, empty, false and fleeting, arising only from the coincidence of the three factors (sense-organ, object and consciousness).
- perception is like a mirage – pool which cannot be laid hand upon; it is an unreal thing (*dharma*) constructed by thought when causes and conditions leading to thirst and craving mistakenly arise.
- impulse is like the banana tree which, though you strip it leaf-sheath by leaf-sheath, you cannot lay hand on.
- consciousness is like things seen in a magic show, brought together by conditions which create the illusion that something exists. But actually there is nothing that can be laid hand upon.

The Bodhisattva *Mahāsattva* also knows in his perfection of wisdom that when each of the five *skandhas* – form, sensation, perception, volition and consciousness – originates, it comes from no-where, and when it is extinguished, it goes nowhere, but that though it neither comes nor goes, yet its origin and extinction do jointly exist (*saṃprayukta*).

Further, he knows that Suchness of each of the five *skandhas* (i.e., selflessness of them) is not subject to origin or extinction (i.e., it is uncaused, unborn); that it neither comes nor goes, is neither foul nor clean, neither increases nor diminishes, is constant to its own nature, is never empty, false or changeful, and is therefore called Suchness. Suchness is the synonym of emptiness (selflessness), the way things (*dharmas*) actually are, lacking their own-existence.

6. Form is Emptiness and Emptiness Itself is Form

The shortest of the *Prajñāpāramitā* texts is the *Prajñāpāramitā Hṛdaya,* which expresses perfectly the concept of *śūnyatā.* It states:

"When the Bodhisattva *Avalokiteśvara* was engaged in the practice of the deep *Prajñāpāramitā,* he perceived : there are the five *skandhas*; and these he saw in their self-nature to be empty.

"O *Śāriputra,* form is here emptiness, emptiness is form; form is no other than emptiness, emptiness is not other than form ; what is form that is emptiness, what is emptiness that is form. The same can be said of sensation, perception, volition and consciousness.

"O *Śāriputra,* all things are here characterised by emptiness: they are not born, they are not annihilated ; they are not stained, they are not immaculate; they do not increase, they do not decrease. Therefore, O *Śāriputra,* in emptiness there is no form, no sensation, no perception, no volition, no consciousness; no eye, ear, nose, tongue, body, mind; no form, sound, colour, taste, touch, objects ; no *dhātu* of vision, till we come to no *dhātu* of consciousness; there is no knowledge, no ignorance ; there is no attainment (and) no realisation ...." (Translated from the Sanskrit by D.T. Suzuki-Beatrice Lane Suzuki, *Mahāyāna Buddhism,* p. 84/85)

We find in the above paradoxical statements like 'Matter (form) is emptiness' and 'Emptiness itself is matter'. The latter is reverse of the former and is positively oriented as against negative orientation of the former. Scholars like G.M. Nagao interpret such a contradictory and paradoxical proposition as a synthesized view originating from direct yogic and intuitive insight of the practitioner. Their view of emptiness is not the result of analysis as in the *Hīnayāna abhidharmic* practice where individual things are minutely analysed, but a synthetic view seen by the intuition, which is called *Prajñāpāramitā* wisdom. This is different from ordinary wisdom, *Vijñāna. Vijñāna* is nothing but an aggregate of conscious experiences, whereas *Prajñā* transcends wisdom.

This emptiness of life and the world is not to be taken in a nihilist sense. The emptiness here is synonymous with dependent origination. It is only the negation of substantive reality to things because they are existing depending on conditions and causes. Things are empty and devoid of self ; they are said to be unborn, unoriginated etc. because they are not self-created, self-established and self-maintained; because they are dependently – originated and dependently – existent on others. They have no birth or existence of their own.

What is meant by 'Matter (form) is emptiness' is that matter is devoid of substantive reality and as such, is transient. When this negative expression is followed by the positive assertion 'Emptiness itself is matter (form)', it only affirms that dependent nature (dependent origination) i.e., selflessness is the essential nature of matter. These *Sūtras* do not negate the world as a fact of experience, but destroy the substantive reality and such other values attached to the world. The real import of these *Sūtras* is the negation of attachments ordinarily held to the values of the world. In this sense, the negation of substance is no other than the negation of attachments to substance. The objective here is to produce a pure mind unattached to anything.

7. *Nirvāṇa* of No Fixed Abode

Vajracchedikā Sūtra states: "A great bodhisattva should produce a mind freed from attachments. That is, he should not produce a mind attached to something." (Translated by G.M. Nagao; *Mādhyamika* and *Yogācāra*, p. 172)

So long as the mind is produced, it is directed to some object, dwells on that object and tends to adhere to what it has grasped. The mind is always clinging to something. Therefore, to state : 'The mind should be produced without clinging (i.e., without dwelling anywhere)' is equal to saying : 'One should think without thinking'. Here, an objectless mind, that is, a mind that is completely free from any thought of an object, unsupported by any objective form, is being suggested. This leads to *Nirvāṇa*.

The basic notion of *abhidharmic* schools assuming *dharmas* to be the ultimate supporters of experience is subverted by *Prajñāpāramitā* movement by denying the very possibility of pinpointing *dharmas* and by suggesting that they too are without a support and indistinguishable like *ākāśa* (space) and without any essence or self-nature of their own. As *Vimalakīrtinirdeśa* states, all *dharmas* are mental constructs and as such, "are supported on roots that have no support."(*Śikshāsamuccaya* 264)

Wisdom perfected or wisdom that has gone beyond is that which transcends all *dharmas* and which remains empty and unsupported like *ākāśa*. Highest wisdom is called the Prajñā which remains steady and unsupported by or without clining to any *dharmas,* any form (matter), any sensation, any perception, any volition or any *Vijñāna* (conscious experience).

Having all possible supports pulled from beneath one's mind (*citta*), it is then said to be 'non-residing' or 'unsupported' (*apratiṣṭhita*). This is the *Nirvāṇa* of no fixed abode or no fixed support. This is the perfection of wisdom.

'To go beyond' or 'to transcend' is the domain of the bodhisattva as explained in the *Vimalakīrtinirdeśa-Sūtra* :

"Not the domain of the ordinary individual and not the domain of the saint, such is the domain of the bodhisattva. The domain of the world, yet not the domain of the passions, such is the domain of the bodhisattva. Where one realizes *Nirvāṇa,* yet does not enter final and complete *Nirvāṇa,* there is the domain of the bodhisattva."

(G.M. Nagao; *Mādhyamika* and *Yogācāra,* p. 170)

This *Sūtra* teaches that the domain of the bodhisattva is the 'non-dwelling *Nirvāṇa'.* A bodhisattva does not dwell in the world of *saṃsāra* owing to his wisdom and does not remain in *Nirvāṇa* owing to his compassion. A bodhisattva is the one who defers his salvation and does not remain rooted in the final bliss of *Nirvāṇa* even though he has attained to that state. He refuses the liberation of *Nirvāṇa* untill all beings are saved. He takes birth willingly and of his own volition to serve and benefit others. The term non-dwelling *Nirvāṇa* does not mean only that one does not enter and remain in *Nirvāṇa* but it also means that one is not attached to *Nirvāṇa* and does not cling to *Nirvāṇa.* That is because *Nirvāṇa* originates in *śūnyatā. Nirvāṇa* was considered one of the *asaṃskṛta* (unconditioned) *dharmas* and made into a concrete substantive reality in the *Sarvāstivāda.* However, here in this philosophy, even that *Nirvāṇa* is considered as *śūnyatā* and the bodhisattva stands in a bottomless void unsupported by anything. He does not cling even to *Nirvāṇa.*

8. The Six Perfections (*Pāramitās*)

The greatness of *Prajñāpāramitā* movement and *Mahāyāna* lies in its concept of bodhisattvas and the underlying spirit of selfless service to humanity. The first step on the march of bodhisattva is the practice of the four great vows and the six *pāramitās.*

The four great vows are :

- To save all beings
- To destroy all evil passions
- To learn the Truth and teach it to others
- To lead all beings towards Buddhahood.

Every disciple of the *Mahāyāna* Buddhism aspires to become a Buddha. It is not mandatory to become a monk. Wherever he is, if he possesses the resolutiom, he may take the vows before his spiritual teacher or he may take it alone; but in order to take it, he must be filled with love and compassion for all creatures and resolve to practise the six *pāramitās* (Virtues of Perfection).

Perfection of Giving *(Dāna)*

The perfection of giving is graded into two – the worldly perfection and the supermundane perfection – in *Mahāyāna* Buddhism

"The worldly perfection of giving consists in this : The bodhisattva gives liberally to all those who ask. .... It occurs to him: "I give, that one receives, this is the gift. I renounce all my possessions without stint. I act as one who knows the Buddha. I practise the perfection of giving. I, having made this gift into the common property of all beings, dedicate it to supreme enlightenment, and that without apprehending anything. By means of this gift and its fruit, may all beings in this very life be at their ease, and may they one day enter *Nirvāṇa* !". Tied by three ties he gives a gift. Which three? A perception of self, a perception of others, a perception of the gift.

"The supramundane perfection of giving, on the other hand, consists in the threefold purity. What is the threefold purity? Here a bodhisattva gives a gift, and he does not apprehend a self, nor a recipient, nor a gift; also no reward of his giving. He surrenders that gift to all beings, but he apprehends neither beings nor self. He dedicates that gift to supreme enlightenment, but he does not apprehend any enlightenment. This is called the supramundane perfection of giving." (*Pañcaviṃsatisāhasrikā* , 263-64)

Total negation of self is the characteristic mark of perfection of giving. *Prajñāpāramitā* emphasizes that, actually to attain to the full degree the perfections of giving and so on, it is necessary to have had direct non-conceptual awareness of emptiness. They are not truly perfections unless they are underpinned with a direct realisation that e.g. the giver, recipient and gift all are empty (i.e., all lack inherent existence).

Giving is explained as being of four kinds: (*i*) material goods; (*ii*) Love and comfort; (*iii*) fearlessness; and (*iv*) the Doctrine (*Dharma*). Fearlessness here indicates that the bodhisattva dedicates himself for the fight against unjust social orders and oppressions of all kinds. He engages in removing poverty and suffering.

Perfection of Morality *(Śīla)*

The perfection of morality of a bodhisattva consists in his staunch adherence to the ten wholesome (virtuous) conducts subsumed under the principles of Right Speech, Right Action and Right Livelihood in the Noble Eightfold Path and also in his efforts to lead others into the Noble Eightfold Path. *Mahāyāna* regards the concentration on positive virtues as of more importance than abstention from evil. In this perfection, three kinds of morality or discipline are considered:

"The three kinds of discipline are the discipline of increasingly giving up what is not good, the discipline of increasingly developing what is good and the discipline of increasingly benefitting sentient beings." (*Buddhist Yoga,* Translated by Thomas Cleary, p. 78)

The bodhisattva not only lives according to the precepts but urges others to do so, both by teaching and example. Here he is walking in the Eightfold Noble Path. Even when his body is dismembered, he does not deviate from his path, he radiates goodwill towards all beings and does not contract himself from the pain. That for him constitutes the Perfection of Conduct. (*Śikshāsamuccaya* 187; *Sāgaramati Sūtra*)

Perfection of Patience *(Kṣānti)*

He always practises patience and forbearance. He never gets angry, impatient or excited over what is done by others because he always bears in mind that all troubles arise because of causes and conditions. Forbearance here is characterized by patiently suffering injury without bearing any ill-will towards the one who causes it, serenity in suffering and adherence to the *Dharma,* Truth and Non-violence.

"In that, even when his body is dismembered, he remains patient for the sake of the deliverance even of those who dismember it, does them no injury even in his thoughts and manifests the power of patience. That for him is the Perfection of Patience." (*Śikshāsamuccaya* 187; *Sāgaramati Sūtra*).

"The Lord: A *Tathāgata*'s perfection of patience is really no perfection. Because, Subhuti, when the king of Kalinga cut my flesh from every limb, at that time I had no notion of a self, or of a being, or of a soul, or of a person, nor had I any notion or non-notion. And why? If, Subhuti, at that time I had had a notion of self, I would also have had a notion of ill-will at that time. If I had had a notion of being, of a soul, of a person, then I also would have had a notion of ill-will at that time.........." (*Vajracchedika* 14)

Perfection of patience consists in returning good to evil and not harbouring any unkind thoughts even against those who cause injuries to us.

Perfection of Vigour *(Vīrya)*

In order to tread the path, it is necessary to be energetic and strenuous, to keep one's resolutions strong, not to give way to weakness or discouragement and not to become attached to wordly pleasures. Vigour is the force or energy one applies in practising the four right efforts and in achieving the six perfections.

'Right effort' consists of effort to prevent the arising of unwholesome mental states (e.g., greed, hatred and delusion) which have not arisen and effort to get rid of unwholesome states that have arisen. It is also effort to arouse wholesome states (e.g., non-attachment, loving kindness and wisdom) which have not arisen, and effort to develop and promote wholesome states that have arisen.

The perfection of vigour of a bodhisattva is his ability to dwell persistently in the six perfections with great application, energy and steadfastness and to lead others to these perfections.

"The three kinds of diligence (vigour) are diligence as armour, diligence of concerted effort to increasingly develop good qualities, and diligence of concentrated effort to help sentient beings." (*Buddhist Yoga,* translated by Thomas Cleary, p. 79)

"That vigour by which he refuses to give up the urge towards enlightenment ...., that vigour by which he remains in *saṃsāra* due to his compassion towards fellow sentient beings (without entering into *Nirvāṇa* though he could) and continues to bring to maturity the roots of goodness – that for him is the Perfection of Vigour."

(*Śikshāsamuccaya* 187; *Sāgaramati Sūtra*)

Perfection of Meditation *(Dhyāna)*

In this perfection, three kinds of meditation are highlighted:

"The three kinds of meditation are meditation in a state of bliss without discriminating thought, still and silent, extremely tranquil and impeccable, thus curing the pains of afflictions (defilements); meditation that brings forth virtuous qualities and powers; and meditation that brings forth benefit for sentient beings." (*Buddhist Yoga,* Translated by Thomas Cleary, p. 79)

"Even when his body is dismembered, the bodhisattva does not become confused in his cultivation of the thought of omniscience he has gained, has regard only for enlightenment and takes care only of the peaceful calm of cessation – that for him is the Perfection of Meditative Concentration. (*Śikshāsamuccaya* 187; *Sāgaramati Sūtra*)

He, through skill in means, enters into the meditative trances, yet he is not intent on being reborn in the corresponding heavens of form even though he could. He "takes birth, willingly, volitionally, in the world of existence" for the benefit of sentient beings.

Perfection of Wisdom

In this perfection, three kinds of wisdom (insight) are stressed: insight focussed on conventional worldly truth, insight focussed on ultimate truth, and insight focussed on benefiting sentient beings.

He does not settle down in any *dharma* (thing or entity) and he contemplates the essential original nature of all *dharmas* as emptiness. He sees all *dharmas* as empty of marks of their own, without true reality, incomplete and uncreated. He avoids the two extremes of affirmation and denial, and always treads the middle path, that is called insight.

"Even when his body is dismembered, he looks upon the phantom and image of his body as upon so much straw, a log or a wall; arrives at the conviction that his body has the nature of an illusion, and contemplates his body as in reality being impermanent, fraught with suffering, not his own, and at peace – that for him is the Perfection of Wisdom." (*Śikshāsamuccaya* 187; *Sāgaramati Sūtra*).

It is the supreme virtue and its complete possession is the same as *Nirvāṇa.*

9. The Bodhisattva Ideal

Har Dayal has summarized the concept of *arahantship* in early Buddhism as below:

"An *arahant* who was thus liberated, knew that he would not be reborn. He had accomplished what was to be done. He attained undefiled and final emancipation of mind and heart. He was alone secluded, zealous, master of himself." (The Bodhisattva Doctrine in Buddhist Sanskrit Literature, p. 2)

In course of time, the Buddhist monks overlooked the ideal example set forth by the Buddha in his own life and became self-centered, concerned only with their own liberation. They were indifferent to the duty of teaching and helping all human beings. But the *Prajñāpāramitā* masters were not satisfied with the narrow selfish ideal of such *arahantship*. For them, the Buddha's life itself is his teaching and is the perfect ideal to be achieved. Buddha's life was characterized by altruism and compassion towards all sentient beings. For *Prajñāpāramitā* masters, the Buddha's life itself came to be understood as an exemplary model of superior ideal. Accordingly, they set forth the ideal path and practices of a bodhisattva whose aim is not just *arahantship*, but attainment of perfect Buddhahood for the benefit of all sentient beings.

His *Nirvāṇa* is *apratiṣṭhita* – *Nirvāṇa* (*Nirvāṇa* of no fixed abode). For him, *saṃsāra* and *Nirvāṇa* both are identical and he does not turn back from either. He is in perfect equanimity in both.

"Since he possesses compassion, a bodhisattva does not become agitated by *saṃsāra* nor feels weary of *saṃsāra;* therefore, he does not dwell in *Nirvāṇa*. Again, since he possesses the highest wisdom, he is not bound by the faults of *saṃsāra*; therefore, he does not dwell in *saṃsāra*." (Vasubandhu, *MSA*.XVII. 32)

A bodhisattva does not dwell in and does not cling to *Nirvāṇa* owing to his compassion. Also, he neither dwells in nor clings to *saṃsāra* owing to his great wisdom. Even though the 'becoming' or further evolution of his *Vijñāna* (blind will to live) has ceased, he takes birth willingly, volitionally, in the world of existence for the benefit of all sentient beings.

A bodhisattva resolves : "I take upon myself the burden of all suffering, I am resolved to do so. I will endure it. I do not turn or run away, do not tremble, am not terrified, not afraid, do not turn back or despond . . . . I must rescue all these beings from the stream of *saṃsāra* which is difficult to cross, I must pull them back from the great precipice. . . . . I myself must grapple with the whole mass of suffering of all beings. To the limit of my endurance I will experience in all the states of woe, found in any world system, all the abodes of suffering. And I must not cheat all beings out of my store of merit. I am resolved to abide in each single state of woe for numberless aeons and so I will help all beings to freedom, in all the states of woe that may be found in any world system whatsoever.

"And why? Because it is surely better that I alone should be in pain than that all these beings should fall into the states of woe. . . . ." (*Śikshāsamuccaya* 280-81 ; *Vajradhvaja Sūtra*)

What is special in the bodhisattva concept is the "skill in means" (*upāya*) which he is said to possess and by which he knows exactly what to teach or do and how to teach any particular individual to lead him to enlightenment and end of suffering.

"It is through his compassionate skill in means for others
that he is tied to the world
And that though he has attained the state of a saint,
yet he appears to be in the state of an ordinary person.

He has gone beyond all that is worldly, yet he has not
moved out of the world ;
In the world he pursues his course for the world's weal,
unstained by worldly taints.

"As a lotus flower, though it grows in water, is not
polluted by the water,
So he, though born in the world, is not polluted by
worldly *dharmas.*

"Like a fire his mind constantly blazes up
into good works for others ;
At the same time he always remains merged in
the calm of the trances and formless attainments."

(*Ratnagotravibhāga* I, vv. 70-73)

It may look paradoxical but the *Prajñāpāramitā Sūtras* consider bodhisattva also as empty. Even through they teach that one should become a bodhisattva, for them there is no such thing as a bodhisattva, as all-knowledge, as path or as realisation. According to them, all are conceptual constructs and are relevant only in the conventional sense ; in the ultimate truth all *dharmas* including *Nirvāṇa* are empty.

"Even *Nirvāṇa,* I say, is like a magical illusion, is like a dream. How much more so anything else ! . . . . Even if perchance there could be anything more distinguished, of that too I would say that it is like an illusion like a dream." (*Aṣṭsāhasrikā Prajñāpāramitā*, Trans. Conze : 99)

What is affirmed as truth in the conventional sense for practical purposes is ultimately unreal. Mixing up the two without realizing the distinction between the conventional truth and ultimate truth will lead to paradoxical contradictions. *Prajñāpāramitā Sūtras* only highlight these contradictions. The main concern or the only concern of these *Sūtras* is liberation through transforming the mind, cutting down the craving and clinging even to the subtlest source of attachment or even to *Nirvāṇa.* It is not possible to eradicate the defilements of the mind and burn away the *karmic* residue without cutting down this clinging even to the subtlest sources.

"If, Subhuti, these bodhisattvas should have a perception of either a *dharma,* or a no-*dharma,* they would thereby seize on a self, a being, a soul, or a person. And why? Because a bodhisattva should not seize on either a *dharma* nor a no-*dharma.* Therefore this saying has been taught by the *Tathāgata* with a hidden meaning: "Those who know the discourse on *dharma* as like unto a raft, should forsake *dharmas,* still more no-*dharmas.*" (*Trans.Conze ; Buddhist Wisdom Books,* p. 34).

We see that *Prajñāpāramitā Sūtras* do not cling to any theory on existence of *dharmas* or emptiness of *dharmas.* They teach us to abandan both the theories and rise above them. These should not be clung onto with craving and attachment. The Buddha Dhamma should be considered only as a raft or boat. It is taught for the purose of crossing over to the other shore and is not for holding onto with attachment. Once he crosses over, the bodhisattva remains unsupported and not clinging to anything. He does not cling even to the theory of *dharma-nairātmya* leave alone *dharma-ātmya.*

Chapter 12

Madhyamaka

1. Madhyamaka Literature

In *Prajñāparamitā Sūtras*, the concept of *śūnya* (emptiness) has been expressed generally in enigmatic intuitive maxims with hardly any logical analysis or systematic exposition. It was Nāgārjuna who logically analysed the various *Sūtras* on *śūnyatā* and systematically organized them into a coherent philosophy that has come to be known as Madhyamaka. With his profound philosophy, *Mahāyāna* Buddhism got a firm philosophical foundation and almost all forms of *Mahāyāna* schools of later times regard and accept him as their founder and a great philosopher and monk second only to the Buddha.

The foundational texts for this school are mainly the following works of Nāgārjuna (100-200 AD) and his disciple *Āryadeva* :-

(*i*) The *Madhyamakakārikā* ('Verses on Madhyamaka', commonly abbreviated as MMK) – Nāgārjuna's main work still extant in Sanskrit.

(*ii*) *Dvādaśa-dvāra* (the 'Twelve Gates') by Nāgārjuna, which is now available only in Chinese translation.

(*iii*) *Śata Śāstra* (the 'One Hundred Verse Treatise') of *Āryadeva*.

(*iv*) The *Vigrahavyāvartanī* ('Averting the Controversy') – Verses extant in Sanskrit together with an auto commentary – a reply by Nāgārjuna to his critics.

(*v*) *Ratnāvalī* ('The Jewel Garland', a long epistle apparently to a king).

2. Emptiness of all *Dharmas* (*Dharma-Nairātmya*)

The concept of *śūnyatā* (emptiness) is a logical corollary of the fundamental Buddhist teachings of *anityam* (impermanence), *asukham* (suffering) and *anātman* (no-self). Emptiness is synonymous with the definition of no-self and signifies the non-being or non-existence of a substantive self in the aggregates constituting the subjective 'I' and the objects called 'mine'. Nāgārjuna defines emptiness by stating that 'all things are empty because they have no essences', that is, because they have no inherent self-nature of their own.

As a rule, *śūnyatā* (emptiness) means '*niḥsvabhāva*' (no self-nature). Emptiness is usually expressed as "no-self, no self-nature, hence emptiness". The term self-nature (*svabhāva*) is defined by Nāgārjuna as "that which cannot be artificially produced (*akṛtrima*) or that which is not dependent (*nirapekṣa*) on others(MMK XV.2). Self-nature, therefore, refers to the inherent essence of a thing, to what exists on its own accord, in and of itself, or to a substantive being unchanging and immovable. In other words, it is an 'absolute existence being neither created nor relative to others'. Yet such essences or self-natures are not particularly evident in our present world where everything exists in relation to something else and where every thing changes.

Nāgārjuna proves that since everything arises co-dependently depending on some other things, nothing in this world of our experience is self-established, self-maintained and self-dependent and that all things including the personal self (*pudgala*) are empty because of this fact of their not having any self-nature of their own. To accept such a self-nature is to negate change and also the core Buddhist doctrine of dependent origination which are the very facts of our experience. Thus it negates experience. The fact of 'That exists' is dependent upon and conditioned by the fact of 'This being'; it is not owing to the fact that 'That' has its own self-nature, an inherent substantive nature of its own. Universal relativity manifested by dependent origination always points to the non-substantiveness of all things. This is the same truth expressed by Nāgārjuna as emptiness or *śūnyatā* of everything which simply means that all entities have 'no self-nature' and, as such, are relative and dependently originating.

Further, the notion of 'intrinsic self-nature' is incompatible with the changes we are experiencing in our daily lives. If a thing or a *dharma* (constituent element of experience) is said to have an 'intrinsic self-nature' of its own, then it is understood that its self-nature is unchangeable and that it is eternal, changeless. In that case, how are we to account for the changes experienced? Nāgārjuna states in MMK 24. 20f :

"According to 'Own-being', the world would be unoriginated, unceased, unchanging and free from varying conditions .... If all this is non-empty, then there would be no arising and no ceasing."

He also poses another fundamental question : How can that which exists by its own being come into existence? If a belief in intrinsic self-nature or an abiding changeless self or essence in any factor of our experience is clung to, then changes experienced cannot be logically explained.

The predisposition, whether of common sense or of philosophical speculation, to view the existing as somehow aboslutely existing, arises from the tendency of language and its users to freeze the flow of experiences into concepts and 'objectify' these concepts (*vikalpa*), thereby creating the illusion that the world of our experience is made up of real, unitary and self-sufficient substances. Due to ignorance, one gets attached to the idea of a fixed self-nature (*svabhāva*) to the internal world of his own 'self' and creates boundaries and distinctions between his 'own self' (internal world) and the 'external' world of objects and other people. It is important to understand that *Niḥsvabhāvatā* (no self-nature theory) is a denial of the self in both of these realms and not just a denial of a personal self. This is the import of the *Mahāyāna* doctrine of '*dharma-nairātmya*'.

3. Truly Empty hence Unfathomable Existence

Śūnyatā concept flows from the core Buddhist doctrine of dependent origination. For Nāgārjuna, *śūnyatā* (emptiness) is identical with dependent origination .

Professor G.M. Nagao has succintly presented the whole philosophy and its implications in the following words:

"On the one hand, dependent co-arising means that all beings are not independent (*svātantrika*) and self-existing (*ātman*) things, but only transient beings brought about by the constellation of cluster of causes. This no-self and absence of any independent self underlying transient being is the emptiness of things .... On the other hand, this emptying and negating of things does not mean that things do not exist at all; non-being is not nothingness. Emptiness signifies only the absence of essence. The evolving, changing world understood through insight into emptiness is not meant to be negated. Beings that exist in emptiness exist just as they are .... This restored and purified second dimension of dependent co-arising is indeed wondrous (*āścarya*). Because of emptiness, the existence of beings together with their causes is ineffable (*avācya*) and inconceivable (*acintya*). In truth, the phenomenal world is first and foremost a beautiful world, and phenomenal being is a being wondrous and enjoyable beyond description. But this is not the beauty or joy of the one–dimensional birth-death cycle, which consists in unlimited suffering. The wonder, beauty and joy of the dependently co-arising world is entirely due to its being free of essence and empty."

The concept of *śūnyatā* has both negative and positive connotations. Negatively speaking, it conveys that everything is empty, and nothing is essentially real! But the beauty of the thing is that it is precisely because everything is empty, anything is possible. This is the positive aspect of the concept. Even though nothing is essentially real, anything is possible. You may create your own hell and suffer or you can create your own heaven of Buddha Nature and enjoy the bliss of *Nirvāṇa.* That is why Nāgārjuna states in *Vigrahavyāvartanī,* Verse 70, that :

"All things are possible for the one for whom emptiness is possible; nothing whatsoever is possible for the one for whom emptiness is not possible."

Emptiness eradicates all boundaries, so anything is possible if everything is empty and not otherwise.

Nāgārjuna explains that an activity becomes possible only when the world is *śūnyatā.* It is inconceivable that an activity takes place in a substantive being, for a substantive being is understood to be an eternal immutable being and therefore could not be active and undergo change. Only when there is no substantiality, that is, only when *śūnyatā* is, can there be change and activity. This point is discussed thoroughly in Chapter XXIV (*Āryasatya*) of MMK. An opponent charges :

> If everything is *śūnya,*
> There can never be any appearance,
> Disappearance or transformation.
> Hence, there can be no Buddha-dharma,
> Such as the Fourfold Truths.
> (And, consequently, no emancipation or salvation).

Nāgārjuna answers the charge with the very same words :

> If everything is not *śūnya,*
> There can never be any appearance
> Disappearance or transformation.
> Hence, there can be no Buddha-dharma,
> Such as the Fourfold Truths
> (And, consequently, no emancipation or salvation).

The first verse depicts an attack by the opponents who mistake *śūnyatā* as mere nothingness. The second represents the Buddhist view that defends the position that everything is dependently originated on account of its emptiness. For Nāgārjuna, all things will be seen to be rational and acceptable only when emptiness is seen to be rational and acceptable. This is because, since emptiness is an implication of dependent origination, the alternative to emptiness would be inherent existence and therefore an unchanging block-universe (or of course literally nothing at all). If X exists and is not empty, X would be inherently existent and thus would never go out of existence. That is how, in a wonderful reversal, Nāgārjuna accuses his opponent who denies emptiness with destroying the teaching of Buddha. Who could become enlightened if their state of unenlightenment were inherently existent and this is not the result of causes and conditions?

Nāgārjuna has linked the idea of *śūnyatā* to the idea of dependent origination (*pratītyasamutpāda*) that has been the core of Buddhism since its beginning and on account of that, his philosophy of *śūnyatā* did not end up being a nihilism that negated the religious efforts of human kind nor did it deviate from fundamental Buddhist tenets.

In later Chinese Buddhism, the very same theory of Nāgārjuna finds beautiful expression in the maxim: "Truly empty (hence) unfathomable existence." This is to be understood, as the recovery of existence from emptiness (non-existence). Here, there is first negation followed by affirmation.

4. Eight-fold Negation

In the expositions above, we have seen how Nāgārjuna has proved *śūnyatā*, based on the doctrines of dependent origination (*pratītyasamutpāda*) and *anātman* (no self-nature). Nāgārjuna's profound philosophical insight delves further deeper and identifies *pratītyasamutpāda* itself as emptiness by discerning eight-fold negation in it.

At the beginning of his work MMK, Nāgārjuna describes *pratītyasamutpāda* as having the characteristics of eight-fold negation as below and hence it is *śūnyatā* :

Neither existence nor non-existence
(Neither birth nor death);
Neither eternal nor annihilated;
Neither one nor many;
Neither coming nor departing.

Dependent origination is an undeniable fact of experience. This is established in the systematic formulations of the laws of cause and effect in all modern scientific enquiries. The doctrine of dependent origination which is the core teaching of Buddha denotes this concept of laws governing the evolution of universe in all the fields. Later day Spinoza equated the higher reality or God with eternal, immutable and necessary laws. These laws explicate the idea of dependent origination. But, in the ultimate analysis, the laws as well as the concept of dependent origination are abstractions from the experience and constructions of the mind explaining that, depending on such and such conditions, such and such things arise. Based on scientific-enquiry, we analyse the experience and formulate the laws. We accept them after verification and proof. We believe that these laws are valid not only in the present but hold good for the future also. In future? new laws will also be discovered and added to the knowledge to enhance the power of man. Can we say that all these laws come into existence only after they are discovered by the human mind and were non-existent in the past? Will they be existent in future? We can only say that they were or they will be neither existent nor non-existent for they come into force depending on the conditions fulfilled.

On similar considerations, they are neither having a beginning (birth) nor having an end (death), they are neither ephemeral nor eternal, they are neither one nor many.

Such is the insight that Nāgārjuna brings to bear in his profound philosophy when he expounds dependent origination as having the characteristics of this eight-fold negation. This eight-fold negation signifies the *śūnyatā* of dependent-origination and also of the things originating and dying. Thus, in Nāgārjuna's philosophy, dependent-origination is itself identified with *śūnyatā*. It is *śūnyatā* and it arises in *śūnyatā* depending on conditions. There is no absolute necessity or essentiality in any of the *dharmas* constituting the experience. Only the conditions and causes determine the *dharmas* and experiences. New set of conditions and causes will lead to a new set of *dharmas* and experiences which are thus changeable.

5. Dependent Origination is also the Middle-Path

Having equated dependent origination with *śūnyatā* (emptiness), Nāgārjuna then proceeds to equate it with the Middle Path. He quotes Buddha in his *Vigrahavyāvartanī* :-

"I pay respect to that incomparable Buddha who taught emptiness, dependent origination and the Middle Path as synonymous."

From this, it can be seen that not only are emptiness and dependent origination treated as synonymous, but the Middle Path also is treated as synonymous with them.

Nāgārjuna's philosophical position is summarized succintly in his *Mūla-Madhyamaka-Kārikā* (MMK) verse XXIV.18 thus:

"What is originating co-dependently,
we call emptiness.
It is a designation based upon some material
(*upādāya-prajñapti*);
Only this is the Middle Path."

(G.M. Nagao's translation; *Mādhyamika and Yogācāra*, p.190)

The first part of the verse equates dependent – origination with emptiness as discussed earlier.

The term '*upādāya-prajñapti*', in the second part of the above verse, is interpreted by scholars variously. G.M. Nagao interprets the same as a 'designation' (*prajñapti*) which depends upon or bases itself upon (*upādāya*) something else or some kind of material (*upādanā*). According to him, '*upādāya-prajñapti*' is designation based on some material or it is our conceptual construction, the name and form we impose on the worldly objects with our minds. It is only conventional talk and has existence based on causes and conditions. Since it is arising depending upon causes and conditions, it is also equated with dependent-origination (*pratītyasamutpāda*). *Pratītyasamutpāda* which was earlier identified with *śūnyatā* is now equated with this conceptual construction (*upādāya-prajñapti*) which because of its impermanence and no-self nature can only be descibed as neither existent nor non-existent and hence empty.

The whole philosophical scheme of Nāgārjuna may be represented diagrammatically as below:

Paramārtha Satya
(Ultimate Truth)
Neither Existence Nor
Non-Existence

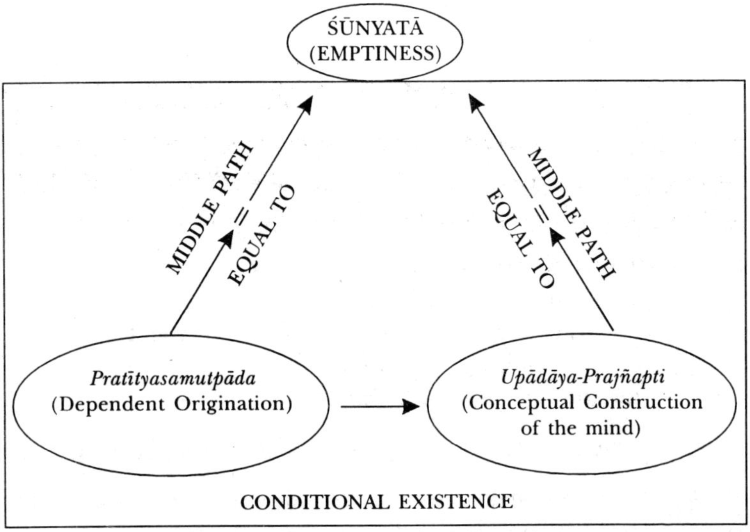

Saṃvṛti Satya (Conventional Truth)

Pratītya-samutpāda and *upādāya-prajñapti* are both equal to *śūnyatā* since they can only be defined by such expressions as 'neither existent nor non-existent', 'neither eternal nor non-eternal', 'neither arising nor going of their own'. By reason of their having no self-nature of their own, but instead having the characteristics of eight-fold negation as expounded by Nāgārjuna, *pratītyasamutpāda* and *upādāya prajñapti* are treated equal to *śūnyatā*. The eight-fold negation denies and avoids the extremes of existence and non-existence, eternalism and nihilism etc. and instead affirms the middle ground in each case. The realisation and practice of this middle ground, the golden mean, is the Middle Path preached by Buddha which, with sustained arduous practice, gives insight into the concept of emptiness and leads one to enlightenment and emancipation.

Since the Middle Path also arises dependently and is not self-made and not self-established, it is also identified with *pratītyasamutpāda* and thus, in the ultimate analysis, it is also *śūnyatā* or empty. The ultimate truth is *śūnyatā* and in this *śūnyatā* arise *pratītyasamutpāda, upādāya-prajñapti* and also even Buddha's teachings such as the Four Noble Truths, Middle Path etc. depending upon causes and conditions. Once the causes and conditions cease, there is no arising, there is no birth or death.

The doctrinal aspect of the Middle Path involves an attempt to avoid what the Buddhist tradition sees as 'extreme views'. From a Buddhist point of view, not only the practical extremes of asceticism and licentiousness, but also the doctrinal extremes of eternalism (based on the belief in a permanent abiding self) and nihilism (nothingness) are also to be avoided. Nāgārjuna adheres to this basic Buddhist position of Middle Path through his reciprocal eight-fold negation as below avoiding the extremes in the doctrinal views:-

No birth – No death (Neither existence nor non-existence)
No permanence – No annihilation
No diversity – No unity
No coming – No going

With this reciprocal eight-fold negation, Nāgārjuna refutes all the phases of 'becoming' or life-conditions. If there be any other extreme views or attachments, Nāgārjuna would deny them also. The final result of Nāgārjuna's negations is the *śūnya* or Void which is not an actual emptiness or nothingness, but is instead the middle position of all stated extreme views.

6. Dialectic of Nāgārjuna

Thus, it is the genius of Nāgārjuna that provided a firm logical foundation for the concept of *śūnyatā* and other core Buddhist teachings of dependent origination and Middle Path. He is opposed to any form of absolutism and denies the reality of any absolute or substantive existence *per se*. The process of his reasoning is exemplified by the so-called *catuṣkoṭi* (*tetralemma*, four alternative propositions), by which he directed his logic to the negation of any form of realism or substantiality to things. *Catuṣkoṭi* conists of any four alternative propositions such as, for example, 'exists' (positive), 'does not exist' (negative), 'both exists and does not exist' (both positive and negative) and 'neither exists nor does not exist' (neither positive nor negative). These are all the possible veiw points that can be advocated and, dialectically speaking, there is no other possibility.

Applying *tetralemma*, Nāgārjuna refutes all theories put forward in the absolute sense. In this sense origination or birth of anything cannot be established. The only four possiblities of 'origination' or 'birth' are origination from itself or from something other or from both itself and other or without any cause. If it is claimed that something originates from 'itself', then this would be a contradiction because what is the need for it to originate as it already exists. Or, otherwise that thing would be continuously originating without end, which is an absurdity. If something is said to originate from 'something other', then something different like fire would originate from something other like water; or otherwise, all things would arise from all other things. If something-originates from 'both itself and something other', then the difficulties involved in the above cases would only be compounded. If something originates 'without a cause', then everything would originate at all times and everywhere.

Thus, it can be seen that the origination of a thing cannot be established as an absolute reality having a self-nature of its own. As such, there can be no origination or birth in the absolute sense. It can only arise depending on causes and conditions. Thus, only emptiness or no self-nature makes possible for the things to arise.

Likewise, the First Cause is also subjected to scrutiny and refuted. (1) Is it caused by itself? (2) Or is it caused by another? (3) Or is it caused by both? (4) Or is it caused by neither? The deconstructive (*prāsaṅgika*) reasoning thus will prove that the First Cause itself is a contradiction in terms.

In this way, through analytical investigation, Nāgārjuna demonstrates the truth of complete emptiness 'like an illusion' asserted in the *Prajñāpāramitā Sūtras*.

"Whatever comes about conditioned by something else is quiescent from the point of view of inherent existence. Therefore both the process of origination and the act of production itself are quiescent ... . Like an illusion, a dream or a castle in the air are production, duration and cessation declared to be"(MMK 7: 16/34).

Thus, the *Mādhyamikas* adopt deconstructive reasoning to analyse the positions of the opponents and refute their theories of existence. They questioned the various categories of Buddhist as well as non-Buddhist thoughts and attacked metaphysics in general. They never put forward any counter-positions. In the eyes of the *Mādhyamika* thinkers, there was no *Mādhyamika* position. According to them, a self-assertion of emptiness is 'an erroneous view of emptiness' and it cannot be '(true) insight into emptiness'. The claim that all is *śūnyatā* is also absurd, for non-assertion or non-maintenance of a position is the real meaning of *śūnyatā*. As dependently origianted, emptiness itself is empty.

> (The *Tathāgata*) should not be described as
> He is void, he is non-void;
> Neither should he be termed
> Void and non-void simultaneously,
> Nor not void and not non-void simultaneously,
> But he is spoken of just for the sake of designation
> (MMK XXII. 11)

"One who accepts *śūnyatā* does not present any *pakṣa* (thesis, proposition) as his own." (*Vigrahavyāvartanī* 23)

Summarizing the foregoing, the ultimate truth is that beings or things have no reality in themselves, that is, they do not possess any inherent or intrinsic existence of their own (*svabhāva*), i.e., self-contained existence not caused by anything outside. The whole world is an ongoing process of causal continuum and all exist only in the manner of dependent origination (*pratītya-samutpāda*).

7. Two-Fold Truth

When the *pratītya-samutpāda* (dependent origination) and *upādāya-prajñapti* (designation based upon some material, conventional talk) are manifested depending on causes and conditions and following the laws of cause and effect, and when they are considered as existent or treated as existent, these are in the plane of conventional truth (*saṃvṛti-satya*). But, the ultimate truth (*paramārtha-satya*) is the true understanding that they are neither existent nor non-existent and that they are subjected to the eight-fold negation as described by Nāgārjuna in MMK; it is *śūnyatā* and all exist only in the manner of dependent origination.

This insight into emptiness (*śūnyatā*) is the ultimate truth of the way the things really are. The ultimate truth is correctly seeing the conventional as conventional and seeing it as existing in the manner of emptiness. It is not seeing a separate independent reality. The ultimate truth is *śūnyatā.*

The Middle Path taught by the Buddha, though it is also a conceptual construction and, as such, belongs to the category of conventional truth, is oriented towards the direction of ascent to the ultimate truth, because it affirms the truth as neither-existence nor non-existence. It denies both the extremes and adheres to the middle ground of flux of continuous process. From conventional truth one ascends to the ultimate truth. This is explained in MMK 24.8–10:

"The teaching of the *Dharma* by the Buddhas rests upon the two truths : worldly conventional truth and truth in the ultimate sense. Those who do not discern the distinction between these two truths do not discern the profound truth in the teaching of the Buddha. Without relying upon the practical, the ultimate is not taught. Without understanding the ultimate, one cannot attain *Nirvāṇa*".

The ultimate truth i.e. the insight into *śūnyatā* (emptiness) is realized when both *pratītyasamutpāda* (dependent origination) and the Middle Path, earlier thought of as having real existence, are correctly understood to be neither–existent nor-non-existent and every thing in the universe is seen as a flux of psycho-physical factors in a causal continuum. There is no self-contained existence in anything in the world and there is not any permanent, abiding, changeless, eternal self in anything. *Niḥsvabhāvatā* in Madhyamaka philosophy is a denial of self in both the internal world of one's own 'self' and the 'external' world of objects. With the negation and denial of 'self' in both these realms–subjective as well as objective–the discriminatory knowledge which consists of distinction between the subject and the object is also negated. This discriminatory knowledge with its incessant proliferation of concepts is based on the illusion that the world of our experience is made up of real, unitary and self-sufficient substances and exists for our enjoyment.

The *saṃsāric* world of suffering is the result as long as there is an adherence and clinging to the view of 'self' and objects and the concepts 'I' and 'mine' as existent reals. Liberation is the cessation of all conceptions and discriminatory knowledge (*vikalpa/ prapañca*).

MMK 18.4-5 states:

"When the views of 'I' and 'mine', whether pertaining to an outer or an inner self, have ceased, there is a relinquishment of grasping. With that cessation, there is the ceasing of becoming (birth). On the cessation of the *karmic* defilements, there is liberation. For the one who constructs, the *karmic* defilements (exist) due to conceptual proliferation (*prapañca*), but this conceptual proliferation ceases with emptiness".

Emptiness, which in the *Prajñāpāramitā* scriptures is a matter of direct religious insight, has thus been systematically elaborated by Nāgārjuna as an object of meditation for the practitioner to aid him in the abandonment of craving and clinging to the false notions of 'self', 'I' and 'mine' and to lead him in the path to liberation. The intent of Nāgārjuna was not merely to construct a philosophical and metaphysical system, but to offer a model for religious practice.

In Nāgārjuna's philosophy, *śūnyatā* is of course a negativity, but negativity of both existence and non-existence and is not mere nothingness. It stands midway between existence and non-existence with complete cessation of suffering. His *śūnyatā* is the ultimate truth and is beyond the reach of verbal designation (*prapañca*) or conceptual construct (*vikalpa*) (MMK XVIII .9).

Thus, we meet here denial of views and conceptions again and again. According to him, negation alone can lead us to the door of the absolute truth. In short, what Nāgārjuna is driving at is the principle of non-acquisition (*aprāptitva*) and non-attachment which is attained by the doctrine of universal negation. It is in fact an infinite negation until the tinge of worldly truth is utterly washed off. Therefore, the ultimate truth thus arrived at by dialectical method is called either the Middle Path of the Eightfold Negation or the Middle Path of the Twofold Truth.

Following the Buddha's practice, Nāgārjuna started, from an evaluation of the worldly or common-sense truth (*saṃvṛti-satya*) and against this he set forth the ultimate or highest–sense truth (*paramārtha-satya*). 'Highest-sense' does not mean the highest-sense truth at the beginning, but is only the highest at any particular time. It is, in fact, only higher-sense truth, as the term *lokottara* ('above the world') indicates. Gradually the common-sense world will reach the higher-sense truth then set forth, which latter then will become the common-sense truth. By the side of it Nāgārjuna would set forth a still higher-sense truth which again will become a common-sense truth in time. Thus the standard of common-sense truth will be raised higher and higher until it attains pre-eminently the Highest-sense Truth which can be taken as the Absolute. But it is not any Absolute entity but only the stage of perfect freedom.

Thus, the Highest-sense truth is taught to be arrived at dialectically and positively. This is the synthetic Void taught by Nāgārjuna by synthesizing and reconciling all opposing views as against the antithetic Void in Negativist School
(Junjiro Takakusu, The Essentials of Buddhist philosophy, p. 207/208).

8. Emptiness—Psychological Analysis

Emptiness that we have so far studied in the Madhyamaka philosophy of Nāgārjuna is based on purely logical analysis ; it is an intellectual theorisation emerging from a rational enquiry into the nature of things (*dharmas*). A psychological analysis of emptiness is given in *Candrakīrti*'s *Prasannapadā.* He quotes from *Ratnāvalī* to prove the unreality of the self:

> "As by means of a mirror one sees a reflected
> image of one's own face
> Though in actual reality this reflected imgage is
> nothing at all ;
> Just so, one apprehends the idea of 'I' through the
> *skandhas*
> Though in actual reality, like the image of one's
> own face, it is nothing at all
> As without the mirror one cannot see the
> reflected image
> Of one's own face so also the 'I' without the
> medium of the *skandhas.*
> ---------------------"
> (*Ratnāvalī* I, 31-34)

With the apprehension and grasping of 'self' arises the discrimination of the objects that are enjoyed and the subject (self) who is enjoying. This discrimination brings into play the mental factors of feeling, attachment, craving, lust, desire and passions. With the discrimination arise the three root poisons – attachment (passion), hatred and delusion – attachment for the objects that are pleasant, hatred for those that are unpleasant and delusion because of those that are neither pleasant nor unpleasant.

Candrakīrti explains in *Prasannapadā* XVIII :

"It is said in the *Sūtra* that all defilements have the false theory of individuality (of self) for their root, for their origin, for their cause.

"But this false theory of individuality is forsaken when one does not apprehend a self or what belongs to a self."

"And by the forsaking of that, one also forsakes the four-fold grasping i.e. grasping at sense – desire, grasping at false precepts and views, grasping at mere rituals and practices, grasping at the false theory of self."

"The extinction of grasping leads to the extinction of birth, the extinction of becoming again and again."

Candrakīrti further elaborates this idea as below:

"All worldly ideas are stopped without exception in emptiness, where there is a vision of emptiness of the own-being of all existents. How does that come about? Because, if one has the apprehension of an object, then the whole net of discursive ideas comes about. If one would not apprehend that, which is really the daughter of a barren woman, as a handsome young woman, then one would not, with her as an object, enter on a trend of discursive ideas; this would not lead to unwise discriminations; the net of thought-constructions, by an inclination to the ideas of 'I' and 'mine', would not give rise to a host of defilements which are rooted in the false view of individuality, one would not do deeds, wholesome, unwholesome and immovable; and in consequence one would not experience the jungle of *saṃsāra*, which is just a network made up of birth, old age, death, sorrow, lamentation, pain, sadness and despair."

"But the Yogins who abide in the vision of emptiness do not at all apprehend the *skandhas*, elements and sense-fields as if they were something in themselves ; in consequence they do not enter upon discursive ideas with these as objects, make no discriminations, by inclination to the ideas of 'I' and 'mine', do not give rise to a host of defilements which have the false view of individuality for its root, do not perform any actions, and, in consequence, do not experience the transmigration which consists in birth, old age and death. It is thus, when one resorts to emptiness characterized as blissful and as the appeasing of all discursive ideas, that all the discursive ideas, which are a net of thought-construction, disappear. When discursive ideas have disappeared, discrimination comes to rest, and with it all karma and defilement, and all kinds of rebirth. Hence one calls emptiness *Nirvāṇa,* as it brings to rest (*nirvriti*) all discursive ideas".

(*Buddhist Texts,* Translated & edited by E.Conze etc. p.167-169)

The above passage explains in a nutshell how *karma* and defilements originate from discrimination and how they are stopped by emptiness. The negation of subject-object duality becomes the cornerstone of *Yogācāra* philosophy as further development of *Mahāyāna* Buddhism and there the emptiness is defined in terms of the non-existence of this duality.

9. *Saṃsāra* and *Nirvāṇa* are Identical

Both *saṃsāra* and *Nirvāṇa* have no-self established natures of their own and arise depending on causes and conditions (dependent origination). Sufferings in the *saṃsāra* induce one to find out ways and means of eliminating them and depending upon the latter, *Nirvāṇa* arises. In as much as both have no self-natures and both arise in dependent manners and since both have in the ultimate reality neither existence nor non existence, *saṃsāra* and *Nirvāṇa* are identical.

As such, the enlightened one who has realized this, clings or attaches himself neither to *saṃsāra* nor to *Nirvāṇa,* and he transcends both *saṃsāra* and *Nirvāṇa.* This realisation, as we have already seen, provides the doctrinal foundation for bodhisattva practice.

CHAPTER 13

Yogācāra

Contrary to popular misconception, *Yogācāra* school, the second most important school of *Mahāyāna* Buddhism, has not arisen in opposition to the Madhyamaka school of Nāgārjuna. In fact, *Yogācāra* school has been built over the edifice of emptiness constructed by Nāgārjuna with firm logical foundations. *Yogācāra* is like an ornamental superstructure or dome raised over Madhyamaka. It inherited the philosophical thoughts of Nāgārjuna and built over it to take *Mahāyāna* Buddhism to new heights.

Nāgārjuna in his MMK verse XXIV.18 has equated both *pratītyasamutpāda* (dependent origination) and *upādāya – prajñapti* (designation based upon some material or conventional talk) with *śūnyatā.* The fundamental position of *Yogācāra* also is the same. *Yogācāra* also affirms that all things are conceptual constructions only and that the selflessness of all phenomena is an incontrovertible fact of experience. But, whereas Nāgārjuna interprets the Middle Path and *śūnyatā* as neither-existent nor-non-existent, *Yogācāra* tends to take them as both existent and non-existent. The Middle Path in the former is conceived as synthetic negation whereas in *Yogācāra* the same is adhered to by accepting and synthesizing both the extreme views of existence and non-existence. Both the schools treat conventional as conventional only and not ultimately true. The ultimate truth for Madhaymaka is *śūnyatā* defined as neither existent nor-non-existent and for *Yogācāra* it is *śūnyatā* defined as both existent and non-existent.

The special feature of *Yogācāra* is that it lays emphasis on the mind or consciousness (*Vijñāna*) behind the conceptual constructions and elaborates the theory of *Vijñāna-pariṇāma*, the evolution of consciousness. The teaching that " the triple–world is nothing but (evolving of) consciousness" is found in a number of *Sūtras* that are quite early such as *Pratyutpanna Sūtra* and *Daśabhūmika Sūtra*, as well as the *Saṃdhinirmocana Sūtra.* Other *Sūtras* from which *Yogācāra* has derived its philosophy include the *Avataṃsaka Sūtra* and the *Laṅkāvatāra Sūtra.* Apart from its theory of *Vijñāna-pariṇāma, Yogācāra* is well-known for its three-nature theory.

The principle of 'representation – only' (*Vijñaptimātra*) has been proposed as an extension to its *Vijñāna* theory. This is later extended to affirm the view that consciousness alone exists. This is the extreme view of *Vijñāna-vāda* school and is a later day development.

This school attached special importance to Buddhist praxis based on yoga and insight meditation, and, as such, it gained the name of *Yogācāra,* the practice of yoga.

1. *Yogācāra* Literature

Yogācāra derives its basic philosophical position from *Saṃdhinirmocana Sūtra* ('Sūtra Unlocking the Mysteries') which is considered by the *Yogācārins* to contain philosophically the most definitive teaching of the Buddha on the ultimate truth which should not give any room for controversy and dispute. According to them, this *Sūtra* is the third and final 'setting in motion the Wheel of *Dharma*', the first being the Buddha's first sermon in the Deer Park at Saranath and the second the *Prajñāpāramitā* literature. The earlier teachings were considered as nothing but the 'skill-in-mens' (*upāya*) of the Buddha adopted to suit the spiritual levels of consciousness of the hearers at those particular points of time. The real philosophically definitive teaching, they felt, had come from this third 'setting in motion the Wheel of *Dharma*'.

It was in the fifth century (CE) that *Yogācāra* school reached its full bloom, having been founded and established on firm footing by two *Mahāyāna* monks, Asaṅga (410-500CE) and his brother Vasubandhu(420-500 CE).

According to legend, Asaṅga received the teachings on *Yogācāra* from none other than the great 'celestial' bodhisattva–to be the very next Buddha here on earth–Maitreya himself. "For many years Asaṅga had tried in his meditations to visualize Maitreya, but without success. In despair, he gave up, but coming across a suffering dog on the roadside, he was filled with compassion and stooped to help it. The suffering dog turned into Maitreya and gave Asaṅga the teachings on *Yogācāra*." The following five works are attributed to Maitreya:-

(*i*) *Abhisamayālaṃkāra* ('Ornament for the Realisations')–a text on the *Prajñāpāramitā* path;
(*ii*) *Madhyāntavibhāga* ('The Discrimination of the Middle from the Extremes');
(*iii*) *Dharmadharmatāvibhāga* ('The Discrimination of *dharmas* and their true nature (*dharmatā*));
(*iv*) *Mahāyānasūtrālaṃkara* ('Ornament for the *Mahāyāna Sūtras*') ; and the
(*v*) *Ratnagotravibhāga,* otherwise known as the *Uttaratantra,* on the *Tathāgatagarbha* or Buddha-nature teachings.

Asaṅga is said to have written commentaries on some of the above. Other important *Yogācāra* scriptures are:

- *Mahāyānasaṃgraha* ("Compendium on *Mahāyāna*") by Asaṅga
- *Yogācārabhūmi* ("Stages of *Yogācāra*") attributed to Asaṅga, but probably of multiple authorship
- *Triṃśikā* ('Thirty Verses') by Vasubandhu
- *Viṃśatikā* ('Twenty verses') by Vasubandhu
- *Trisvabhāvanirdeśa* ('Teaching on the Three Natures') by Vasubandhu

Vasubandhu's works also include some commentaries on the five scriptures attributed to Maitreya.

2. *Yogācāra* Classification of *Dharmas*

The *Yogācāra* school, though idealistic, accepts the model of the analytical method used in the Realistic School of *Sarvāstivāda* and classifies the world of becoming into five categories subdivided into one hundred *dharmas* as below:-

(1) Mind or consciousness (*citta/ Vijñāna,* 8 *dharmas*)
(2) Mental concomitants (*caitesika,* 51 *dharmas*)
(3) Form (*rūpa,* 11 *dharmas*)
(4) Compounded–factors independent of the mind (*citta– viprayukta,* 24 *dharmas*)
(5) Uncompounded (unconditioned) elements (*asaṃskṛta,* 6 *dharmas*)

The analytical classification here is more elaborate than in *Sarvāstivāda.* But the special point of interest is that mind has been divided into eight consciousnesses:

Functional cognitions

- The five primary *Vijñānas* (consciousnesses associated with the five sense-organs and the corresponding sense-objects)
- Mano-Vijñāna (minding consciousness, sense centre)
- Klista-manas (defiled manas or intellectual discriminating consciousness which gives rise to the duality of subject and object, thought-centre)

Store Consciousness

- *ālayavijñāna* (the seed or store consciousness)

The first five consciousnesses are simply the sense consciousnesses. The eye contact and form and colour are the conditions producing eye-consciousness. Likewise, the ear, nose, tongue and body with contacts, and sound, scent, flavour and feeling are the conditions producing ear – consciousness, nose-consciousness, tongue-consciousness and body-consciousness respectively.

The sixth is the minding consciousness (sense-centre) which co-ordinates the first five primary consciousnesses and forms conceptions out of the perceptions of these first five. The seventh is the intellect-the discriminating conceptual consciousness-, the thought-centre which analyses, thinks, reasons and also wills. This is the one responsible for self-consciousness, self-interest and selfish-motives arising from the discrimination of object and subject, self and others.

The eighth consciousness is called by the *Yogācārins* as clinging consciousness and also as seed or store consciousness. This consciousness arises because of two kinds of grasping and clinging. One is the craving and clinging to the sense perceptions and the feelings of pleasant, unpleasant and indifferent induced by them. The other is the clinging to the habit energy of emotions arising from feelings i.e. emotions of lust for those that are pleasant, hatred for those that are unpleasant and delusion towards those that are neither pleasant nor unpleasant. These emotions in turn give rise to the tendencies to impose attributes and qualities on the things that are arbitrary conceptual constructions. This is the breeding ground for all passions, desires and volitions.

This eighth consciousness is called clinging consciousness because it arises and clings in the body as explained above. It is also called store (repository) consciousness because it receives and stores all seeds for breeding and development and also because it accumulates and increases the corpus of passions, cravings and volitions. This is a sort of collective unconscious which stores within it all the seeds of potential phenomena. This is in fact an explication and elaboration of the concept of *Vijñāna* studied in Early Buddhism as one of the five *skandhas* constituting the individual being. This is the consciousness that is continuously in the process of 'becoming' according to the twelve-limbed Wheel of Dependent Origination.

The eighth, the *ālaya*-consciousness itself, is not an unchangeable fixed substance (*dravya*) but is itself ever-changing instantaneously (*kṣaṇika*) and repeatedly. It is like a torrent of water which never stops at one place for two consecutive moments. In the *Saṃdhinirmocana Sūtra*, this *Vijñāna* has been described by the Buddha as below:

"*Ādāna-Vijñāna* (i.e. *ālayavijñāna*) is highly profound and subtle;
It is the All-seed consciousness (*sarva-bījaka*) and is like a violent current.
I do not reveal it to common man,
Lest they imagine it to be *ātman*".

The sixth, seventh and eighth consciousnesses always interact with each other. The sixth, which is the general centre of perception and cognition inwardly, acts outwardly on the basis of commands from the intellect (discriminating conceptual consciousness) which derives its energy and efficiency from the all-seed store consciousness.

3. Evolving of Consciousness *(Vijñāna-Pariṇāma)*

According to the *Yogācārins*, "the triple world is nothing but (evolving of) consciousness". This is nothing but a reassertion of the idea contained in the Buddha's Dhammapada Verse 1 : "All *dharmas* (things or elements of experience) are born from mind and made up of mind". The same idea is explicated in the *Vijñāna-pariṇāma* (evolution) theory of *Yogācāra*.

Evolving means undergoing a change in form or developing from one form to another in a successive causally determined manner. Unlike *Sāṃkhya* System which talks about *pariṇāma* as the evolution of a substantial material principle *prakṛti*, *Yogācāra* maintains that what evolves and becomes the manifold phenomena is consciousness i.e. *Vijñāna* and not the material principle. It follows from the theory of Karman and the inviolable moral laws. *Karman* is volition according to the Buddha. It is the volition or moral intention that turns around and shapes the world of our experience. Thus it is the consciousness with its intentions and volitions that is ultimately responsible for the evolution of the triple-world. In the Buddhist tradition, the core principle dependent-origination is also understood as 'the fruition of *Karma'*. In *Mahāyāna*, this is explicated and taught as Dependent Origination as the function of *ālayavijñāna* (seed or store consciousness).

The volition in the *ālayavijñāna* produces a corresponding phenomenal activity through the seven functioning consciousnesses. This is the 'producing' aspect of the evolving of *ālayavijñāna*. The wholesome or unwholesome intention i.e. the ethical intention behind the volitional activity, on the other hand, is said to impress the seed in the *ālayavijñāna* continuum with a new fragrance or say a code, as an automatic and spontaneous reaction determined by the moral retributive principle which is operative in a causal law-like manner. The reaction influence on the *ālayavijñāna* caused by the wholesome or unwholesome intention is understood as the 'perfuming' of the *ālayavijñāna* in *Yogācāra* philosophy. The *ālayavijñāna* is thus perfumed and imbued with a different fragrance (or code). This is the 'perfuming' mode in the evolution of *ālayavijñāna*. The seed or impression is getting perfumed (*vāsanā*) and matured in the *ālayavijñāna* to flower in appropriate pleasant or unpleasant effects in due time. Thus the *Kamma* nature modifies the *ālayavijñāna* which again acts and produces further phenomena. This evolutionary process is aptly summarized in the following stock saying:

> A seed (*bīja*) produces a phenomenon (manifestation);
> The phenomenon perfumes a seed;
> The three elements (seed, phenomenon and perfume)
> turning on and on ;
> The cause and effect at one and the same time.

Here, it is said that the three *dharmas* – seed, phenomenon and perfuming of seed – are simultaneous, mutually being cause and effect. Seed is the cause of phenomenon (effect) which in turn is the cause of perfuming and imbuing the seed with a different fragrance. Thus the law of *Kamma* is active and determines the evolution of *ālayavijñāna* as a causal wheel of cause and effect. The 'seeds' and 'perfuming' occur at the sub-conscious level in the *ālayavijñāna.*

The *ālaya* is on the one hand the 'receptacle' or store consciousness where all impressions (*vāsanā*) of past influences (activities) are deposited and preserved and, on the other, it is the seed which matures according to the Laws of *Kamma* active in dependent origination and becomes the 'source' of all future phenomena. According to this school, the impression itself acts also as a seed of future phenomena.

In the ultimate analysis, every phenomenon in the world of our experience originates from the volition or will in the *ālayavijñāna* of one individual or another. The phenomena produced by the *ālayavijñāna* of one will affect the others and in turn cause phenomena from the other sides. Thus the whole world of experience is nothing but the inter-play of phenomena produced by the various individual corpus of *Vijñānas.* Hence, the *Yogācārins* hold on to the theory that the triple-world is nothing but the evolution of *ālayavijñāna.* In fact, *Mahāyāna* Buddhism sees infinite horizon of interconnectedness of these *Vijñānas.* These are also knitted together by various kinds of bonds – myths, legends, common history, culture, tradition, religious teachings etc. Therefore a collective unconscious *ālayavijñāna* may be conceived as containing all seeds for potential development and unfolding of the universe.

4. Three-nature (*Trisvabhāva*) Theory

The three-nature theory of *Yogācāra* school follows logically from the theory of evolution of *ālayavijñāna* studied above. Since the world around us is nothing but the evolution of this *Vijñāna,* its nature is determined by the way the *ālayavijñāna* is evolving. It assumes any of the following three natures or characteristics depending on the manner the evolution of *Vijñāna* takes place:-

(1) The imagined nature (*parikalpita-svabhāva*)
(2) The other-dependent nature (*paratantra-svabhāva*)

(3) The consummated (perfected) nature (*parinispaññā-svabhāva*)

The world is of the basic other-dependent nature which results when the "five defilements of the mind and the factors that impede wisdom" are removed and the world is approached without craving and clinging and avoiding habit energies of negative subjective passions and prejudices that are nothing but unreal imaginary conceptual constructs.

The analogy may be the world as viewed by the pure scientist or pure astronomer where the laws of nature are studied objectively. This is the world characterized by essential relativity. The same world slips into the 'imagined or conceptualized' (*parikalpita*) nature when the subjective factors like the cravings and passions come into play in the view and the world-view is coloured by *vikalpa* (discrimination, conceptual construction).

Saṃdhinirmocana Sūtra compares this to a clear crystal which when viewed through a blue glass looks like a sapphire, seen through red looks like ruby, seen through green looks like emerald and changes to gold when seen through yellow glass.

"The misapprehension of the crystal as sapphire, ruby, emerald or gold is like clinging to conceptualisation imposed on dependent existence. The clear cystal itself is like dependent existence. Just as the appearances of sapphire, ruby, emerald or gold imposed on the crystal never have any reality, never have intrinsic being, the characteristics imposed on dependent existence by conceptual clinging never have any reality or intrinsic being ......" (Buddhist Yoga, trans. by Thomas Cleary, p. 24).

False discriminations and impositions of attributes and qualities are because of inner craving and clinging to habit energies.

In *Tattvārtha* chapter of *Bodhisattvabhūmi*, Asaṅga describes eight types of discriminations (*vikalpa*) caused by incomplete knowledge of reality:

Discrimination of intrinsic nature
Discrimination of particularity
Discrimination grasping a whole
Discrimination of 'I'
Discrimination of 'mine'
Discrimination of the pleasant
Discrimination of the unpleasant
Discrimination of neither pleasant nor unpleasant.

These *vikalpas* ultimately lead to the three primary afflictions (*kleśas*) i.e. attachment, hatred and delusion. This is the world of bewilderment/affliction filled with ignorance and error, the world of false imagination (like snake seen in a rope in twilight or like a ghost that exists merely in one's imagination but not in reality). By virtue of clinging to what is imagined as the substantive real, the imagined world that is a falsified world, becomes established with the genuine dependently originating world as its basis. This, in effect, is transformation of the genuine other dependent world into the imagined world.

Just as the false existence of the imagined world, the genuine other-dependent world has also temporary or transitory existence having no permanent character (*asvabhāva*) and it is like a house that is built with timbers, stones, tiles etc. It exists only by a combination of causes and is not self-existent. It has no permanent reality.

When attachment and false imagination are removed and a virtuous and holy path is followed and as a result of Yoga-praxis, the world becomes thoroughly purified and consummated as the pure world. This consummated world is the one experienced in the emptiness of *Nirvāṇa*. This is the turning around of the basis when the world of other-dependent nature turns around and becomes totally devoid of the imagined nature with the impurities and defilements annihilated completely and absolute purity and perfection attained.

Thus, the same world assumes three different characteristics depending on the perspective or approach in which the interaction takes place: the other-dependent as viewed in an objective scientific enquiry or the other-dependent as in the imagined perspective with our subjective and conceptual constructs superimposed on it or the other-dependent as the consummated or perfected in the view of the enlightened ones with their non-discriminative wisdom. This shows the convertibility of the nature of the world which is basically other-dependent or which works basically in dependently – arising mode. It is in this world of dependent-origination that we make our continual rounds of birth and death and it is therein that we become liberated from *saṃsāra*. Hell, and likewise the heaven, too, are to be found in this world, not elsewhere. It is the world itself that converts depending on our approach, behaviour and perspective. Thus, the three nature theory accounts for the structure of this world and sets forth the ground on which these conversions occur. This shows the possibility of path for the ordinary, un-enlightened people to get enlightened (G.M. Nagao, Mādhyamika And Yogācāra, p.133,135).

5. Turning Around of the Basis (*Āśraya-Parāvṛtti*)

The tenth limb of 'becoming' in the Buddhist Wheel of Life has been explicated and further developed by *Yogācāra* with their *Vijñāna-pariṇāma* theory and Three-Nature theory. Dependent origination is the axis or the ground on which the *ālayavijñāna* evolves and constructs the world of other-dependent nature, imagined nature or consummated (perfected pure) nature. Dependent origination with its Laws of *Kamma* and laws of cause and effect is the ruling principle or the axial principle that determines this evolution of *ālayavijñāna.* The conversion of the nature of the world constructed by the *ālayavijñāna* from other dependent to imagined or consummated is termed "turning around of the basis (*āśraya-parāvṛtti*)" in the Three-Nature theory. What is called 'basis' here is 'the *ālayavijñāna* which is the seed for everything'. With the core principle of dependent origination as the axis or ground, the *ālayavijñāna* turns around from other-dependent nature to either imagined or consummated. The conversion from the other-dependent nature to the consummated nature is the proper 'turning around of the basis (*āśraya-parāvṛtti*)' in the *Yogācāra.* It is directly opposite to the conversion of the other-dependent to the imagined and requires arduous practice and sustained effort through Yoga praxis, unlike the other conversion to the imagined.

The term 'turning around' (*parāvṛtti*) has been explained in the *Mahāyāna-saṃgraha* (IX.1) as below:

"The turning around [of the basis] means that, when the antidote for it arises, the impure division of the other-dependent becomes annihilated and the pure division comes to the fore".

G.M. Nagao writes in his 'Mādhyamika And Yogācāra' (p.144) that, in the translation by *Hsüan-tsang* into Chinese, the Chinese word with the meaning of 'turn and reject' has been used for the term 'becomes annihilated' and the word meaning 'turn and acquire' for the term 'comes to the fore', thus conveying well the meaning of turning around. Sthiramati amplified the meaning further and gives in detail an interpretation of the word in his *Triṃśikā-bhāṣya* as follows:

"In overcoming the gross turbidities of the two kinds of hindrances, intellectual and afflictional, the turning around of the basis is attained. The 'gross turbidity' (*dauṣṭhulya*) means that the basis (i.e. the personal mind/body existence) lacks the power to function freely (i.e, lacks the power of agility or dexterity *karmaṇyatā*). When there occurs the turning around of the basis, the gross turbidity changes into agility ; the maturation of body which comes about as the fruit of past karma ripens into the dharma-body; and knowledge which comprises the subject/object dichotomy transforms into non-discriminating wisdom. In short, the contaminated impurity is eliminated and a state of purity, freed of contaminations, is attained".

Sthiramati defines the 'consummated' in his commentary on Vasubandhu's *Triṃśikā*, k. 21, :

"When the other-dependent is at all times absolutely free of the subject-object dichotomy, this is the consummated".

Thus, consummated (perfected) is the *nirvikalpa-jñāna* (non-discriminative wisdom) where the subject-object duality ceases absolutely. It is '*rahitatā*', getting rid of or to be absolutely free of subject-object duality and becoming utterly selfless.

6. Three-Knowledges/Three-Truths

From the three-nature theory follows the theory of three-knowledges or three-truths. The terms 'nature', 'knowledge' and 'truth' may be interchangeably used here. Thus the knowledges and truths are classified into three kinds as below in *Yogācāra* school:-

Imaginary or Illusory
Other-dependent or Relative
Consummated or Perfected (Ultimate–*Paramārtha*)

As we have already seen, the imaginary or illusory knowledge stems from discrimination of subject and object, "I" and "mine", which is a false conceptual construct arising from the free play of cravings and clingings due to ignorance. In this, ultimate or true reality is not realized and it is assumed that everything is in reality what it appears to be or imagined to be. This is the false "*saṃvṛti*" caused by the veil of ignorance, false perception and delusion which obstructs the instrinsic nature of things. A favourite example cited by the *Mahāyānists* to illustrate the point is the snake-rope-hemp simile.

A man encounters a snake lying on a road at twilight and becomes frightened. He starts to run away but then decides to examine it more closely. A close inspection of the snake form reveals that it is not a snake after all but a rope. He realizes that the snake is illusory and does not exist ; what really exists is the rope. He is enlightened to the fact that his knowledge of seeing a snake was illusory and imaginary. But then he perceives that the rope is also illusory and less than the final reality. It can be analyzed into strands of hemp and further reduced into elements such as earth, water, fire and air, or even further. Thus, what exists in reality is hemp or elements or atoms or electrons, protons and neutrons or waves of energy and not rope.

In this simile, the snake is equated with the imagined nature or thought, the rope with the other-dependent nature and the hemp or elements with the consummated truth or ultimate reality. Both snake and rope should be negated to reach the ultimate reality here of hemp, elements or waves of energy.

The second form of knowledge is relative, generally, spoken of as conventional truth or accommodated truth which concerns the conditions of this phenomenal world which have to be taken as real for practical purposes. This is the true worldly convention (*tathyasaṃvṛti*) as against the false worldly convention (*mithyāsaṃvṛti*) according to the distinction recognized by Bhāvaviveka in later day Madhyamaka. The ultimate truth is devoid of subject-object duality, utterly selfless, perfect nonduality which is most subtle, profound and inexpressible in words. Sages detach from names and words through the consummated knowledge and insight and realize enlightenment as to the ultimate truth. Because they want to make others aware of this ultimate truth which is beyond words, they provisionally set up names and characteristics and describe things. Thus comes about the relative truth or accommodated truth. Buddhism believes that such of its own doctrines that are not the result of direct spiritual insight and experience belong to this form of knowledge, the doctrines, scriptures and practices of all religious including its own being regarded as relative, accommodated or conventional. All scientific knowledges and enquiries and most of the philosophical teachings also belong to this category.

The third is the ultimate truth. It is the way things actually are and not as they appear to be. It is the identitylessness or selflessness of things with no inherent self-existence of their own. This selflessness or emptiness pervades everything, pervades the whole world. It is the suchness (thusness) the way the world is *Saṃdhinirmocana Sūtra* states:

"——————the selflessness of phenomena in the ultimate sense in true thusness is not said to have a cause, is not causally produced, is not created. This is the ultimate truth. Having realized this ultimate truth, one no longer seeks any other ultimate truth."

"Based on this principle, Subhuti, you should know that ultimate truth is everywhere one. Just as the space in all kinds of different forms is signless, undifferentiated, unchanging, all-pervasive, and uniform, so is the ultimate truth within all things which are different in nature and form, all-pervasive and uniform."

(*Buddhist Yoga,* Translated by Thomas Cleary ; p. 18)

The enlightened one realizes this ultimate truth of selflessness (emptiness) and becomes one of selflessness personified and devoid of subject-object duality.

7. Emptiness in *Yogācāra* School

Yogācāra treatise '*Madhyāntavibhāga*' (MV) employs the following logic to establish the principle of *Madhyamā-pratipad* (Middle Path) through its concept of *śūnyatā* (emtpiness):-

"There exists unreal imagination ; duality does not
exist therein
Emptiness, however, exists in it, and also the
former exists in the later." (M.V. I.1)

"Therefore it is stated that all entities are
neither empty nor non-empty
Because of existence, because of non-existence,
and again because of existence. And this is the
Middle Path."

(M.V.I.2)

Professor Gadgin M. Nagao has explained these verses diagrammatically as below:-

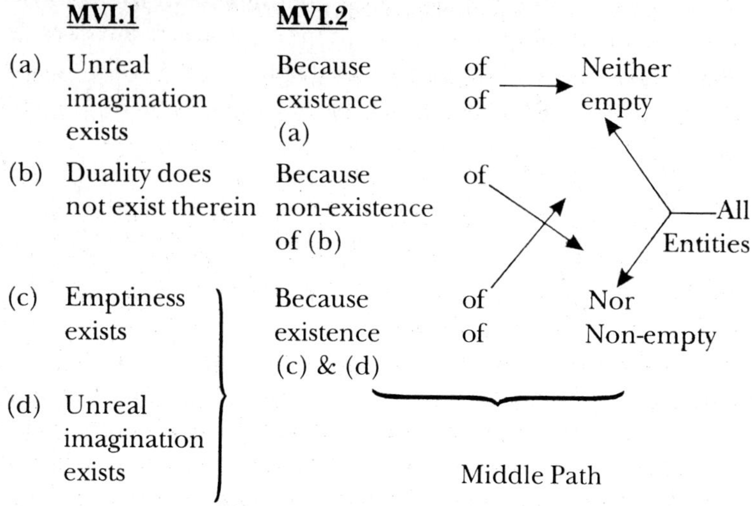

(*Mādhyamika* and *Yogācāra,* p. 197)

The actualities of daily life in the world made up of imaginary constructions are here summed up as 'unreal notions' or 'unreal imagination'. What Nāgārjuna has called *upādāya-prajñapti* (conceptual construct) in his MMK, *Yogācāra* identifies here as *abhūtaparikalpa* (unreal imagination). These are constituted of a discrimination between, and attachment to, two things – the subject grasping and the object grasped. This duality, though indispensable for conceptualisation and practical purposes, does not have any ultimate existence and reality. This is the source and origin of the three root poisons. Only emptiness is found to belong to this differentiation, the unreal notion or 'imagination' because the latter singles out as existent things that are 'not reals' and hence that is empty. At the same time, however, this 'unreal imagination', in spite of its emptiness, is constantly operative. Hence, unreal imagination exists in some manner in emptiness.

MVI.2 states that all entities are neither exclusively empty nor exclusively non-empty. These are not empty because of the existence [of the 'unreal imagination']. The existence of the unreal imagination is in the conventional sense and not in the ultimate sense. Therefore what is meant here is that all entities are not empty in the conventional sense. As such 'Neither empty' stated above conveys a conventional truth. These are also not non-empty because of the non-existence and unreality (of the duality of subject and object) in the ultimate sense. Therefore, 'Nor Non-empty' in MVI. 2 stands for ultimate truth. Summing up, what MV states is that all entities are 'Neither empty' in the conventional sense and 'Nor Non-empty' in the ultimate sense. This is the 'Middle Path' for MV avoiding the two extremes.

This is basically not different from the stand-point of Madhyamaka which, as we have already seen, adheres to the Middle Position and defines emptiness as the middle position of neither existence nor non-existence of things i.e. neither Being nor Non-Being. Emptiness there is neither existence nor non-existence of things, but stands for universal relativity i.e. relative existence causally determined, in the sense of what is ultimately unreal but phenomenally real for conventional worldly purposes.

The same truth is expressed in *Yogācāra* in a slightly different way. Here all entities are described as 'Neither empty nor Non-empty', where empty means non-existence, void, unreality. This also amounts to saying that all entities are neither existent nor non-existent as in Madhyamaka and sticks to the golden mean of avoiding the two extremes. But at the same time, MV adds a new element of thought in the above verses, by affirming the existence of 'emptiness' in the unreal imagination. Thus, MV talks about existence of 'Non-existence' in the unreal imagination in the above verses. This is further elaborated in MVI. 13 as below:-

"Truly, the characteristic of emptiness is the non-existence of the duality (of subject and object), and the existence of (that) non-existence."

As against the complicated logic of neither empty nor non-empty in MV I.1. and I.2, MVI. 13 succinctly defines emptiness as the existence of that non-existence of the duality of subject and object. In defining emptiness, the emphasis in *Yogācāra* philosophy is on the negation of subject-object duality whereas in Madhyamaka the core principle defining it is dependent originatin. Concentrating and negating the subject-object duality, selflessness is perfected in Yoga praxis. It is a means for perfection of selflessness that is the ultimate goal of realisation. It is the practical guide in *Yogācāra* for realizing the ultimate truth whereas in the Madhyamaka of Nāgārjuna emptiness, even though projected as an object of meditation, is mainly an intellectual theorisation.

The existence of that non-existence of subject-object duality in *Yogācāra* can only be interpreted to mean the existence of selflessness in the consciousness stream as its characteristic mark on enlightenment. Dependent origination is also selflessness. Thus, both *Madhyamaka* and *Yogācāra* converge in stressing the selflessness.

Professor G.M. Nagao quotes passages from the *Yogācārabhūmi*, *Abhidharma-samuccaya* and *Āryadeśanā-vikhyāpana* to show that similar idea of "non-existence and existence of non-existence" occurs in these literatures also as in the MV (*Mādhyamika* and *Yogācāra*, p. 55/56).

Abhidharma-samuccaya of Asaṅga negates '*ātma-ātmīyatva*' ('self-hood and possessin'), but states that '*anātmakatva*' ('selflessness') remains as real. That is, the Reality of 'selflessness' is affirmed here. Likewise, a commentary in the *Āryadeśanā–vikhyāpana* of Asaṅga reads : (1) the two-kinds of selfhood, that of person (*pudgala–ātman*) and that of things (*dharma–ātman*), do not exist, but (2) the two kinds of non-self (*nairātmya*) do exist. These are identical with the idea of 'non-existence and existence of non-existence of subject-object duality' found in MV. I.13. This negation and affirmation can be reconciled as explained by Candrakirti in the *Madhyamakāvatāra* in the following passage:-

"In the *paratantra* (i.e the other-dependent), the duality of subject and object does not exist (and is not real). Thus the *paratantra* is *śūnya* with regard to duality. (What exists and is real) is the knowledge of this *śūnya* with regard to duality."

The Reality of subject-object duality is denied by every Buddhist school. When *Yogācāra* talks about the "existence of that non-existence of subject-object duality", what exists here can be interpreted to mean only the knowledge or conscious awareness of the unreality and non-existence, in the ultimate truth, of the subject-object duality i.e. *śūnya* with regard to duality as explained above by Candrakirti. This is the realisation of *śūnya*, the realisation of selflessness or becoming utterly selfless.

This means that, in the evolution of *ālayavijñāna* in the path to perfection, there comes a stage where it exists without the subject-object duality, utterly selfless, without any *karmic* formations and without any defilements i.e. utterly purified. This is the supermandane cognition of the nirvanic stage where the *ālayavijñāna* is totally empty of all defilements and *karmic* formations because of the eradication and non-existence of the subject-object duality and becoming totally selfless. This is the ultimate consummated (perfected) stage.

Some scholars tend to see in the assertion of "existence of that non-existence" in *Yogācāra,* the existence of an absolute consciousness. But, according to Vasubandhu (*Triṃśikā* 27), one forsakes the apprehension of any consciousness in this state. However, the scholars take the *ālayavijñāna* in *Yogācāra*'s *Vijñāna-pariṇāma* theory as one primary existent (*dravyasat*) which constructs all the *dharmas* (i.e. all elements of experience) and the three worlds. They tend to freeze the flow of *ālayavijñāna* at a particular state and treat it as an absolute substantive entity. But this is contrary to the Buddhist understanding.

Even after attaining the perfect state, the *Vijñāna* continues to be active. For instance, following the example of the Buddha, the bodhisattva relinquishes the exquisite pleasure of *Nirvāṇa* to descend into *saṃsāra* with the best altruistic motive of serving the sentient beings. "His mind, like fire, constantly blazes up into good works for others." His *ālayavijñāna* is thus very active and not remaining an unchanging block entity. It is empty of all defilements and is totally selfless. Selflessness characterises his *ālayavijñāna.* We see here only the existence of selflessness and not any absolute unchanging static consciousness. Thus what is described in *Yogācāra* as the 'existence of that non-existence' is the existence of the characteristic nature selflessness in the *ālayavijñāna* and not the existence of the latter as an unchanging absolute entity.

This interpretation conforms to the basic Buddhist teaching. The early *Yogācārins* did not accept the ultimate reality of subjective consciousness (*Vijñāna*). But later '*Vijñānavāda*' took to the doctrine that 'Consciousness (alone) exists'. In later formulations, the view came to prevail that at enlightenment the consciousness that was the substratum (*ālaya*) consciousness would continue to exist for ever in a completely radiant and purified form as a transformed consciousness or Buddha consciousness. In China, the Indian missionary Paramārtha (490-659 CE) gave the special name of *amala-vijñāna* for the pure and taintless consciousness that arises at enlightenment replacing the *ālaya*-store consciousness. Thus, his school divided the consciousness to nine including this *amala-vijñāna* as against eight in *Yogācāra.* This, it may still be seen, only defines *vijñāna* as *amala,* that is selfless and cannot be viewed as confirming the existence of an absolute *vijñāna.* Postulating an absolute existence for it is a conceptual construct and it only shows the lingering desire in the heart for continued exitence for ever.

Nāgārjuna started out from Buddha's core teaching of dependent – origination and saw emptiness (*śūnyatā*) therein. In contrast, it may seem as if the three-nature theory of *Yogācāra* with its concept of *ālaya-Vijñāna* as the basis (*āśraya*) is closely aligned with existence (Being) rather than with emptiness. But this is not correct. Their three-nature theory has the theory of "three non-natures" (*niḥsvabhāva*, lacking inherent existence) built in it and therein has emptiness been explicated.

First, with regard to the 'imagined' nature, there is 'non-nature' or 'non-existence' of marks, specific characteristics (*lakṣaṇa niḥsvabhāva*). Marks, forms, characteristics and so forth are discriminated here; but, because they are products of imagination, they are said to have no 'self-nature' and to be empty and non-existent.

Secondly, with regard to the 'other-dependent' nature, there is 'non-nature' or 'non-existence' of origination (*utpatti niḥsvabhāva*). This means that all are empty, because, as everything is dependent on some other things, nothing can originate on its own accord nor exist in and of itself.

Lastly, with regard to the 'consummated' nature, there is "non-nature" (non-existence), selflessness in an ultimate sense (*Paramārtha niḥsvabhāva*). This is non-existence in the ultimate sense, true non-reality, selflessness, emptiness, far transcending all specific characteristics and conditions of life.

What is meant by "non-nature in reference to origination"(*utpatti niḥsvabhāva*) exactly corresponds to Nāgārjuna's statement, 'dependent origination is identical to emptiness' in his MMK XXIV. 18. From all the foregoing, it is clear that *Yogācārins*' ideas of non-being or non-existence are built over the concept of emptiness (*śūnyatā*) inherited from Nāgārjuna. But, the scholars classify *Yogācāra* as the school affirming both 'Being and Non-Being' in view of its assertion of 'existence of that non-existence of subject-object duality' and passages like the following in the *Madhyāntavibhāga*:-

"The 'imagined nature' is always non-existent. The 'other-dependent' is existent, but not as real Reality. The 'consummated' is both existent and non-existent in an ultimate sense." (MV III.3).

The first species of imagination is not real and as such, is not existent. Hence, it is empty. The second species of causal combination has only temporary or transitory existence. The

Middle Path in the *Yogācāra* is neither real nor empty (because of conditioned existence), or, stated in another manner, neither empty nor non-empty. The third species of consummated (*parinișpaññā*) is both existent and non-existent because it is *śūnyatā* (emptiness) signifying non-existence of the subject-object duality and existence of that non-existence. This is designated as both the 'True Non-being' and the 'True Being'. The True Non-being is *śūnyatā* (*niḥsvabhāva*, absense of own inherent existence) in the highest sense and the True Being is *parinișpaññātva* (perfected state of selflessness).

8. Representation-Only (*Vijñaptimātra*)

Another important contribution of *Yogācārins* is their theory of *Vijñaptimātra* or 'Representation-Only'. This is the insight into the fact that what we perceive as objects is in actual fact only the representation of objects in the mind, and not the objects themselves. This leads to the realisation that the presence of an external object is not a prerequisite for its perception by us. The analogies of dream experience and perception of water in the mirage will illustrate this point. Every night in a dream we have a whole host of experiences and representations of objects without any corresponding objects 'out there'. The arguments from dream experience and water in the mirage are the characteristic features of *Yogācāra* philosopy. When a mirage makes its apperance, no real water is there, and yet the notion of real water arises.

The mental experience is also compared to the perceptions of echo, reflected image, moon reflected in water and magical objects in a magic show. These analogies reinforce the *Yogācāra* view of 'Representation-Only'. Further, what takes place in the mind is the thought-constructs and further build-ups and false imaginations superimposing attributes and qualities on them based on the inner cravings, lusts, passions and desires. These are not in the things themselves but only the mental constructs.

The logic in this theory is extended to deny the reality of subject-object duality i.e. perceiver-perceived distinction. Explaining *Madhyāntavibhāga* verse I.7, Vasubandhu states:

"Depending upon the perception that there are only 'Representations', there arises the non-perception of objects. Depending upon the non-perception of objects, there arises the non-perception of mere-representations (*Vijñaptimātra*) as well.

Thus, one understands the definition of the non-existence of the perceived and the perceiver."

Vasubandhu further elucidates this theory and liberation in his *Triṃśikā* as below:

> "As long as consciousness does not abide in
> Representation-Only,
> So long does one not turn away from the
> tendency towards the twofold grasping."
>
> (*Triṃśikā*, 26)

What is perceived as 'Representation-Only' and further thought on it is purely a mental construct. This is the true nature of thought. When this truth is realized and consciousness is established in this truth, then there is no tendency towards the twofold grasping. 'The twofold grasping' means the grasping of the object and grasping of the subject. This twofold grasping vanishes with the inward realisation of the truth of Representation-Only, that is: "This is mere representation only, it is devoid of an object, there is here no external object." This inward realisation also leads to the forsaking of the apprehension of one's own consciousness, the subjective self.

When he thus abides in 'Representation-Only', 'he does not apprehend', not see, not grasp, not take as real, any object whatsoever, - be it the demonstration (of *dharma*) and instruction in it, or an ordinary object, like form, sound etc. – and that because he sees that what really is, and not because he is as one born blind. At that time, there is a forsaking of the grasping at consciousness, and he is established in the true nature of his own thought. This is because "where there is nothing to grasp, there is no more grasping." This is the stage of no-mind where mind does not produce any thought and simply 'drops down'. This, Vasubandhu describes as the true nature of mind and thought.

Where there is an object, there is a subject; but there is no subject where there is no object. The absence of an object results in the absence also of a subject and not merely in the absence of grasping. The tendencies to treat object and subject as distinct and real entities are forsaken, and thought is established in just its own true nature forsaking the consciousness of anything. Vasubandhu describes this as below:

> "It is without thought, without basis, and is the
> supermundane cognition

The turning-around of the basis (i.e. the substratum,
ālayavijñāna) results from the elimination of the
twofold corruption."

(*Triṃśikā*, 29)

"This is the element without outflows,
inconceivable, wholesome and stable
The blissful body of emanicipation, the
Dharma-body of the great sage."

(*Triṃśikā*, 30)

"————It is where one understands that everything is merely that which is seen in (of) one's own mind only; where there is no inclination to believe in outside existents or non-existents ; where one is free from the four logical possibilities (i.e. it is, it is not, it both is and is not, it neither is nor is not); — ————where one does not apprehend either subject or object; ————where the two forms of egolessness (*pudgala-nairātmya, dharma-nairātmya*) are understood; where the two forms of defilement are kept away and where one is purified of the twofold covering; ———— and where there is a revulsion from thought, mind and mind-consciousness" (*Laṅkāvatāra Sūtra*, 184-85). (*Buddhist Texts*, Translated & edited by E.Conze etc, p. 208, 210, 211).

The two forms of defilement and the twofold covering are those arising from evil inclination and realistic error. But these vanish in emptiness i.e. negation of subject-object duality.

9. Suchness

Nāgārjuna defined emptiness equating it with dependent – origination. MV defined the same in terms of the non-existence of subject-object duality. In *Mahāyāna*, emptiness is also described variously as suchness, reality limit, the signless, the ultimate reality, the element of *Dharma*, non-duality, the realm of non-discrimination, the true nature of *Dharma*, the inexpressible, that which has not been stopped, the unconditioned, *Nirvāṇa* etc.

Suchness or Thusness is the most important synonym of emtpiness in *Mahāyāna*. It is expounded in *Saṃdhinirmocana Sūtra* ('*Sūtra* Unlocking the Mysteries') as of seven kinds:

"The nature of Suchness means the true suchness in all defiled and pure pehnomena. Of this there are seven types.

"First is the suchness of the mundane whirl; this refers to the beginninglessness and endlessness of all events."

"Second is the suchness of characteristics; this refers to the identitylessness and selflessness of all phenomena."

"Third is the suchness of discernment, which means that all events are essentially consciousness (i.e. all events evolve from consciousness)."

"Fourth is the suchness of setups, which is the holy truth of suffering that I explain".

"Fifth is the suchness of wrong action, which is the holy truth of causes of suffering that I explain."

"Sixth is the suchness of purity, which is the holy truth of extinction that I explain."

"Seventh is the suchness of right action, which is the holy truth of the path that I explain."

(*Buddhist Yoga,* Trans. By Thomas Cleary, p. 51,52)

When we embarked on our search for reality, we set before ourselves the goal of finding out the ultimate reality that is uncaused (that is in itself and of itself), unborn, not-become, not-made ; reality that is free from evil ; reality that is eternal, immutable and unchanging. What is that ultiamte reality? Buddhism teaches that there is no such absolute entity or reality ever-existing and remaining the same and answering these criteria. The ultimate truth is contained not in 'What exists', but only in 'How it exists', that is, in the manner of existence, of the way things truly are. This is the way of selflessness, emptiness or thusness (suchness), the manner of dependent origination. The ultimate Truth or Reality is emptiness or Suchness and this is described in *Saṃdhinirmocana Sūtra* as denoting the following seven truths:-

- Beginninglessness and endlessness of all events i.e. the cyclic nature of life.
- Identitylessness and selflessness of all phenomena i.e. continuously flowing nature of phenomena as a process dependently originating, continuing and decaying.
- All phenomena evolve from *ālayavijñāna* (all-seed consciousness continuously flowing like a torrential flow).
- The Four Noble Truths of : Suffering, Cause of suffering, Cessation of Suffering and Path leading to cessation of suffering.

Suchness encapsulates all the above and exists uncaused, and unborn, in the true sense. It is there in itself, of itself. It is the way things are truly.

10. *Cittamātra* (Mind only)/ *Vijñānavāda*

Early *Yogācārins* held the view that what we perceive as objects is in actual fact only the representation of objects in the mind. That is the view of *Vijñaptimātra* as we have seen.

This line of thought was further extended by later *Yogācārins* to the view that what we perceive in actual fact is nothing more than the mind itself (*cittamātra*). From *Vijñaptimātra* (representation only) they moved to the position of *cittamātra* (mind only). Further extreme view has been : 'Consciousness (alone) exists', the doctrine of *Vijñānavāda* which denies the existence of any external objects and asserts that subjective consciousness (*Vijñāna*) alone exists as the ultimate reality.

Early *Yogācāra* school does not subscribe to this extreme view that denies the existence of external objects and treats everything as absolutely non-existent. According to Asaṅga, this is an extreme and erroneous view and it cannot be denied that there exists a 'bare given-thing (*vastu-mātra*) as the basis for the *rūpa-skandha* etc. In as much as the triple-world is nothing but *Vijñāna* in the sense that it is after all the product of the will-action in the *ālayavijñāna* and, as such, the evolute of *ālayavijñāna,* the outer substances and the bare-given things talked by Asaṅga as the basis for *rūpa* etc may also be considered as the products of *Vijñāna* and as owing their physical existences to *Vijñāna.* They all, including *Vijñāna,* exist in the manner of dependent origination. Here the emphasis should have been on the creative evolutionary potential of *Vijñāna* and the emptiness of all as conceptual creations. But the later *Vijñāna-vādins* shifted the focus to the cognitive, mental aspect of *Vijñāna* away from the creative aspect of *Vijñāna-pariṇāmavāda* and came to assert that cognition alone exists and that there is no external reality. But their assertion of 'cognition alone exists' as an ultimate reality deviates from the main stream philosophy of evolution of *Vijñāna.*

CHAPTER 14

Selflessness of Buddhism Vs Self of *Upaniṣads*

1. Self Vs Selflessness

In spite of very clear expositions in the Buddhist teachings that *Nirvāṇa* is selflessness, it is baffling how some scholars try to read in the concept of *Nirvāṇa* some sort of an absolute self akin to the self in the *Bṛhad-āraṇyaka Upaniṣad* and interpret Buddha's teachings as an extension of the ideas of non-dualism found in that *Upaniṣad* (*BU* IV. 3.29, 5.15).

First and foremost, the concept of an absolute self is incompatible with the fundamental Buddhist doctrine of dependent origination. If everything exists in dependence on others as taught by the Buddha and life is cyclic as depicted in the Buddhist Wheel of Dependent Orinination, with no beginning and with no end, then there cannot be any absolute self that exists in itself. As Nāgārjuna questions in MMK 24.20 f , "How can that which exists by its own being come into existence?" If the self is posited as a First Cause, does it mean that causation first started with it and there was no causation prior to that? 'First cause' itself is a contradiction in terms and is a misnomer. Such a theory of causation cannot be logically sustained. Does this not violate the concept of the cyclic nature of life and the beginninglessness and endlessness of life cycle? Analysing the facts of experience, the Buddhists arrive at the conclusion that no such self, unborn, uncaused, not-become and not made is truly ever found. Such epithets and descriptions can be applied not to any self or thing, but only to the selflessness, emptiness and suchness found in the things.

Bṛhad-āraṇyaka Upaniṣad in the above mentioned passages emphasizes the non-duality of Self and Brahman. The non-duality of *Upaniṣads* is concerned with proving the existence of Brahman as the one and only reality and concentrates on the same. But the import of non-duality in Buddhism is different and much deeper. Here all dualities arising from conceptual constructions like the polar opposites of existence and non-existence, created and not-created, birth and death, eternalism and nihilism, asceticism and hedonism, subject and object, are denied. Non-dualism stands for the middle position avoiding the extremes and not for any absolute entity. From this, selflessness and emptiness logically follow.

The *Upaniṣads* assert the one reality of Brahman and exhort one to realize this and become Brahman. Brahman is to be realized by meditative concentration. On the other hand, Buddhism asserts the truth of selflessness in everything and teaches one to become utterly selfless by negating and denying all dualities and conceptual constructions and making the mind pure and empty of all defilements, because the defilements arise from these dualities and conceptual fabrications. Here the emphasis is on eradication of defilements and burning away of all *karmic* residues. For this, the thrust in Buddhism is on insight meditation and the practice of the four *Brahma Vihāras* (the immeasurables: all-pervading loving kindness, compassion, sympathetic joy and equanimity) till one becomes utterly selfless and empty, and realisation dawns on him that all his *karmic* residues are burnt and there is no more birth of suffering for him.

The non-duality in Buddhism is the Middle Path or emptiness with the denial of subject-object duality i.e. non-dual nature of experience (*advaya*) and attendant purity of utter selflessness, whereas in the *Bṛhad-āraṇyaka Upaniṣad* the focus is on the non-duality (*advaita*) of Self within and Brahman. The aspects of defilements and purity are not talked about in the *Upaniṣads* as logically and coherently as in Buddhism. Further, the *Upaniṣadic* philosophy is beset with the problem of how to reconcile the emergence of impure and imperfect world from the pure Brahman. Buddha has developed a logically coherent and consistent system with no inner contradictions found in the *Upaniṣadic* philosophy.

Even when the supramundane cognition of the nirvanic state of emptiness is talked about by the *Yogācāra* masters Asaṅga and Vasubandhu, they emphasize the cardinal point that the practitioner should forsake the apprehension of his own consciousness. But some scholars seize upon the statement of 'existence of that non-existence' in *MV* I.13 and equate the meditative awareness of that state with *ātman* or self in the *Upaniṣads.* This results from the normal tendency of the human mind to freeze any particular state in the flow of experiences and ascribe a substantive reality to it. It is undeniable that the consciousness is continually changing and flowing, not remaining the same at any two consecutive moments and as such, no state of consciousness can be truly called as the permanent abiding self. The Buddha and the Buddhists are not denying the existence of flowing consciousness or self in conventional terms for practical purposes; but for them, the ultimate truth is only the selflessness or emptiness in things, the way things actually are, i.e. suchness as explained in the *Saṃdhinirmocana Sūtra.* What *MV* I.13 calls the 'existence of that non-existance' is misinterpreted. It is nothing but the existence of selflessness that characterizes the flow of illumined consciousness as we have seen. It is about the characteristics or nature of the flowing *vijñāna* after enlightenment and not about any absolute unchanging entity.

To free the mind from the defilements and impurities, things have to be seen in their true nature of having no-self (no substance) and existing in their selfless Suchness, and this universal truth of Selflessness (Suchness) which is not normally realized should be comprehended and made the guiding principle in life's activities to direct the life stream towards *Nirvāṇa* (i.e. cessation of suffering). This is the core element of the teaching in Buddhism as against the concept of *ātman* or self in the *Upaniṣads.*

The concepts of purifactory insights and practices of the four *Brahma Vihāras* to destroy the *karmic* seeds and see nakedly within one-self and realize emptiness and utter selflessness are unique to Buddhism.

2. *Īśvara* Vs Dependent Origination

The theories of Brahman, *Īśvara* and Self in the philosophies of Hinduism are inextricably mixed up with the notion of absolute power – call it wonderous power or magical power according to one's conceptual construction – the power of creation, sustenance and destruction. In such a conception of an omnipotent *Īśvara* wielding this absolute power, the very same *Īśvara* who is the cause of action and creation determines and imposes the consequences and effects also i.e. the rewards and retributions over the actions of the indiviiduals. This concept is further mixed up with the ideas of sacrificial rituals, *karmic* consequences, divine will and divine grace. The whole universal process including the modification and evolution of the individual selves with their sufferings and sorrows is attributed to His divine will and it is all a sort of sport or play (*līlā*) for Him. The moral view holding the universal ethical principles as the sole determining factors in the evolution of the individual selves is diluted and in fact undermined in these philosophies, even though the theory of Law of Karma taken from the alien *śramaṇic* culture is incorporated and talked about.

Unlike these philosophies, Buddhism is uncompromising in its position that moral and ethical principles alone determine the evolution of the individual *vijñānas* and the flow of the universal processes. As Richard Gombrich points out (Theravāda Buddhism, p.66), it is the Buddha who is primarily responsible for 'ethicizing' of the concepts of *karman* (action) and *saṃsāra.* For the Buddha, the principle determining the evolution is the moral intention or volition itself behind the actions. If any power or God can be thought of as implied in the Buddhist philosophy, it is the power or law of 'dependent origination' only. The Law of Karma and the laws of cause and effect themselves are gods. These arise and decay with the corresponding *karmans* and, as such, they are also dependently originated. They can be described only as neither existent nor non-existent as in the Madhyamaka or as both existent and non-existent as in the Yogācāra. As Nāgārjuna with his incisive logic proves, dependent origination itself is emptiness ; it is selflessness.

Bṛhad-āraṇyaka Upaniṣad (V.2.1) describes the Absolute Brahman as fullness (*pūrṇam*). From this, it is argued that, conditioned by the finite modes of thought, we cannot talk of changes, imperfections, injustices or evils of the world affecting the integrity of the Absolute Brahman, because It is *pūrṇam* and nothing can affect the *pūrṇam* or infinity. Even if we take away infinity from infinity, infinity still remains. But this is only a play in words. In this age when global warming and total environmental degradation are being apprehended, talk of infinity not being affected cannot be maintained. Infinite changes are taking place in the infinity. However, infinity is nothing but the word used to inficate what is inconceivable. It is beyond any conception and void of any conception. Even though the words "*pūrṇam*" and "infinity" are used, these only point to the emptiness or voidness of conceptions. If It is a "*pūrṇam* "or" infinity", "*pūrṇam*" of what? *Neti, neti* (not this, not this) ! It only leads to the emptiness or selflessness of Buddhism. What rules in this emptiness is only dependent origination ; but this is also empty (selfless). This is the ultimate truth in Buddhism.

CHAPTER 15

Paths and Stages of Bodhisattva

1. Five Paths

Mahāyāna Buddhism teaches five paths (*mārga*) for a bodhisattva and talks of ten stages (*bhūmi*) of development of bodhisattvahood. The five paths are not different paths, but in fact they are five stretches of the path a bodhisattva has to tread in his mission of realizing perfection. The first is the path of accumulation (*sambhāra-mārga*). Here the bodhisattva accumulates the merits accruing from virtuous practices.

The second is the path of preparation (*prayoga-mārga*) which is the preparatory stage of arduous practice of calming and insight meditations to gain non-discriminative wisdom (*nirvikalpa-jñāna*) where all conceptual constructions and subject-object duality are transcended. When direct non-conceptual awareness of emptiness i.e. intuitive insight into emptiness first occurs in meditation, the bodhisattva is said to attain the path of seeing (*darśana-mārga*). This is the indescribable state in which one awakens to the Buddha-nature within. This state is characterized by utter selflessness with no notion of a separate 'I' to be appeased and satiated. This is followed by the path of cultivation (*bhāvanā-mārga*) where the perfections are further refined and mastered and the bodhisattva engages himself actively in the *saṃsāric* world for the benefit of all sentient beings.

This is the stage in which the Four-fold Noble Truth is investigated more fully and actualized by the practice and perfection of the following Seven Limbs of Enlightenment as

Life-Culture:-

Mindfulness
Thorough investigation of the mental states and *dharmas*
Vigour (Effort)
Tranquillity (Peace)
Rapture (Joy)
Concentration
Equanimity

In this path of cultivation (*bhāvanā-mārga*), the bodhisattva is guided by *tat-pṛṣṭhalabdha-jñāna*, the knowledge acquired subsequent to the *nirvikalpa-jñāna* (the non-discriminative wisdom). This subsequent knowledge has its basis in the non-discriminative wisdom he has already gained with his insight into emtpiness. It is also referred to as '*śuddha–laukika–jñāna*', that is, purified mundane knowledge. It is a pure form of knowledge that flows out of non-discriminative wisdom (G.M. Nagao, *Mādhyamika* and *Yogācāra,* p. 223). It is the knowledge in which *prajñā* (insight into emptiness) and *karuṇā* (compassion) are fused into one wisdom and this transcends the insight into emptiness.

The system of the five paths (*mārgas*) expounded in *Mahāyāna* Buddhism ends with *niṣṭha-mārga,* the final goal, the path of "no-more learning". The final goal is reached at the end of the path of cultivation and this is the Buddhahood with the fusion of *prajñā* and *mahā-karuṇā* into one enlightened consciousness. This is the realisation of the **Life-Ideal**. Thus, by descending into the *saṃsāric* world, after gaining insight into emptiness, with *mahā-karuṇā* towards all sentient beings, the true Buddhahood is attained.

2. Ten Stages (Bhūmis) of Bodhisattva

(1) Joyous

The stage, when the direct insight into emptiness occurs first at the end of the path of preparation (*prayoga-mārga*) and when the path of seeing (*darśana-mārga*) begins, is called the first bhūmi (stage) of bodhisattva. At this stage he or she is no longer an ordinary person, but becomes a full-fledged *ārya-bodhisattva.* Accomplishing a great aim and attaining a world-transcending mind for the first time, he or she becomes very joyful. With this, Kamalaśīla says, the bodhisattva attains the first of the ten bhodhisattva stages (*bhūmis*), the stage called that of 'Joyous' (intense joy). This stage is associated with the particular (although by no means exclusive) cultivation of the perfection of giving (*dāna*).

He feels joy because by the fruit of his actions and meditation he is born in the family of Buddhas; he feels joy in his affection for the Buddhas and joy in the fact that he is devoting himself to the work of a bodhisattva; he also takes joy in his feeling of goodwill to all creatures and to the vow he has made.

All the perfections practised are permeated and purified by the insight into emptiness. His practice of giving is characterized by seven purities : purity of gift, purity of conduct, purity of vision, purity of mind, purity of speech, purity of knowledge and purification of defilements.

The other nine bodhisattva stages all occur on the fourth of the five paths, the path of cultivation (*bhāvanā-mārga*).

(2) Stainless

The second bodhisattva stage is called the "Pure" ("Stainless", Vimala). At this, the bodhisattva attains total freedom from all defilements and reaches the very perfection of morality, having avoided all transgressions even the minute ones. Not only his conduct and speech but also his or her inner thought remains perfectly pure even in his or her dreams.

The bodhisattva avoids all transgressions and maintains constant discipline, stable discipline, consciously performed discipline and subconsciously operative discipline.

(3) Radiance

At the third stage, the stage of 'Radiance', the concentration and mental control attained provide a firm basis for immeasurable light of knowledge to shine forth. Here the bodhisattva perfects the virtue of patience. He or she reflects upon the nature of things and practises patience, which really means forbearance towards people and things as they are. To be tolerant and patient with the sins, frailties, vanities and oddities of others is an important virtue that he perfects. Also he is capable of putting up with any misery. He resists evil not with the force of hatred but with the force of loving kindness.

The bodhisattva has deep faith and maintains equanimity when the results of his actions develop variously. He does not get upset when anything unfavourable occurs. He never gets angry or violent. Fear or humiliation does not touch him. He does not retaliate in anyway, does not hold grudges; he is not angered by admonition and he does not wait for others to admonish and correct him. He practises forbearance without fear and without expecting any reward or favour. These are the various kinds of purity of his forbearance (patience).

(4) Blazing Intellect

Then the bodhisattva attains the fourth stage called the stage of 'Blazing Intellect'. It is so called because the elements of enlightenment one attains in this stage burn out the afflictions with knowledge like flames of fire. This is the stage where the bodhisattva gains the perfection of effort/vigour and practises good works as well as meditation most strenuously with the greatest diligence and vigour. Good works predominate in this stage whereas meditation predominates in the next stage.

The bodhisattva realizes the equal nature of all and he neither elevates himself nor looks down on others because of his own great diligence. He is imbued with great strength and great energy, is capable, steadfast and vigourous and does not deviate from the Noble Eightfold Path. These are the various kinds of purity of his diligence.

(5) Difficult to Conquer

The fifth *bhūmi* (stage) is called the stage 'Difficult To Conquer' because the bodhisattva now attains complete mastery in practising the techniques of the elements of enlightenment. He attains the perfection of meditative concentration. He eradicates all attachments–attachments even to concentration states of bliss and religious practices.

(6) Approaching or Presence

Then comes the crucial sixth stage. The sixth *bhūmi* (stage) is called the stage of 'Approaching' or 'Presence' because one observes the flux of events as a causal continuum and understands 'dependent origination' (*pratītyasamutpāda*) in all its implications. *Arūpa-jhānas* (ecstasies of formless meditation) become manifest in this stage.

The bodhisattva avoids the two extremes of affirmation and denial and travels the middle path. Through his insight, he truly knows the three doors to deliverance – wishlessness, signlessness and emptiness. He fully understands the true nature of things in its various aspects of the imagined nature, the other dependent nature and the consummated (perfected) nature. He truly knows the meaning of *niḥsvabhāva* (i.e. having no inherent self nature) with reference to the essencelessness of appearances, origination and ultimate truth. He truly knows the conventional truth, referring to the five fields of knowledge. He truly knows the ultimate truth, referring to the sevenfold suchnesses or thusness encapsulating the seven truths.

His mind has attained the state of no-mind and he shines as it were by the light of *prajñā* (the supermundane cognition or direct insight into emptiness). He has now reached the end of the six perfections. The *Hīnayāna* does not mention any further stages ; but the *Mahāyāna* conceives of four more.

According to *Mahāyāna*, the bodhisattva still continues for a long time, attaining a further series of four additional perfections (as per sources like *Daśabhūmika Sūtra*) and the seventh to ten stages.

(7) Gone Afar

The seventh *bhūmi* is called the stage of "Gone Afar" because the bodhisattva in this stage realizes flawless, uninterrupted formless concentration to a great extent and is on the brink of purity. Here conscious effort is applied to enter into the formless meditations (*Arūpa-jhāna*) whereas in the next stage this is achieved effortlessly.

Of the four additional perfections, the most important is *upāya*. (skill in means). *Upāya*, meaning 'expedient', 'strategem', 'device' or 'craft' has a technical sense in Buddhism. It is used to contrast wisdom (*prajñā*) and is synonymous with love (*karuṇā*).

He is now skilled in all means of leading others to Bodhi (Enlightenment) and attains the perfection of skill in means (*upāya*). This perfection of skill in means is to further aid and deepen the first three perfections of giving, morality and patience for the benefit of all sentient beings. Although he no longer has worldly thoughts, he can, through his great compassion, assist others in their troubles in this world and he turns over his accumulated *karmic* merit to assist them. He carries out his benevolence and mercy, not only to human beings but to animals and plants and all sentient beings. He treats animals with kindness and cares for plants and does not act as if the lower forms of life exist only for the benefit of the higher forms and have no significance of their own.

This *upāya* includes special knowledge whereby he knows exactly what is the right thing to be done to any particular individual to aid him in the path to enlightenment. Here, *Mahāyāna* ascribes magical powers to him.

The bodhisattva is now free from rebirth according to *Madhyamakāvatāra.* Were he or she not a bodhisattva with the bodhisattva vows to attain perfect Buddhahood for the benefit of all sentient beings, it would have been possible for him to become an *arahant.*

(8) Steadfast or Immovable

The eighth stage is called the 'Steadfast or Immovable' by virtue of attainment of effortlessness in entering the formless (*Arūpa-jhānas*) and freedom from any afflictions while immersed in the *rūpa-jhānas.* This is the stage of nonregression in the path of cultivation and there is no looking-back in the ascendancy to Buddhahood.

This stage is characterized by the bodhisattva's mastery of the *rūpa-jhānas* and effortlessness in entering the *Arūpa-jhānas.* The bodhisattva makes formless meditation (*Arūpa-jhānas*) flawless and uninterrupted and highly cultivated.

This stage is associated with the perfection of the four vows taken by the bodhisattva:

(i) To save all beings
(ii) To destroy all evil passions
(iii) To learn the Truth and teach it to others
(iv) To lead all beings towards Buddhahood

The vows are taken to deepen and strengthen the perfection of vigour and diligence (effort).

The characteristic of this stage is the 'will in action', the state of divine mind, a state of consciousness inconceivable and inexpressible, in which the idea of duality has been totally lost. The subconscious will of the bodhisattva is constantly acting in all kinds of merciful ways, but his conscious mind is quiet and serene. From this stage, all the activities of the bodhisattva become instinctive ('spontaneous'), the natural outflow of his or her great vows of compassion. There is no more striving but all actions are spontaneous.

(9) Good Intelligence

The ninth *bhūmi* is called the stage of 'Good Intelligence' because the bodhisattva now attains mastery of all kinds of spiritual teachings and tremendous unobstructed knowledge.

The bodhisattva associates with good people, listens to true teachings and reflects on the same. He perfects the transcendent way of power (bala) and he makes it an aid to the perfection of meditative concentration. He thereby transforms inferior will and knowledge to superior will and wisdom. He now becomes adept in teaching with different techniques, different forms and different expressions to all kinds of people. He has acquired inner mental stability and mastered the capability in teaching. He has attained higher powers and aspiration to benefit all sentien being.

(10) The Cloud of Doctrine or Law (Dharma Megha)

The tenth stage is called the '*Dharma Megha*' ('the Cloud of Doctrine or Law') because the bodhisattva here is enveloped by the perfect spiritual body of selflessness like a cloud that can cover all. He acquires the supermundane wisdom of selflessness and realizes the Ideal or Truth, the *Dharma.* This is the Truth body or spiritual body (*Dharmakāya*).

This is the perfection of gnosis (*jñāna*) which aids and deepens the perfection of wisdom (*prajñā* or insight) of the sixth stage. Here the insight is perfected and he sees and assumes the spiritual body (*Dharmakāya*).

(11) Buddhahood

The eleventh stage is called the stage of 'Buddhahood'. Even the most subtle barriers of afflictions are here permanently stopped, and unattached and unobstructed knowledge acquired for dealing with all kinds of objects of knowledge.

This is not merely the supermundane realisation of *śūnyatā* or insight into emptiness and eradication of all defilements without even any subtlest trace, but this is the final goal of Buddhahood where *prajñā* and *mahākaruṇā* are conjoined and become one beatific consciousness of enlightenment.

There is only one religion, the religion of truth; but there are many ways, many means, many *upāyas,* all issuing from the all-embracing love of the *Dharmakāya* and equally efficient to lead the masses to supreme enlightenment and universal good.

3. Bodhisattva Model and Seven Purifications in *Hīnayāna*

Compared to the model of 'Seven Purifications' in the *Visuddhimagga* of *Hīnayāna* school, there appears to be different views as to when one becomes an *arahant* in the bodhisattva practice. Is it on completing the sixth stage or the seventh stage?.

Some scholars opine that the bodhisattva becomes an arahant and enjoys the bliss of *Nirvāṇa* on completing the sixth stage. It is true that, in this stage, he attains the *Arūpa-jhānas* and enters into the state of cessation of perception and volition. But, as *Saṃdhinirmocana Sūtra* explains, he is still unable to penetrate the continuing cycles of his 'becoming' and see through his remaining *karmic* formations and burn them out complete with all defilements. His *arūpa-jhānas* (formless meditative trances) are still not completely flawless and uninterrupted and not highly cultivated. He has to still press ahead with further arduous and diligent practices to realize flawless and uninterrupted *arūpa-jhānas* and attain perfect purity. This he attains in the seventh *bhūmi* (stage) and thus, the seventh bhūmi corresponds to the *arahantship.*

Bhāvanā-mārga (path of cultivation) of the bodhisattva in *Mahāyāna* does not end with the attainement of this *arahantship,* but continues with the descent of the bodhisattva into *saṃsāra* and voluntarily taking on others' sufferings on himself for the purpose of benefitting all sentient beings. He goes through three more stages before achieving the ultimate goal of perfect Buddhahood, that is nothing but selflessness personified. His consciousness is transformed into Buddha consciousness, the consciousness suffused with selflessness. He becomes utterly selfless and empty ; empty of all defilements, but full of innumerable Buddha virtues arising from selflessness.

The differing emphasis in the two schools may be noted (Figure 19).

The emphasis in the *Hīnayāna* model is on :

Cessation of perception and volition (will).

Destruction of defilements and the *karmic* formations

Cessation of suffering

Nirvāṇa

Hīnayāna – Buddhaghoṣa's Visuddhimagga Model of Seven Purifications

Stages	Characterized by:	
1. Purification by proper moral conduct (śīla)	Perfection of morality	ASCENDING TO NIRVĀṆA ↓
2. Developing serenity and calmness	Calming meditation (samatha)	
3. Purification of view	Insight meditation	
4. Purification by over-coming doubt	Insight meditation (deepened)	
5. Purification by distinguishing between the right and wrong path	Insight meditation (further deepened)	
6. Purification of vision in the knowledge of progress	Calming and insight meditations combined to culminate in arūpa-jhānas	
7. Final purification – Purification by knowing and seeing	Destruction of defilments	
i) Stream – winner (sotapanna)	Destruction of the first three fetters	
ii) Once-returner (skadagamin)	Partial destruction of the next two fetters	
iii) Never-returner (anagamin)	Complete eradication of all the five fetters	
iv) Sainthood (arahant)	Complete eradication of all NIRVĀṆA	

Mahāyāna Bodhisattvabhūmi Model

Stages	Characterized by:		Path	Perfections
1. Joyous	Insight into emptiness	ASCENDING TO NIRVĀṆA ↓	Darśana-mārga ↑	1. Giving (Dhana)
2. Stainless	No moral transgressions even minute ones			2. Morality (Śila)
3. Radiance	Meditative concenetration resulting in immeasurable light of knowledge		Bhāvanā Mārga (Path of Cultivation)	3. Patience (Forbearance)
4. Blazing Intellect	Knowledge burns out affictions/difilments			4. Vigour (Diligence)
5. Difficult to conquer	Mastery in insight meditation and concentration			5. Meditation (Dhyāna)
6. Approaching or Presence	Attainment of arūpa-jhānas			6. Wisdom
7. Gone Afar	Flawless uninterupted form-less meditation (arūpa-jhānas); attains perfect purity PEAK OF NIRVĀṆA		↓	7. Upāya (Skill in means)
8. Steadfast or Immovable	Effortlesseness in entering arūpa-jhānas; all activities spontaneous	DESCENDING TO SAMSARA ↓	↑	8. Vows
9. Good Intelligence	Mastery in spiritual teachings		Bhāvanā Mārga Continuous in saṃsāra	9. Power (Bala)
10. The Cloud of Doctrine or Law (Dharma-megha)	Suffesed with the spirit of selflessness and attaining Dharma-body (Dharma-kāya)		↓	10. Prajñā (Insight, Jhāna)
11. Buddhahood	Consciousness transformed into Buddha consciousness		Bhāvanā Mārga Continuous in saṃsāra	

Fig. 19 Comparison of Models of Hīnayāna and Mahāyāna for Sainthood

On the other hand, the emphasis in the bodhisattva model is on :

<u>not only:</u>

Cessation of perception and volition (will) (i.e. cessation of *Vijñāna-pariṇāma*)

Destruction of defilements and the *karmic* formations

Cessation of suffering

<u>but also:</u>

Cultivaton of virtuous qualities and powers (i.e love and compassion and powers to benefit all sentient beings).

Renunciation of the exquisite bliss of *Nirvāṇa* and entering *saṃsāra* with higher aspiration to benefit all sentient beings wihtout any expectation of rewards.

Saṃcintyabhavopapatti (i.e. taking rebirth volitionally and willingly for the benefit of all sentient beings).

Apratiṣṭhita Nirvāṇa (i.e. Nirvāṇa of no-fixed abode or Non-abiding Nirvāṇa)

Attainment of Buddha consciousness and *Dharma Body* (*Dharmakāya*)

The path of cultivation (*Bhāvanā-mārga*) extends till Buddhahood is attained.

In a similar way, the bodhisattva model may be compared with the meditation practices and the salvation suggested in the *Upaniṣads*. The *Turīya*, the highest meditative state of union with *Ātman* (Brahman), presented in the *Māṇḍūkya Upaniṣad*, may be equated with the sixth *bhūmi* or at best with the seventh *bhūmi* of the bodhisattva model. The utter selflessness of Buddhism stands in stark contrast to the clinging to a subtle self or *Ātman* in the *Upaniṣads*. The emphasis in Buddhism is on destruction of the defilements and transformation of the consciousness whereas in the *Upaniṣadic* philosophies it is more on the apprehension of an absolute unchanging *Ātman* (Brahman).

4. How to Become a Buddha

The proper commencement of the path of the boddhisattva, who has taken a vow to become a perfect Buddha for the benefit of all sentient beings without any distinction, is to practise the six perfections (*pāramitā*). At the core is the right effort to effect a fundamental switch in orientation from self-concern to concern for others, to compassion – a real deep wish and intention to be kind in every way to all without discrimination. This fundamental switch is called the 'arising of the Awakening Mind (*bodhicitta*)'.

Take Residence in the Four Brahma-Vihāras

'Mind resolved on Awakening' next proceeds 'towards Awakening'. Originally the so-called 'divine abidings' (*Brahma Vihāras*) also known as the 'four immeasurables' were themselves thought to be sufficient means for attaining enlightenment itself. The aspirant meditates and takes up residence in the four states of consciousness celebrated as the *Brahma Vihāras.*

These are *maitrī, karuṇā, muditā and upekṣā*: loving-kindness, compassion, sympathetic joy and equanimity. Elaborating on these states in his commentary in the *Visuddhimagga* (The Path of Purification), the scholar *Buddhaghoṣa* points out that they are a practical means by which the individual may step out of his narrow individuality to realise the larger oneness of life. Absorbed in meditation, the disciple lets his mind pervade the four quarters of the world with thoughts of loving-kindness. And so, recognising himself in all, he suffuses the whole world with love beyond measure.

From this attitufe of *maitrī,* loving-kindness towards all, non-possessive love, is born *karuṇā,* that takes the active form of empathy with those who suffer, who have lost hope, who are sunk in anguish. As a condition of understanding, *karuṇā* melts down all the barriers of separateness. It leads, also, to *muditā,* a sharing in other's happiness, a joy in others' joy, the renunciation of envy and malice. Finally, having shared in the emotions of others, the meditator enters upon a condition of serene detachment, *upekṣā.* He responds to the world neither with attachment nor with aversion ; he stands as a quiet witness to the flow of events, watching with equanimity as every action brings into being its own series of consequences, and passes into the kaleidoscopic pattern of life.

In effect, the practice of the *Brahma-Vihāras* traces the *bodhicitta–utpāda* (literally, the production of the illuminated consciousness) and opens up the transcendental possibility of becoming a Buddha within the realm of ordinary human existence.

Equalising Self and Others and Exchanging Self and Others

Later Tibetan traditions have isolated two analytic meditation patterns from the Indian sources which it is thought will facilitate the awakening and transformation of the mind.

The first meditation pattern, called "equalizing self and others and exchanging self and others" can be traced to the eighth chapter of Śāntideva's *Bodhicaryāvatāra.* Morality is nothing but the simple principle that you should do to others what you would like others to do to you and you should not do to others what you would not like others to do you. We must be completely objective. As for morality, to treat everyone equally, that is all there is to it. Viewed objectively there is nothing special about me such that I strive for just my own happiness and the avoidance of my own suffering.

"I should dispel the suffering of others because it is suffering like my own suffering. I should help others too because of their nature as beings, which is like my own being." Everyone loves life and longs for happiness. All try to avoid suffering. As such, all are equal. With this knowledge, one actually 'exchanges self and others' by seeing all the evils that arise from cherishing oneself and the benefits that accrue from cherishing others. One meditates that :

"All those who suffer in the world do so because of the desire for their own happiness. All those happy in the world are so because of their desire for the happiness of others."

"Why say more? Observe this distinction : between the fool who longs for his own advantage and the sage who acts for the advantage of others."

(Paul Williams, *Buddhist Thought,* p.177 / 178)

Repayment for Kindness Received in One's Previous Lives

The other meditation pattern can be traced in the second *Bhāvanākrama* of *Kamalaśīla* and in the commentary to *Atiśa*'s *Bodhipathapradīpa.* This is based on the inward realisation that, in the course of the infinite series of previous lives we have gone through, all sentient beings must have been one's mothers, fathers, brothers, sisters and friends many times. In truth, all are one's 'mother sentient beings' at some time or other. From this realisation arise the spontaneous identification with all beings and also the deep wish to repay for all the kindnesses we must have received from them and to which we are indebted. From that, in turn, arises love and compassion for one's 'mother sentient beings' that are suffering so much.

One is in All and All are in One

Dependent Origination is the core principle of Buddhism. This means that every thing arises depending on some others ; all beings and all things are mutually co-arising and interdependent, with their causes and effects all interwoven together. All are woven in an infinite network of interconnectedness. One meditates on this interconnectedness and merges himself in the infinity of this network.

Buddhism has a unique theory of freedom which states that freedom comes from mutual identification and exchanging with others. One is free insofar as he identifies himself with others and abides in the same consideration of well-being for all as much as his own well-being and happiness. Mutual identification flows from selflessness. Identifying oneself with another, one can synthesize with another. Negating oneself and identifying oneself with another constitute synthetical identification. This is a peculiar theory or practice in *Mahāyāna*. It is applied to all practical situations. Even two opposed theories or incompatible facts are often identified. Often a happy solution to any conflict is arrived at by the use of this method and finding the middle path. As the result of mutual penetration and mutual identification, there arises the inward understanding and deep realisation : "One is in All; All are in One; One behind All and All behind One"; the great and small, the high and low all moving together harmoniously. Even the humblest partaking of the work in peace, no one stands separately or independently alone. It is the world of perfect harmony.

These are the meditative patterns in Buddhism to effect total transformation of the mind and to attain the state of perfect Buddhahood for the benefit of all sentient beings without distinction.

Part IV

EARLY ADVAITA VEDĀNTA

CHAPTER 16

Gauḍapādīya-Kārikā

Advaita Vedānta as a distinctive philosophical school seems to have developed only from seventh century CE and has its roots in *Gauḍapādīya-kārikā* (GK). Even though Śaṅkara is traditionally considered to be the founder of this school and its most famous exponent, the central doctrines of non-dualism (*advaita*) of this school have been derived from GK. GK consists of four *prakaraṇas* of which the first deals with the various creation theories and expounds the doctrine of the four states of experience taught in the *Māṇḍūkya Upaniṣad.* It is intimately linked to the teachings of this *Upaniṣad* and, as such, is traditionally interspersed between its prose passages. It also contains an explanation on the meaning and significance of the syllable *OM* and exhortation to meditate on the same. The other three *prakaraṇas* propound the theories of non-origination (*ajātivāda*), non-dualism (*advaita*) and *māyā. Asparśa-yoga* is taught as the means of deliverance.

Tradition has it that *Gauḍapāda* (7th Century CE) is the author of GK and he is said to be Śaṅkara's paramaguru (i.e. guru's guru, teacher's teacher). But modern scholarship tends to attribute multiple authorship to GK. Even though GK maintains the absolutist position of Vedānta on Self (*Ātman*), it no doubt has been greatly influenced by the thoughts, ideas and arguments of Madhyamaka and *Yogācāra* schools of Buddhism. The theories of non-origination and equality of the waking and dream states found in GK are all drawn from the earlier Buddhist philosophies.

GK acknowledges in its verse IV.90 :

"From the *Agrayāna* (i.e. *Mahāyāna* tradition) one should know that which is to be abandoned, that which is to be known, that which is to be acquired and that which is to be perfected........."

1. Creation Theories Rejected

GKI cites many creation theories and rejects them on logical grounds.

"It is the firm conclusion (of sages) that there is an origin of all existing entities. *Prāṇa* creates the universe, *Puruṣa* creates each separate ray of consciousness" (I.6).

Puruṣa radiates all the rays of consciousness that appear divergently as Viśva (consciousness in the waking state), *Taijasa* (consciousness in the dream state) and *prājña* (consciousness in the deep sleep state) in all the living creatures. *Prāṇa* here is equated with the Self. *Prāṇa* as the vital breath infuses life into the creatures and causes them to come into being. This theory of creation by *Puruṣa* and *Prāṇa* is suggested here as the view of some wise men, but not endorsed by the author of GK as will be clear from the subsequent verses.

"Some creation–theorists, however, think of creation as an outflowing (emanation) (i.e. *vibhūti*, exuberance, a demonstration of the superhuman power of God). Creation is imagined by others as having the same form as dream and illusion (*māyā*)"(I.7).

"Creation is merely the will of the Lord so (think others who have) a firm conviction about creation and those who speculate about time consider the creation of beings (to be) from time"(I.8).

Four more theories of creation are mentioned here. In one view, creation is considered to be the *vibhūti*, exuberance of God, an outflowing from Him due to His superhuman power. An emanation from God or a sort of transformation of God with the world created out of Him is suggested here. In another view, creation is a mere will of the Lord; He creates the world with all its beings like a potter creates a pot. Here the creation is due to His unfailing will. Creation is considered by some others as comparable to dream or magic. The world and its beings arise as in a dream of the Lord or as in magic show where the Lord creates these entities as illusory phenomena. Yet some others, the *Kālācintakās* (i.e. astronomers and astrologers) think that creation emanates from time alone.

The mode and nature of creation have so far been talked in verses I-6,7 and 8. In the next verse, the purpose of creation itself is questioned and all theories of creation rejected.

"Creation is for the sake of enjoyment (or experience)–so say some. Others say it is for the sake of sport. This again is the lordly own-nature of the divine, for what desire is there for the one who has obtained all wishes?" (I.9).

The views that creation by the Lord is for the sake of his enjoyment or experience or sport do not do justice to the concept of God. God cannot be said to be subject to any desire whatsoever. If He be desiring any of these things, then He is not the Lord of Himself. As such, all theories of creation by the Lord including creation by magic are refuted by asserting: "What desire can one have whose desire is ever fulfilled?".

It is true that there are *Upaniṣadic* texts supporting creation; but, according to GK, such passages have some other purpose.

"The creation that has been multifareously set forth with the help of the examples of earth, gold, sparks etc, is merely by way of generating the idea of (oneness); but there is no multiplicity in any way" (III.15).

For instance, *Muṇḍaka Upaniṣad* (II.i.1) states that, just as sparks of fire fly off from a fire fully ablaze, different kinds of creatures originate from the Imperishable. This view, according to GK, has a different purpose, the purpose of engendering in us the idea of the oneness of the individual and the supreme Self. There is no creation of multiplicity in any way.

Not only the theories of creation are rejected by GK as above, but also the theories of evolution like the *Sāṃkhya* theory of evolution from *prakṛti* and some *Upaniṣadic* theory of *Brahma–pariṇāmavāda* (i.e. a real transformation, *pariṇāma,* of Brahman into the world) are also refuted by GK.

2. *Pariṇāma* Theories Refuted

The *Sāṃkhya* theory of evolution of the world and its beings from *prakṛti* has been refuted by GK in the following verses in the fourth *prakaraṇa* :

"The cause must undergo birth according to one who holds that the cause itself is the effect. How can a thing be birthless that takes birth, and how can it be eternal when it can be subject to (partial) disintegration" (IV.11).

"If the effect be non-different from the cause, on that account the effect, too, is birthless (unoriginated). (This is a contradiction because how can a thing, that is a product, be still considered birthless) (Further contradiction). How can your cause be still eternal, it being non-different from its effect which is subject to birth?" (IV.12).

"That disputant has certainly no supporting illustration, who holds that the effect is produced out of an unborn cause. If the produced effect is held to be born out of another born thing, that too leads to no solution"(IV.13).

According to the *Sāṃkhyans*, the eternal principle *prakṛti* evolves into the effects like *Mahat, ahaṃkāra* and other twenty-one principles. If it is born and changes into these principles, how can it be said to be eternal and birthless? For it is a contradiction in terms to say that a thing is eternal and unborn and yet has birth. How can it be eternal if it is split up and transformed into some other things? It becomes a contradiction to say that a thing may be broken up partially and yet be birthless and eternal.

If the effect be non-different from the cause, then the effect also should be birthless like the cause or the cause is also not eternal like the effect. There is no illustration to support the view that the effect is originated from the unoriginated (unborn). On the other hand, if it is held that the effect is born out of another born thing, then since the latter must come out of another born thing, and the last one again from another born thing, this will lead to infinite regress and not to any solution of the problem.

Likewise, *Brahma-pariṇāmavāda* (i.e. evolution of the universe and life-forms from Brahman) of some *Upaniṣads* are also refuted by GK.

Brahman is eternal, immutable and unborn. But how can such a positive entity that is unborn and immortal undergo mortality? (III.20, IV.6)

"The immortal cannot become mortal. Similarly the mortal cannot become immortal. The mutation of one's nature will take place in no way whatsoever"(III.21, IV.7).

"How can an immortal entity continue to be changeless from the stand point of one according to whom a positive entity which is immortal by nature can pass into birth, it becoming a product". (III.22, IV.8)

How can a beginningless, birthless, changeless, immortal thing give birth to changing, decaying and mortal things? How can a positive entity that is unborn, eternal and immortal undergo mortality? How can an immortal entity continue to be changeless when it gives rise to the birth of multifarious things that are constantly changing, decaying and dying? By considering the eternal, immutable, changeless, birthless self as the source of all, the integrity of the self is violated. How to reconcile the ever-identical unchanging self with the ever-changing empirical variety and diversity of objects? The former is permanent, immutable whereas the latter are impermanent and ever-changing. How to establish a causal relationship between the two without compromising the integrity of the eternal and immutable self?

GK asserts that this relationship is only through *māyā*. The external world, the inner subjective dream world of the mind stuff, *Prāṇa*, vital powers and the inner controller of these are all appearances or illusions as in a dream or magic and are imagined on the auspicious non-dual self of the *Turīya* state. For GK, all excepting the non-dual Self are unreal.

Since birthlessness is the very nature of Brahman, transmutation of its nature can take place in no way whatsoever (IV.29).

As we have already seen in Madhyamaka philosophy, Nāgārjuna proves by means of the tetralemma (four alternative propositions) that 'origination' as an absolute attribute of Reality cannot be established. Following the same logic, GK states:

"Nothing (*vastu*) whatsoever is originated either from itself or from something else (or) (from both together). Nothing whatsoever existent, non-existent or both existent and non-existent is originated" (IV.22).

As a jar does not come out of that very jar, so nothing can be born out of its own form by itself. Nor does it take birth from another, as something different from another, just as a cloth is not born of a pot or a cloth from another cloth. Similarly a thing is not born both out of itself and another, just as a jar or cloth is not born out of a jar and cloth, for this involves contradiction.

The difficulties of causation lead GK to say that nothing is produced either by itself or by another, nor is anything in fact produced. The causal law requires a relation between the cause and effect and all relations of this kind are unintelligible because they lead to contradictions. We cannot say that God or Brahman is the cause of the world or *jīva* is born from Brahman. Nothing is born and nothing is destroyed.

For Nāgārjuna, there is no birth in the absolute sense. GK also establishes that nothing whatsoever is born. But, from this, GK has jumped to the conclusion and assumed that 'there is an unborn'. This is debatable and we shall come to this later.

But, continuing our consideration of the *Sāṃkhya* theory of evolution of *prakṛti* and *Upaniṣadic* ideas of evolution of Brahman (*Brahma-pariṇāmavāda*), we find that these are conclusively refuted by GK. Such a view of evolution of Brahman in the

Upaniṣads, according to GK, "is merely by way of generating the idea of unity of the individual and the supreme Self."

3. *Māyāmātra*

If the evolution theories of *Sāṃkhya* and *Upaniṣads* are rejected, then how are we to explain the coming into existence of the universe with all its beings? GK explains that these are only appearances (*māyāmātra*) and not real. The phenomenal world is negated and non-duality is considered the only reality.

"It is beyond question that the phenomenal world if it had any existence would cease to be (upon enlightenment). All this duality that is nothing but *māyā,* is but non-duality in reality" (I.17).

The *Bhāṣya-kāra* gives the following exposition on this verse.

The phenomenal world does not exist because it is only a mistaken superimposition like a snake on a rope. There is no doubt that if it had existed (in the mistaken view of ignorance), it would cease to be (upon enlightenment). Certainly, it is not that the snake, fancied on the rope through an error of observation, exists there in reality and is then removed by correct observation. Verily, it is not that the magic conjured up by a magician exists in reality and is then removed by curing the optical illusion of its witness. Similar to the illusion of snake on a rope and the magic show, the phenomenal world and the duality seen therein are not real, but only *māyā.* In the supreme truth, there is only non-duality in reality just like the rope and the magician; there is no such thing as the world, which may be considered as appearing and disappearing. (Eight Upaniṣads with the commentary of Śaṅkara, Vol.2, Trans. By Swāmī Gambhīrānanda, p.213).

Richard King adds: "If this world really existed then it would vanish with the experience of non-duality (i.e. the realization of *Turīya,* the fourth state); but it remains precisely because it is duality and is to be taken as merely illusion (*māyāmātra*). The mistake is in thinking that duality even exists in the first place"(*Early Advaita Vedānta and Buddhism,* P.28, 29).

"Vedic texts are equally in evidence with regard to creation in Reality and through *māyā.* That which is ascertained (by the *Vedas*) and is supported by logical reasoning only can be the meaning and nothing else"(III.23).

"Since it is stated (in the *Vedas*), 'There is no diversity here', 'The Lord, on account of *māyā,* (is perceived as manifold)' and the '(the Self) without being born (appears to be born in various ways)', it follows that He is born on account of *māyā* alone". (III.24)

As already mentioned, according to GK, the *Upaniṣadic* texts supporting creation theory are meant for the purpose of engendering the idea of oneness of the individual with the supreme Self and as a help to enable comprehension of the non-duality of the Self. Other *Upaniṣadic* passages are cited in verse III.24 as supporting the *māyā* theory. For instance, BU II.v.19 states: 'The Lord, on account of *māyā* is perceived as manifold'. Further, according to *Kaṭha* II.i.11, 'There is no diversity here whatsoever'. This denies the existence of duality.

As earlier discussed, logical reasoning proves that the immortal Self cannot become mortal, cannot be born into mortal things. Mutation of its nature cannot take place in any manner, just as fire cannot change into water. That which is proclaimed by the *Vedas* to be one without a second, birthless and immortal and that which is supported by logical reasoning is only the truth. The conclusion is that it is through *māyā* alone He who is unborn appears to be born in various ways.

"Just as dream and magic are seen to be unreal, or as is a city in the sky, so also is this whole universe known to be unreal from the *Upaniṣads* by the wise"(II.31).

This whole universe is viewed by the wise as unreal just as dream or magic or an imaginary city in the sky.

"The aggregates (of bodies and senses) are all projected like dream by the *māyā* of the Self. Be it a question of superiority or equality of all, there is no logical ground to prove their existence." (III.10)

This verse also states that all composite things and the phenomenal world arise like dreams projected by the *māyā* of *Ātman*. These are compared to dream and magic show conjured up by a magician (IV.68-69).

4. Analysis of *Māyā*

GK has used various analogies to illustrate its theory of *māyā* as we have seen above. These are summarized and analysed below for a proper understanding of this theory.

The phenomenal world is condemned as unreal and false like:

- a dream
- an imaginary city in the sky

- a magic show
- many shapes assumed by Indra
- fear of snake superimposed on a rope in darkness

The analysis of the first two analogies – dream and imaginary city in the sky – leads us to the concept of *māyā* as a mere illusion or imagination of a thing where nothing exists really. The *māyā* here is a sort of power of *Ātman* or Self to project a dream or imaginary city in the sky from out of nothing. Two ways of interpreting these are possible. The first is that, because of His wonderous power, the dream and the sky-city projected by Him become the conventional practical realities of the phenomenal world. This is only a restatement of the conventional creation theory in a new form with the idea of unreality of these in the ultimate sense emphasized. The second interpretation may be that *Ātman* or Self Himself is dreaming this dream or imagining a sky-city. Here *māyā* is the illusion suffered by the *Ātman* or Self.

The next two analogies – magic show and many shapes assumed by Indra – illustrate the deceptive power of *māyā* possessed by Brahman? In this view, Brahman becomes a deceiver and what for should Brahman resort to this deceptive power is a valid question.

The last analogy – snake on a rope – points to an entirely different, qualitatively different concept of *māyā*. Here something exists but attributes of some other thing are superimposed on the first thing due to *avidyā* (ignorance) and the first thing is mistaken for the other thing. The veil of ignorance conceals the first thing. *Māyā* is this veil of ignorance.

In this last analogy, there are three entities: rope, snake and the seer. Rope is *Ātman* or Brahman. The snake is the phenomenal world. Who is the seer? The seer (whoever he may be) superimposes the qualities of the phenomenal world (snake) on the *Ātman* or Brahman (rope). But where does the mind of the seer (which superimposes) come from? This mind is only a derivative of the consciousness of *Ātman* or Brahman and grows from it. This growth itself is a phenomenal occurrence, which takes place before the superimposition. For the superimposition to take place, in fact, the phenomenon should have already occurred. Therefore, the theory of *māyā* as a superimposition is flawed. Further, the root cause of the superimposition lies ultimately in *Ātman* or Brahman only. That means, the *Ātman* itself is deluded and imagines the phenomenal world on itself. This amounts to saying that rope itself imagines itself as snake. This much is conceded by GK when it says in the second *prakaraṇa*:

"The self-effulgent Self imagines Itself through Itsellf by the power of Its own *māyā*. The Self itself cognizes the objects. Such is the definite conclusion of *Vedānta*" (II.12).

The *Ātman* imagines himself by himself and expresses himself as the *jīvas* and the world through the power of his own *māyā*.

"First He imagines the individual (soul) and then He imagines the different objects, external and mental. The individual gets his memory in accordance with the kind of thought impressions He has" (II.16).

"(This Self) is imagined to be the infinite objects like *Prāṇa* (the vital force) etc. This is the *māyā* of that self-effulgent one, by which He himself is deluded"(II.19).

The conclusion is that *Ātman* deludes itself through its own *māyā* and imagines itself to be the *Prāṇa*, individual souls (*jīvas*) and different things, external and internal i.e. all objective and subjective things. The wonderous power in the earlier creation theory is now replaced by the 'delusive power' inherent in *Ātman*. *Ātman* himself is subject to this delusive power which is termed his own *māyā*. The *māyā* becomes the *svabhāva* or the very nature of the *Ātman*. The inevitable questions arise as to how and why the non-dual, omnipotent and omniscient *Ātman* or Brahman could 'delude himself'. If He is subject to delusion, then He cannot be considered omniscient and omnipotent. Another flaw in the theory is that the *Ātman* or Brahman deludes himself and becomes the source of all defilements, impurities in moral behaviour, evils and injustices. In their conception of the working of the universe, the Buddhists postulate a universal impersonal moral principle that determines the retributions over the actions and the evolution of *Vijñāna* as the various worlds (*Vijñāna-pariṇāma*). The Law of Karma is an inviolable principle in Buddhism. In the *māyā* theory of the *Advaita Vedānta*, is such law of *Karma* also imagined by the deluded Brahman and as such unreal? How can it be logically conceived that the same deluded Brahman is the source of evils and injustices and at the same time dispenser of justice? These are the nagging questions on the status given to the moral aspects of the universal order in the *māyā* theory.

As the scholars opine, the māyā-theory has only been suggested broadly and not systematically developed and presented in the GK. In its view, *māyā* in the final analysis is incomprehensible (IV.52). In spite of the various confusing analogies given, it seems what GK wants to emphasize is that the phenomenal world of variety has only the status of a false imagination (*vikalpa*) or dream. This world is the false imagination or dream of *Ātman* or Brahman at the macrocosmic level and of the individual selves at the microcosmic level. Ignorance is the root cause. However, ignorance which remains as ignorance at the microcosmic level is transmuted and raised to the level of *māyā-śakti*, a mysterious power, at the macrocosmic level.

5. Proof of Unreality-Equality of Waking and Dream States

GK tries to establish its fundamental position that the phenomenal world of diversity experienced is a dream by proving the equality of the waking state with the dream state. GK first proves the falsity of the objects seen in dream thus:

"The wise declare the falsity of all objects in a dream because of the location of the objects inside (the body) and by reason of (the space) being small" (II.1).

"All entities are unreal in dream, since they are seen (perceived) within the body. How can there be vision of creatures within this narrow space here?"(IV.33).

In dream, objects like elephants or mountains are perceived and these are obviously inside the dreamer's mind and not outside the body. They ought to be false because mountains and elephants cannot possibly exist within the limited space inside the nerves in the dreamer's body.

Besides one does not see places in dream by going anywhere outside the body. One may dream that he is going to a far away place; but it is not real because there is not sufficient time for him to reach there and come back. Moreover, every dreamer, when awakened, does not continue in the places that he dreamt. Should one go to a different region in dream, he should wake up in the region of his dream, but this is not so (II.2).

In dream states, an actual concrete world is presented to us. But, we do not call that world real since on waking that is contradicted.

GK sees the following similar or common features between the dream states and the waking states:

(1) In both the states, consciousness does not come into contact with any object. (IV.26-27).

(2) In both the states, things (objects) are seen to be within the narrow space of the body. (IV.33, II-3)
(3) In both the states, the objects are 'perceived through consciousness' (II.4-5)
(4) Both the states have the common feature of having a beginning and an end.
(5) In both the states, two aspects of consciousness are involved–consciousness of objects directed outward and consciousness of objects directed inward (i.e. mental constructs of attributes or qualities on the objects observed). We may call these as objective consciousness and subjective consciousness respectively (II.9-10).

Verses II.3 and IV.33 aim at proving the falsity of all things seen. If falsity in dream follows from the fact that things are seen within the narrow confined space of the body, then all things even in the waking state must be false since they are also seen within the narrow space of the body (*Ānandagiri; Eight Upaniṣads* with the commentary of Śaṅkara , Translated by Swāmī Gambīrānanda, p. 351-352).

Richard King differs and comments :

"Although the 'spatial limitations' argument can be used against the veridicality of dream experiences (there being no problem here since common sense beliefs do not attribute externality to dream objects), the same argument fails to stand up to rational consideration when applied to waking experience.................... ."

" 'Enclosure within the body' can hardly be the meaning of the term in the context of GK II.4 since it would make no sense to argue that the 'external world' of waking experience existed within our own body because the body itself is a material object and part of that world. Besides, IV.33 is discussing *dharmas* (objects of consciousness), not *bhāvas* (entities), which may be a different case altogether. In this context, it seems more likely that the argument refers to 'enclosure within' the mind. This makes statements such as IV.36–"all things perceived by the mind (*citta*) are insubstantial"–appear more appropriate........... ."

(*Early Advaita Vedānta and Buddhism*, p.170-171)

In both the dream and waking states, the consciousness does not actually come into contact with any object, but only experiences the appearances or representations of objects. This closely resembles the *Vijñaptimātra* (Representation-only) theory of *Yogācāra* School. The experiences in both the dream and waking states are equal in as much as what is perceived is the appearance of an object and not the object itself.

Another argument of GK to prove the equality of waking and dream states is that, since the fact of "being perceived through consciousness" is equally present in both the states and since the objects perceived there in a dream are false, they are false in the waking state also. The body that is seen in dream to be walking about or doing something is unsubstantial since another sleeping body as distinguished from the one in the state of dream exists separately (IV.36). As the body perceived through consciousness in dream is unreal, so also things seen through consciousness even in the waking state are unreal for they are all equally perceived through consciousness.

The point made is that the waking state is also unreal since it is similar to the dream State.

Even in the dream state, a distinction is inwardly realized between the subjective consciousness and objective consciousness experienced in dream. The dream objects like elephants, pots and the like perceived by the objective consciousness are taken to be real and true in the dream and it also happens that the attributes or qualities imagined by the subjective consciousness on the objects and the emotions of the subjective consciousness are realized to be false in the dream itself. Nevertheless, the reality of the objective consciousness and the unreality of the subjective consciousness experienced in dream are both unreal.

In the waking state also, similar distinction of true and false can be seen for whatever is perceived by the objective consciousness and whatever is imagined by the subjective consciousness. GK's view is that, just as in the dream state, it is reasonable to assume that both the so-called true and false are unreal in the waking state also, because they are equally imagined either by the subjective consciousness or objective consciousness (GK II.9-10).

The common fact of 'being perceived through consciousness', that is equally present in both the states, is adduced as proof of the equality or sameness of the waking and dream states and unreality of both. On the other hand, objections may be raised to treating these two states as same on the ground that the objects of the waking state have utility and serve some purpose or other whereas dream objects have no such utility. For this, GK replies that the utility experienced in the waking state of food, drinks, etc., is contradicted in dream. For, a man who has got his hunger appeased and thirst quenched by eating and drinking in the waking state, may on going to sleep dream as though he is hungry or thirsty and he has been fasting for long. Similarly, he may dream of full satisfaction from eating and drinking; but on waking up he feels hunger and thirst. Thus, the objects of the waking state are seen to be contradicted in dream. These contradictions and also the fact that the objects seen in dream and those experienced in the waking state possess the common feature of having a beginning and an end, lead to the conclusion that the objects of the waking state are also unreal just like the objects seen in dream. (II.7)

No doubt dream objects and dream experiences are false because they are contradicted immediately on waking. Similarly, the unreality of the waking world also will be known when we realize the Truth and attain to the state of *Turīya* (meditative *samādhi*). The world as we experience it in the waking state is contradicted by the experiences in the other states of consciousness i.e. dream, deep sleep or meditation (*Turīya*).

Impermanence, ephemeral transient nature, of things (*anityam*) stressed in Buddhism as a mark of unreality is also suggested in GK. GK echoes this where it states that both the dream and waking states are false since both are limited, having a beginning and an end.

"That which does not exist in the beginning and in the end, also (does not exist) in the present" (II.6, IV.31).

That, which comes into existence and subsequently ceases to be, cannot be treated as real. It does not exist in the middle also really. To be real, it must exist always.

These are the various logical reasonings adduced by GK in proof of the equivalence of the waking and dream states and unreality of the waking experiences just as dream experiences.

There is no denying the fact that the inner subjective world created by the mind-consciousness under the influence of the assailing cravings and passions and the attributes and qualities assigned to the outer objects on the sole criteria of whether these satisfy or hinder our desires, are false. These are the ones superimposed by our cravings and passions on the things. This superimposition is truly the dream in the waking state. But the waking state has another aspect where we analyse the various states of existence, explore the truth, collect and correlate data, form hypothesis, prove by facts and experiments, establish the laws of cause and effect, propound scientific and religious theories, control the nature and shape the future. Unlike the dream state, the waking state is subject to the laws of cause and effect and is characterized by acquisition and accumulation of knowledge and establishment of holy path to attain liberation from the *saṃsāric* experience. Hence, equating the waking state totally with the dream experience will be an erroneous position. In recognition of this distinction, the two truth system of Madhyamaka has been expanded to three-truths or three-natures in the *Yogācāra* philosophy. The conventional realm has been divided into two: imagined (*parikalpita*) and other-dependent (*paratantra*). Following *Yogācāra* formulation, GK also seems to endorse this distinction as may be seen in verse. IV.73, but does not elaborate on the theory:-

"That which exists according to the imagined conventional (reality) (*kalpita-saṃvṛti*) does not exist in ultimate reality. It may exist in the relative aspect (*paratantra*) of conventional (reality), (but it) does not exist in ultimate reality"(IV.73).

This distinguishes between that which is merely imagined or fabricated (*kalpita*) and that which has some form of relative existence, dependent upon causal conditions and worldly consensus. This is in line with the philosophical position of *Yogācāra* in Buddhism.

6. No Objective Reference

Having made the distinction between the objective consciousness and subjective consciousness and recognized the possibility of true and false natures in these, GK draws the conclusion that since both these are unreal in dream, these are unreal in the waking experience also, as we have already seen. The proof adduced is the common fact of "being perceived through consciousness" in both the states. This means, according to GK, that whatever is perceived through consciousness is unreal. This is the axiom on which GK's arguments are based. The world exists only in the mind of man. GK reduces all experiences to mental impressions and declares that the latter have no objective causes.

GK does not agree with the view that knowledge, perception of sound, etc., has objective reference apart from its own subjective existence through the consciousness. It may be argued that perception of sound and the rest of such experiences cannot be contentless and unrelated to objects. How to explain experiences of burns, pains and the like, if there were nothing externally present to cause them? GK does not accept the logic that external objects are the basis of experience.

"From a logical point of view it is held that a designation (*prajñapti*, knowledge) has an objective reference (*nimitta*) ; from the point of view of reality, it is said that (there is) no objective reference for an objective referent" (IV.25).

Bhāṣya-kāra explains that a jar does not exist apart from clay after being recognized as clay that it really is, nor does a cloth exist apart from the yarns, nor the yarns apart from the fibres. Thus, if the reality is pursued successively till words and notions cease, we do not perceive any external cause of knowledge at all (*Eight Upaniṣads,* Vol.Two, Trans. By Swāmī Gambhīrānanda, p.344).

The objects in the ultimate analysis reduce to molecules, atoms and finally to electrons and protons or waves of energy and a set of mathematical formulae. Breaking up further, we come to void or nothingness. This is the destructed or abstracted void, antithetic void propounded by one of the Buddhist Schools, namely Satyasiddhi School of Harivarman (C.250-350 CE).

7. Duality is Vibration of Consciousness

GK's position is that external object is non-existent (*abhūta*) and its illusory appearance is not separate from or different from consciousness (IV.26). It is perceived through consciousness and hence unreal as already established. GK concludes that the consciousness never actually touches an object and the division of our experience into a 'subject' and an 'object' is nothing more than a vibration of consciousness.

"This duality of perceiver and perceived is merely vibration of consciousness (*cittaspandita*). This consciousness is declared to be unrelated to an object (*nirviṣaya*), permanent and non-relational i.e. without any relations"(IV.72).

"As in dream consciousness (*citta*) vibrates as though having dual functions, so in the waking state consciousness vibrates as though with two facets"(III.29, IV.61).

"There is no doubt that, in dream, the consciousness, though one, appears in dual aspects ; so also in the waking state, consciousness, though one, appears to have two aspects" (III.30, IV.62).

Analysis of dream state reveals that, apart from consciousness, there do not exist two things – the cognizer and the thing cognized – in dream. So is the case in the waking state also, for in either state there exists only the consciousness. The duality as a whole, comprising the moving or the motionless, that is perceived by the mind, is nothing but the mind. When the mind ceases to be the mind, duality is no longer perceived.

It is consciousness alone that is imagined in the forms of diverse objects and creatures in dream. Similarly, the creatures – egg-born, moisture-born and other *jīvas* – seen by a waking man are non-different from his consciousness, since they are perceived through consciousness, just like the creatures perceived by the consciousness of a dreamer. That consciousness again is the experiencer. Both consciousness and the diverse objects can be understood only in terms of each other (IV.63-67).

Just as creatures seen in a dream or conjured up by magic or charms and incantations, undergo birth and death, so also creatures are merely imagined by consciousness and they are verily non-existent (IV. 68-70). The birth, death etc, of creatures within the realm of phenomenal existence are verily like those of the creatures in dream or magic. They appear and disappear. There is no birth in the absolute sense in the ultimate reality (IV.71).

From the foregoing, GK concludes that it is consciousness (*vijñāna*) that has the semblance of birth, appears to move and simulates a substance possessed of qualities; but it itself is unoriginated (birthless) and motionless, insubstantial, tranquil and non-dual (*advaya*). The objects of consciousness (*dharmas*) and the creatures that appear in the consciousness are also considered to be birthless as established above.

What is it that causes the appearance of these objects and creatures? It is the vibration of consciousness, as it were, that is set in motion by ignorance.

GK IV uses the analogy of fire-brand to illustrate the non-dual substratum that underlies the world of appearances. When a firebrand is moved in a circular motion, there appears to be a wheel of fire (*alātacakra*) hovering in the air. Indeed it creates various images as per movement. These images depend upon the fire brand for their appearance, yet they are not real.

"Just as with a moving firebrand there are straight and crooked images etc, likewise with vibrating consciousness (*vijñāna*) there are the images of a perceiver and perceived"(IV.47).

Consciousness (*vijñāna*) is the non-dual reality behind the appearances of the various objects and creatures, just as the fire brand is the single reality behind the varied images. The images are neither part of the fire brand itself, nor are they different from it. They do not come to it from anywhere else. When the fire brand comes to rest, the images do not go anywhere else nor do they enter it. In the same way, it may be said of consciousness that the appearances of various objects and creatures are neither part of the consciousness nor different from it. When consciousness is in vibration, these appearances do not come to it from anywhere else. When it is not vibrating, these appearances do not go anywhere else, nor do they enter into consciousness. (IV.49-52)

Thus, the appearances of various kinds of objects and creatures are because of the vibration of consciousness and this vibration in turn takes place because of ignorance. Ignorance is the *māyā-śakti* of the Self. Under the influence of this *māyā*, the Self deludes itself and imagines the various kinds of objects and creatures. The Self Itself cognizes them and becomes the support of their cognition and memory (II.12). The *Ātman* (Self) first imagines the *jīva* (individual soul) and then different things, external and internal (objective and subjective) (II.16). The aggregates of bodies and senses are all projected like dream by the *māyā* of the Self. (III.10).

The *Ātman*, turning the mind outward, manifests diversely the mundane things existing in the mind and creates the well-defined things such as the earth etc, as also those not well-defined. Similarly He manifests diversely such things as mental desires by making His mind turn inward. In this way, the Prabhu (Self) imagines and creates. (II.13)

8. Ātman is Like Space

Ātman (Self), infinite and all-pervasive, remains in the individual souls just as space exists within the jars. He imagines and projects the aggregates of bodies and senses that separate and differentiate the individuals, just as in dream, through the *māyā* of His own Self. (III.3).

Just as, when the space within one jar is contaminated by dust, smoke etc, the spaces within the other jars are not affected, in the same manner, the happiness, suffering or sorrow afflicting one individual soul will not affect the others. (III.5)

In the cases of the spaces created by individual jars and the like, there may be differences in forms, functions and names; but space itself is undifferentiated and there is no multiplicity therein. Similar is the case with regard to the individual souls and *Ātman*. In spite of the differences in the forms, functions and names of the individual beings, *Ātman* is one since these differences are unreal, mere imaginations due to ignorance. (III.6)

As the sky becomes darkened by impurities in the opinion of children, similarly *Ātman* in the opinion of the unenlightened, becomes tainted with impurities (III.8). GK maintains that *Ātman* (Self) in all the bodies is quite similar to space and that, just as space is not contaminated by impurities in the confined space of a particular jar, *Ātman* is not contaminated by impurities. This does not stand to logical scrutiny. In the case of the space, differentiating barriers of jars etc, are not created by space. But, in the case of *Ātman*, He creates or imagines the differentiating factors of bodies of the individual beings. It may be argued that these are only imaginations and not real. Even if this be conceded, the impurities and defilements of the individual beings flow from his imaginations. In as much as he is deluded by ignorance and imagines these impurities and defilements, he cannot escape the criticism. This is the inevitable contradiction that will arise if an absolute being is assumed and attempt is made to reconcile the imperfections and impurities of the phenomenal world with the perfection and integrity of the absolute being. It may argued that, in the ultimate analysis, these are all *māyā* and *māyā* is incomprehensible (*acintya* – GK IV.52) and unexplainable. All such views ultimately take recourse to a belief system where logical reasoning has no place.

9. *Ātman*, The Non-Dual Self

"This Self is imagined to be the unreal things and also to be non-dual; these perceived things are also imagined on the non-dual Self. Therefore non-duality is auspicious." (II.33)

In the translation of the above GK verse II.33 (*Eight Upaniṣads*, Vol. Two, Translated by Swāmī Gambhīrānanda, p.256-257), certain ambiguity has been introduced on the question who is imagining the unreal things on the non-dual Self. The *Bhāṣya-kāra* explains the above verse as follows:

"...... The Self is imagined to be such multifarious unreal things as *Prāṇa* etc. which do not exist. But this is not done from the standpoint of reality, for nothing can be pointed out by anybody unless the mind is active, nor can the Self have any movement. And things, perceivable to the unsteady mind alone, cannot be imagined to subsist in reality ("Diversity perceived on the motionless Self cannot be fancied to have real existence"- according to *Ānandagiri*). Therefore, though the Self is ever of the same nature, it alone is imagined to be such unreal things as *Prāṇa* etc and again as existing in its own nature of non-duality and absolute reality. It is supposed to be the substratum of everything, just as a rope is of the snake etc. And those perceived entities too, viz. *Prāṇa* and the rest, are imagined by virtue of the existence of the Self that is verily non-dual, for no illusion can be perceived that is without a substratum. Thus since non-duality is the substratum of all illusion and since this non-duality is ever unchanging in its own nature, it is auspicious, even in the state of illusion. But the illusions alone are evil, for they generate fear like that from the snake seen on a rope for instance. Non-duality is free from fear, hence that alone is auspicious."

In the above interpretation, it is implied that mind alone is active and imagines unreal things on the non-dual Self whereas the latter is ever unchanging. As we have already pointed out earlier, for the mind to be active, it should have been created or imagined first by the Self. Rope only imagines the snake on itself. and nothing else is there. This has been conceded by GK also in verses (II.12,16) where it is clearly stated that the self-effulgent Self deludes itself through its own *māyā* and imagines itself to be the unreal things such as *Prāṇa*. After *Prāṇa* and life comes the mind in the process of evolution (imaginery). The root cause is ignorance in Self itself which may be called euphemistically the *māyā-śakti* of the Self.

The above verse II.33 is rendered by Richard King as follows so as to be inconformity with other verses of GK (II.12, 16):

"And this is imagined to be non-existing entities themselves by means of the non-dual (*advaya*). The (dual) entities exist only by means of the non-dual. Therefore there is auspicious non-duality". (*Early Advaita Vedānta and Buddhism*, p.248).

Another point in the above interpretation of *Bhāṣya-kāra* on verse II.33 is that "no illusion can be perceived that is without a substratum." This is contradicted by the illusion in dream which springs from within and does not require any separate substratum.

"(This Self) is imagined to be the infinite objects like *Prāṇa* (the vital force) etc. This is the *māyā* of the self-effulgent one, by which He Himself is deluded" (II.19).

The Self imagines itself to be the various kinds of objects and creatures (*jīvas*) through its own power of *māyā*. In turn, *jīvas* themselves imagine the Self to be diverse and varied. GK verses II.20 to 28 give an account of the various views of *Jīvas* regarding *Ātman*. The *jīvas* consider reality that is *Ātman* variously as *Prāṇa*, the great elements, *guṇas*, *tattvas*, the three quarters (*pada*) of *Viśva*, *Taijasa* and *Prājña*, the sense-objects, the worlds, the gods, the *Vedas*, the sacrifices, the Enjoyer, the object of enjoyment, the subtle, the gross, the form, the formless, the time, the four directions, the mind, the intellect, the consciousness, the virtue and vice, the twenty-five or twenty-six (including God) principles (of *Sāṃkhya* theory), the people, the stages of life etc.

"Through these things that are (really) non-different from the Self, this One is presented as though really different. He who truly knows this grasps (the meaning of the *Vedas*) without any hesitation." (II.30)

We have seen how GK started with the proof of the unreality of the phenomenal world and things by equating the waking experience with dream experience. GK has posited the idea of the reality of a supreme Self who imagines this unreal world and the multifarious unreal things such as *Prāṇa* etc, as described above. The *jīvas* in this unreal world view the reality and describe it variously as *Prāṇa* etc. All are descriptions about the same reality, the Self or *Ātman*. These do not have separate existence except as the imaginations or creations of the Self. As such, they are really non-different from the Self though they appear to be different. All are really just the non-dual *Ātman*. The imaginations of the Self become conventionally real but ultimately unreal. In the final analysis, this is what the *māyā* theory reduces to; this is nothing but the traditional old creation theory with *māyā* introduced as the specific power of the Self in place of the wonderous power earlier assigned to the Self or Brahman.

GK's position is that whatever view anyone has is the attempt to understand and define the ultimate reality and every view, as such, is the view about reality and becomes non-different from it. The different views are different conceptions of the same reality that is the non-dual *Ātman* or Brahman. As *Māṇḍūkya Upaniṣad* sums up, "All this is truly Brahman." Thus, GK propounds its theory of no-conflict with any view (*avirodhavāda*), firmly grounding itself in the belief expressed in *Ṛg Veda*: "Him, who is the one existent, sages name variously" (I.164.46).

"The dualists are firmly convinced in the establishment of their own conclusions and contradict one another; but this (non-dual view) does not conflict with them" (III.17).

"Non-duality is indeed the ultimate reality. Duality is said to be a differentiation of it. For them (the dualists) there is duality both ways; therefore this (view) does not conflict (with theirs)." (III.18)

Thus, GK maintains that its view of non-dual Self remaining the substratum of everything encompasses and holds within its fold all views and, as such, it is not opposed to them. It is the holistic view whereas the others are partial attempts of comprehending the same reality. The dualistic views engender negative passions of dislike and hatred to others; but on the other hand the non-dual (*advaita*) view is the perfect and blemishless one because it sees the same Self in everything.

10. *Ajātivāda* (Doctrine of Non-origination)

"Neither does an existent nor a non-existent originate in any manner (whatsoever). Those dualists (*dvaya*), (through their) disputing, in fact reveal Non-origination. We approve of the Non-origination revealed by them; we do not dispute with them. (O disciples), know how it (this philosophy) is free from dispute (*avivādam*)"(IV.4.5).

Here GK refers to the theories of *Sāṃkhyas* and *Naiyāyikas*. The former hold that the effect (the phenomenal world of things and creatures) pre-exists in the cause (*prakṛti*) from which it evolves. The other disputants oppose this view stating that the effect is separate from the cause and does not pre-exist in it. GK counters by saying that if, according to the *Sāṃkhyas*, the effect already exists in the cause, it is a self-contradiction to say that the already existent thing originates or comes into birth. If the effect is non-existent as held by the other disputants, then also it cannot come into birth because of the very fact that it does not exist. How can a non-existent thing give rise to birth? Therefore, whatever opposing views are taken, all reduce to the conclusion of birthlessness (*ajāti*). GK declares that *ajātivāda* is the supreme view of reality. Having arrived at the conclusion that there is no birth, GK derives therefrom that there is an unborn and that unborn is the non-dual *Ātman*.

"(There is) neither cessation nor origination, neither one bound nor one practising spiritual discipline, neither one aspiring for liberation nor one who is liberated. This is the supreme truth." (II.32)

"Nothing (*vastu*) whatsoever is originated either from itself or from something else ; nothing whatsoever existent, non-existent, or both existent and non-existent is originated"(IV.22).

"No *jīva* whatsoever is ever born; there is no origin of it. This is that ultimate truth where nothing whatsoever is born"(III.48).

Duality is not real because it is not found to be existing always. For instance it is not perceived in deep sleep state or in meditative concentration (*samādhi*). It is a mere figment of the imagination. All the empirical experiences of duality like *Prāṇa* and the various kinds of things are superimpositions on the Self like a snake on a rope. This is a mental illusion and the birth or death of an illusion is equally illusory. Origination or cessation can belong only to a thing that has existence. Since the things do not exist in reality, the supreme truth is that there is neither cessation nor origination of these, no *jīva* whatsoever is ever born. All of them take birth only through imagination like a snake on a rope.

"All is born according to the conventional (i.e. from empirical point of view); therefore in fact there is no eternal. In terms of reality, all is unborn; thus, there is no annihilated." (IV.57)

Everything is produced by delusion inherent in the conventional outlook due to concealment of truth by ignorance. In the ultimate reality, there is no birth, no death ; all are unborn.

"Those *dharmas* (objects of consciousness) said to be born by convention are not born in reality. Their birth is like *māyā* (magic), and that *māyā* itself does not exist"(IV.58).

"Like a māyā-made seed, a sprout of the same nature (i.e. illusory) is born. It is neither permanent nor destructible (because it has no existence); so likewise is the logic (of birth and death) for the objects"(IV.59).

From the standpoint of supreme reality, there can be no real birth or death for the objects in the phenomenal world of existence. The birthlessness of things is proved by citing the unreality i.e. non-existence of these things and the presumed duality. Does this prove the existence of the non-dual *Ātman*? The argument given is that the appearances of duality and phenomenal things arise from super-imposition, which requires a substratum. This substratum is the non-dual *Ātman.* An attempt is made to support this view with the analogy of snake on rope and the contention that such illusions of a snake on rope cannot occur without a substratum. However, analogies cannot prove the point. Further what about the illusions or imaginations in dream? There is no substratum here. The illusions in dream arise from within because of inherent cravings and passions.

The existence of non-dual *Ātman* is presupposed as a basic assumption in the view that phenomenal world is imagined by the *Ātman* or on the *Ātman.* It is a presupposition and no proof is given in support of the same. The real and the unreal are polar opposites. How can an absolute and unconditioned real like the *Ātman* either imagine the unreal or support the unreal? The theory of *māyā* is brought in to link the two opposites and a stand is taken that *māyā* is incomprehensible. Thus the Advaita Vedānta of GK becomes mystifying and confounds the seeker of reality. For a proper understanding and evaluation of the same, we have to compare it with the teachings in Buddhism, particularly *Mahāyāna* Buddhism, from which many of its points have been derived.

11. GK's Philosophy Compared with Buddhism

We have earlier studied how the philosophical position of Buddhism after the Buddha shifted from its initial naive realism of *Sarvāstivāda* (the doctrine that all exists) to the emptiness of *Prajñāpāramitā* movement and how Nāgārjuna established the concept of emptiness on firm logical footing. His concept of emptiness is fully in conformity with the fundamental Buddhist tenets of dependent origination and Middle Path and with the triple marks of existence highlighted in Buddhism viz. *anityam* (impermanence), *asukham* (suffering) and *anattā* (no-self). Nāgārjuna has also used the analogies of dream and illusion to explain the phenomenal world of change:

"Like an illusion, like a dream, like a castle in the air, thus is origination, thus is duration, thus is destruction declared." (MMK XVIII.34)

The similarity of GK verse II.31 (that we have studied above) with this verse of Nāgārjuna is quite striking. For *Prajñāpāramitā* and Nāgārjuna, the analogies of dream, illusion and the like illustrate the emptiness (*śūnya*) of all things, their impermanence and no self-nature (*Niḥsvabhāva,* selflessness in everything) because everything is dependently originating and nothing is self-created, self-established and self-maintained. All are nothing but conceptual constructs. Emptiness for them is the eight-fold negation (No origination, No extinction etc) and is the Middle Path avoiding the two extremes of eternalism and nihilism. It is the Middle Path adopting the middle view of neither existence nor non-existence. *Yogācāra* masters interpreted the same as both existence and non-existence, which is another understanding and formulation of Middle Path. What is defined as neither existence nor non-existence in Madhyamaka and as both existence and non-existence in *Yogācāra* becomes *māyā* or illusory appearance in GK. It is unreality for GK.

The equivalence of waking and dream states and the idea that consciousness does not come into contact with any object and what we perceive as objects is in actual fact only the representations of objects in the mind and not the objects themselves are some of the *Yogācāra* ideas that have been adopted by GK in the formulation of its philosophy. Impermanence (*anityam*) is highlighted in Buddhism as a mark of emptiness of things. In GK, this is suggested as a mark of unreality of things in its oft-repeated pronouncement : "That which does not exist in the beginning and the end, does not exist in the middle also". Phenomenal existences are unreal and false because they are limited, having a beginning and an end.

Ātman and *Vijñāna*

The *Ātman* appearance (*māyā*) theory of GK may be contrasted with the 'becoming of *Vijñāna*' or '*Vijñāna-pariṇāma*' theory in Buddhism.

The tenth limb of 'becoming' in the Buddha's Twelve-limbed Wheel of Life or Dependent Origination and the theory of *Vijñāna-pariṇāma* (i.e. the triple-world is nothing but evolution of the consciousness) and the three-nature theory of *Yogācāra* give a clear exposition of the World-view in Buddhism. As against the theory of *Ātman* (the ever-existent reality) imagining itself as *jīva* and other creatures in GK, the blind 'will to become' (*Vijñāna*) acts and creates the body-mind complex according to Buddhism. It becomes a bundle of inner drives and volitions. Driven by cravings and attachments it acts and impinges on the external environment. It creates phenomena in the external world and the phenomena in turn recoil and modify it leaving their imprints as morally deserving retribution (*karmic* seeds). The modified *Vijñāna* again acts and creates fresh phenomena which in turn impress new seeds or impressions (*vāsanā*) on the *Vijñāna*. The *karmic* seeds mature in due time and give effects according to the Law of *Karma*. The evolution (the becoming) of *Vijñāna* is thus continually taking place with the Law of *Karma* and the laws of cause and effect determining this evolution as the universal principles (*tattvas*).

The whole world process is nothing but the evolutions of the innumerable individual *vijñānas* (i.e. the bundles of inner drives and volitions) mutually depending on each other and interacting and interpenetrating among themselves. They are all dependently originated, dependently holding together and dependently evolving according to the universal laws of cause and effect. All the developments in the means of livelihood – agriculture, industry and others – and all the civilisational growths with their concepts of family, village, society, city, state and nation and with their advancements in the scientific, religious and spiritual realms – all these are the creations of these fundamental *vijñānas* which are ever-changing and evolving.

The individual *vijñāna* identifies itself wrongly with its cravings and clingings (attachments) without knowing the true nature of things due to ignorance (*avidyā*) and develops false notions of 'self' and 'mine'. It differentiates 'self' from others and discriminates and in this process creates its own world of likes and dislikes, attachment and hatred, good and bad, ugly and beautiful, lust and pride, delusion and deceit. This is the world of its conceptual construction or fabrication assigning names and characteristics and attributes simply based on its like and dislikes, attachments and hatreds. This is the dream world arising out of the subjective passions and prejudices which have their basis on the false theory of individuality and self. Strifes and discords, evils and sins, sufferings and sorrows in this world – all have their origin in this false conceit of self which in the ultimate analysis has ignorance (*avidyā*) as the root cause. This dream world is *anityam, asukham* and *anattā* (selfless).

GK also talks about *Vijñāna* (consciousness), sometimes as the *Ātman* itself (nondual unchanging reality) and sometimes as a *dharma* (object) imagined on the *Ātman* or superimposed on the *Ātman*. If at all there be any superimposition on the (rope) *Ātman*, that can occur only later after the development of mind, the faculty that imagines and superimposes its ideas. The superimposition theory is fundamentally fallacious as we have already discussed.

A satisfactory explanation can only be that *Ātman* itself becomes the *Vijñāna* as propounded in *Brahma-pariṇāma* theory of some *Upaniṣads*. But this *pariṇāma* theory is rejected by GK and it concedes that *Ātman* itself is deluded and imagines itself as the *Vijñāna* and the rest. These are phenomenal appearances which have no existence in the ultimate stand point of reality. In the ultimate Truth, *Ātman* only is the existent. But, the question why *Ātman* becomes subject to ignorance and imagines the consciousness (*Vijñāna*) and various other things remains unanswered. This undermines the integrity and omniscience (all-knowing nature) of *Ātman*. The ignorance to which the *Ātman* is subject and because of which he imagines the things is now extolled as the *māyā-śakti*, the power of *māyā* inherent in the *Ātman* or Brahman. The idea here corresponds to the *māyā* theory presented in the *Paiṅgala Upaniṣad*. This is only a sophisticated, but more mystifying reformulation of the earlier theory of wonderous power of creation of God found in the *Vedas*. The wonderous power extolled in the *Vedas* is now replaced by the illusive power with the suggestion that the world emerging is unreal. Even with this reformulation *Ātman* (Brahman) is still very much open to all the criticisms leveled by the Buddhists against the creator God. The concept of creative power may now have been changed to illusive power of *māyā* ; but how can that free the *Ātman* from all the objections and criticisms and evil and sin.

In the ultimate Truth, *Ātman* only is the reality according to GK. In the conventional realm, the various kinds of things and creatures imagined by the *Ātman* are only phenomenal appearances and do not exist in reality. In this nebulous theory of *māyā* and appearances, how the Law of Karma and the moral principles (that turn round the wheel of *saṃsāra* in the world) fit in is not clear. Are these also unreal and *māyā*? Does the *māyā-śakti* of *Ātman* which is conditioned by ignorance operate the moral laws also and become the moral retributive principle and dispenser of justice? It is rationally inconceivable how the same *māyā-śakti* which is characterized by ignorance and which gives rise to the defilements, evils and injustices can be considered as the dispenser of justice against the very same evils it gives rise to? This is like the criminal himself acting as a judge to try his crime or the player himself acting as a referee in a game. How can a universal moral order based on Law of Karma arise in ignorance? These are the inner contradictions in the concept of *māyā*. All these questions cannot be brushed aside taking a position that *māyā* is indeterminable and incomprehensible. This position simply means that the Theory of *māyā* is not amenable to rational analysis and enquiry and this has to be simply believed. This may be contrasted with the crystal clear and rational expositions in Buddhism where no contradictions are involved and no appeal to faith is resorted to.

GK maintains that, in the phenomenal appearances in the conventional realm, the non-dual *Ātman* remains as the sub-stratum supporting these appearances just as the rope supports the illusion of snake in the snake-on-the-rope analogy. This theory is also flawed on two counts. First, as already discussed, it is the *Ātman* itself that is deluded and imagines itself or superimposes. Rope only imagines itself as the snake. Second, delusions as in dream occur without any sub-stratum at all. They occur from within driven by the inner dispositions and cravings without any substratum. The conclusion is that the *Ātman* is not supporting but becoming the phenomenal appearances through its own imaginations and by the power of its own *māyā*.

In the Buddhist view, the *Vijñāna* (consciousness) is continually evolving and becoming the triple world. The objective and subjective worlds arise from its cravings and passions and conceptual fabrications. They are dependently originated and have no birth or no death. Dependent origination (*pratītyasamutpāda*) is in fact no origination (*an-utpāda*) at all. They have no self-natures of their own because they are dependent on others for existence. Ignorance in Buddhism is 'not knowing' the things as they really are i.e. not knowing the true nature of selflessness (emptiness) of all things. On the other hand, in the philosophy of GK, *Ātman* is not becoming the phenomenal world of existences, but only appearing or imagining as the phenomenal world. This phenomenal appearance is through the power of its own *māyā*. It is said to be not undergoing any change. It is the eternal, immutable and ever-existent reality. Ignorance in the view of GK lies in not seeing the ever-existent *Ātman* behind the phenomenal appearances. Considering its philosophical position that *Ātman* himself is imagining those appearances, this becomes a mystifying doctrine.

Change Versus Appearance

Niḥsvabhāva is the keystone in the philosophical edifice of Nāgārjuna's Madhyamaka. It is 'no self-existence' signifying the cardinal Buddhist principle of dependent origination. Nothing in this world is self-made, self-created, self-established, self-existent. Everything is dependently originated. Dependent origination is no origination in Buddhist Philosophy. Eightfold negation of Nāgārjuna like "No origination (No birth)–No cessation (No death)" points to the middle path of avoiding the extremes or opposites. Birth can never be in the absolute sense of ever being there, because, if so, birth will continuously be taking place. Likewise death also cannot be in the absolute sense. Truth is neither birth nor death, but dependent birth. This is the truth embodied in *śūnyatā*. Problem with speech and language is that they always tend to be in the absolute sense investing a fixed nature to things.

Change is the fact of experience. But what is change? It is defined as transformation of one thing with a nature of its own into another thing of another nature. The tendency in the use of language is to assume a fixed own-nature to a thing. But, if the thing has its own fixed nature, it cannot change ; it will remain as an unchanging bloc. Paradoxically, if the thing does not have its own-nature, then also it cannot change because question arises: 'What is it that changes?' Nāgārjuna's position is that change always occurs and there is no such thing with a fixed nature. Absolutism of fixed nature creeps in because of the specific tendency in the use of language and all views expressed entail absolutism and presupposition of fixed own-nature. For Nāgārjuna it is a problem of language and that is why he avoids taking any philosophical position. His position is no position. It is *śūnyatā* (emptiness).

On the other hand, GK opts for the fixed own-nature and denies the possibility of any change. For GK, change is only an appearance and not real. There is only eternal, immutable and unchanging *Ātman* of fixed own-nature and change is only an unreal appearance on the *Ātman*. The theory of 'appearance' implies another entity that sees the appearance on *Ātman*. But according to *Advaita* philosophy of GK, this entity is also an appearance or imagination of *Ātman* himself on himself. This is ascribed to his power of *māyā*.

If the *Ātman* is unchanging and ever remaining the same as an unchanging bloc, then how do appearances arise? GK explains that these are due to the vibration of consciousness. Consciousness is identified with *Ātman*. Thus it propounds a theory of *Vijñānaspandita* (vibration or oscillation of consciousness) which reminds us of the *Vijñāna-pariṇāma-vāda* of *Yogācāra* school in Buddhism. The *pariṇāma* (transformation) of *Yogācāra* is replaced here with *spandita*, vibration or oscillation. It is implied that, with this spandita theory, the manifestation of dualistic phenomena is explained and accounted for without necessitating an actual transformation (*pariṇāma*) of *Ātman*. But, it is baffling how the unchanging, ever quiescent *Ātman* or consciousness undergoes vibration and how it is still considered unchanging even with these vibrations. The question is: Is not vibration change of the fixed thing?

We have already studied the analogy of firebrand given by GK to illustrate its theory of appearances. The single firebrand when moved creates various images that are unreal. In the same way, it is explained, the phenomenal unreal appearances occur with the non-dual *Ātman* as the underlying reality just as the single firebrand underlies the various unreal images. But this illustration also presents a problem and negates the very unchanging nature of *Ātman* that GK tries to uphold. For, without movement, firebrand cannot create the various images. Likewise phenomenal appearances cannot also be conceived without movement of the *Ātman* either by itself or by another. This goes against the presumed unchangeability of the *Ātman*.

Nāgārjuna accepted change as a fact of experience and denied *svabhāva* (self-existence or own-nature) to anything. On the other hand, GK assumes an unchanging *Ātman* with a fixed own-nature and denies change as really happening. According to GK, there are only phenomenal appearances that are unreal. What is change for Nāgārjuna is appearance or *māyā* for GK. But, the illustrations given by GK contradict the unchangeability of *Ātman* assumed. For giving rise to appearances, *Ātman* will have to change in some way. Appearances also cannot be explained and accounted for without taking recourse to change. But it may be stated that this is *māyā* and *māyā* is incomprehensible. Such *māyā* theory may satisfy a belief-oriented religious mind and not a rational mind.

Non-Origination

Birthlessness is an established cardinal philosophical doctrine in Buddhism for it flows logically from the basic Buddhist tenet of dependent origination. For Buddhists, everything is unoriginated because it is dependently originating and dependent origination is no origination. As repeated often in our study, nothing is having self-nature or inherent existence (*svabhāva*) of its own. Nothing in this world is self-created, self-made or self-originated. Since things have no *svabhāva* (inherent self-existence) of their own and since they are dependently originating, they have no origination. If they have no origination, then they have no extinction. Further, birth (origination) and death (extinction) cannot be there in the absolute sense because in such a case the things will be born continuously or dying continuously. This doctrine earlier earlier established by the Buddhist schools has been adopted by GK also but with a different logical reasoning. GK's ideas on this have been presented in section 10 above. Birthlessness is proved logically in GK verse IV.22. Basically its position is that since everything is an appearance and only an illusion, the birth or death of that thing is equally illusory; there is neither birth nor death.

This theory that 'there is no birth (no origination)' has been extended by GK to assert that there is an unborn. For Buddhists, the words 'birth', 'death', 'creation', 'dissolution', etc are all verbal expressions arising from conceptualization which tends to freeze the continuously flowing experiences into segments. Birthlessness or non-origination (*ajāti*) means 'not originated' and Buddhist scholars like Bhāvaviveka maintain that it is not logical to stretch this to imply an unoriginated absolute existent thing. i.e. an unborn *Ātman* .

Assumption of an unborn absolutely existent thing contradicts the fundamental Buddhist doctrine of the dependent origination, which is an unquestionable fact of experience. If an unborn absolute is postulated as in GK, this goes against 'dependent origination' and denies the fact of experience. The question then, as Nāgārjuna asks, is "How can that which exists by its own being come into existence?" (*MMK* XXIV.22).

Truth/Reality

According to GK, reality must have an own-nature, which cannot change. The very fact that we are discussing about reality presupposes a reality. All views entail absolutism. All views, philosophical and religious, are views about reality. Even though the views may be different, they talk about the same reality. Here GK seems to assert that, since the mind thinks about reality and holds some view of reality, that reality must perforce be existing. An ideal is assumed to be existing as reality because it is existing in the mind. This goes against the very theory of GK that what we see and experience in the world are only appearances because they are imaginations and conceptual constructs of the mind. On this logic, the view about reality is also an imagination or conceptual construct.

However, GK maintains that the reality must exist as an unchanging substratum to support all views. It must have a fixed nature of its own. What is that fixed own-nature? GK answers that it is the one that is realized in the *Turīa* state of deep meditative *samādhi.*

"When the individual, sleeping under the influence of beginningless *māyā,* is awakened, then he realizes the birthless, sleepless, dreamless, non-dual (*Turīya*)" (I.16).

According to GK, the search for reality must involve analysis of all the states of experience. Waking experience is contradicted by dream experience, which again is sublated by deep sleep state. In deep sleep state, the sleeper loses his identity and experiences perfect non-dual bliss. *Bṛhad-āraṇyaka Upaniṣad* accords the highest status to this state and identifies the Self (*prājña*) in the deep sleep state as the ultimate Reality. But *Māṇḍūkya Upaniṣad* and GK pass beyond this state in search of highest reality. They interpret the deep sleep state differently and consider it in essence as unawareness of reality. According to them, it is a mere "mass of cognition" and does not comprehend anything–neither himself nor others, neither truth nor falsehood.

"*Prājña* does not comprehend anything–neither himself nor others, neither truth nor untruth. That *Turīya* (however) is always all-seeing" (GK I.12).

The suggestion here is that the Self in the *Turīya* state is the one that exists in all beings in the other three states of waking, dreaming and deep sleep also and is the seer and witness of everything. He simultaneously supports and transcends the other three states. In verse I.10, *Turīya* is described as the ordainer (*Īśānaḥ*), the lord (*Prabhuḥ*), the non-dual (*advaitaḥ*) and all-pervading (*vibhuḥ*) God (*deva*) of all beings. Again in verse I.13 it is contrasted with *Prājña* of the deep sleep state as below:

"Non-perception (non-grasping) of duality is common to both *Prājña* and *Turīya. Prājña* is associated with the causal state of sleep, while it (i.e. the causal state of sleep) does not exist in *Turīya*". (I.13)

Even though *Prājña* experiences perfect bliss of non-duality, it is in the causal state of association with *avyakta* where the blind will to become and the *karmic* formations are still active subconsciously. It has not yet dissolved the *avyakta,* defilements, impurities and *karmic* formations that cause the rebirth and obscure the vision of reality. It has still the seed of false-perception and the seed of rebirth. On the other hand, according to GK, *Turīya* is where all the tendencies and propensities producing defilements and impurities and *karmic* formations have been eradicated and freedom from causation of rebirth attained.

Thus, it is seen that a state akin to the Nirvanic state described in Buddhism is suggested here, but with the assertion that highest reality *Ātman* or Brahman is seen therein. Reality is what exists always, not only in the four states of waking, dreaming, deep sleep and *Turīya,* but also in other states like fainting and the existence in the mother's womb as an embryo. Can we say that consciousness in these other states and in the post-mortem existence after death is of the same kind or nature as the self-consciousness or pure awareness experienced in the *Turīya* state? Buddhism does not accept that the consciousness in all these states is the same and unvarying. What we can truly say is that the consciousness in those other states is indescribable or it is enveloped in darkness, void of any conceptions. According to the Buddhists, consciousness is nothing but a conglomeration or bundle of inner volitions, impulses, passions, cravings, feelings, thoughts and other mental states, which is an ever-flowing stream, continuously changing and not remaining the same at any two consecutive moments. If it is claimed that the *Turīya* consciousness is the ever-existent unchanging reality *Ātman,* then it is merely a conceptual construct or belief superimposing the bliss or awareness in this state on all other conceivable states and asserting it as an ever-existent reality. If *Turīya* apprehends a consciousness, then it descends from no-mind to mind.

GK adopts the final position that this reality *Ātman* (Brahman) is incomprehensible.

"The explanation 'This is not this, not that......' denies explanation, by reason of its incomprehensibility; the unborn (nature) of all shines forth"(III.26).

Bṛhad-āraṇyaka Upaniṣad II.(iii) starts with: "Brahman has but two forms-gross and subtle" etc. And at the end of the section it is stated, "Now, therefore, the description (of Brahman): 'Not this not this'" (*B.U.*II.iii.6). Whatever was earlier explained through various ways again and again for the sake of establishing Brahman is negated by the *Upaniṣad* subsequently with 'neti, neti' because Brahman is incomprehensible. The traditional interpretation of this negation is that everything is negated here so that the absolute Brahman alone may be comprehended as the only reality. G.K concludes that this Brahman or *Ātman,* the only reality, is birthless and gets revealed by itself. Nāgārjuna surpasses and soars beyond *Yājñavalkya*'s above famous proposition of 'neti, neti' in the *Bṛhad-āraṇyaka Upaniṣad*, establishing emptiness with a wholesale negation of all categories of existence in the absolute sense. Nāgārjuna negates everything and does not accept any 'That' beyond 'neti, neti'.

The clear-cut principles of Dependent Origination and Emptiness in Buddhism stand in stark contrast with the theories of incomprehensible Brahman and indeterminable *māyā* in the Advaita Vedānta. The idea of existence of any absolute unborn entity militates against dependent origination, which is an incontrovertible fact of experience. In the final analysis, if there be any fixed own-nature in the universe that can be said to be unborn, not causally produced and not created, that in truth is the self-evident nature of selflessness in things. This is the ultimate truth, ultimate reality and there is no other truth apart from this, according to Buddhism. GK's idea of a non-dual *Ātman* as an ever-existent unchanging reality is a conceptual construction. Like *Yogācāra,* the later Upaniṣads and GK accept *nirvikalpa-jñāna* as the highest wisdom but in the end they descend to imagine and construct (*vikalpa*) a 'self' where there is only 'selflessness'.

As we have seen earlier (Section 8), GK equates *Ātman* with space (*ākāśa*). In Vedānta, this is a very familiar and oft-quoted illustration. Space is merely the non-existence of anything ; it is the absence of any dharma or entity as the *Sautrāntikas* have defined. Then, the *Ātman* also would amount to the non-existence of anything or any dharma. Thus, it would become the emptiness or selflessness as in Buddhism.

12. Asparśa-Yoga

GK teaches '*Asparśa-yoga*' as a means for realization of ultimate reality and merger in the same. '*Asparśa*' means no sense-contact and '*Asparśa-yoga*' is a form of meditative practice with negation and denial of all sense–contacts i.e. withdrawal of all senses from sense objects, and mind from any sensation, perception or volition. Mind remains a sort of no-mind without any of its functions of thinking, willing and feeling.

The concept of '*Asparśa-yoga*' flows logically from the basic philosophical position of G.K on perception that "consciousness does not come into contact with any sense object". GK's theory is akin to the *Vijñaptimātra* or 'Representation – only' theory earlier propounded by the *Yogācārins.* According to GK, the external objects, sense organs and the mind are all only imagined entities like a snake on a rope and as such have no inherent existence in truth. The only reality is the underlying *Ātman* or Brahman. This reality though underlying all entities is not touching any of the sense-objects ; it in no way comes into contact with anything. It remains all alone (*kevaladvaiṭa*, sole non-dual) untouched and untouching. This is the ultimate truth in G.K's philosophy. In the light of this, *Asparśa-yoga* is not simply the withdrawal of the sense organs (including mind) from their objects like the "*pratyāhāra*" prescribed in the conventional yogic praxis. It is not only a meditative practice to achieve a state of non-contact (*Asparśa*) and total separation between consciousness and sense objects, but it also stands for the ultimate truth or reality which shines in such a mode of non-contact. Practising *Asparśa-yoga*, one could gain insight into the ultimate truth and become merged in the *Ātman* or Brahman who himself is without *sparśa* or contact with anything.

This is the 'contactless' yoga difficult to be mastered by all the Yogins (III 3.9) and free from all relationships (IV.2). This is the state of the absolute where there is no fear. Where is the question of fear for those who have become identified with Brahman? They have attained to the ever-lasting peace called emancipation. Thus, *Asparśa-yoga* stands for the ultimate goal of liberation itself.

"For all Yogins, depending upon the complete control of the mind (*manas*), are fearlessness, the removal of suffering, complete enlightenment and eternal quiescence itself" (III.40).

"When the mind does not become lost in sleep and is also not distracted, when it is objectless and motionless, then it becomes Brahman" (III.46).

"They say it is quiescent within itself, calm, in *Nirvāṇa*, indescribable, ultimate bliss (*sukha-uttama*), the unborn known by the unborn, the omniscient (Brahman)" (III.47).

"All this that there is, comprising the moving and the motionless, is perceived by the mind (and therefore all this is but the mind); for when the mind ceases to be the mind (i.e. becomes non-mind, *amanībhāva*), duality is no longer perceived". (III.31)

"When, following the teachings of the scriptures and the guru and by knowledge of the truth of *Ātman*, the mind ceases to imagine, it attains the state of non-mind (*amanastā*); it is without cognition in the absence of a cognizable entity". (III.32)

"They say that the unborn gnosis (*jñāna*, the non-discriminative knowledge), free from imagination, which is birthless, is non-different from the knowable (Brahman). The knowledge that has Brahman for its content is birthless and everlasting. The birthless (Self) is known by the birthless (knowledge)." (III.33)

In the *Asparśa-yoga*, the path itself i.e. control of the mind to become contactless and attain the state of no-mind becomes the ultimate goal and ultimate reality. With the help of the dual process of detachment and practice of non-discriminative wisdom, one should wake up the mind that is merged in deep sleep i.e. in non-perception of reality and engage it in the realization of the Self. When the mind becomes distracted and tends to be afflicted by passion and desire, one should control and bring it to tranquillity not allowing it to fluctuate. The mind should be established in equipoise. In this state of equipoise, there will arise some happiness; but one should not get attached to this happiness realizing that this is also a creation of ignorance and as such, is false. He should withdraw his mind not only from the perception of sense objects but also from the perception of this joy. When the mind is thus brought under control and becomes objectless (i.e. without any image of any object therein) and motionless like a still lamp in a windless place, then it becomes Brahman i.e. lost and merged in Brahman. This quiescent state is described in GK not only as Brahman but also as *Nirvāṇa*, a Buddhist term (III.47). Thus, it is clear that GK equates its concept of Brahman with Buddhist *Nirvāṇa.*

As we have already studied, *Nibbāna* in Buddhism is not only the negation and extinction of the craving for worldly pleasures, the negation and extinction of attachment, hatred and delusion, the negation and extinction of the conceit of 'I' ness and 'mine' ness, the negation of enjoyable objects, the negation of sensation, the negation of perception, and the negation of volitions, but also the negation of consciousness i.e. the underlying will to become. At *Nibbāna,* the individual aggregate, call it a person, is never more to be conditioned by causation in space and time (compare GK I.13 discussed above). He gains absolute and perfect freedom. Buddhism has spawned two concepts of *Nirvāṇa.* The first as propounded in *Hīnayāna* Buddhism is total liberation from the cycle of birth and death with the person's *karmic* residue and the will to become completely burnt out, and that person is no more born. There is no more creation, no more causation and no more becoming. He transcends all the four alternative possibilities of: is, is not, both is and is not, neither is nor is not. The second concept of *Nirvāṇa* as in *Mahāyāna* is that the person attains perfect enlightenment and perfect freedom with all his *karmic* residues totally eradicated. He becomes the personification of utter selflessness. He will not be born again but for his wish to take birth again willingly and volitionally for the benefit of all sentient beings with the altruistic motive of leading all beings to *Nirvāṇa.* His *Nirvāṇa* is *Prājña* and *karuṇā* combined into a single wisdom, as exemplified in the Buddha's life.

The conception of *Asparśa-yoga* in GK with its emphasis on the negation and denial of the external sense objects and the cessation of sensation and perception resembles the *nirodhasamāpatti,* the highest level of Buddhist meditative attainment which is characterized by complete cessation of all perceptions, conceptions and volitions . In the *Asparśa-yoga* also, the mind ceases to be the mind and ceases to imagine or conceptualize just as in *nirodhasamāpatti.* It attains the state of non-mind (*amanastā*). There is no perception of any sense-object and there is no thought. The mind becomes tranquil, controlled and withdrawn like fire that has no fuel. There is no perception in the absence of a perceptible object (III.32). The mind has become no-mind and there is no perception of duality of subject and object, perceiver and perceived. This is *nirvikalpa samādhi.*

This concept of 'no-mind' has been very elaborately explained in Buddhist literatures. For instance, Vasubandhu gives the following exposition in his *Triṃśikā* verses 27 and 28 :

One may realize that what he perceives is only a representation of the objects in the senses and not the objects themselves. But when he persists in the idea: "This is mere representation-only, it is devoid of an object, there is here no external object", he grasps this idea as the basis and clings to the consciousness of this idea. But to achieve the state of no-mind, one should forsake the apprehension of his own consciousness also. Only when he does not apprehend, not see, not grasp, not take as real any object or any idea whatsoever, and when he forsakes completely the grasping at consciousness of any idea, then only he is said to be established in the true nature of his own mind. No-mind only is the true mind with no grasping involved. Where there is nothing to grasp, there is no more grasping. There is a subject only where there is an object, but not where there is no object. The absence of an object results in the absence also of a subject and not merely in that of grasping. (*Buddhist Texts,* Trans. & Editated By E. Conze etc. p. 210).

Since there is no object, there is no cognizing subject also. With the denial of object, the idea or consciousness of the same is also denied. Whereas the Buddhist masters insist on the forsaking of the consciousness also, GK clings to a consciousness in this state as perception of reality which in its term is *Ātman*. In Buddhist concept of no-mind or emptiness, even the consciousness of emptiness is denied and rejected. Buddhism considers this meditative state also as impermanent whereas GK takes this as *Turīya* remaining identical with Brahman, ever-existent and eternal. According to Buddhists, the idea of ever-existent eternal *Ātman* or Brahman is a conceptual construction, imaginary, without any basis.

13. Ultimate Goal

According to GK, the *Turīya* is the ultimate state and the final goal in the path to realization of Brahman. As we have already noted in our study of Buddhism, this state of *Turīya* may at best be compared to the sixth or seventh stage in the bodhisattva path to perfection.

In the philosophy of GK and Advaita Vedānta, the problem of the defiled consciousness at the sub-conscious level and the *karmic* formations already lying dormant in the sub-conscious and the techniques for transforming the defiled consciousness are not properly and adequately addressed. In their philosophy, it is tacitly assumed that the cessation of perception of external objects and the non-discriminative wisdom attained will not only prevent the accumulation of any fresh *karmic* demerits but also destroy the old *karmic* residues that are yet to become active. With such cessation of perception of external objects and non-discriminative wisdom, prevention of fresh *karmic* results in the present or future is understandable, but not the destruction of the old *karmic* residues and the deep-rooted propensities of the mind. The *karmic* residues basically arise from false notions of self and individuality and the concomitant acts of self-aggrandizement at the cost of and injury to others. Proper antidotes have to be administered to overcome the effects of these poisonous acts and eradicate the *karmic* residues resulting therefrom. Buddhism considers the cultivation of the four Immeasurables (i.e. the *Brahma Vihāras*) – the all-pervading loving kindness towards all sentient beings, all-pervading compassion, sympathetic joy and equanimity – as the necessary prerequisites and efficacious means for totally transforming the defiled consciousness at the deepest level and eradicating all the *karmic* residues which have their roots in the greed, anger, hatred, lust and stupidity. Hence great importance is attached in Buddhism to the path of cultivation to be perfected even after gaining the highest state of meditation and insight into the reality or emptiness.

Buddhist literatures elaborate various models of combining calming meditation (*śamatha*) and insight meditation (*Vipaśyanā*) to achieve the desired results of burning away the old *karmic* residues and gaining the knowledge of the destruction of the defiling impulses at the roots. The elimination of all defilements and contaminated impurities lying deep within the *ālayavijñāna* and attainment of perfect purity free of all contaminations is generally equated with *Nirvāṇa* or *arahantship*. This state of *arahantship* characterized by the knowledge of destruction of the defiling impulses and *karmic* residues and the realization of perfect and absolute freedom from the sorrows of birth-is still only the sixth or seventh stage of bodhisattva's ten stages of cultivation and perfection in *Mahāyāna*. The ultimate stage is the attainment of perfect Buddhahood with *Prājña* (i.e. wisdom or insight into the selflessness and emptiness of all things) and *karuṇā* (i.e. compassion pervading the infinite network of interconnectedness of all existences) combined into the one blend of consciousness, pure Buddha Consciousness. The nobility of the ultimate vision here may be contrasted with the ultimate ideal in GK and Advaita Vedānta.

Part V

ADVAITA OF ŚAṄKARA

CHAPTER 17

Advaita of *Śaṅkara*

Advaita Vedānta of Śaṅkara (C.eighth century CE) derives its philosophical position basically from the teachings in the *Māṇḍūkya* and *Paiṅgala Upaniṣads.* The suggestion of *māyā,* contained in the *Paiṅgala Upaniṣad* in its description of Brahman as four-layered existence or as constituted of four selves with different degrees of reality in a hierarchical scale, has been taken up by Śaṅkara and built into a formidable philosophical system. His Advaita is considered to be the acme of philosophical development under the banner of Hinduism.

Advaita means 'not two' or non-dual. Śaṅkara's *Advaita* philosophy aims to establish that reality is one and it is not to be differentiated. This philosophy maintains that the souls animating the different bodies, the universal soul (*Īśvara*) underlying the universe and the *Ātman* (= Brahman) of the *Upaniṣads* are not different. The innumerable souls, *Īśvara* and the universe are but the appearances of the one reality *Ātman* (= Brahman), the divine power, knowledge of which leads to *Mokṣa,* liberation. In the *Gauḍapādīya-kārikā* and the *Paiṅgala Upaniṣad,* we saw the suggestion that the ultimate reality Brahman (= *Ātman*) deludes himself and becomes *Īśvara* by identifying himself with the unreal *mūla-prakṛti* and energizing it. *Īśvara* is the creator, preserver, inner-controller and destroyer of the universe. He also creates the individual selves. But, in the Advaita Vedānta of Śaṅkara, the refinement is in establishing the theory that the ultimate reality Brahman remains just the light of consciousness and substratum like space for the appearance of *Īśvara* with his *māyā-śakti* and its illusory projections. The products evolving from the *māyā-śakti* of *Īśvara* are not real but only appearances. Here the idea stressed is that, since these are not real but only appearances, the imperfections of these will not affect the purity and integrity of the reality that is Brahman.

Brahman is Pure Consciousness and ever exists without any attributes. This is the only reality and it is non-dual i.e. not-two. The *Īśvara* that enters into creation or evolution, the individual souls (selves) and the multiplicity of the world that we experience are ultimately unreal and are only appearances superimposed on the ground of Brahman. This superimposing principle is called *māyā* as a metaphysical concept in Śaṅkara's philosophy. Essentially this metaphysical principle *māyā* is the same as the *prakṛti* in *Sāṃkhya* philosophy. The theory of evolution of *prakṛti* under the influence of consciousness earlier propounded by the Sāṃkhyaites has been basically accepted by Śaṅkara with the difference that the energizing consciousness here is *Īśvara* consciousness that takes *prakṛti* as its own body and is one with it. The *prakṛti* of *Sāṃkhya* is talked here as *māyā-śakti* that creates and accounts for the appearances of the individual living beings and the multiplicity of the world. According to Śaṅkara, this evolution of *māyā-śakti* is not real in the ultimate sense, but only an appearance or an illusion. *Pariṇāma* (evolution) theory of others is reduced to *vivarta* (appearance) theory in Śaṅkara's philosophy. Even though it is described as an appearance or an illusion, the suggestion seems to be that it is unreal only in the ultimate sense, when the insight into the knowledge of non-dual Brahman is attained.

1. Māyā

In Śaṅkara's philosophy, *māyā* is said to be absolutely dependent on Brahman and is coeval with him. It is inseparable from him. If we understand Śaṅkara correctly, what he says is that *māyā* is the physical body of Brahman but unreal. He also adds that it is the inherent power or potency of Brahman; it is his *māyā-śakti* or illusory power.

What are the characteristics of *māyā* according to Śaṅkara? He describes *māyā* as having two aspects-negative and positive. In its negative aspect, it conceals (*āvaraṇa-śakti*) the reality and acts as a veil to hide it. In its positive aspect, it projects (*vikṣepa-śakti*) the world of plurality on the Brahman ground.

The philosophical ideas of Śaṅkara on *māyā* may be summarized as below : (References : Chandradhar Sharma, *A Critical Survey of Indian Philosophy* (Chapter 15) ; Pandit Rajmani Tigunait, *Seven Systems of Indian Philosophy* (Chapter 8)).

(1) Like the *prakṛti* of *Sāṃkhya,* it is something material and unconscious (*Jaḍa*) as opposed to Brahman which is pure consciousness, though unlike *prakṛti* it is neither real nor independent.

(2) It is the inherent power or potency (*śakti*) of Brahman. It is coeval with Him. It is absolutely dependent on and inseparable from Brahman. It is non-different from Him. The relation of *māyā* and Brahman is unique and is called *tadātmya*; it is neither identity nor difference nor both. *Māyā* is energized and acts as the medium of the projection of the world of plurality on the non-dual ground Brahman.

(3) It is beginningless (*anādi*).

(4) It is something positive though not real. It is called positive in order to emphasize the fact that it is not merely negative. It has two aspects. In its negative aspect, it conceals (*āvaraṇa*) the real non-dual nature of reality and acts as a screen to hide its purity. In its positive aspect, it projects (*vikṣepa*) the world of plurality (qualified by names and forms) on the Brahman ground. It is non-apprehension as well as misapprehension.

(5) It is indescribable and indefinable for it is neither real nor unreal nor both. It is not real for it has no existence apart from Brahman. It is not unreal, for it projects the world of appearance. It is not real for it vanishes at the dawn of knowledge; it is not unreal, for it is true as long as it lasts. It is not real to constitute a limit to Brahman and yet it is real enough to give rise to the world of appearance. And, it is not both real and unreal, for this conception is self-contradictory. From the standpoint of the world, *māyā* is comprehended as real, but from the standpoint of the absolute reality it is unreal. Thus it is neither real nor unreal, nor both real and unreal. Because of its complex nature, it is indescribable.

(6) It has a phenomenal and relative character. The one absolute Brahman appears in many forms, and its power of becoming finite is called *māyā.*

(7) It is of the nature of superimposition (*ādhyāsa*). It is an error like that of a 'rope-snake' or a 'shell-silver'. It is the superimposition upon one thing of the character of another thing. It is wrong cognition or misapprehension.

(8) It is removable by Right Knowledge.

(9) The substratum of *māyā* is Brahman and yet Brahman is really untouched by it, even as a magician is unaffected by the

illusions of his own his magic or the colourless *ākāśa* is untouched by the dark colour attributed to it.

(10) Thus *māyā* is the power of the absolute Brahman. It has no independent existence, but rests on Brahman. From the practical point of view, however, it is not totally illusion. There are certainly some differences between hallucinations, illusions and dreams on the one hand and the experiences of the waking state on the other. Compared to the experiences of dreams, the experiences of the waking state are more real. But, from the absolute point of view, hallucinations, illusions and dreams, and the experiences of the waking state are all equally unreal.

Summarizing : *māyā* is the unreal body of Brahman, the body not having the same order of reality as Brahman.

It will be most illuminating and instructive to compare this philosophy of *māyā* in Śaṅkara *Vedānta* with Buddhist thoughts because it was after all the *Prajñāpāramitā* movement in Buddhism that first gave birth to such an idea of illusion and treated the whole world and everything in it as unreal and illusory like a dream or magic.

2. Ignorance and Transmigratory Existence

The Wheel of Life and Becoming, the arising of the world of sufferings and sorrows, the *saṃsāra*, has been explained by the Buddha in his very first discourse on *Dhamma* higlighting ignorance (*avidyā*) as the root cause. This scheme of the Buddha has been adopted by Śaṅkara also as can be seen from his *Upadeśasāhasrī* (I. 1, 3&4). Here Śaṅkara says:

"*Karmans* (as the results of actions, good or bad, in the past existence) produce association with a body. When there is association with a body, pleasant and unpleasant things are inevitable. From these result passion and aversion (and) from them actions (*kriyā*)."

"(From actions) merit (*dharma*) and demerit (*adharma*) result (and) from merit and demerit there results an ignorant man's association with a body in the same manner again. Thus this transmigratory existence rolls onward violently for ever like a wheel."

Thus, Śaṅkara explains the wheel of transmigratory existence as consisting of the following limbs:

(1) *Karmans* resulting from actions, good or bad, in the previous existence.

→(2) One's connection with the body (new) because of *karmans* in the past.

(3) Experience of pleasure and pain.

(4) Arising of passions and aversions (= *doṣa, Upad.* I.1.7)

(5) Actions (*kriyā*) – verbal, mental and physical – good or bad.

(6) Merit and demerit (= *karmans*) accruing from the above actions.

The cycle repeats. The transmigratory existence is thus the continuously recurring process of the performance of actions (*karmans* of the previous existence and *kriyās* of the present existence) and experience of the sweet and bitter fruits of the actions. Close resemblance of Śaṅkara's exposition with the Buddha's Wheel of Life and Becoming is quite striking.

In *Upad.* I.1.5 and II.2.110, Śaṅkara identifies *ajñāna* (ignorance) as the ultimate cause of this transmigratory existence. *Ajñāna* is also called the controller of the transmigratory existence (*niyāmaka, Upad.* I.16.61). In another place (*Upad.* II.3.112), the cycle of transmigratory existence is described as : (1) nescience (*avidyā*)-(2) faults (*doṣa*)-(3) verbal, physical and mental activities-(4) accumūlation of *karmans* of which the results are desirable, undesirable and mixed. In this way, the root cause of the transmigratory existence is traced to ignorance or *avidyā* just as in the Buddha's Wheel of Life and Becoming (Sengaku Mayeda, Śaṅkara's View of Ethics, Philosophy : East And West, p.193/194).

In the Buddhist scheme, ignorance (*avidyā*) is defined as not knowing things as they truly are i.e. not knowing their true nature of *anityam, asukham* and *anattā* and getting attached to them. It is ignorance of the Law of Becoming and the Law of Karma, in short, ignorance of the four Noble Truths, that is the root cause of craving and clinging, becoming and *saṃsāra.*

On the other hand, in Śaṅkara's philosophy, ignorance is not knowing *Ātman* i.e. absence of the discriminating knowledge (*aviveka*) concerning *Ātman* (Self) and non-*Ātman* (non-Self).

"........ And the absence of discriminating knowledge (*aviveka*) is beginningless; this and nothing else is thought to be transmigratory existence"(*Upad.* I.16.61).

In the Buddhist philosophy, the ultimate truth is selflessness (*anattā*) and ignorance is not realizing this truth, whereas Śaṅkara maintains that the ultimate truth is Self (*Ātman*) and ignorance is "not discriminating this Self from non-self and realizing this Self".

3. Ignorance (*Avidyā*) and *Māyā*

The ignorance (*avidyā*) which is the fundamental root cause of the individual transmigratory existence at the microcosmic level becomes *māyā* in Śaṅkara 's philosophy at the cosmic level when the universal existence is considered. *Avidyā* and *māyā* are said to be synonymous in Śaṅkara 's philosophy and are interchangeably used.

How the power of projection and the power of hiding or veiling the truth are both rooted in ignorance (*avidyā*) has been clearly explicated in the Buddhist Wheel of Life and Becoming. The ignorance veils the Four Noble Truths and also the truth of how things actually are and how they become and, because of this ignorance, the 'blind will' lapses into craving and clinging and conceptual fabrication and creates its world of becoming. The innumerable worlds of the individuals are mutually dependent on one another and interact with each other and evolve resulting in a dynamic world process that rolls on according to the universal principles of causation (dependent origination) and Law of Karma. Thus, Buddhism recognizes three elements – the blind wills of the individuals to become, their dream worlds of cravings and conceptual constructions, and the universal principle of dependent origination and conditioning – in the totality of the world process which rolls on like a chariot wheel with ignorance as its kingpin.

In Śaṅkara's Advaita Vedānta, all these are replaced by the *māyā-śakti* of *Īśvara* which, with its twin powers of projection and veiling, manifests itself as the world and the individual *jīvas* in an illusory evolution from top-to-down. The *māyā-śakti* here is not only the creative will power acting under the influence of ignorance; it also subsumes within itself the universal power that dictates and operates the laws of cause and effect and the Law of Karma. There is a contradiction in the concept here to which we shall come later.

According to Śaṅkara : "This *Māyā* is not pure illusion. It is a cross between the real and the unreal. In fact, it is indescribable. It is neither existent nor non-existent nor both. It is not existent because the existent is only the Brahman. It is not non-existent because it is responsible for the appearance of Brahman as the world. It cannot be both existent and non-existent for this conception is self-contradictory. It is called neither real nor unreal. It is false or *mithyā.* But it is not a non-entity like hare's horn. It is positive. It is potency. It is also called superimposition".

Śaṅkara's description of *māyā* closely follows the description given by Nāgārjuna to elucidate the concept of emptiness (*śūnya*) in his Madhyamaka philosophy propounded some six centuries earlier to Śaṅkara. Nāgārjuna describes emptiness (*śūnya*) as neither existence nor non-existence (because of dependent existence), neither having an end nor eternal, neither one nor many, neither coming nor departing (all because of dependent origination). This is the eightfold negation meant to be a wholesale negation of all categories of existence and definition of emptiness. Śaṅkara's description of *māyā* is also as neither real nor unreal. It is undeniable that the concept of *māyā* in Śaṅkara's philosophy is derived from the concept of emptiness in Buddhism.

The two philosophical schemes are represented diagrammatically in Figures 20 and 21.

4. *Māyā* and *Śūnyatā*

Śaṅkara's theory of *māyā* will be clearly understood only from the concept of *śūnyatā* (emptiness) and the two systems of truths established in Buddhism i.e. conventional truth (*saṃvṛti-satya*) and ultimate truth (*paramārtha-satya*).

The various aspects of conceptual construction and the resulting world of conventional truth (which can be described only as neither real nor unreal or as neither existent nor non-existent) have been thoroughly analysed by Buddhist philosophers of different schools and explained in detail in a rational manner without getting obfuscated in abstruse metaphysical terminology. Nāgārjuna started with identification of all the three – conceptual construction of the mind, dependent origination and middle path – with emptiness and established his concepts of emptiness and the two-truths.

Candrakīrti of Madhyamaka school, who followed him, defined the conceptual construction and the conventional truth (*saṃvṛti-satya*) as encompassing and covering three aspects (Ref: *Prasannapadā,* 24.8/492.10-12) as below:

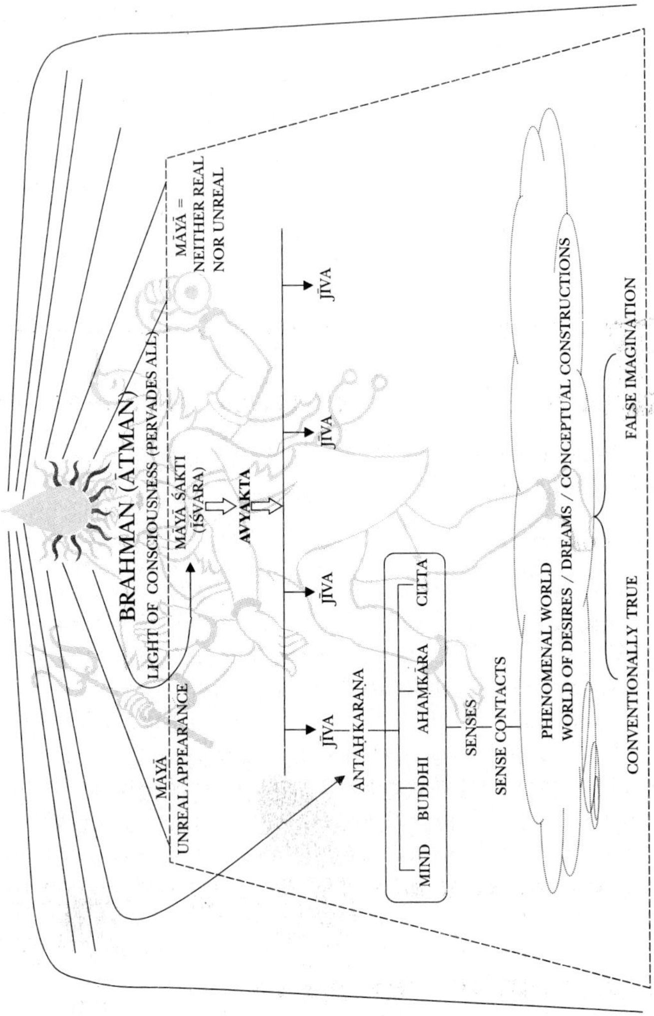

Fig. 20 Brahman/Māyā theory of Śaṅkara

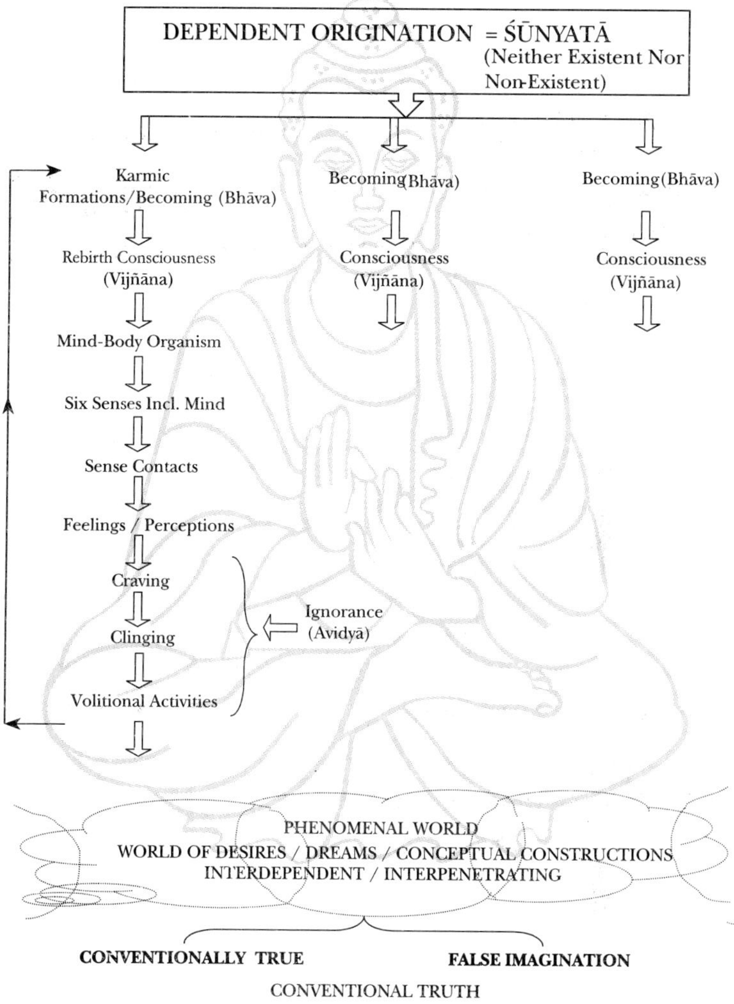

Fig. 21 Śūnyatā of Buddhism

(1) Falsehood through ignorance (*avidyā*).
(2) Contingent existence without substance or self (Interdependent existence).
(3) Symbolic and worldly discourse.

The first aspect is the covering or masking of the truth on all sides because of the veil of ignorance, and as such, not-knowing (*ajñāna*) things as they actually are and superimposing the conceptual constructs.

The second is the 'interdependent existence' derived from the meaning of *saṃvṛti* as 'causing each other to come into being' which is further explained as *anyonya-samāśrayeṇa*, that is, "with one depending upon another" (G.M. Nagao, *Mādhyamika* and *Yogācāra*,, p.15). It occurs on the basis of mutual support of component factors.

The third aspect covered in the conventional truth is the "symbolic and worldly discourse" by which dependent existence in the world is enabled. It is the set of conventions set up through linguistic symbols, social discourse and custom. It involves differentiation of the perceiver and perceived (i.e.that which names and that which is named).

Sthiramati (belonging to the *Yogācāra-Vijñānavāda* school) later expounded the conventional truth interpreting the same as '*saṃvṛtti*' (with root *vṛt*) instead of '*saṃvṛti*' (having root *vṛ*) considered by Candrakīrti. His definition of conventional truth includes three aspects:

(1) Prajñapti-saṃvṛtti
(2) Pratipatti-saṃvṛtti
(3) Udbhāvanā-saṃvṛtti

The first is exactly the same as Candrakīrti's third definition i.e. 'Conventional symbols' or 'symbolice and worldly discourse'.

The second aspect refers to '(wrong) discrimination (*vikalpa*)' and covers the conceptual constructs (i.e. falsehood through ignorance) and interdependent existence (*paratantra*) of Candrakīrti's definition.

Udbhāvanā is 'manifestation' and it stands opposed to the first definition 'to cover universally' and 'to be concealed universally' given by Candrakīrti. It aims to display and to point to reality which remains alway beyond *vikalpa*. *Saṃvṛtti* is thus an utterance, attempting to express the inexpressible truth. In this respect, *Saṃvṛtti* is raised to a position higher than those of the other two and placed closer to *Paramārtha*. *Saṃdhinirmocana Sūtra* explains this attempt in the following words:

"......... sages detach from names and words by knowledge and insight and therefore realize enlightenment. Then, because they want to make others aware of this real nature which is beyond words, they provisionally set up names and characterstics and call things created or uncreated (i.e. pairs of opposites)............ ."

(Buddhist Yoga, Translated by Thomas Cleary, p.8)

Here language functions as the vehicle for the appearance (*saṃdarśana*) of ultimate truth. The linguistic conventions are used to describe things 'just as they are' (*yathābhūta*). They function as pointers (*prajñapti*) to the ultimate truth and allow for its manifestation (*Udbhāvanā*) in conventional discourse.

Further development of thoughts in the *Yogācāra/ Vijñānavāda* school has led to the distinction between what is conventionally true and what is false imagination and the elaboration of the two-truths system into three-truths as below:

(1) *Paratantra* (Other dependent) - Conventionally true
(2) *Parikalpita* (Imagined) - False imagination
(3) *Pariniṣpanna* (Perfected) - Ultimate truth

Both *paratantra* and *parikalpita* belong to the conventional realm. The first is conventionally true whereas the other is simply false imagination. But, in the ultimate sense, both are unreal because conventional truth is not an ever-existent truth and also not a self-existent one in itself, of itself and by itself without any dependence on others. It starts after birth and develops from childhood only, with impact from environment and education. It is not existent in the states of deep sleep and fainting and also in the embryonic state of existence in the mother's womb. It depends on causal factors and it arises and becomes extinct depending on other causes and conditions. Hence the world of the conventional truth cannot be said to be either existent or non-existent and, as such, is empty. On the other hand, the ultimate truth of selflessness and voidness of conceptions stands totally opposed to the conventional truth and is not said to have a cause i.e. it is uncaused and unborn.

The conventional truth and emptiness expounded in Buddhist philosophy have been discussed in some detail above because these only become *māyā* in Śaṅkara's philosophy and will serve to clarify and throw more light on his abstruse theory. More emphasis and prominence are given in his philosophy to the aspect of 'covering universally' or 'veiling universally' as defined in Candrakīrti's exposition. *Māyā* as an illusion has come to prevail more than other aspects in Śaṅkara's theory. Because of this, his theory is vulnerable to the criticism that, if every thing is *māyā* or an illusion, what he teaches also is illusory and unreal and the entire foundation of his philosophy is undermined. On the other hand, Sthiramati's exposition includes *Udbhāvanā* (manifestation) also as one of the aspects or ingredients of conventional truth and makes a distinction between what is conventionally true and what is false imagination in the conventional realm. Thus it provides a sound philosophical footing to validate the relevance and significance of the religious teachings and holy life. On the other hand, mere *māyā* theory of Śaṅkara will render the religious life meaningless.

5. Māyā-Śakti (*Īśvara*)

From the above, it will be clear that the conceptual constructions and the resulting world of conventional truth, that are described as empty (*śūnya*) in Buddhist philosophy, become *māyā* or illusory appearance in the Advaita Vedānta of Śaṅkara.

The ignorance (*avidyā*) in the individual microcosmic level, that veils the truth and creates the world of the conceptual construction and conventional truth blinded and driven by inner passions and cravings, becomes *māyā* in Śaṅkara's philosophy in the cosmic context. In the Buddhist philosophy, this conventional world arises and revolves because of the interplay of the conceptual constructions of the innumerable individual *vijñānas* (i.e. packets of will energy) and their evolutions according to the universal laws. The Law of Karma and the universal laws are the determining principles which operate spontaneously in the suchness of this realm and in these evolutions. But Śaṅkara breaks ground here with the Buddhists and differs radically from them and postulates a metaphysical entity called *Īśvara* behind this world of *māyā* to conform to his Vedic tradition. He describes *Īśvara* as the Lord of *māyā* and accepts the traditional religious philosophy associated with *Īśvara*.

Īśvara is immanent in the whole universe and is the inner controller. He is the universal soul of souls as well as the soul of nature. As the immanent inner ruler, he is called *antaryāmin*. He is also transcendental for in his own nature he transcends the universe. He is the creator, sustainer and destroyer of the universe.

He is the source of everything. He is the final haven of everything. He is the object of devotion. He is the inspirer of moral life.

According to the basic theory, *Īśvara* is conditioned by *māyā* (*avidyā* or ignorance). In the case of *Īśvara* also, just as in the case of individual *jīva*, the root cause of creation, conceptual construction and projection of the miserable world of sufferings and sorrows, is *avidyā* (ignorance). In the case of the individual *jīva*, he is subject to ignorance ; he is deluded and he suffers. But, in the case of *Īśvara*, it is said that he is the Lord of *māyā*, even though he is subject to ignorance and enters into creation of this sorrowful world replete with evils and iniquities, strifes and atrocities, inequalities and injustices. There is a logical inconsistency here in defining ignorance involved in the two cases although *māyā* and *avidyā* are said to be the same and are synonymous terms in Śaṅkara *Vedānta*. The individual *jīva* wrongly identifies itself with the physical body due to *avidyā* and commits acts and reaps the fruits of its actions according to the Law of Karma. The same ignorance applied to *Īśvara* is transmuted into *māyā* which is now said to have the power of creating the Law of Karma and the universal laws of cause and effect and also controlling these laws according to a divine will. The untenability of this conception has already been discussed in our study of Early Advaita Vedānta of GK.

For Śaṅkara, *Īśvara* and *jīva* are the inexplicable appearances of Brahman due to *māyā* (*avidyā* or *ādhyāsa*). He seems to hold the view that, even though both *Īśvara* and *jīva* are appearances due to *avidyā*, this *avidyā* in its negative aspect of concealment operates only on *jīva* and never on *Īśvara*. 'Why so?' and 'How so?'– these are treated as illegitimate questions by Śaṅkara. We are asked to accept this difference in the way *avidyā* operates without questioning. This is an insoluble mystery according to Śaṅkara.

In this view, *Īśvara* is the Lord of *māyā* while *jīva* is subject to *māyā*. *Īśvara* always enjoys the bliss of Brahman while *jīva* is afflicted by the bondage of *avidyā*.

Compared to the above, Buddhism is very clear and rational in its understanding and explanation of the world process. As already shown in the foregoing, Buddhism recognizes only three elements – the blind will to 'become' (with its volitions) of the individual beings conditioned by ignorance, the world of conventional truth arising out of their cravings, clingings and conceptual constructions and the universal principle of dependent origination and causation i.e. the Law of *Karma* and other laws of cause and effect which determine the world of becoming. There is nothing metaphysical and mysterious in this philosophy to warrant blind faith. Apart from the universal principle of dependent origination and causation, there is no other metaphysical entity such as *Īśvara* postulated in the Vedic and *Upaniṣadic* thoughts. The entire world process and its dynamics are governed by eternal and immutable laws that invariably and inviolably act depending on causes and conditions. A separate law-giver or law-enforcer apart from the laws is an imaginary construction. Moreover, the concept of the same *Īśvara* who creates the *jīvas* and causes them to do deeds, becoming also the law-giver and dispenser of retribution against these deeds, is incongruous and illogical.

Further, there is also the problem of how to reconcile the idea of the all-powerful and all-merciful *Īśvara* with the evils and injustices in his creations. Apologists of the theory of God come out with weak replies such as: "there is no good or no evil; these are relative terms which do not touch *Īśvara*". What is relative about the passions and impurities like lust, greed, covetousness, pride, arrogance, conceit, indolence, malevolence, anger, hypocrisy, treachery, obstinacy and other wicked impulses and forces lying deep within? What about the natural calamities and also atrocities committed by man against man, by man against other living beings? These are the vile stuffs of which creation is made. If creation theory is maintained, the creator cannot be absolved from his responsibility for these evils and injustices in the world. In the ultimate analysis, the theory of *māyā* adopted in Advaita Vedānta is itself an attempt to shield and insulate its highest reality Brahman from the iniquities and imperfections of the world. But, the unreality adduced for the world and *Īśvara* is only in the ultimate sense according to Śaṅkara, and reality is claimed for them as conventional truth. But, as a truth in the conventional realm also the criticisms leveled by the Buddhists against the Brahman/*Īśvara* theory remain valid and have to be conceded.

The analogy of magician and his magical acts is cited by Śaṅkara to show that the acts of creation are mere appearances and Brahman is not affected by these appearances just as the magician is not affected by the magical appearances (illusions) he is creating. Is creation then an act of skillful deception Brahman is performing like a magician? Brahman may not be affected because he knows it is a deception. But why should he resort to this deception? Such analogies do not prove anything but succeed only in obscuring the truth and giving wrong ideas.

Magician is resorting to deception for his livelihood. For what purpose does Brahman stoop to his acts of deception? Action is involved in the magic performed by the magician. Is it claimed that, in making the world appear, no conscious effort is involved in Brahman? From such expositions, we get only confusing and contradictory ideas. Such theories appeal only to the imagination and belief of the ordinary mind.

Brahman or *Īśvara* is not the magician, but the real magician is in fact only the craving within that is creating the illusory world. This truth is obscured and totally lost sight of in these philosophies.

These are the opposing view-points and objections that arise when we consider the theory of creation and *Īśvara* asserted by Śaṅkara as conventionally true. But Śaṅkara himself concedes that in the ultimate analysis *Īśvara* and the individual selves are unreal and non-existent. This may be contrasted with the Buddhist philosophical position that *Īśvara* and the concept of Self are false and unreal not only from the stand point of ultimate truth but also from the conventional stand-point. The creation theories and the *Brahman-Pariṇāmavāda* have been rejected by the Advaita Vedānta on logical grounds as we have already seen in our study of GK's early Advaita Vedānta. Śaṅkara accepts these theories as true and real in the conventional realm until they are sublated by the realisation of oneness and union with the ultimate reality Brahman. The logical inconsistencies and contradictions in these theories are brushed aside taking a philosophical position that these are because of the incomprehensible nature of *māyā-śakti* and that questions on these are illegitimate. Now this becomes a matter of faith not to be questioned.

6. Unreality of Transmigratory Existence

As we have earlier seen, one of the descriptions given by Śaṅkara for *māyā* is that it is of the nature of superimposition (*adhyāsa*)– superimposition upon one thing of the character of another thing. It is an error like that of a 'rope-snake' or 'shell-silver' cognition. Just as the qualities of the snake are superimposed on the rope and the rope is mistaken for a snake in the dark, in like manner, due to *avidyā* (ignorance), qualities are being superimposed on Brahman or *Ātman* and multiplicity of the world and the *jīvas* is seen where only Brahman is actually there. Thus, the multiplicity of the world and the *jīvas* is only an appearance and a projection on the ground of Brahman. It is a false superimposition (*mṛṣādhyāsa*) according to Śaṅkara .

"Just as, when there is (the existence of) a rope, a snake, (though not a reality), exists in the rope before there is discrimination (of them), so because of (the existence of) the transcendentally changeless *Ātman*, this transmigratory existence, though not a reality (exists in *Ātman* before the two are discriminated)" (*Upad.* I. 18.46).

The transmigratory existence of the self and the multiplicity of the world derive their existences from the superimposition in the absence of discriminating knowledge (*aviveka*). All these are nothing but nescience (*avidyāmātra*). Who is the transmigrating self (*saṃsārin*)?

"As the Seeing is changeless, (It) is not (the transmigrator) nor is the reflection (the transmigrator), for the reflection is unreal. Nor is the bearer of the 'I'-notion (the transmigrator) since it is non-conscious. Who could be the transmigrator?" (*Upad.*I.18.44)

According to Śaṅkara's view of transmigratory existence, there is no transmigrator anywhere. Transmigratory existence is unreal. So is the transmigrator. As the immovable *Ātman* exists, It is only regarded as the transmigrator because of nescience. (Sengaku Mayeda, Śaṅkara's view of Ethics, Philosophy: East And West, p.194/195).

In our study of Early Advaita Vedānta of GK, we have seen how according to GK's conception the *Ātman* (rope) is getting deluded and imagines itself as *jīvas* and other things of the world (snake) on itself (rope). This is the logical explanation based on the snake-on-the rope analogy in GK's philosophy. On the other hand, Śaṅkara takes an opposite view and asserts that snake (i.e. individual *jīva* in the transmigratory existence) only imagines itself on the rope (i.e. non-dual Brahman ground). Since the individual *jīvas* (selves) are imagining themselves, they are unreal and non-existent. Their existences are imaginary and, as such, they do not touch the non-dual Brahman and affect his integrity according to Śaṅkara. On the same logic, the existence of *Īśvara* is also an imaginary existence and unreal (*māyā*). Unreality of the selves is also the philosophical position of Buddhism because they are impermanent (*anityam*), they suffer (*asukham*) and they are indentityless and selfless (*anattā*). They have no substance of their own and they depend on others for existence. According to the Buddhists, the individual 'will to become' (*vijñāna*) wills and creates its body-mind complex and gives rise to the phenomenal world of existence. There is only the collection of individual *vijñānas* (bundles of wills and cravings), ever-changing and ever in flux of becoming, and not any *Īśvara* or universal soul, omnipotent, omnipresent and omniscient creator God. In the Buddhist world-view, there is no permanent unchanging self behind the flux of experiences and becoming. The concepts of permanent self and *Īśvara* are imaginary and false both in the conventional sense (*saṃvṛti-satya*) as well as in ultimate sense (*paramārtha-satya*).

Even though the individual *jīva* imagines and creates itself, Śaṅkara maintains that this imagination takes place as a false superimposition (*mṛṣādhyāsa*) on the non-dual ground Brahman. His argument seems to be that, just as the existence of a rope there in the twilight is necessary for the false notion of snake to take place, in the same manner, the existence of an unchanging *Ātman* is considered necessary for the superimposition of *jīva* in transmigratory existence to occur (See *Upad.*I.18.46 quoted earlier).

This is a strange and convoluted logic stretching an analogy and wrongly applying it. In the analogy, there is something (rope) there; but in the darkness mistaking it and overcome by fear induced by that something external, one imagines and constructs a world of his own (snake) through superimposition. But in the actual existential situation obtaining what exactly takes place is that one imagines himself (not induced by anything external) to be possessed of a self, a permanent entity, and considers pleasing his own self as the sole concern and aim in life. Ignorant of the true nature – *anityam, asukham* and *anattā* (no substance, no self) – of his personality, he indulges in actions driven by craving, greed and other self-centred passions surging from within. The root cause of his transmigratory existence is his ignorance and the cravings, clinging, conceptual constructions and actions arising therefrom. It is not that he sees something external and, overcome by fear, imagines and superimposes on that 'something' as in the snake-rope analogy. He is driven by inner passions and cravings which make him to dream and conceptually construct where nothing is there. He dreams, not superimposes. The superimposition theory of Śaṅkara misses the vital point of the craving from within being the fundamental factor that makes one wallow in the *saṃsāric* existence. Instead of stressing this point, Śaṅkara tries to prove the existence of a permanent Self or *Ātman* as a substratum to support the superimposition. Just as in a dream, imagination and creation can take place from within even in the absence of any substratum to support it. Creation may best be described as a dream rather than a superimposition. Therefore, the superimposition theory held by Śaṅkara is not sustainable.

If it is asserted that *Ātman* exists as pure light of consciousness and induces consciousness in the *jīva*, then that *Ātman* is the cause of, and as such is directly responsible for, the imagination, conceptual construction and creation of the *saṃsāric* world, in as much as it is the one that gives the consciousness and initiates the whole process. GK concedes this point and adopts a philosophical position that *Ātman* deludes itself and imagines itself as the *jīvas* and the various things of the world. But Śaṅkara is disinclined to concede this. He takes a philosophical position akin to the theory of "blind will to become (*Vijñāna*)" in Buddhism and states that the *jīva* imagines and creates itself but at the same time adding that this imagination is a sort of superimposition. The *jīva*'s world is an imaginary world and, according to Śaṅkara, the *jīva* (the transmigrator)., who imagines, is also imaginary and hence unreal. But, when he adds that this unreal imagination takes place as a superimposition and a real permanent substratum is necessary for this unreal superimposition to occur, he passes beyond logic.

Śaṅkara adopts contradictory positions. He tries to insulate his highest reality *Ātman* or Brahman from the imperfections and evils of the world by suggesting that whatever is taking place in the transmigratory existence of *jīva* or *Īśvara* is imaginary, illusory (*māyā*) and as such, has no reality. Unreality cannot touch and affect the integrity of the reality that is the transcendentally changeless *Ātman*. But, on the other hand, he also maintains that the non-dual *Ātman* is also the ground and support of the individual *jīvas* and the worlds created by them. Here he argues that the real supports the unreal. How can it be logically conceived that real supports the unreal? If the real supports the unreal, then the evils and imperfections of the unreal are bound to affect and tarnish the real.

7. *Badha* (Sublation)

Unlike in Buddhism, Śaṅkara treats the individual *jīvas* and *Īśvara* as unreal only in the ultimate sense. In the conventional sense, they are taken to be real whereas for the Buddhists the concepts of permanent unchanging self and *Īśvara* are false conceptual fabrications in the conventional realm also. Notwithstanding the difference in these concepts, Śaṅkara accepts the distinction between the conventionally true and false imaginary constructs. Śaṅkara's notion of *badha* is the same as the three-nature theory and the three-truths system earlier propounded by the *Yogācārins.*

Badha is sublation or cancellation, and involves correcting a judgement once one has an experience that contradicts it. Three layers of truth or reality are recognized by Śaṅkara also. Absolute truth or reality is the one that cannot be sublated by any other experience or knowledge (compare ultimate truth in Buddhism). This is the non-dual *Ātman* without any differentiation i.e. the Absolute reality with nothing really apart from it, whereas in Buddhism the ultimate truth is selflessness, emptiness or suchness.

Then there is the ordinary world of experience which appears to be real but which is sublated according to Śaṅkara on attaining the correct knowledge and realisation of the non-dual *Ātman.* This may be compared with the other-dependent truth (*paratantra*) described in *Yogācāra.* For the *Mahāyāna* Buddhist, who has attained the highest state of selflessness, conventional (other-dependent) truth is conventional truth and he regards conventional as conventional. For him, *saṃsāra* and *Nirvāṇa* are both equal and there is no separate realm of ultimate truth; he treats what is conventionally true as conventional truth and what is conceptually fabricated or imagined as false. The logic in his life is the logic of selflessness and love (compassion). On the other hand, Śaṅkara Vedānta seems to suggest a separate realm of Absolute Truth. It is stated that, once the saint apprehends the non-dual *Ātman,* he realizes that the ordinary world of experience is not real at all.

Finally, there are illusions which are themselves sublated when evaluated with respect to our other normal experiences. This concept of illusions is equivalent to imagination, *parikalpita* in *Yogācāra.*

Thus Śaṅkara Vedānta also recognizes three levels of truth or reality as in Mahāyāna Buddhism:

Absolute truth
Relative truth of the ordinary waking world
Illusory (imaginations, hallucinations, dreams and the like)

8. The Four States of Experience and the One Consciousness

According to the above hierarchy of truth (reality), what is most real is what cannot be contradicted or sublated by something else. The unreality of the imaginary standpoint will be realized only when the conventional truth is accessed. Similarly the unreality of the conventional realm will be realized only when the absolute truth is comprehended. The falsity of the dream-objects is realized when the dreamer gets awake. Śaṅkara points out that in this condition even though these dream objects are sublated, the consciousness that the dreamer had experienced these objects in the dream is not sublated even in the waking state. Similarly, when the deep sleep is sublated and we wake up, we intuitively know the presence or continuance of the consciousness in the deep sleep state also for, immediately on waking up, one is aware that he had a good sleep undisturbed by dreams. If the experience of bliss in the sleeping state had not been presented direct to one's consciousness, one would never be sure that he was the one that had slept blissfully. Thus, even though the deep sleep state is sublated, the consciousness of bliss experienced therein is carried over to the ensuing waking state.

Just as the fish swims from one shore to the other and back and forth, one passes from waking state to dream state, from dream state to deep sleep state and from deep sleep state to waking state again. Even though one state is sublated by another and experiences in the three states vary, there is an eternal unchanging consciousness underlying all these experiences according to the *Vedānta.* This, Śaṅkara asserts, is the ultimate reality, *Ātman* or Brahman. This is pure consciousness, devoid of any attribute or quality.

The existence of the consciousness in the three states of waking, dreaming and deep sleep as asserted by Śaṅkara may not be denied. But the question is whether the consciousness remains the same unchanged in all these three states. All consciousness must be conscious of something. Consciousness is so called because it is conscious of something. When that something varies, consciousness also varies. From the various sets of experiences of consciousness, one particular element cannot be abstracted and presented as consciousness *per se.* Further what about the states of fainting and existence as an embryo in the mother's womb? Can it be said that the same consciousness of the three states of waking, dreaming and deep sleep is present in these other states also? Obviously the awareness proved by Śaṅkara to exist in the former three states cannot be ascribed to the state of fainting. The problem in Śaṅkara's philosophy is that it seems to restrict consciousness to the aspect of awareness or cognition only. On the other hand, Buddhism has a more clear and comprehensive concept of consciousness. Consciousness for the Buddhists is a bundle of wills, volitions, impulses, desires, feelings and thoughts in ever-changing formation and in continuous flow. For conventional practical purposes, a name has to be assigned for this ever-changing bundle and that name is consciousness.

According to Śaṅkara and other Hindu philosophers, equating self with a flux of states or a stream of consciousness would be to confuse the principle of consciousness with the portions of its contents. If all these varying contents are to be connected, there has to be a unifying consciousness. Buddhists also recognize this unifying consciousness, but according to them the unifying consciousness itself changes with the contents in the stream. When the contents change, the consciousness holding them also has to change.

According to Śaṅkara, the fact of memory and recognition gives a death blow to the theory of momentariness and flux of mental states in Buddhism. The past is recognized and remembered in the present and this implies the existence of a permanent synthesizing subject without whom perception will remain at the level of scattered sense-data and knowledge shall always remain an impossibility. But, if a permanent synthesizing subject is always there and accounts for the fact of memory and recognition, then how is it that one is not able to remember all that is experienced and why does memory become weak and faint and sometimes get lost? Memory comes and goes. Memory of the infanthood is completely lost. Sometimes we remember and recognize somebody. The same somebody we fail to remember and recognize at some other times. Memory and recognition do not prove the existence of a permanent self or subject; in fact, they disprove the theory of existence of such a permanent self (consciousness).

"When it is said, it is 'I' who now know, who at present exists, it is 'I' who know the past and what was before the past, it is 'I' who shall know the future and what is after the future, it is implied in these words that even when the object of knowledge alters, the knower does not alter, for he is the past, present and future as his essence is eternally present" (Dr. S.Radhakrishnan, *Indian Philosophy,* Chapter VIII: The Advaita Vedānta of Śaṅkara).

The statement above that the knower does not alter even when the object of knowledge alters is an assumption and an assertion, not proved by facts of experience. It is asserted that nobody doubts that he is. No one thinks 'I am not'. Śaṅkara tries to prove the truth of the self by citing the self-certainty in such statements as 'I am'. According to him, no one doubts his own existence and no doubt can be cast on one's own existence. This is like Descartes' famous argument : 'I think, therefore I am'. However much you delve deep within or without, you will not find this self 'I', but only the thought of 'I'. Whatever you find is only a conglomeration of thoughts and other mental states. You only give a name 'I' to this bundle and this is a conventional designation for practical purposes.

It is true that doubt about the existence of this changing bundle 'I' does not arise; but doubt about the existence of a permanent self residing within does arise. The man who has fainted and also the infants have no notion of self or 'I am'. In morally exacting situations, a person is assailed by conflicting sets of passions and desires; different personality traits are fighting within to gain mastery over him. Which set of personality traits constitutes his real 'I'? Mad people, intoxicated ones and drugged ones have not only no notion of self but also think themselves to be of multiple personalities. Who is such a one's 'I'? It is baffling how Śaṅkara can assume that such statements as 'I am' are true because this amounts to asserting the reality of the ego self. One may call the bundle of his five aggregates as 'I' and be sure of its existence, but if he thinks that this bundle is a permanent and unchanging entity, then it is nothing but his ignorance. This is only a name, not a reality.

9. *Ātman* (Brahman)—The Ultimate Reality

But the entire philosophy of Śaṅkara hinges on this conept of *Ātman* or Self as the Pure Consciousness and the one (non-dual) reality. This non-dual *Ātman* (Brahman), Pure Consciousness, is devoid of all attributes and all categories of the intellect. According to Śaṅkara, this stands self-revealed, self-proved, as the background of all knowledge, affirmations and denials. It is the highest truth, the absolute beyond all phenomena in existence, beyond time, space and causation. It cannot be experienced by the senses or the mind.

Śaṅkara's concept of *Ātman* is very difficult to understand. The various descriptions and analogies given tend to confuse. He abstracts an element of consciousness from experience that is completely separated from all its concomitant aspects of creation, cognition, thinking, willing and feeling. In spite of all his protestations, it is a conceptual abstraction. Despite this, Śaṅkara asserts that the moment we try to bring this Brahman within the categories of intellect or try to make this ultimate subject an object of our thought, the mind modifies it and its essential nature is missed. Then it no more is unconditioned consciousness, but becomes conditioned as it were.

This conditioned consciousness (conditioned Brahman), Śaṅkara calls *apara* Brahman (lower Brahman) or *Īśvara* as contrasted with the unconditioned Brahman which is called *para* Brahman (higher Brahman), the ultimate reality. Śaṅkara asserts that the *apara* Brahman or *Īśvara* is the highest which the intellect can reach and comprehend; as against this, *para* Brahman, the ultimate reality, can be realized, not by intellect, but by only immediate intuitive perception or deep spiritual insight. For the liberated one who has realized his identity with the ultimate reality, *Īśvara* and the multiplicity of this world become unreal. For others in the phenomenal world, *Īśvara* is all in all. Finite thought can never grasp Brahman. And therefore all talks about Brahman are in fact talks about *Īśvara* in the unreal phenomenal world.

The consciousness shed by the Brahman (*Ātman*) energizes the physical body to become *jīvātma* which only acts and experiences. Thus, the *Ātman* is the subject element of subject-object complex constituting the *jīva* or individual self. It is called the *Sākṣin* (witness) in Śaṅkara's philosophy. It is always known to be actionless. The object element of *jīva* is the internal organ called *antaḥkaraṇa*. The internal organ differs from individual to individual and functions within varying limits which are defined and determined by the past conduct of the individual to whom it belongs. The internal organ is so called because it is the seat of the functions of the senses as distinct from the outer organs. It receives and arranges what is conveyed to it through the senses. It has transparency by which it reflects objects, even as the mirror has the lustre to reflect our faces. In Śaṅkara's theory of perception, when a sense-organ comes into contact with an object, the internal organ assumes the 'form' of that object. It is the *vṛtti* or the mode of the internal organ.

This *vṛtti* illuminated by the *Sākṣin* takes the form of empirical knowledge. The power to reflect objects i.e. to become conscious of them is not innate in the internal organ ; but it becomes conscious by being illuminated by the *Sākṣin*. Though the internal organ is said to shed its lustre on the objects and reflect them, it is still the *Sāksin* that reflects in it. *Sākṣin* is the illuminator and by means of it, the internal organ perceives. It is because of the radiation of light from the *Ātman* (*Sākṣin*) that all the names and forms of the world become perceptible to the senses and the internal organ.

The *vṛtti* or modes of the internal organ are of four different kinds: indetermination (in this mode it is called mind), determination (in this mode called buddhi), self-consciousness (called *ahaṃkāra*) and concentration and remembrance (*citta*).

In this account of Śaṅkara, *Ātman* (*Sākṣin*) is the light (*jyotis*) which illumines the *antaḥkararạ* and gives rise to the development of mental faculties – mind, intellect, *ahaṃkāra* and *citta*. It is the light permeating the *antaḥkararạ* and energizing it. This account talks about the development of mental faculties from *antaḥkararạ* and deals only with the aspect of knowledge or cognition. It is stated that knowledge (cognition) becomes possible only because of the consciousness induced in the *antaḥkararạ* by *Ātman* with its light. The development of *antaḥkararạ* itself is relegated to the objective realm. This may be contrasted with the theory in Buddhism, according to which, it is the fundamental consciousness, *Vijñāna* (the will to become), that descends into the ovum-sperm combination and develops into the body-mind complex. Not only the body, senses, nerves and brain centres but also the mind, intellect and volitions grow from the all-seed consciousness which is equivalent to the 'That' in the 'That Art Thou' teaching of the *Chāndogya Upaniṣad*, where it is explained with the example of the seed of a nyagrodha tree how this vast universe arises from non-being.

But in Śaṅkara's philosophy, *Ātman* is conceived only as the light illuminating the *antaḥkaraṇa* and making knowledge possible. Thus, here, the conception of *Ātman* is restricted to only knowledge or cognitive aspect of existence and no creative or development potential is admitted therein. It is as if this light of *Ātman* exists separately and illumines the individual's *antaḥkaraṇa* to make knowledge possible after he is born from the mother's womb. Whatever drive or inner power or will, which grows the individual being inside the mother's womb, is not supposed to belong to the light of consciousness (*Ātman*) according to this school. That drive or will is understood to be in the realm of *māyā* or *avidyā*. The question arises whether this drive or will which develops the body, senses, nerves and brain centres has the power to grow and develop upto the brain centres only and thereafter a separate principle of light of consciousness has to step in to continue with the evolution and develop cognition process. Śaṅkara's Advaita Vedānta School makes this arbitrary division between the will to grow (the sub-conscious or superconscious activity) and the consciousness of knowledge activity, and assigns one a reality and condemns the other to the *māyā*. This arbitrary division of the one conscious process which is a continuous flow and development is an imaginary conceptual exercise and is untenable.

Furthermore, the very theory of perception in this school which suggests that the light of consciousness just remains there shining and the *antaḥkaraṇa* becomes consciously activated stretches the limit of credulity. The mere presence of a principle like light cannot explain the whole mechanism and process of cognition and knowledge and subsequent actions. On the other hand, Buddhism has a very rational theory which accords well with science. Here the same fundamental consciousness, the will to become, contains the potential within it, not only the will-power to grow body complex, but also the will power to develop the mechanism of perception and knowledge and the will-power to actions. The will to gain knowledge is one of the off-shoots of the very same fundamental consciousness. Postulation of a separate transcendental light of consciousness to explain a part of this whole process is untenable. Further, the idea of an unchanging consciousness is also a conceptual abstraction and construction as already pointed out.

In all the intellectual exercise and conceptual abstraction by Śaṅkara, an attempt to insulate his *Ātman* (Brahman) from the imperfections of the created world is apparent. The analogies given in his *Vedānta* to illustrate his concept of *Ātman* reinforce the idea of separation from the created realm. Space-pot analogy is often cited to stress the point that *Ātman* is all-pervasive and non-dual like space. There is a definite suggestion in this that just as the pot barriers are not created by space, the *jīvas* and the world are not created by the *Ātman*. Also take another analogy quoted:

Ātman is like an ocean of bliss and consciousness and the physical appearances of individuals are like waves in the ocean of bliss. When the wind of *saṃskāras* and desires blows, the waves appear and disappear. The appearances of the individuals are like these waves. Here also the suggestion is that just as the wind is separate from the ocean, desires are separate from the ocean of consciousness. If desires do not arise from the consciousness of *Ātman*, they are self-created or they arise from a different source.

The non-duality professed in the *Vedānta* is only in the ultimate sense. In the conventional realm the duality and separation are recognized. Despite this separation, Śaṅkara maintains that, for the appearance of the *jīvas* and the world, the existence of *Ātman* as the substratum to support this appearance is necessary, just as a rope is necessary to support the imaginary existence of snake (*Upad.* I. 18.46). Śaṅkara constructs only an imaginary relation between the *Ātman* and the transmigratory existence. We have already seen how, for the imagination and conceptual construction of this transmigratory world, imagination of a separate *Ātman* is not necessary. Transmigratory world arises depending on causes and conditions as explained by Buddhism in a rational and logical manner.

But Śaṅkara takes a philosophical position that the proof of ultimate reality *Ātman* (Brahman) is based on the revelations in the *śrutis* and it cannot be apprehended by such intellectual exercises. Deep spiritual insight only will reveal *Ātman*. Any description of *Ātman* or Brahman will only be a futile intellectual exercise because It is indescribable ; no description of It can be complete. Best description of *Ātman* is only 'neti, neti' (not this, not this) as in *Bṛhadāraṇyaka Upaniṣad*. But, extend the negation one step higher to its logical end. We are in the emptiness of Buddhism.

10. Ethics

In Śaṅkara's Advaita Vedānta School, the Law of Karma and the ethical and moral principles that govern the world-process have not been given due weightage and importance. These stand precariously in this philosophy on uncertain footing within *avidyā*. On the other hand, the main focus and thrust in Buddhism are on these ethical and moral aspects and on transformation of the consciousness (*vijñāna*). Whereas in Śaṅkara's philosophy the emphasis is on discrimination of *Ātman* (Self) from non-*Ātman* (non-Self) and apprehension of *Ātman* to attain salvation and final release, the emphasis in Buddhism is on transformation of the consciousness. Buddhism stresses that what the *Upaniṣads* call non-*Ātman* or non-self–all arise from the defiled consciousness which should be stripped thoroughly and seen nakedly to bring about total transformation.The root cause of all the defilements and all the evils and sins in this world is the persistent attachment to the idea of self and the attendant selfishness and self-aggrandizement. As we have already seen, Buddhism proves that selflessness is the ultimate truth and it is the ideal, dharma-body for Buddhists. As against this ideal of selflessness, Śaṅkara posits an *Ātman* or Self adhering to the Vedic tradition and clings to a Self where there is none according to the Buddhists and according to the rational enquiry.

The notion of *Ātman* or Brahman always connotes power. One who knows Brahman is traditionally held to have the power to control the universe. Brahman denotes power, permanence and sovereignty over everything. Even though Śaṅkara makes a distinction between *apara* Brahman (*Īśvara*) and *para* Brahman, this idea of Brahman signifying power still lingers on in his philosophy when he talks of *Īśvara* as the all-in-all Brahman in the phenomenal world. This idea of Brahman or Self is totally rejected by the Buddhists as a false conceptual construct even in the conventional realm leave alone the ultimate truth. It is an erroneous view that will lead us astray from the correct path.

Many scholars rightly or wrongly hold the view that Śaṅkara's Advaita Vedānta is indifferent to ethical and moral actions and in fact, is a-moral. For instance, Rudolf Otto in his 'Mysticism East And West' comments:

"............ (Śaṅkara's) mysticism has no ethic. It is not immoral, it is a-moral. The *Mukta*, the redeemed, who has attained *ekatā* or unity with the eternal Brahman, is removed from all works, whether good or evil. Works bind man. He leaves all activity and reposes in oneness........."

But Dr. S. Radhakrishnan disagrees and dedicates a chapter in his book 'Indian Philosophy', (Vol.II, p.621-634) answering the criticisms raised against Śaṅkara's ethical views and *Advaita Vedānta* by Western scholars. Sengaku Mayeda makes an objective analysis in his paper on 'Śaṅkara's view of Ethics' and observes:

"He does not intend to make void the moral laws through knowledge of *Brahman* and *Ātman*. He affirms now and then, though with reservation, that the performance of action, including the observance of the moral laws, is indispensable for final release.

In his *Upad.* (I.17, 44) Śaṅkara says that there is action only before acquisition of knowledge of *Ātman,* since a firm belief 'Thou art That' removes such notions as that one belongs to a certain caste and the like, which are indispensable in the performance of action. This statement is indeed negative but it implies paradoxically a positive meaning that action should be performed before one can achieve cessation of nescience. Before the cessation of nescience, abstinences from injury (*ahiṃsā*) and other abstensions (*yama*), the permanent rites, and even sacrifice (*yajña*) should be observed to purify the mind, since knowledge appears when the mind becomes pure like a mirror (*Upad.* 1, 17, 22). According to Śaṅkara, the cessation of nescience is nothing but final release. Practically speaking, therefore, the aspirant should perform action until his attainment of final release"(*Philosophy: East And West,* Paper 14, p. 201/202).

The final conclusion of Śaṅkara's teaching is that salvation or liberation is merely the removal of nescience (*avidyā*) and realisation of knowledge of oneness with Brahman (*Ātman*). For such a one who is thus liberated and acquired the knowledge of *Ātman,* there is no action. There is complete cessation of all willing and doing. He has attained the state of pure, immovable, changeless and actionless Brahman (*para*). The world outside is now unreal and non-existent for him.

This state may be equated with the *Nirodhasamāpatti* in Buddhism. But *Mahāyāna* school soars higher and teaches attainment of Buddhahood as the highest ideal where the juices of *Prajñā* (wisdom or realisation of oneness with emptiness, i.e. realisation of utter selflessness) and *karuṇā* (love of all living beings) – are combined into the one honey of consciousness, Buddha consciousness. For the *Mahāyāna* yogin now, *Nirvāṇa* and *saṃsāra* are equal. He has realized the ultimate truth of emptiness and burnt away all *karmic* formations. He is now only selflessness (emptiness) personified. Love alone is now the logic of life which governs every action of his life. For him, ultimate truth is not in a separate transcendent realm as in Śaṅkara's philosophy but only the realisation of the conventional as conventional and immersion in it with selflessness and love.

Nāgārjuna describes this perfection stage as below in his "The Five Stages":

"Abandoning the two notions of the *saṃsāric* life-cycle and the nirvāṇic liberation, there where they become the same, that is called 'integration'. Knowing the addictive and the purificative both as the absolute itself; who knows them as just the same, knows this integration. Knowing wisdom and compassion as the same, who acts in such a way is said to have attained integration. Freedom from the two notions of subjective selflessness and objective selflessness is the nature of integration. Free from mindfulness and carelessness, having a constantly spontaneous character, the yogi who acts as he pleases abides in the stage of integration........." (The Tibetan Book Of The Dead, Translated by Robert A. F. Thurman, p.79).

The Yogin attains perfection as below:

He constantly meditates on the infinite horizon of his interconnectedness with all sentient beings and reflects on the tenderness, love, affection and kindness, he received in his life right from the infant stage and the debt he owes to the other beings.

"Once you feel close to all beings in such a visionary network of blood and milk connections, you realize how they constantly suffer, life after life; you remember the relief you now feel at the prospect of liberation; and you generate a powerful ambition to liberate them as well. At the conclusion of this meditative process, you lock in this ambition with the heroic vow to serve all beings. You turn your aspiration to help the world into a solid determination. At that time, you will have generated the spirit of enlightenment of universal love and compassion..... ." (*The Tibetan Book of The Dead,* Translated by Robert F. Thurman, p.61).

On the other hand, Śaṅkara's philosophy treats the realm of ultimate truth as a transcendent one far removed from the conventional realm and from all works, whether good or evil. In this regard, Śaṅkara misinterprets even the teachings of the *Gītā* and denounces all actions. As Rudolf Otto remarks, he "uses all the powers of his dialectic and his penetrating intellect to cloud and twist the clear meaning of the *Gītā*" (*Mysticism East and West,* p.225).

Gītā acknowledges that for the liberated one who has realized the Self, there is nothing to be done. He has nothing to gain by doing an action or by abstaining from an action. The results of action and non-action are one and the same as far as he is concerned (*Gītā,* III.17&18). But he has a duty to nature and duty to the society and world at large. Therefore, *Gītā* enjoins that duty should be performed without any desire for the fruits of actions (*niṣkāmya karma*), as a *yajña* or sacrifice dedicating the results to the supreme Brahman.

"Therefore, do perform always without attachment actions that should be done i.e. obligatory duties, for, by performing action without attachment, one attains to the highest (the Brahman)" (*Gītā*, III-19)

Unfortunately, *Gītā* links the duty and *dharma* with *varṇa* and class thereby giving room to misinterpretation of its teachings by vested interests in the society. Injustices should be fought by everybody irrespective of his class or *varṇa.* "You are a *kṣatriya* ; therefore you have to fight", "You have to perform the duty prescribed for your particular class or caste", - this sort of arguments and teachings in *Gītā* lend themselves to distortions. Even the learned Śaṅkara holds the view that the Vedic teachers should initiate only those belonging to the *Brahmin* caste into the knowledge of Brahman – *Ātman* (*Upad.*II.1.2). How can knowledge be held as the exclusive preserve of a particular caste? What *dharma* is it? Whatever *dharma* or duty is talked about in these scriptures – that is as laid down by the powerful and privileged ones in the society according to their own conceptual constructs and prejudiced world-view.

Consider the whole set of arguments in *Dhṛtarāṣṭra's* assembly hall in *Mahābhārata* where the dicing match had taken place between *Pāṇḍavas* and *Kauravas* and in the aftermath of the same *Draupadī* was disrobed and dishonoured. To the repeated questions of *Draupadī* on the *dharma* of a faultless woman like her being dragged and brought before the assembly, *Bhīṣma* only replies:

"What a powerful person sees as *dharma* in the world is accepted as *dharma* by others when *dharma* is at issue. I cannot speak to your question with certainty for this matter is subtle, obscure and serious" (MB 2.62. 14-16).

Bhīṣma evades the questions always exclaiming that *dharma* is subtle and right answer cannot be given. *Karṇa* argues that *Draupadī* has been won according to *dharma.* The whole episode exposes the utter hollowness of the talks on the *dharma.* Unless universal principles like love, equality and justice are made the overriding defining elements in the concept of *dharma* or duty, the fate of *dharma* will be like that in the above episode in *Mahābhārata.*

The advocates of *Vedānta* may claim that their philosophy also teaches the equality of all selves because the one Self is in all beings and all beings are in the Self. But their claim has a false ring to it in as much as they do not reject and disown the class and caste distinctions which they take as divinely ordained following the Vedic injuctions. This is also compounded further by the fact that they are not able to establish a coherent relationship between the *Ātman* and the individual beings in their philosophies. If the *Ātman* (= Brahman) is the creator of the world and all the beings, then He becomes responsible for all the evils and injustices in the world. Hence, this is rejected. With the theory of *māyā* proposed to safeguard the integrity and purity of *Ātman,* equality and inequality all become imaginations and illusions and as such, they are irrelevant and of no concern. Sometimes, *Ātman* is equated with space (*ākāśa*) and theory advanced that, just as space, *Ātman* supports all beings. But from this support theory also, the equality of all beings does not logically follow. Because of these inner contradictions in their philosophies, the concept of equality of all beings remains hanging in their systems without any philosophical underpinning; hence the ambivalent and equivocal attitiude towards it.

The teachings of *Gītā* on the performance of duty and *niṣkāmya karma* are exemplary inasfar as they go. But duty should be defined properly without giving room for misinterpretations. Duty is repayment of the kindness and indebtedness one has received in life from others and society. Whatever kindness and good things one received in life, he should extend the same to all others unreservedly. *Dharma* is nothing but selfless love. *Dharma* is equalizing oneself with others and exchanging oneself with others. Buddhism excels in its moral and ethical teachings and in its emphasis on the practice of *ahiṃsā* and returning only good for evil. For the Buddhists, love (compassion) is the logic of life as well as the rule of life which determines and dictates every action.

Part VI

ULTIMATE TRUTH

CHAPTER 18

Ultimate Truth

1. A Brief Review of the Philosophies

Our search for reality (truth) has taken us through some major philosophical theories like:

- Theories of Creation and *Brahman-pariṇāmavāda* in the *Upaniṣads.*
- Theory of *Puruṣas* and *prakṛti* in the *Sāṃkhya.*
- Theory of 'Becoming' in the Buddha's Wheel of Life.
- Emptiness of *Prajñāpāramitā* literatures and Nāgārjuna.
- *Vijñāna-pariṇāmavāda* of the *Yogācārins.*
- *Vijñāna-spandita* in the *Gauḍapādīya-kārikā* (GK).
- *Brahman-vivartavāda* and *Māyā* in GK and the works of Śaṅkara.

The theories of creation by a primordial all-powerful creator God through his marvellous power and also *Brahman–pariṇāmavāda* (i.e. real transformation of Brahman as *jīvas* and the world) found in the *Upaniṣads* have been rejected by GK and Śaṅkara as leading to logical contradictions.

A pure absolute unchanging entity cannot account for the dynamic world process and the world of imperfections resulting therefrom To tide over this untenability, GK and Śaṅkara take a philosophical position that the world is unreal, *māyā* or illusion and the only reality is *Ātman* or Brahman. But the questions, as to how the real Brahman can support the unreal world of appearances and why it supports such unreal appearances, have not been satisfactorily answered in their philosophies. We are asked to believe with unquestioning faith that *māyā-śakti* is absolutely dependent on and inseparable from Brahman ; but still the phenomena, good or evil, arising from the *māyā-śakti*, do not touch him.

On the other hand, Buddhism does not accept the theory of *Ātman* or Brahman being the cause, support or the underlying essence of the world. According to Buddhism, the truth is that the world of things is the result of the craving and the conceptual construction of the individual *Vijñānas* i.e. the packets of will energy (that are in continuous states of transformation), and, as such, it can be described only as neither existent nor non-existent (Madhyamaka) or both existent and non-existent (Yogācāra). It is empty and selfless. It is only because the world is empty and selfless, anything is arising and decaying and everything becomes possible. Otherwise it will be an unchanging block. As we have earlier quoted Nāgārjuna from his *Vigrahavyāvartanī,* verse 70 :

"All things are possible for the one for whom emptiness is possible; nothing whatsoever is possible for the one for whom emptiness is not possible".

Thus, for Buddhism, the underlying essence or reality in everything in the world is its emptiness or selflessness.

In fact, the concept of emptiness in Buddhism has been taken by Śaṅkara and adopted as *māyā* in his philosophy, but bereft of its perfound inner meaning and ethical connotations. Further, he enters into contradictions when he tries to marry it with the theory of Brahman in the Vedānta. Even though GK and Śaṅkara teach an appearance and *māyā* theory, the real import of their teachings is that *Īśvara,* the *jīvas* and the world are appearances and *māyā* only in the ultimate sense i.e. for the one who has realized union with the ultimate reality that is Brahman, but they are real in the conventional realm. In fact, Śaṅkara Vedānta tends to accept the *Brahman-pariṇāmavāda* or creation through the wonderous power of *Īśvara* as real in the conventional realm in spite of the logical inconsistencies and contradictions involved in these theories.

The concept of ignorance (*avidyā*) identified by the Buddha in his Wheel of Life and Dependent Origination as the root cause of *saṃsāric* existence and sufferings and sorrows has been adopted by the Advaita Vedānta also. But the same ignorance in the case of the individual *jīvas* becomes *māyā-śakti* in the case of *Īśvara.* The wonderous power in the earlier creation theories are now ascribed to this *māyā-śakti.* The logical inconsistencies and contradictions in these theories are explained away as the incomprehensibility and the inexplicable mystery of the *māyā-śakti.* In the ultimate analysis, all these theories rest on blind belief We are asked to suspend rational analysis and enquiry and look for spiritual intuition. Does it mean that spiritualism has to be divorced from logical reasoning and rational enquiry to realize the truth? This may be contrasted with the Buddha's attitude to spiritualism and inner realization. He never asks his disciples to accept his teachings on blind faith; he always appeals to reason and logic. Intuition and inner realization are only finer refinements and spontaneous culminations of the continuous intellectual process of enquiry within. Spiritual life not based on logic and reasoning cannot be expected to lead to the truth. How can blind faith, which clings to untruth, lead to truth? Buddhism proves the unreality of *Īśvara* and Self in the conventional realm also and treats them as mere conceptual fabrications.

Śaṅkara takes consciousness as the ultimate reality, but considers it only in its cognitive aspect ignoring creative aspect to fit in with his theory of actionless *Ātman* (Brahman) and to free it from all the defiling impulses involved in creation. But the cognitive aspect is secondary in as much as it evolves from creative impulses and comes into play after the development of body, senses, nerves and brain centres. It may be argued that Śaṅkara suggests a higher principle of consciousness transcending both the creative and cognitive aspects. But this is belied by the fact that Śaṅkara emphasizes only the cognitive aspect when he maintains that *Ātman* as the light of consciousness makes knowledge possible by energizing the *antaḥkaraṇa* (inner organ). His arbitrary division of the knowledge aspect of consciousness from the creative willing aspect and abstraction of the same separately to present it as the ultimate reality is unconvincing and untenable. Śaṅkara's theory of the light of consciousness of *Ātman* (Brahman) providing a base or support for the appearance of the *saṃsāric* world is in fact not in consonance with the import of the teaching of the 'That art thou' in the *Chāndogya Upaniṣad* where the 'That' points to the seed of the nyagrodha tree i.e. source and not to any support.

In the Vedānta, the highest goal is the apprehension of *Ātman* (Brahman), and the meditative consciousness realized in the *Turīya* is equated with the light of consciousness of *Ātman.* This concept of *Ātman* as the permanent unchanging consciousness is negated and countered in Buddhism with its *Vijñāna-pariṇāma* (evolution of consciousness) theory. The ultimate goal here is transformation of consciousness to Buddha consciousness rather than mere apprehension of an unchanging consciousness which is only a conceptual fabrication.

Buddhism recognizes the will energy as the fundamental consciousness in contrast to the light of consciousness talked about in the *Vedānta* with emphasis only on the cognitive aspect. This 'will energy' is continuously changing and, according to Buddhism, there is no fixed absolute unchanging entity in existence. All is continuous flow. *Vijñāna-pariṇāma* (i.e. evolution of consiousness) and dependent origination define this flow of life. The idea of *Vijñāna-spandita* (vibration of consciousness) in GK is also in the final analysis akin to the *Vijñāna-pariṇāma* theory of the *Yogācārins.* The term '*spandita*' (vibration) is used by GK to differentiate its concept from *pariṇāma* (actual transformation) and maintain the unchanging nature of *Ātman* (consciousness). But vibration is also a change which produces the *jīvas* and the world. In the ultimate analysis, it is only a difference in the use of words to describe the change. The cravings and passions within are euphemistically called 'vibration' here in GK.

In the beginning when we set out in our search of reality, we noted the definition of ultimate reality as the one that exists always, that is uncaused and uncreated and that is free from evil and sin. But, we do not find any absolute real thing in the world conforming to this definition. Everything in the world is *anityam, asukham* and *anattā.* The search for reality must not be restricted or confined to the analysis of only the four states of experience-waking, dreaming, deep sleep and *Turīya*-as in the *Upaniṣads* and the Advaita Vedānta Philosophy; but extended to other states of fainting, existence as a speck in the mother's womb and also the post-mortem existence after the death. No self-consciousness or self-awareness of bliss can be said to be present in these states. If at all, these states can be described only as void of conceptions. Therefore, the ultimate reality which exists always can only be defined as void of conceptions or selfless. The assumption of a permanent unchanging consciousness in all these states is nothing but superimposition of a self on the void in these states and, as such, is a false conceptual construction.

The Buddhist philosophical position that the consciousness is nothing but the name given to the bundle of cravings, impulses, volitions, thoughts, feelings and other mental states is unassailable. This bundle is ever-changing and in continuous flow. The entire life is the 'becoming' or evolving of this bundle called consciousness. This, according to Buddhists, is unreal (but to be precise, empty: neither real nor unreal) because it is impermanent (*anityam*), sorrowful (*asukham*), substanceless (*anattā*) and impure, and not because of any magical illusory power of a transcendent being as claimed in Advaita Vedānta. Creation is by the craving and conceptual construction from within. It may best be described as a dream rather than as a false superimposition (*mṛṣādhyāsa*) on some other thing as in Śaṅkara's theory.

As taught in Buddhism, everything in life is substanceless and selfless (*anattā*) because it depends on others for existence and arises and decays according to causes and conditions. Dependent origination is the only undeniable fact of experience. Everything is dependently originated, causes and conditions bringing them into existence. Nothing is originated by itself, in itself and of itself. The idea of existence of an absolute unborn entity militates against the principle of dependent origination, which is an incontrovertible fact of experience. As Nāgārjuna asks: "How can that which exists by its own being come into existence?" There can be no such thing as an absolute ultimate reality. The ultimate truth is only in the way things actually are i.e. in the Suchness of things and not in any absolute thing.

The last word on the subject of ultimate reality is pronounced by *Saṃdhinirmocana Sūtra* which summarizes the ultimate truth succintly in the following words:

"................. the selflessness of phenomena in the ultimate sense in true thusness is not said to have a cause, is not causally produced, is not created. This is the ultimate truth. Having realized this ultimate truth, one no longer seeks any other ultimate truth (for there is no other). ...." (*Buddhist Yoga,* Translated by Thomas Cleary, p.18).

Selflessness–this is the ultimate truth because it exists in things uncaused by any other and unborn ; it is also free from evil and sin. It always exists in things. Without realizing this selflessness in every thing, we indulge in conceptual constructions and actions clinging to false notions of self, 'I' and mine and discriminating self and others. These false notions of individuality and self are the breeding ground of afflictions like greed, hatred and delusion which lead to the sufferings in the *saṃsāric* existence. On the other hand, realisation of the ultimate truth of selflessness in oneself and in all things is the attainment of Dharma-Body (*Dharma-kāya*) from which flow all saintly *dharmas.*

2. Essencelessness/Emptiness

The selflessness (*anattā*) is also called substancelessness, suchness, essencelessness and emptiness in Buddhism. These are all synonymous terms. *Anattā* is the core theme underlying all Buddhist philosophies right from the days of Early Buddhism. But it was in the *Prajñāpāramitā Sūtras* that this selflessness was given particular emphasis and raised to new heights as universal emptiness (*śūnyatā*) which was made an object of meditation for deliverance. These *Sūtras*, which were considered as the second "setting in motion the Wheel of *Dharma*", proclaimed as the very perfection of wisdom that everything is a conceptual construct, is like a magical illusion or a dream and, as such, is empty. By their very nature, these teachings were liable to be misinterpreted, and misunderstood as advocating absurd nihilism or nothingness. But as we have already seen in our study of Madhyamaka philosophy, Nāgārjuna established these teachings on emptiness on firm logical foundation by linking the same to the core Buddhist doctrine of dependent origination.

In the Madhyamaka of Nāgārjuna, dependent origination (*pratītyasamutpāda*), conceptual construction of the mind (*upādāya-prajñapti*) and middle-path (*madhyamā-pratipad*) are all equated with emptiness(*śūnya*). These are all shown as characterized by eightfold negation. Nāgārjuna describes them succinctly as neither existent nor non-existent. A salient feature of the philosophical position of *Prajñāpāramitā* and Nāgārjuna is their refusal to cling to any theory adopting a position that no philosophical theory can be maintained in the absolute sense. If at all, the theory will have only a truth in the conventional sense. They prove all theories on the ultimate reality wrong and adopt a philosopohical position of no-position. For them, the ultimate knowledge or supreme wisdom is *nirvikalpa jñāna* in which there is no conceptual construction and it is all void of conceptions as in the embryonic state in the mother's womb, the clean slate of the mind of infant just when it was born, the state of deep sleep or the state of the post-mortem journey of the evolving *Vijñāna.*

Subsequently, *Yogācārins* added further refinements to these ideas on emptiness. They defined emptiness as the non-existence of subject-object duality or any conceptual construction and also as the existence of that non-existence. Thus, for them, emptiness is the existence of that state where all dualities and conceptual constructions cease i.e. the existence of selflessness. With their assertion of both existence and non-existence, the *Yogācārins* gave a positive orientation to the concept of emptiness. But, a little reflection will reveal that this is not basically different from the Madhyamaka position of neither existent nor non-existent which also implies existence as well as non-existence. The difference is only in the way the principle is expressed. For them also, the ultimate wisdom is the *nirvikalpa jñāna.*

The major contribution of the *Yogācārins* to the Buddhist philosophical corpus lies in their exposition of the 'Three Nature' theory and in making a distinction between the 'imagined' (*parikalpita*) false nature and the 'other dependent' (*paratantra*) conventionally true nature in the conceptual constructions of the mind.

The *Yogācārins* derive their philosophical position from the *Saṃdhinirmocana Sūtra* ('Scripture Unlocking the Mysteries') which is considered to be the third and final "setting in motion the Wheel of *Dharma*" establishing the final, definitive teaching of the Buddha without any room for controversy and dispute. In addition to the Three Nature theory, this *Sūtra* also teaches three No-self-natures (*Niḥsvabhāva*) or three essencelessnesses (substancelessnesses) (*Buddhist Yoga,* Translated by Thomas Cleary, Chapter 5) :

Essencelessness of characteristics.
Essencelessness of birth.
Ultimate essencelessness.

The characteristics we attribute to the things in defining them have no inherent existence of their own because they are conceptually constructed and imposed by the mind on the things by the force of its inner passions and cravings. These are only artificial names given by the mind and are by no means inherent definitions of the things. These, being products of imagination and conceptual construction, are essenceless (substanceless, empty).

Everything arises depending on the power of various causes and conditions and does not exist by, in or of its own inherent power. The *Saṃdhinirmocana Sūtra* calls this dependently originated character of things as essencelessness (substancelessness, emptiness) of birth.

The things are also said to be essenceless in the ultimate sense because of the fact of their dependent origination. The ultimate essencelessness of things is revealed by their dependent origination and selflessness. This is the eternal and constant real nature of all things ; this is permanent and uncreated ; this is free of any defilement. This is the suchness of things.

The Buddha further elaborates in the *Saṃdhinirmocana Sūtra*:

"...it is in allusion to the essencelessness of characteristics that I say all things have no origination or extinction, are fundamentally quiescent and inherently nirvanic.

"Why ? If inherent characteristics of things have no existence at all, then they have no origination ; if they have no origination, then they have no extinction. If they have no origination and no extinction, they are fundamentally quiescent. If they are fundamentally quiescent, they are inherently nirvanic..."

The Buddha then goes on to add that the people should not make a rigid literal interpretation of the above teachings and conclude that all things have absolutely no essence, definitely and absolutely are not originated or extinguished, definitely and absolutely are quiescent and definitely and absolutely are nirvanic; they should not misunderstand and acquire a view of nothingness or a view of non-existence of characteristics in regard to all things. The above teachings are the truth in the ultimate sense with a subtle hidden inner meaning that is profound, and these should be distinguished and understood correctly in contradistinction to the relative or conventional truth.

These teachings of essencelessness (selflessness) are expounded by the Buddha with a view to enable people to investigate and contemplate them so that they realize their truths inwardly and become truly disaffected and detached from all transient things which are *anityam, asukham, anattā* and impure. People should become truly free from all desires, cravings and conceptual constructions, and thereby totally liberated from the three-fold defilement of afflictions (passions), actions and *saṃsāric* existence. The real purport of these teachings is to make people realize the ultimate truth of selflessness and cease from superimposing their conceptual constructions and fabrications on the dependent nature.

"Because of knowledge that is not conditioned by words, not thinking in conformity with words, free from the lull of words, they are able to extinguish dependency. Sustained by the power of knowledge in the present state, they are able to extinguish the causes of the future"(*Buddhist Yoga,* Translated by Thomas Cleary ; p.31).

The wise detach themselves from names and words and shed off all conceptual constructions of dualities and opposites of characteristics and thereby attain enlightenment burning away and exterminating all causes of any future impurities and defilements.

When the Buddha teaches the essencelessness of characteristics and the ultimate essencelessness, he is not denying the arising of the transient things and their temporary existence and characteristics, but is only pointing to the conceptualized and fabricated nature of these characteristics imposed on the things by the force of the inner desires and cravings of the mind. Dependent origination is the defining principle in the Buddhist philosophy. But in the ultimate analysis, this is also dependently originated and conceptually constructed. When the conceptual constructions cease on the realisation of the ultimate truth, this also ceases.

Without realising this most subtle and profound truth of selflessness lying hidden within, people indulge in egotistic and self-centred actions based on false theories of individuality and self which disturb the rhythm and harmony of the interdependency realm of the world. These become the root causes of all defilements and *karmic* formations and the perpetuation of the sorrowful *saṃsāric* existence. Thus ignorance of the ultimate truth of selflessness is the cause of all sufferings and sorrows and not the ignorance of any permanent unchanging entity within such as Self, *Ātman* or *Īśvara* as maintained in the philosophies of Hinduism.

3. Praxis

Realize the ultimate truth of selflessness in yourself and become self-less to lead a pure, virtuous and holy life. This, in a nutshell, is the teaching of the Buddha.

Various meditative techniques have been prescribed in Buddhism to realize this ultimate truth of selflessness in one and become selfless. The practitioner attains *nirvikalpa-jñāna* (non-discriminative wisdom) where all duality, discrimination and conceptual construction cease and perfect non-duality prevails. This non-duality is the cessation of the duality of not only subject-object, but all dualities-dualities of birth-death, created-uncreated, existence-non-existence, eternalism-nihilism, pleasure-pain, one-many, coming – going etc. This is the negation of all dualities and polar opposites. This negation of all dualities and opposites is in essence the negation of all conceptual categories of existence and adoption of the middle position neither affirming nor denying the extreme opposites, but synthesizing them.

The practitioner simulates and assumes in his meditative concentration the state of deep sleep, or the state of the mind of the infant just when it is born, or the state of his existence as an embryo in the mother's womb, where there is no desire, no craving, no dream and no conceptual construction. He becomes one of emptiness (*śūnya*). This is beyond the scope of all thought and deliberation ; this is inexpressible. This cannot be verbalized and described.

His *nirvikalpa-jñāna* and meditation on the four *Brahma Vihāras* (all-pervading loving-kindness, all-pervading compassion, sympathetic joy and equanimity) burn away all his *karmic* residues and he becomes empty of all defilements and attains *Nirvāṇa.* This state is one of negativity and cessation. But he comes back (or descends as Professor G.M. Nagao suggests) to *saṃsāra,* still as selflessness personified, but the selflessness this time manifesting in the positive forms of love and compassion. He now immerses himself in *saṃsāra* to serve all sentient beings with love and compassion. His ultimate goal is the attainment of Buddha Consciousness.

In *Mahāyāna* Buddhism, three bodies of the Buddha are talked about:

- Truth-body or Dharma-body (*Dharma-kāya*) which is the ultimate truth of seflessness personified i.e. with the *ālayavijñāna* (the store or seed consciousness) totally transformed obliterating without any trace all ideas and considerations of own-self and filled with only selflessness. This is the body of Buddha consciousness completely immaculate in nature from which the other two bodies (saintly *dharmas*) arise.
- Enjoyment-body, the *Sāṃbhoga-kāya,* which is the embodiment of the enjoyment of bliss/emptiness of *Nirvāṇa* and immersion in *Nirvāṇa.*
- Transformation-body, the *Nirmāṇa-kāya,* which is the immersion in the *saṃsāra* with loving kindness and compassion for the benefit of all sentient beings.

The Buddha had all these aspects. For the bodhisattva who aspires to follow in the foot-steps of the Buddha and attain perfect Buddhahood, *saṃsāra* of loving kindness and compassion is the same as the *Nirvāṇa* of cessation and emptiness. He attains the state of the Transformation-body of the Buddha which is said to have neither a mind nor a no-mind. He has no-mind relative to his self and has mind only relative to others. His ultimate goal is the attainment of perfect Buddhahood and becoming utter selflessness personified i.e. **Vajra-self (diamond-self) of selflessness.**

4. *Tathāgatagarbha*

The concept of *Dharma-kāya* is further extended and elaborated as *dharma-dhātu* (dharma-realm), *buddha-dhātu* (Buddha-nature) and *Tathāgatagarbha* in the second phase of development of *Mahāyāna* movement in the post-Nāgārjuna period.

The *Tathāgatagarbha* theory emphasizes that the Buddha-nature or the germ of Buddhahood is essentially present in all beings and that, as such, beings are potentially *Tathāgatas* (Buddhas). Buddha called himself *Tathāgata* i.e. the one who had thus come in *saṃsāra* and thus gone in *Nirvāṇa.* This Buddha-nature or Buddha-consciousness is said to be present in all living beings as a latent seed but obscured by the inherent ignorance and covered by defilements (*kleśa*). The assertion of Buddha-nature within ordinary living beings became an important element of religious philosophy later in Chinese, Japanese and Tibetan Buddhism. *Śrīmālādevisīṃhanāda Sūtra* (abb. *Śrīmālā,* probably third century CE), *Mahāparinirvāṇa Sūtra* (fourth century CE) and *Ratnagotravibhāga* (fourth/fifth century CE) are the Indian Buddhist scriptures that expound the doctrine of *Tathāgatagarbha.*

All these theories of *Dharma-kāya,* Buddha-nature and *Tathāgatagarbha* are constructed over the fundamental philosophical truth of ultimate essencelessness or selflessness in things we have studied above. This ultimate truth of selflessness reveals the existential nature of things, that is, the way the things truly are. But, the individual *Vijñānas* (i,e. the packets of will energy), without realizing this ultimate truth due to ignorance, indulge in actions based on the false notions of self, 'I' and 'mine' and driven by the defiling impulses of cravings, passions and prejudices. The result is the *saṃsāric* world of disharmony, discord, strife, sufferings and sorrows. On the contrary, when this universal principle of selflessness is realized and translated in practice as an ethical, moral and spiritual principle and nature governing the actions and the evolution of the *Vijñāna,* then the *Vijñāna* (*ālaya* consciousness, the will energy) turns into a consciousness totally filled with selflessness, love and compassion and the result is the world of harmony, peace and happiness. This *ālayavijñāna*, thus filled with selflessness totally, is the *garbha* (womb) from which all saintly Buddha-dharmas mature and become manifest ; this is the *garbha* (womb) of the *Tathāgata*. This *Tathāgatagarbha* is empty of all seeds of defilements, these seeds having been burnt away by the fire of selflessness and the practice of the four *Brahma Vihāras* ; it is filled totally with seeds producing immaculate Buddha-*dharmas*.

The *Śrīmālā* describes:-

"Lord, the *Tathāgatagarbha* is void (*śūnya*) of the all the defilement stores, which are discrete and knowing as not liberated (i.e. which do not lead to liberation). Lord, the *Tathāgatagarbha* is not void (*aśūnya*) of the Buddha *dharmas* which are nondiscrete, inconceivable, more numerous than the sands of the Ganges, and knowing as liberated (i.e. which lead to liberation)".

The '*Tathāgatagarbha*' is interpreted by scholars variously as 'embryo', 'seed'. 'womb', or 'matrix' of the *Tathāgata*. When it is defined as a womb, what is implied is the store-consciousness (*ālaya Vijñāna*) containing the immaculate seeds of Buddha consciousness (will). The '*Tathāgatagarbha*' is also called the Element of *Tathāgata* in *Ratnagotravibhāga*, the 'Element' having the meaning of root cause. Thus, in the ultimate analysis, the '*Tathāgatagarbha*' is the immaculate seed of Buddha consciusness (will) producing the Buddha *dharmas* or the transformed *ālaya* (store)–consciousness that has turned around its basis (*āśraya–parāvṛtti*) and acquired the perfected nature (*pariniṣpanna*) and that now holds the immaculate seed of Buddha consciousness. This is the root or ground from which the inconceivable Buddha *dharmas* (cessation of suffering, *Nirvāṇa* and also the bodhisattva practices) more numerous than all the sands of the river Ganges grow and flow. The scholars argue whether the term '*Tathāgatagarbha*' stands for the 'container' (i.e. womb) or the "contained (i.e. the seed of Buddha consciousness)". It is better to bear in mind that Buddhism generally does not believe in the existence of consciousness as a distinct hard-core entity in the manner of a container, but only as a flow of mental states causally connected. Thus, the *Tathāgatagarbha* is the source or origin of the flow of the saintly Buddha *dharmas*.

"Like the Buddha covered in withered lotus flowers,
Like honey covered by a swarm of bees,
Like the kernel of rice with the husk,

Like gold covered within dirt,
Like a treasure buried below ground in a poor man's hut,
Like the fruit covered in rough skin,
Like the jewel studded image wrapped in tattered garments,
Like a future emperor in embryonic form in the vile belly of the pregnant, abandoned woman,
Like a precious golden statue covered in the clay mould,
So is this Element (of the *Tathāgata*) established in beings who are covered with the stains of adventitious defilements."

(*Ratnagotravibhāga* I)

What is the precious thing or treasure lying hidden in beings in the manner as illustrated in the above analogies? It may be interpreted as the universal truth of selflessness or as the consciousness suffused with the spirit of selflessness (Buddha consciousness). Whatever be the interpretation–the ultimate truth or a particular consciousness stream-, the defining element is the spirit of selflessness; this is the source of the flow of all saintly *dharmas* or Buddha *dharmas*.

As we have already seen, selflessness is the ultimate truth and it is the true nature or the way things are ; it is the Buddha-nature, but only this nature is not normally realized and applied as the guiding principle of life stream. The potentiality for realizing this ultimate truth and developing the seed consciousness of selflessness and becoming a Buddha always exists in beings. That is why it is said that in each being there exists in embryonic form the Element of the *Tathāgata* ; but people do not look through to that. Anything is possible because it is all empty and selfless as Nāgārjuna proves. *Saṃsāra* or *Nirvāṇa* or blooming of the Buddha consciousness–anything is possible because of emptiness and selflessness of beings and it is only a question of effort, diligence causation and dependency.

Some scholars tend to give an absolutist interpretation to the concept of *Tathāgatagarbha. Ratnagotravibhāga* (RGV) is often cited as subscribing to the view of *Tathāgatagarbha* as an absolute ever-existent entity. This absolutist interpretation and view arise basically because of a mix-up of the two notions – the first of selflessness as the ultimate truth denoting the way things actually are and the other of a consciousness that has actualized this selflessness as a life-governing principle – without distinguishing them properly as a universal principle and as an actualisation respectively. The unborn-nature of the former i.e. selflessness is superimposed and ascribed to the conscious entity also that has realized this selflessness. This is unbuddhistic. But, if RGV maintains this view, it shows its religious fervour to deify Buddha as an absolute principle that inspires devotion. This passes on into the realm of religious philosophy based on faith and belief. The aim seems to be to encourage people in the path highlighting the potentialities of becoming Buddha and to inspire devotion as a means of salvation.

In conclusion, it may be summarized that the Element of *Tathāgata* is the ultimate truth of selflessness which is the root or basis of enlightenment (*Nirvāṇa*) and the fountain-head of all saintly *dharmas* and which is there as suchness, uncaused, uncreated and unborn. The spirit of selflessness may arise in any consciousness-stream and blossom into *Dharma-kāya* depending on causes and conditions just as Prince Gautama Siddhartha got enlightened and became the Buddha. The Buddha – nature is *Dharma-kāya,* the body of selflessness, that can be attained by any consciousness – stream with arduous and unremitting practice of faith, vigour, mindfulness, meditation and wisdom. This body of selflessness is revered and made the object of worship in *Mahāyāna* Buddhism generally, not as an absolute ever-existent entity, but as an ideal nature to be acquired by man: the Buddhahood.

Thus, the truth of selflessness is the ultimate truth. There is no other truth to be known higher than this.

Our search ends here.

Bibliography

Alladi Mahadeva Sastry, *The Bhagavad Gītā with the commentary of Śrī Śaṅkarācārya*, Samata Books, Madras, 1977.

Chandradhar Sharma, *A Critical Survey of Indian Philosophy*.

Conze, Edward, *Buddhist Wisdom Books*, George Allen and Unwin, London, 1958.

Conze, Edward, *The Prajñāpāramitā Literature*, The Reiyukai, Tokyo, 1975.

Conze, Edward etc, *Buddhist Texts Through the Ages*, Translated & edited by Edward Conze etc., Research Press, New Delhi, One World Publications, Oxford, England, 1999.

Coomaraswami, A.K, *Buddha and the Gospel of Buddhism*, 1956.

Dayal, Har, *The Bodhisattva Doctrine in Buddhist Sanskrit Literature*, Motilal Banarsidass, Delhi, 1970.

Eknath Easwaran, *The Dhammapada*, Translated with A General Introduction by Eknath Easwaran, Penguin Books India, New Delhi, 1986.

Gambhīrānanda, Swāmī, *Eight Upaniṣads, Volume One*, Advaita Ashrama, Calcutta, 1996.

Gambhīrānanda, Swami, *Eight Upaniṣads, Volume Two*, Advaita Ashrama, Calcutta, 1998.

George Grimm, *Doctrine of The Buddha*.

Gethin, R., *The Foundations of Buddhism*, Oxford and New York: Oxford University Press, 1998.

Gombrich, R, *How Buddhism Began : The Conditioned Genesis of the Early Teachings*, London and Atlantic Highlands, N.J. : Athlone Press, 1996.

Gour, Hari Singh, *The Spirit of Buddhism*, Rupa & Co., New Delhi, 1924.

Julius Lipner, *Hindus – Their Religious Beliefs and Practices*, Routledge, London, 1994.

Junjiro Takakusu, *The Essentials of Buddhist Philosophy,* Motilal Banarsidass, Delhi, 1947.

King, Richard, *Early Advaita Vedānta and Buddhism,* State University of New York / Indian Books Centre, Delhi, 1995.

Krishna Moorthy, K.S., *Essence of the Upaniṣads,* Krishna Moorthy, K.S, Bangalore, 2001.

Merv Fowler, *Buddhism – Religious Practices & Beliefs,* Sussex Academic Press / Kusum Publishing Services, New Delhi, 2000.

Nagao, G.M., *Mādhyamika and Yogācāra; A Study of Mahāyāna Philosophies* – Collected Papers of G.M. Nagao, Translated by L.S. Kawamura, State University of New York Press, New York / Indian Books Centre, Delhi, 1991.

Ñāṇamoli, Bhikku, The Life of the Buddha : According to the Pāli Canon, Buddhist Publication Society, Kandy, 1992.

Narada Thera, *The Buddha – Dhamma or The Life and Teachings of the Buddha,* Asian Educational Services, New Delhi, 1942 Kendy.

Oliver Leaman, *Key Concepts in Eastern Philosophy,* Routledge, London, 1999.

Radhakrishnan, S. *Indian Philosophy*

Radhakrishnan, S., *Basic Writings of S. Radhakrishnan,* Edited with an Introduction by Robert A. McDermott, E.P. Dutton, Inc., New York / Jaico Impression, 1972.

Radhakrishnan, S., *The Principal Upaniṣads,* Harper Collins Publishers India, New Delhi, 1994.

Rajmani Tigunait, Pandit, *Seven Systems of Indian Philosophy,* The Himalayan International Institute of Yoga, Pennsylvania, USA., 1983.

Ranjit Hoskote, *Four Ways of Embracing the World,* The Hindu Folio, Chennai, 2001.

Robinson, Richard, *Early Mādhyamika* in India and China, Motilal Banarsidass, Delhi, 1967.

Sengaku Mayeda, Śaṅkara's View of Ethics, Paper 14 in *Philosophy : East And West.*

Stephen Hawking, *A Brief History of Time,* Bantam Books, UK, 1988.

Suzuki, Beatrice Lane, Mahāyāna Buddhism, Mandala, An Imprint of Harper Collins Publishers, 1990.

Thomas Cleary, *Buddhist Yoga – A Comprehensive Course,* Translated by Thomas Cleary, Shambhala South Asia Editions, Boston, 1999.

Thurman, Robert A.F., *The Tibetan Book of the Dead* – Liberation through Understanding in the between, Translated by Robert A.F Thurman, Harper Collins Publishers India, New Delhi, 1998.

Upadhyaya, Kashi Nath, *Early Buddhism and the Bhagavadgītā,* Motilal Banarsidass Publishers, Delhi, 1971.

Warren, Henry Clarke, *Buddhism in Translations,* Atheneum Press, Edition, New York, 1962.

Williams, Paul, with Anthony Tribe, *Buddhist Thought, A Complete Introduction to the Indian Tradition,* Routledge, London, 2000.

Woodward, F.L., *Some Sayings of the Buddha according to the Pāli canon,* Oxford University Press, 1973.

Index

B

T